IWR

Culley

# Cattle, Horses & Men

*The drawings by Katherine Field illustrating this volume are used with the kind permission of the Union Stockyards Company of Los Angeles who own the copyright.*

JACK CULLEY

# Cattle, Horses & Men
## OF THE WESTERN RANGE

KatherineField - 1940

*By* JOHN H. (JACK) CULLEY

ILLUSTRATIONS BY KATHERINE FIELD

THE WARD RITCHIE PRESS
LOS ANGELES, CALIFORNIA

TO

THE STOCKMEN OF THE WEST

# Table of Contents

## III. CATTLE AND MEN

# List of Illustrations

# Introduction

ONE OF the most colorful and important periods of American history had to do with the development of the range cattle business in the western half of the United States. Many romantic tales have been written about that period from about 1865 to 1900. The locale was that great portion of our country that lies westwards of the one hundredth Meridian. Most of the men who made that history have passed on and, others, being of a practical vein, did not consider the work, the hardships, the trials and tribulations worthy of written pages in history. They considered their accomplishments ordinary because of their environment. They were so accustomed to dangers and hardships that these very things became the ordinary things of everyday life.

The result has been that all too much of the writing of the history of that great saga of human accomplishment has been in the hands of men who were admittedly good writers, but who in the main, were men who did not have first-hand knowledge of the early days of the western range. Therefore, most of them drew heavily upon their all too vivid imaginations. It is indeed a pity that so much of the so-called history of the West has been handed down in distorted form.

I have had the privilege of having for my personal friends many of the men who took active part in the actual handling of cattle in the latter half of the 19th Century. They are a great lot of men; most of them hard and rough, but endowed with the virtues of faith in their own abilities; a high degree of integrity and honesty; men who were truly rugged individualists, ready to fight for what they thought were their own rights and men who had to fight for self preservation. Some of these men were illiterate, others were highly educated. Yet all carried very much the same characteristics. Mainly due to the character of their range work, they learned to think things out for themselves and to act accordingly.

In any true history of the western range, due credit must be given the many men of British and Scotch descent who were so active in the development of the cattle business. Most of these men from the tight little British Isles were men of means; it was their money that capitalized much of the beef cattle development in the United States. Any man who understands livestock breeding knows that from the British Isles have come the foundation for most of our improved livestock in this country. The British Isles developed the Hereford, Aberdeen-Angus, Shorthorn, Galloway, Devon—all beef breeds—as well as our popular breeds of sheep and horses in this country. America owes a great debt to the British Isles for the improved livestock its breeders have passed on to us; and for the men who came over to the North American continent to pioneer the development of our vast livestock industry.

One of those men was Jack Culley. As the publisher of the *Western Livestock Journal*, it has been my privilege to carry many articles from the gifted pen of this famous range cattleman, true horseman and fine gentleman. His writing have always earned a warm response alike from the experienced cowman and the lover of pure literature. Even when he deals with an episode from a historic angle his narrative is always full of action and stirring incident from his own and others' lives, while at the same time he is careful to stay within the facts. I know that those who peruse *Cattle, Horses and Men* will come away from it with a vivid and authentic impression of life and character in the most romantic period of American history.

A few words about Jack Culley will give some insight into

the background of his very successful career and at the same time explain his exquisite literary form.

Jack Culley is the product of the English countryside. In his veins courses the blood of generations of Englishmen who were fighters, empire builders and livestock improvers. His family was originally French and the family name appears in the Roll of Battle Abbey among the barons and knights who went to England with William the Conqueror. The family many centuries ago settled in the North of England and remained there to become noted in the production of improved horses, cattle and sheep in a sound agricultural program for which England is noted.

The first history of livestock was written by George Culley, Jack Culley's great uncle. This book, *Culley on Livestock,* was the leading livestock authority for the 18th Century. An intimate friend of the family was Robert Bakewell, the most celebrated livestock breeder of all time. Mr. Culley's great grandmother was Elizabeth Bates Culley, a first cousin of Thomas Bates, the famous Shorthorn breeder.

Jack Culley was "born in the purple." The family home since early in the 18th Century was Coupland Castle on the border line of England and Scotland. Mr. Culley succeeded to this grand old castle and the estate in 1921 upon the death of his brother, Monsignor Mathew Culley. With his family, he spent some time in England after his long and colorful career as a southwestern range cattleman, but the love of the west was in his veins and eventually, he sold the entire family estate and returned to the United States to establish there a permanent home in Los Angeles. Upon the walls of the family home in Los Angeles are many of the family portraits which for many years graced the walls of old Coupland Castle.

Jack Culley was educated in one of England's most famous preparatory schools, Harrow School, and completed his schooling at Oxford University, which was also his father's college. Mr. Culley's literary background will become clearer for students of literature when I tell them that he was a pupil and close friend of Walter Pater at Oxford. Today Jack Culley's style reflects in some aspects the influence of the great esthetic stylist, blended rather curiously with the forthrightness and simplicity which characterize the diction of the southwestern cowman and which Mr. Culley greatly admires.

When a young man, in good old English tradition, Jack Culley traveled to the United States where a relative, William Pinkerton, operated a sheep and cattle spread on a large grant in New Mexico. He spent several years in New Mexico working far various horse and cattle outfits, including the A1 Bar, Rail 12 and others. After a few years, he was joined by his brother, Chris, who left England to join with Jack in starting in the stock business in a small way in New Mexico. The two brothers were successful and gradually extended their operations into one of the large units of the Southwest.

In 1893, Mr. Culley and his wife went to the famous old Bell Ranch in San Miguel County, New Mexico, Mr. Culley becoming ranch manager. This ranch is still one of the largest in the United States, and is now under the management of Albert Mitchell, one of America's best known and highly regarded cattlemen. A section of this book is devoted to this celebrated cattle ranch.

The Bell Ranch was a Mexican Grant and in 1893 comprised a total of 750,000 acres. It was far removed from any town or railroad and had a rather tough reputation. Recalling his days on this enormous cattle spread, Mr. Culley once told me: "It is a magnificent tract of range country and I have always looked back with peculiar pleasure to my life there. Here my boy Matt started his young life as a child among the cowboys."

Mr. Culley was a member of the firm of Culley & Martin, one of the oldest concerns in New Mexico. The company was formed by Mr. Culley and his sister, Mrs. Theodore Martin at

Wagon Mound, New Mexico. The concern ran about 2,000 cattle under the Rafter C Bar brand. The company was bought by New England capitalists in 1916 but still operates under the old name.

Again running true to English tradition, Mr. Culley offered his services in World War No. 1. When the United States entered the war in 1917 he sold the last of his cattle interests and joined the U. S. Army under the Military Department of the American Red Cross. He served as Field Director with assimilated rank of Major. Later he was transferred to the Navy Department at San Francisco and served until 1921, when he resigned to take his family to England, remaining there nine years.

Mrs. Culley was Constance McKellar, daughter of John McKellar who farmed extensively in New Zealand before coming to New Mexico. Matt J. Culley, only son, has been in the U. S. Forest Service since leaving New Mexico State College at the age of 21. He is now in charge of the Santa Rita Range Experiment Station, U. S. Forest Service, Tucson, Arizona. He served fourteen months with the A.E.F. in France during the world war. His wife was Idelle Grumbles of a well known Texas-New Mexico cattle family. There are besides two daughters in the family, Mary and Margaret, the former, Mrs. Harold Lund.

In addition to his interest in livestock, Mr. Culley is widely recognized in literature and art. During his stay in Europe, he made a close study of modern art and has lectured to schools and colleges extensively, since retiring from the livestock business. Such services are given gratuitously. He is a collector of contemporary prints and his collection of wood cuts is considered the most comprehensive in existence.

That in brief, is the story of Jack Culley. George E. Crocker, an oldtime Southwestern cattleman and former neighbor, writes: "Jack Culley had the reputation of being the best rider in our district of New Mexico. We picked out what we considered the worst horse in the Wagon Mound outfit for Jack to ride one time. He rode the bronco and made fun of him. I've heard Jack could ride a bucking horse in an English saddle."

Dean C. W. McCampbell, distinguished head of the department of Animal Husbandry, Kansas State College, Manhattan, wrote me: "Jack Culley is one of the finest and most interesting of the many great personalities that have played an important part in developing the range country. I enjoy his writing more than anything else I read. They are so splendidly written—such excellent depictions of the range life of an earlier day and so full of human interest appeal."

When Mr. Culley flattered me by asking that I write this foreword, I promised to do so with no little trepidation; for mine is the style of the newspaperman—his the elegance of the polished essayist. But it is a pleasure to tell you something about this fine gentleman and good friend. I know that you will treasure these records of the real Western range which he has prepared for you, and for posterity.

NELSON R. CROW

# I
# The Bell Ranch

# I

# We Make Entry into the
# Famous Bell Ranch

COME with me if you have time today and we'll take a little
trip in north-eastern New Mexico. I propose to start from
a ranch about five miles south of the Santa Fe railroad
at the little town of Wagon Mound. It is a high dry country,
sixty-three hundred feet above sea-level, with pine and pin-
yon and oakbrush brakes and a dark reluctant soil; where the
summer comes late and goes early, and if snow falls in December it may lie two months with the thermometer ten or even
twenty degrees below zero. The grama grass grows short and
the rim rocks are black malpais. All along to the north of it lie
the Rockies.

But we are going east, or south-east today. On horseback, for
there are no wagon roads directly across the Mora and Red
River brakes in the direction of the place we are heading for.
The riding will be rough, but I'll give you a good rock horse
that won't make a mistake all day. The way lies over mesas and
across canyons, through pine timber and oak brush, till at the
end of thirty miles or so we are halted suddenly by a great bluff
or mesa side. It's not a foot less than a thousand feet deep, and
pretty near perpendicular. Standing on its edge, behold a new
world stretching below us. It is—for I know it—a world where
the summers are long and hot and if in winter a flurry of snow
comes, it is gone by noon; where things grow readily in the loose
red soil and the rim rocks are vermilion. A world where few
pines are to be seen, but the hill and mesa sides are covered with
juniper and the flats with mesquite, and the sunflowers grow
higher than a man on horseback in the bottoms.

The land we are standing on is known as the "mesa." The land we are contemplating, as the "lower country," or "below the mesa." I wonder where else you can stand in one country and by merely riding down a trail pass into an entirely different one.

Well, let's scramble down to the foot of the long Mexican made trail and, crossing Red River below Canyon Largo, ride on south till we pass through a gate in a long fence. That puts us in the famous Bell pasture; a pasture containing seven hundred and fifty thousand acres under fence, without challenge, I believe, the finest body of pure grazing land in America.

It was originally a Mexican grant, and the old grandee who selected it certainly knew the country and the requirements of a stock ranch. Watered by the Canadian (or Red River) throughout its entire length and by a number of considerable streams, La Cinta, Trementina, Atarque, Conchas, as well as by numerous creeks and permanent springs, no cow needs to go more than a few miles to find natural water. There is shelter everywhere alike from winter cold and summer suns. Everywhere between the mesas rich grass flats reach down to the river bottoms. In the southern part mesquite bushes offer their foliage and pods for feed in dry seasons. Even the roughest country in the Atarque is clothed with good grass and accessible to stock that knows it.

When I went down there from the mesa, where I lived and worked, I found a number of things different in the ranch life besides the climate and vegetation. On the Mesa they used tents on the roundups. Every man a tepee. I never saw a tent in the Lower Country unless the manager's wife might take a fancy to visit the wagon! We had to depend on our bed tarps to keep our beds dry, and when it rained much they didn't do it very satisfactorily. The "tarp" was an oblong sheet of duck, one half of which extended under your bed, and the other half over it. Just wide enough so you could fold the sides in a little. When this was done you rolled it up from the end and tied it with a cord. Hence its name of "bed roll," and they were piled high on top of the chuck wagon. Next to your horse and saddle the bed roll was the most important thing in your young life. All our possessions, such as they were, went into it. It was a sort of range safety deposit box, and it wasn't exactly healthy for a man to be found probing around in another fellow's bed roll. In most New Mexico outfits the boys kept their six-shooters in their bed, it being illegal after 1885 to tote a gun on a roundup. On the whole the bed roll was a great institution—I use one today—but after two or three days out in the rain it became pretty damp.

Then it was not the custom to employ any Mexican hands on the Mesa. The Texas prejudice against the native governed us up there. With the Bell outfit we always had a few, including the horse wrangler, and very good ones they were, though I never thought the cooks as good as the American ones. But as for cowhands, it would have been hard to find a better one than Jake Munyiz.

Some of the terms too they used were different. In the upper country they called the horse herd the "cavyard" (spelling unknown) which was a beautiful cowboy version of *caballada* (cavah-yahtha), a bunch of horses. Down below it was known as the *remuda*. That's another Spanish word, signifying "change": a change of horses. An appropriate term and soft on the tongue (the "d" pronounced as a soft "th".) But we "wrangled" horses just the same below the mesa as above it. That word, derived from *caballerango*, a horse herder, has always struck me as the most delightful of all the cowboy shots at the Spanish language. It has stuck too and been recognized by the high-brows that compose our dictionaries.

When I went to the Bell Ranch barely ten thousand head of cattle carried the Bell brand. Under a reorganization of the property we raised that number to about twenty thousand, and, later, considerably more. I remember our buying one southern bunch: ten thousand head of good cows at ten dollars a head. It was a period of disbandment of many range outfits, following

the great blow-up of the range cattle boom, and in order to fill
up our pasture we winter pastured a number of herds of cattle
that had been moved off their own ranges: the GOS and CA Bar
from southern New Mexico, and all the Tee and Smith cattle
from around St. John, Arizona. When it came time to turn them
over to their respective owners in the spring, we had to run five
wagons, with sixty or seventy men and a thousand horses, to
gather and divide them, as well as do our own work, and things
were a-movin' around the old Bell Ranch. Ah, those were the
days!

II

Yes, the old Bell Ranch had a pretty tough "rep" when I
went down there in the middle nineties. My reason for going
was to take the place as range manager under Arthur Tisdall of
"Baldy" Haynes. The company had been reorganized and Tisdall brought in from Texas where he had been in charge of the
JA ranch. Everybody in the West knows the JA ranch in the
Paloduro canyon, out from Clarendon. It had been founded—
one of the earliest in the Panhandle—by the famous frontiersman
and cattleman, Charlie Goodnight, and eventually the whole of
its five hundred thousand acres of land and its great herd of
Hereford cattle had come into the hands of Mrs. Adair, beautiful
ex-New York debutante, and widow of the Irishman John Adair.
There you have a brief history of the JA ranch. It had a number
of links with the Bell Ranch under Tisdall.

It was the fall of the year and getting late, and Baldy had
found a terrible lot of work to be got through. Baldy was a
number one cowman and an all around good man, but there is
no doubt that what with overwork and worry he had allowed
himself to get rattled and irritable and at outs with some of the
boys, who thought he was "ridin'" them. At length, however,
he got the work pretty well cleaned up, the fat cows cut and
on the trail for the railroad, the late calves branded; and the
wagon drew in to the headquarters. Headquarters at the Bell's

consisted of a long row of one-storied rooms opening on the outside, Mexicanwise. Haynes' room was at the far end from the store and office, and he went straight into it on reaching the ranch. Almost immediately one of the boys, a young fellow whose name I never got, followed him along the narrow board walk and into the room. A moment after several shots were heard. The cowboy came out and when they went in to investigate they found Baldy lying face down across the center table, quite dead. There was nothing could very well be done about it. The cowboy took out his pay, saddled his horse and pulled out.

When I got down there, they showed me Baldy's room, which was to be the sitting room for myself and wife and small son. Baldy had bled quite freely and I recall still, oddly enough, that they hadn't troubled to clean up the blood stains from the table. Folks those days were kind of casual—and my wife and kid just moving into the room!

I had run into a chapter of accidents. A day or two before one of the Turner boys, son of old man Turner of the Atarque fence camp, had been shot and killed on the roundup with his own gun. His horse had started to pitch, and the pistol had flown out of his hip pocket and gone off. The bullet went through his stomach and he died before they could get his mother to him. They buried the boy on the ranch, in the little *campo santo* down on the river, and from that day on old Mother Turner's heart, wherever her body might be, was on the Bell Ranch. "Mother won't ever go fur from that thar boy a' hern," the old man would say.

Turner had just come from the Dry Cimarron country to take over the fence camp on the Atarque. It was hard to get a man to stay at this wild and lonely camp at any time, but more so now because only a few days before I came old Mike Lantry, the fence-rider, had been murdered there—presumably by Mexicans. No one could guess any cause for it or ever did, but signs indicated that a number of men had attacked him in his camphouse with axes. Mike was Irish and much of a man, and it was plain he had put up a terrible fight before they had almost hacked him to pieces. I've often sat and listened to old man Turner—it was his favorite amusement—trying to trace the course of the fight by the axe blows on the walls where they had missed Mike and hit the wall. Some of the blows were low down near the floor, showing that at the end the old man had fought them on his hands and knees.

Turner himself was a Texan, and he and his missus were of the frontier kind. His eldest son was an outlaw, though for what trouble I never knew, but I fancy he used to drop in at the old folks' camp once in a while by night. You could have hidden out in that wild Atarque country—the wildest I ever rode over—for years without ever being even seen. And many an outlaw did, both man and beast. It was eighty miles, too, from any town or railroad. Another of these old folks' sons was Tom Turner who died in 1937, after many years of splendid service in the Southwest as cowman and peace officer.

The old man was a splendid specimen of the older Southerner: tall and clean-cut, spare and powerful. Looking at him I thought I realized how the Confederates "fit" so stubbornly in the Civil War. He had a great contempt for some of the younger cow-punchers. "Yesterday," he would say in his slow drawl, "one o' them fancy cowhands rid up to the door. I looks him over and I sez: 'Yes, sir! it's a mighty fine outfit! . . . a seventy-five-dollar horse, and a hundred-dollar saddle,' "—here the old man would pause—" 'and a twenty-five dollar man.' " But in spite of his bitter tongue I liked him well, and I think he liked me, for he acted towards me always as gently as you would to a child. He must be dead these a-many years. One of the boys I knew used to say there was a special pen in Hell reserved for cowpunchers. If that is so, that's where old man Turner and I will meet again someday, I hope.

# 2

## Outlaws of the Range

I'VE told you how rich in grazing land the Bell pasture is. The rim rocks are about the only part that doesn't grow feed. For all that there is plenty of as wild country as I ever rode over. It is mostly around the edges. I remember when I first went down there, I thought I'd take a look at the main grant fence. To my surprise, that job occupied me just two weeks. I never took so long, before or since, to ride one hundred and twenty-eight miles. And then I'd sometimes be afoot, or just taking a bird's-eye view of the fence from the rim rock of a canyon. Every old fence rider will recall the little labor saving dodges, like that, we used in "ridin' fence!"

Well, wild country, such as that is, makes wild cattle and horses; and some of them become outlaws, as we used to call them. It's about that kind of outlaws I thought I'd tell you now.

The tendency to resist restraint seems to be strong in every normal living thing—human or of the animal order. You will notice it in the little tot in your own family the minute he begins to toddle. He indicates a determined desire to escape. In the same way you'll find the average bunch of rested horses reluctant to enter a corral, and they'll make wild whoopee as soon as they are turned out of it. Whenever, in consequence of rough country and the advantages it gives an animal to get away, or through bad handling or any other cause, a horse succeeds for a number of times in dodging the corral gate and effectually escaping his pursuers, there becomes established in him what we may call the "habit of escape." Thereafter, actually, he would sooner break his neck than submit to being driven or corraled. In short

RUNNING BRONCS

—if you happen to be the owner of him—you've got an outlaw on your hands.

At best, corraling broncos was not a light job. You had to have a horse with a right good turn of speed, and long-winded. There must be plenty of the good readers of these pages who have run broncos in the old range days. It won't be necessary for me to tell *them* what a fellow's inner feelings are when, after chasing a band of mares for half a day, it suddenly stops and scatters on him just as he gets it to the corral gate. You'll agree with me, I believe, that at that moment life touched the bottom. And you'll sympathise with my old friend, George Crocker.

George was out one day after a bunch of bronco mares. He aimed to corral them at a stockyard on the Santa Fe railroad which runs through that part of the country. They had been giving him and his boys some considerable helluva time, but at last they had them straightened out for the corral gate and almost within the wing. It so happened that at that moment a freight train was coming along, and just when the engine got opposite the corral gate, the engineer, thinking to have a little fun, gave three sharp toots with his whistle. That was enough; the broncos stopped short in their tracks, wheeled, broke—and away to the tules!

George is one of the quietest men I ever knew, but he got down off his horse, unlimbered his .44 carbine, and sent three bullets in quick succession through the engineer's cab. Fortunately—or unfortunately, according as you view the matter— the engineer was not hit. He lived to run other trains, I suppose, but not, one believes, to try out practical jokes on range men corraling broncos.

When I first went down to the Bell's, there were about twelve hundred broncos scattered all over the large range. This was unsatisfactory for many reasons. The bunches were hard to find when we wanted to brand colts in the fall or to break them in the spring. Then, gentle saddle horses would get out of the horse pastures and go off with them. So we decided to gather up everything and locate the whole lot on the Mesa Rica, a large mesa fenced on two sides by the south and west grant fence, and on the remaining sides by rim rocks.

There was a well known brown mare running on the range at that time. She had been roped years before, but had broken the rope and got away, and from that day to the time I'm writing of, no one had ever been able to corral her. The rope they had caught her with had been a rawhide one and it broke right at her throat, and the noose stuck there around her neck and had been there ever since. So the Mexicans called her La Vaqueta (bah-ka-tah), which is Spanish for "the strap"; and by that name the brown Bell mare was known the length and breadth of that country. My last words to Tom Kane, the wagon boss, when he started on the hunt, were, "Be sure and get La Vaqueta." "Never fear," said Tom.

As soon as the boys got the general range worked and the mares gathered and on the mesa, I rode over to see the thing finished up. I found them driving somewhere between one thousand and twelve hundred head. The ground was broken, and I thought the herd, with La Vaqueta, fat as butter, in the lead of it, inclined to be restive, so, taking an opportunity, I slipped in at the head of them. It's not usual to drive horses from the point like that, and when Tom Kane saw me there he hollered to me he was afraid I'd break up the herd. I hollered back, "Look here, Tom Kane; you leave this job to me. I'll lead this here bunch of broncs into the ranch post-office, if you say you want them there."

Of course it's a ticklish job riding right bang in front of a bunch like that. It's like handling a six-shooter with a hair trigger. Yet, as a matter of fact, the wilder the individual animals in a herd, the more sensitive to the point, and, therefore, the easier to control. What you need is a quick pair of eyes and a good horse—alert, yet perfectly steady. Anyhow, I never remember in all my range experience enjoying anything more than pointing that herd of broncos. It isn't every day you get a chance at over a thousand of them, all wild, in one lot. To see the whole herd swing, and sway, and swerve, this way or that, as easy as water flowing—in response to the slightest movement on my part—was a beautiful and exciting experience.

At length the fellows on circle had all the pockets worked, and we started down the long draw leading to the corrals. Once inside, Tom wanted to catch La Vaqueta, to take off the strap and see how she'd act. So we ran her off with a few others into a catching pen, and someone caught her by the neck, and we lined up on the rope to choke her down. She proved hard to choke, but finally she began to sway and stagger, and down she went. I ran up with a few others to loosen the rope around her neck and hold her down. But it wasn't necessary. She never stirred. The brown mare lay there as dead as a doornail. Too bad, La Vaqueta! We had broken your heart.

## II

I have just told you how we corraled the brown outlaw mare, La Vaqueta. How we roped her and threw her, and how we broke her heart. Too bad, indeed, I remember thinking; and I don't believe there was one of the boys of the outfit but felt a pang of sympathy for the brave old mare that died sooner than surrender. May we all be as stout-spirited as that!

But, as every cowman knows, cattle on a rough range get every bit as wild as horses. The roughest country we had on the Bell Ranch was the brakes of the Atarque. It isn't rough in the sense that much of Arizona is; it's on an altogether smaller scale, and not really mountain at all. But it's as rough as a country can be, and yet be good grazing. It might, perhaps, be best described as a wild scatter of parks and pockets, cut up in every possible direction by steep and rocky ridges, over which narrow trails lead from park to park. The boys on circle were always cautioned to work carefully and make as little noise as possible. You might sight a bunch of cattle in an open park and slip around it; but let them once get wind of you and they would hit it for the nearest trail and be gone like a flash. And with the best rock horse in the world you'd be lucky to get sight of them again that day, much less catch them.

I suppose we could have got a lot of these outlaws out by making a special work, or by contract. Up on the Mesa the Wagon Mound and Watrous cattle associations, which represented the range cattlemen of those districts, paid ten dollars for every outlaw animal brought out of the Mora and Red River brakes. I remember planning, one time, with my brother-in-law, Harry McKellar, to take over a contract. Harry was a crack hand, and I thought I had the best horse for roping in rocks in New Mexico. (And I'm still not sure I hadn't.) But the Bells during my time never made any special effort; just depended on the regular outfit to get out whatever it could.

Under such conditions there were "critturs" that got away every year and finally became outlaws. Cows and steers were running in those brakes, as old as 15 or 20 years, that had never been in a roundup since they were branded. One old spotted steer all the old Bell hands knew. A perfect specimen of Texas Longhorn he was, tall and gaunt and narrow, with a tremendous spread of horn; and warier and speedier than a deer.

One day on the fall roundup two of the boys came upon this old chap and succeeded in cutting him off. Riding good horses, they ran onto him and laid their lines on him, brought him in to camp and joined him with the day herd. A day or two after he was driven down to the headquarters ranch and corraled there, with the idea of dehorning him and turning him loose in the horse pasture till we got ready to ship. The wildest cowbrute will become tractable if you take off his horns.

Well, they got his horns off, opened the corral gate and turned him loose. The poor old fellow was sore and wrathy as he came out of the corral. He looked all around him for someone to take it out on. But not a soul was to be seen. The ground floor of that ranch at that particular moment was totally deserted. What population there was, was situated on the top rail of corral gates and other objects off the ground. There was a large open shed in the center of the yard and the old man went over there, moving with a queer little scuttle, and rummaged around for a while among the buggies and chuck-wagons and blacksmith's outfits, etc. But there was clearly no business to be done there, as the only man in the shed had climbed on top of a chuckbox, and the steer seemed on the point of quitting the premises altogether when his eye fell on a narrow gap in a brick wall that formed an enclosure around the main ranch dwelling.

I was standing inside this enclosure, tinkering with something close beside the kitchen door, the steer having passed out of my mind for the moment, when all of a sudden, lo and behold, his bovine nibs pops through the hole in the wall within a few feet of me and, tickled to find a victim at last, comes at me head down, snuffing. I did not wait to argue the point with him; I executed an immediate retirement through the kitchen door, lowering all records for events of that sort. The old fellow seemed puzzled at my sudden disappearance, but, after a moment's consideration he turned and trotted back through the wall and, finding no one outside, scuttled away along the road leading east through the pasture and disappeared in a dip of the creek.

A couple of hours or so after, about sundown, someone coming in to the ranch reported seeing an animal lying in the creek a hundred yards or so below the house. So I went down to investigate. There, sure enough, was the old spotted steer, stretched out full length in the middle of the creek. It was dusk and the water flowing past his body gave an appearance of movement to it. But as I came up to him I saw at once that the old steer would range the pastures no longer. When he left the kitchen door and disappeared from view in the dip of the creek, he had run into the first pool he encountered, shoved his head under the water and deliberately drowned himself.

Too bad; we had broken another old outlaw's heart.

# 3
# The River ("The Old Canadian")

WHEN I look back on my years on the Bell Ranch, the thing that seems to have played the principal figure in our lives was the River.

A number of my range readers must have "pulled bog" on the old Canadian in one part or another of its long course from where it heads on the Colorado-New Mexico line to where it slips into the Arkansas in eastern Oklahoma. Nine hundred miles the old man has meandered before that—through lofty mountains, along the foot of deep canyons, across wide flats—at one time just a succession of dry sand reaches; at another a red terror, dealing ruin and death.

Everywhere the river had the same reputation for sudden alternations of complete dryness and flood. The drying up is due, perhaps, to the narrow watershed it drains on either bank. For, parallel with the Canadian throughout nine-tenths of its course flow two other large streams, sometimes not forty miles distant: the Cimarron on the north, and the Red River to the south. The latter is one of the big rivers of the country, measuring fifteen hundred miles from its source forty miles south of the Bell pasture to where it yields its waters at last to Ol' Man River, the great Mississippi, clear down in Mississippi.

The Canadian went usually by the name of Red River in New Mexico. I suppose this was because the Mexicans called it Rio Colorado, on account of its red waters in flood time. I never followed it beyond the line of New Mexico, but always I heard of it as the same old wicked stream, treacherous alike to man and beast.

Yet the old river, in our district at least, opened its wide banks to a host of fine streams that served to make the Bell pasture the grand grazing range it is. And in summer when the bottoms were yellow with sunflowers, or in fall when the Indian summer haze softened the outlines of the surrounding mesas, and the wide draws that sweep down to the river on both sides were rich with grama grass, the Canadian offered many a memorable picture to the lover of nature. I use the word memorable because my own memory of it, after all these years, is still fresh and delightful.

I think the first time I got to know the Red River was when a mustang cowhorse I had on the mesa got away from me one day. A week or so after I got word from Dolph Harmon, who rode for the Red River Cattle Company (owned by H. M. Porter of Denver), that my horse was in their pasture in the brakes of the Red River. So I went over to Dolph's to hunt for him. Dolph's camp was surely a wild and lonely place, and I recall him, as we talked that night, telling me it was hard to get a man to stay there alone, as the place was haunted. On wild nights a wagon drove around the house and up to the door. "If you listen close," Dolph said, "you can hear the clucking of the wagon wheels." It was in those same brakes that Ira Gail, range foreman for the V cross T's, perpetrated, it was believed, a killing that must have caused ghosts to haunt those canyons for all time to come.

But I was to get to know the river well enough when I went down to the Bell's. The nature of my position there took me on many long solo trips to all parts of the grant. And since the river must have meandered fully sixty miles through the dead center of the pasture, the greater number of my trips took me across it. You never knew what to expect. You would come down to a regular everyday crossing, to find a sheer cliff of sand five or six feet deep where you entered on the level a week before. What was a mere thread of water in the morning might be a roaring torrent when when you rode back to it in the afternoon. That might not be so bad in the northern end of the river, because there were Mexican settlements there, and I've often paid a Mexican fifty cents to go ahead of me on foot: they knew every ridge and rock in the river. But in remote parts, far from any human habitation, one just had to take a chance: I'd strip, and wade or swim beside my horse, hoping for the best. But I've stood on those banks, hesitating many a long minute. Some of us, too, had had close calls in floodtime crossing cattle.

But what we dreaded most were the quicksands. You can only tell them when your horse begins to shift his feet uneasily, or you feel a kind of tremor beneath you. They were the worst things for the cattle, too. You know, when a cow sinks in one of them and stays there all night, the sand gradually settles around her till she might as well be in a bed of concrete. You have to dig her out—if she's alive—and then you find the circulation clean gone out of her legs.

O yes, it was a helluva mean old river, all right. And that is why I said at the start the River played the principal part in our lives down there. If you met a Mexican on the road—and anyone you met down there was likely to be a Mexican—you'd greet him, "*Cómo le va, amigo?* (how goes it, friend?)" and then you'd say, "*Cómo está el río?* (how's the river?)" I remember one time starting off with my wife and small boy for Las Vegas, which was our nearest town, eighty miles to the west. We used to drive a team of mules to the buggy, Biddy and Judy. Judy was as mean as they make mules. I used to have to throw my rope around her forelegs to harness her or even to hang a nose-bag on her. And she had most of the other tricks mules learn. Well, we got off from the ranch and reached the river, to find it in flood. You can imagine, when you were starting on an eighty-mile trip by buggy, you hated to be stopped ten miles from home, so I whipped up the team and we drove in. When we got to where the water was belly deep to the mules, Judy decided that was far enough and indicated her decision by lying down. I whipped her up and was for going on when, somehow, something in me said the black mule might know best, and I turned the team—with some difficulty—and we scrambled back onto dry land.

It occurred to me to go and look up Ysaias Munyiz, an old Bell hand who lived a short piece up the river, and enquire about the flood. "How about the river, amigo?" I said. "*O, señor, lleva mucha agua* (it carries much water)." But when I told him we had started to cross it, he exclaimed, "*Ah, que carambas!* what good luck *la* Judy lay down. You would have been swept away and drowned *con tu señora y el muchachito y todo* (with your lady and the little boy and everything.)" There remained nothing to do but go back to the ranch and await the subsidence of the river.

So the ornery old black mule saved us—me and, which is more important, my good wife and boy—from the red terror of the Canadian. And if ever I meet up with you again on the other side, Judy, I'll sure rope you by the forelegs (just like old times) and hang a nosebag on you full up to the top with whatever the stuff is they feed to mules in those regions.

II

But they weren't all grim, my recollections of the old Canadian. I will try and show you now why I have some pleasant memories of the river, too.

The title to the Bell Ranch, or to give it its official name, the Pablo Montoya Grant and Baca Location, was perfect. Nevertheless, the northern part of the river from the mouth of Las Conchas to the grant fence contained several settlements of Mexicans, who farmed little plots of land and ran their goats and milk cows in the surrounding brakes.

Now the general management and running of the ranch before the Eastern company acquired it and brought Arthur

Tisdall from the Paloduro ranch in Texas to be general manager, had been in the hands of Western men of the old stamp, reared under pioneer principles. They believed in the strong arm, and there doesn't appear to have been any attempt made to get the settlers off the grant other than by scaring them and doing them dirt whenever an opportunity showed up. As a result the feeling between the employees of the company and the settlers was about as bad as it could be. One of the first things I was warned about, on going down there, was to keep strictly out of the Mexican *placitas* or settlements, and never to go about the grant unarmed.

However, a short while after the new ownership came into effect it was decided to start a movement to get the settlers off the grant, and it fell to me to take the principal hand in this proceeding. There were one or two things that were of help to me in this task. To begin with, I had a good working knowledge of the Spanish language, both to speak and write it. A second point in my favor was that I did not have to the full the prejudice against Mexicans that prevailed almost universally among the cattlemen of the West. I had, I must confess, something of that contempt for what we are pleased to consider "inferior races," which is characteristic of all Anglo-Saxon peoples: I remember sharply resenting being arrested, once, by a Mexican peace officer. But, raised in one of the older countries, I never felt that active animosity against the "greaser" that characterized almost all western Americans.

This attitude and state of feeling spread over the West from Texas, along with the cattle business which originated there. Its roots were in the Alamo. Numbers of the good people of the East have never heard of the Alamo. But for the Texan of those days—it is even true of the present generation—the memory of that spot with its record of Mexican savagery kept alive a never failing flame of hatred and contempt for everything Mexican. As a consequence, the range men of those times treated the

entire Spanish-American people as if they had no rights at all;
refused to have any social relations with them, although some
were of proud Spanish blood, killed them, dispossessed them of
their lands, scattered their sheep and drove off their cattle. The
Mexicans, being without means of self-defense, became completely cowed and browbeaten. Few there were, like Elfego
Baca, to learn the expert use of the gun, and meet and defy
the Gringo on his own ground. Nevertheless, underneath smoul-
dering fires of resentment burned, and I have seen a Mexican
give a toy pistol to the child he was dandling on his knee with
the words: "*Mata al Americano* (kill the American)!" It was
under some such conditions of feeling between the Bell Ranch
personnel and the Mexican settlers that we undertook to get the
settlers off the grant.

I remember distinctly the day I rode down into the little settlement of Alamosas to break the ice, so to speak. I took with
me Shorty Horne, one of the boys. We both packed our guns,
there being no knowing what kind of reception we might get.
The Mexicans had many an old score against the Bell outfit to
pay off. But nothing untoward happened as we visited one or
two families and talked about things in general. So I decided
to tackle the business of getting the settlers off the grant without
any further delay. We selected Jake Munyiz—whom I have
mentioned before—to start in on, because he was a kind of leader
among the Mexicans of the river. Jake had a fine *rincon* fenced
off by itself. He had been born there, I believe, and certainly
the idea of leaving it had never entered his head. I recall clearly
how, when I brought up the subject of getting him off it, he
flinched as if I had shot him.

Now seven hundred years back, in old England, it was enacted
by King Edward the First, that title to property could be acquired by possession. That enactment became part of the old
English Common Law which still prevails throughout the United
States, except Louisiana. The time required to establish title by

possession varies, but in New Mexico during the '90's it was ten years. When established, such a title is known as an "original title" and takes precedence over all others. It was the purpose of the company to recognize and respect any legal rights of the settlers, and doubtless some of them were in a position to prove a possessory title. I made it my business to identify these as far as possible. From those who consented to sell we took a quit-claim deed and paid them the price agreed on in cash; it was never a large amount. It so happened that there was plenty of vacant public land *outside* the grant where, at least, water could be gotten by wells with good surrounding range, and we encouraged the idea of their locating claims on these lands and gave them what assistance we could in that direction. Many had no show of legal title, but even from these we took a quitclaim deed, and gave them a small cash compensation to help them reestablish themselves.

Jake was the first to leave the grant. He located a good claim outside the fence, and it actually came about that before long others caught the idea of getting them a piece of Government land and abandoning the grant. By the time I left the Bell's there were only a few families remaining, and these had gone by 1898 or 1899, a few years later.

Never was a more bloodless eviction! If there was any ill feeling, there was but little outward sign of it. The Spanish-American is quick to appreciate just and straight-forward treatment and it was the management's aim to give these people that. It was an advantage, too, to be able to handle cases directly in their own language. The availability of Government land helped a lot. As for *el manijador*, as the Mexicans called me—if I may be allowed to speak personally—I can truthfully say that throughout these transactions the very reaches of the river I had been most warned against, became the places where I felt entirely safe to go unarmed. Such hospitality as these people could offer was open to me day or night. I might even happen in, occasionally, on one of their simple functions or ceremonies—a wedding or the like—which so often contain picturesque and touching customs and ritual. O, certainly, some of my memories of the old river are pleasant ones!

# 4

## The Bartender from Clayton

I
T was—if my memory serves me right—just one hundred and
twenty-eight miles around the original Bell pasture. Measuring, say, six or eight miles outwards around the entire fence,
you have a good big tract of country. It was fortunate for us
that the greater part of this tract was very sparsely peopled, for
we used to figure that the entire population of it fed off Bell
beef. It wasn't easy to correct this condition. You couldn't expect
the average fence rider, living off by himself in an isolated camp,
to risk his life trying to detect beef thieves. I told you what
they did to Mike Lantry at the Atarque fence camp, in retalia-
tion for some act or other of his. We found the old man hacked
to death with an axe.

But of actual cattle stealing there was, I believe, comparatively
little. The population was largely Mexican, and the Mexicans
had not up to that time—at least in New Mexico—learned all the
practices of the "superior" race which occupied the country
alongside them. A little later, in the days of the Whitecaps, we
were to find to our cost that they had been apt enough pupils.

Up on La Cinta creek, however, about three miles above its
entry into the Bell fence, and where it runs through a narrow
canyon, lived an American—of the name of Lester Hall—who
had the reputation of stealing stock on a considerable scale and
devoting special attention to the Bell brand. Hall had a claim
up there and ran a small bunch of cattle. He was a tall, powerfully built fellow, with a loud voice and blustering manner.
There is no doubt he had for long had the fence riders on that
string of fence completely hoodooed. When Tisdall and I came

BEEF STEALERS

in, we decided to try to put a stop to Mr. Hall's activities. The problem was to find the man for the job.

Now, over in Clayton, Union county, which was the town we shipped our cattle from, there was at this time a bartender of the name of Jack Pressley. Clayton was a considerable shipping point, and a good many lively doings took place there from time to time. But in the Union saloon where Jack worked, there was seldom any trouble. Jack's reputation for preserving order was widely known and got results. Not but what he was pleasant and friendly enough with the patrons of the place and interfered but little with them under ordinary conditions. They were mostly cowboys and Jack was an ex-cowpuncher himself. Only, on the rare occasions when he did see fit to intervene Jack had never been known to back down, and while he was slow to draw, he was deadly quick on the trigger.

To make a long story short, we hired Jack Pressley to take over the La Cinta line of fence and watch Lester Hall. We established him and his wife in an old adobe house about two miles below Hall's place. Mrs. Pressley was a pleasant and refined lady who made that old 'dobe shine, as far as that was humanly possible, and who cooked and served their simple meals as delicately as a chef at a Ritz-Carlton.

I used to take a whirl around the fences from time to time, and many a pleasant night I've spent with that couple, and many a long ride taken with Jack. He was a quiet-spoken, rather retiring sort of fellow, and I never got much out of him about his past life. A good big man by nature, some malady, I guessed, had wasted the flesh from off his frame, and his face was as pale as paper in the circle of his black hair and beard. He was not a robust man: he used to tell me how after an extra hard day cutting cattle he would be feverish and not sleep. But the black eyes always looked out from that pale face, clear and direct; and with, I used to think, some secret fire in them.

And how did our arrangement for the La Cinta fence camp

pan out? That was the point. It's often hard to judge results in such cases. But one day I was riding along with Shorty Horne, one of the boys, and the subject of Lester Hall cropped up. Shorty was a young Englishman, a friend of Arthur Tisdall, who had gone completely cowboy. He had worked for the X I T's and other big outfits, was a good cowhand and a great favorite with the boys. Oftentimes we would talk over the affairs of the ranch together. This day, when Lester Hall's name came up, Shorty said sharply: "You better look out for that fellow! He has it in for you the worst kind." And he described how Lester had come to the outfit one day and told them what he was going to do to the new range manager, whenever he met him. And he had told them stories about me, intended to discredit me with the boys. Each one—as Shorty related it—a lie out of the whole cloth.

Now you couldn't expect to run a big outfit like the Bell's, especially in those lawless times, without making at least one deadly enemy. And as for one's reputation with the men, I took the view, always, that that must rest ultimately with your own character and acts, rather than with anything that was said about you. So I didn't allow Lester's lies and threats to disturb me unduly. Moreover, from another point of view, Shorty's information afforded me great satisfaction. For, as I had it figured out in my mind, the only possible reason for this cow thief's feeling such enmity towards me was that our new set-up on the fence had put the kibosh on his customary operations. It seemed that, without so much as pulling a gun, our man, Pressley, had been able to put the fear of the Lord into Mr. Lester Hall.

I wish I could have given you a more exciting story than this is. There is nothing I'd have liked better than to be able to describe for you what took place when big and blustering Lester Hall, driving off a bunch of Bell cattle, met in with the frail, quiet-spoken bartender from Clayton, on his round of the fence. I can tell you one thing: It wouldn't have been Jack that backed water. But nothing of that kind happened.

Jack Pressley is not the sort of man the historians will tell about in their history books. No saga will ever be written around his name. But this cowboy-bartender was one of a select company of cool, courageous, firm-willed men who helped, far more than some self-important officials, to make the Old West a place where you could conduct legitimate business, and where a fellow could keep pretty well out of trouble, unless he was hunting for it. And I'm glad of this opportunity to put on record—however inadequately—one of these men whom I knew well.*

---

*On rare occasions in these stories it has seemed better to give a fictitious name to a real character. "Lester Hall" is a case in point.

# 5

## The Easterner and the Ranch Cook

PERHAPS some of you haven't heard the story of the Arizona cowpuncher and the traveling man, so I'll tell it to you. A cowboy came in off the range one day to one of the small Arizona towns and proceeded to celebrate at the one saloon of the place. As the rot-gut began to get in its work he started shooting out the lights, making people drink with him, and generally rendering life unpleasant for everybody. And no one seemed to have the nerve to try and stop him. Now there happened to be a shoe drummer in the town that night and he sauntered into the saloon to while away the time. He observed the cowpuncher for some time with evident disfavor. Finally, as the fellow pulled an extra rough stunt, he walked quietly up to him and said: "Look here; I'll give you five minutes to get out of town." And the cowboy put up his gun, walked out of the saloon to where his horse was hitched and rode out of town. After he was gone, someone went up to the drummer and asked him: "What would you have done if that fellow hadn't got out when you told him to?" And the drummer considered a moment and said: "Well, I'd have extended the time."

I suppose most people have been at some time or other in the situation of the traveling man. I have, on several occasions. One of them was at the Bell Ranch.

One day we received notice from the company headquarters in New York to expect a young fellow as guest at the ranch for several months. In due course he arrived at Las Vegas, whence we brought him out to the ranch. He turned out to be the son of a widely known Chicago millionaire—we will call him Mr.

J.P— who had married a famous ex-actress and society leader; and he had an uncle who was a well known Episcopalian bishop. In spite of these plentiful supplies of worldly and spiritual riches the young man, J. P— Jr., had turned out no account, and it was thought it might settle him down to send him to a far-West ranch where people live the simple life and you had to go eighty miles to get anything stronger than Hostetter's Stomach Bitters.

J.P— Jr. himself turned out to be a handsome, if rather dissipated looking youth, with a remarkably fine physique; and a pleasant enough companion. But, like some other young Easterners I have met, he apparently inclined to the opinion that nice manners were thrown away on the uncivilized Western ranchman and his women folk.

The management of the Bell's had quarters and a cook to themselves, separate from the bunkhouse where the boys ate and slept. We had at this time a married couple doing for us, Mr. and Mrs. Duggan. Duggan was a big powerful man, and his wife a pleasant and attractive young woman. They were, however, town folk and not overly well suited with ranch life. One day we were having our midday meal and some of the food apparently was not cooked to the taste of our Chicago guest. The natural thing for him to have done was to ask my wife to have the trouble corrected, but no, Mr. J. P—Jr. had other ideas. He ups and out to the kitchen, yanks a skillet off the dresser, slaps it on the stove and cooks his food over to suit his taste, without so much as by your leave to the lady, Mrs. Duggan, presiding there. Then he comes back with his plate to the dining room, my wife and I saying nary a word, only wondering if this was the latest society stunt of the Chicago millionaire group.

After dinner I was on my way over to the office when I was accosted by Duggan. He was evidently in a high state of excitement and enquired where Mr. P— was. I asked him what he wanted him for. He replied that J. P— had insulted his wife—he then told me what had happened in the kitchen—and that he wanted to talk to him. Now it was perfectly clear that Mr. Duggan was in no condition at that moment to carry on an amicable conversation with anyone, let alone J. P—; and while I secretly agreed that the latter was a cad, and, moreover, I was debating in my mind which of these two husky guys would win out in a scrap, yet J. P— was my guest, and it didn't agree with my ideas for him to be assaulted on our premises. So I said, quite quietly, to Duggan: "I don't propose for you to see Mr. P—."

Duggan looked me over. I weighed a hundred and forty-five pounds to his one hundred and eighty.

"How do you propose to stop me?" he said.

The faint sneer accompanying his words did not escape me, but I replied, still quite quietly: "That's not the point. I now propose for you to go to your own quarters, Duggan, and stay there. I'll give you one minute to decide." And Duggan turned away without another word and walked off to his own room, and that was the last I ever heard of the matter.

Now if any of you have managed to get this far with this long story about next to nothing, you may wonder if I really intended to prevent Duggan meeting J. P—, and if so, how I proposed to do it. (I may say that I had only one man on the ranch that day, Willis Dorset, an old Bell hand.) Or whether I was prepared, like the drummer, to extend the time.

In the first place, I most certainly never for a moment entertained the idea of "blocking" Duggan by fighting him myself. Long ago I decided that there was neither money nor glory in engaging in physical encounters with people you were sure could whip you. I learned this lesson young. As a kid at "prep" school I had quite a liking for a scrap and, although a lightweight, would take on most anyone. (It's my belief kids never really hurt each other.) One day I had a row with one of the biggest boys in the school and cheerfully attacked him. We belabored each other for some time and when we quit it seemed to be a draw. Later on, however, I turned quite sick and had to go to bed. Next day when I came back to school I expected to be hailed by the boys as a hero on account of my good stand against Big Johnson. But don't you believe it! What I got on all sides was, "Well, boy, how did you like your licking?" or "You better pick on one of your own size next time!" So, as I said, I never entertained the idea of taking on Duggan myself. As a matter of fact there were but few fist fights in the West in those days. Difficulties were generally settled with that useful instrument, the .45 Colt, which, as old Joe Matt used to say, "makes all men equal."

And that brings up the question of the gun, and I think I could have fixed Mr. Duggan there. I doubt if he was used to firearms; while I, though certainly no Wild Bill Hickock on the draw, had not shot the heads off several millions of sunflowers and such like with my little .41, without learning to hit something. But I was brought up with a wholesome respect for human life, and most certainly wouldn't have risked any lives on account of Mister J. P—Jr.

There remained, however, one weapon which it occurred to me during the moments I was talking to Duggan, that I could use. The rope! Most of us fellows were pretty handy with that in those days, because we used the rope often for things that would be done today in a pen and chute. We did not, of course, *time* our performances at that period; when we laid our string on an animal it was to do something to it, brand or blab it, or the like. But I fancy—to consider the matter in modern terms— that I could, with some assistance from Willis Dorset, have roped and tied down Mr. Duggan in somewhere around thirty seconds. Then I would have left him till he cooled off.

And that's just what I intended doing.

# 6

## The Bandits Visit Us:
## Turkey Canyon Fight

### I

THE modern bandit belongs to an organized syndicate. He is probably armed with a machine gun, and may make his escape in an armored car. He hides out amid the mazes of a crowded city. Things were a bit different for the Western bandit of the '80's and '90's. Sometimes he held up trains in solitary places, single-handed or with one associate, depending solely on his skill and nerve in the use of his weapons. He almost always had to make a getaway through rough country, stealing fresh horses as he went, and securing food by any means possible. He hid out in wild outdoor places. He was an example of rugged individualism sufficient to satisfy ex-President Hoover.

Of such an order was Black Jack (Tom) Ketchum. A name, around the turn of the century, to awake alarm in the breast of every man, woman and child throughout the Rocky Mountain region.

I have told you the Bell Ranch had much wild country and was far removed from town or railroad—a good place, in fact, to be in if you were wanted by the sheriff. Every year when the spring work opened up, men from all parts of the West would come to look for work with the wagons. Some of them were likely to be outlaws, we knew. We asked no questions, only if a man could work cattle.

One spring day in the '90's a tall, finely built man, wearing a square black beard, rode up to Tom Kane's wagon and asked for work. Being short-handed Tom took him on. He turned out to be a good hand, but it was noticed that he never parted with his gun by day or night. His general deportment, too, inclined to be of the tough order, and the boys decided that a "bad hombre" was in camp. The fellow was an expert juggler with his six-shooter. He could twirl the big .45 round and round on the trigger finger, cocking and firing it at each turn with astonishing speed and accuracy. And he seemed fond of exhibiting his prowess. However, after a few days he picked a quarrel with the wagon boss and quit. He came into headquarters, settled up with Henry Winn, the bookkeeper, and rode away north. That same afternoon Tom Kane came in on us from camp and word went out to the country that Black Jack had been working with the Bell wagon.

A few days later Juan, an old hand of the Bell's, rode in to the ranch from his fence camp on La Cinta creek. He reported that some men were camped in the willow brakes of the creek just below the north fence. That they never showed themselves, but their horses were staked out and hobbled around and the stake changed by night. I told him to keep as close a watch as possible and report, and to look out for his saddle horses.

We heard nothing more from Juan, but a few mornings later, the storekeeper, Henry Winn discovered that a little storeroom where we kept ranch stores, had been broken into in the night. It stood in a small horse pasture just across the creek from the house. Examination showed that two men had left their horses just outside the fence, and we saw the tracks of their high-heeled boots down to the storeroom and back. They had evidently taken only what they needed for their journey, and their horse tracks showed they were headed south.

Tom Kane, the wagon boss, was at the ranch that night. Tom had served often as a deputy sheriff and liked that kind of work. He undertook to follow the men and started off well armed amid considerable excitement.

News traveled slowly on the Bell ranch and we heard no more of Tom, but several days after the following word reached us. The little store at Liberty, a small settlement thirty miles south and just outside the Bell fence, had been broken into by night, the post-office robbed and a few blankets stolen. The next morning Levy Herztein, the little Jew storekeeper, had taken two Mexicans and started out to track the robbers. After riding an hour or two they came to a slight rise. As they surmounted it, they saw two men crouched alongside their horses. But that was all they did see, because an instant later a perfect rain of bullets showered upon them, and Herztein and both Mexicans fell to the ground. The gun play exhibited by the "bad man" in the cow camp had evidently been no bluff!

The bandits then, as we heard the story, came up to where the men had fallen. They rolled the body of one of the Mexicans over. He was evidently dead. Then they turned to the Jew and one of them, bending over the body, fired shot after shot into it as it lay. Every time he would pump the lead into it he would say, "You son of a ——! You son of a ——!" Finally they desisted and went off, and the Mexican they thought dead got up and mounted his horse and rode back to Liberty to carry the news. He had only been wounded but had been smart enough to "play possum" and had lain there quietly taking in with his ears the whole proceeding. And by the way, folks, I've always maintained that that Mexican had an excellent brand of nerve. The two bandits were never exactly identified with this crime, but there is no doubt they were Tom (Black Jack) Ketchum and his brother Sam.

And Tom Kane didn't run into the bandits after all. Tom was nervy, all right, but experienced. Unlike poor little Herztein, he was wise to the kind of fellows he was following. 1 shall never doubt that from the moment he left the ranch in pursuit he was quite determined to keep one good day behind Black Jack and his companion.

II

I have said that the two bandits described above were undoubtedly Tom and Sam Ketchum. Although the finely built man with the black beard, who worked with the outfit and showed off his skill with the six-shooter, was Sam Ketchum, not Tom, as the boys believed. Neither they, nor any one else, seem ever to have been connected up, legally, with the killing of the little Jew. We didn't, unless there were some special reason, go to very much trouble over little affairs of that kind in those days. We will leave aside for the present the fate of Tom Ketchum. As for Sam, he was taken wounded a few days after the fight in Turkey canyon between bandits who had held up a Colorado and Southern train and Sheriff Edward Farr of Huerfano county, Colorado, and his posse. I am going to describe for you briefly the circumstances that led up to and followed that fight, as well as the fight itself, because it is one of the most remarkable in Western annals.

Somewhere in the month of April, 1899, says my friend George Crocker, old-time cowpuncher and cattleman of Cimarron, New Mexico, two tough looking hombres rode into Cimarron, leading a pack horse. They made camp in Turkey canyon, a branch of the Cimarron canyon. Although evidently ordinary cowpunchers, they seem to have had plenty of money to spend on their frequent visits to town, planking down fifty-dollar bills from time to time at the bar. One of the men was known as Franks, the other proved to be Sam Ketchum.

Along in early June of the same year there was brought into the district a train of WS cattle from the Mogollon country in south-western New Mexico. With it came a fellow called William McGinnis who took a room at the Lambert hotel in town. He and the two hombres camped in the canyon seemed to know each other and to be on friendly terms. Towards the middle part of the month and about the same time all three men left the neighborhood.

A little later still in July word went abroad that the Denver and Fort Worth express had been held up near Folsom, New Mexico. Three men appeared to have been engaged in the holdup and it did not take the good citizens of Cimarron long, says George, to decide who they were. The express messenger had hidden the contents of the safe, so the bandits got nothing. After some days Sheriff Farr of Huerfano county, took three deputies and a Colorado and Southern special agent and started from Trinidad in pursuit of the robbers. They tracked them to a point near Cimarron where the trail turned off towards Turkey canyon. Coming on to Cimarron, Farr added five local men to his posse, making ten in all, and the party made for Turkey canyon. As they came over a rise the smoke from a camp fire became visible ahead. Concluding it was the bandits' fire Farr took steps at once to surround them. They had chosen a steep and rugged country for their camp. He divided his men into three groups, sending one to the south side and another to the bottom, of the canyon, while he himself with three men occupied the north slope. The robbers had apparently been taken by surprise. As Farr started to go forward a man appeared on an open spot carrying a coffeepot, evidently on his way to get water. Farr opened fire on him and he fell shot in four places. It proved to be McGinnis. The body lay right out in the open; they could have shot him again and killed him, but they thought he was dead—which was a stroke of luck for the bandits.

It was about four o'clock in the afternoon when the battle began, and the survivors said the firing on both sides was very severe. Before they had been at it long, Sam Ketchum came running down towards Farr and lay down under a log, but presently a shot that shattered his right shoulder rendered him helpless. This left the third man, Franks, to handle the situation single-handed. Running across an open space into a bushy side canyon he planted himself behind a ledge of rock and held the posse at bay till darkness fell and the bandits were able to escape. At this point too he must have had to assist his two wounded companions to mount their horses and get away. There is some question as to who this man Franks was. George Crocker has evidence and believes that he was Will Carver, the most desperate man and the finest shot in the entire Black Jack gang. But I think he is shown by Captain French to have been Tom Capehart, who had just before this been riding for French's WS outfit in the Mogollons.

Such was the battle of Turkey canyon, in which three cowboy bandits fought and stood off a posse of ten men, well armed, killed its leader, Farr, on the ground, wounded two others, one mortally, and made a clean getaway. Just how and when this last was effected is not quite clear, but legend still recites how William McGinnis—tall, elegant, soft-spoken bronco rider—as he rode off wounded in four places, stopped and wheeled his horse on the top of the first rise and waved his hat to the survivors of the posse. "*Adiós*, boys!" he shouted; then turned and disappeared over the crest of the hill.

Sam Ketchum didn't get very far. He rode up to the McBride ranch in Ute Park about twenty miles away and said he had been hurt in a saw mill. Only Mrs. McBride and the children were at home but Mrs. McBride gave him a room. A fellow called Pearl Claws who was staying at the ranch put him to bed and, sensing that he was one of the bandits, told him he would help him to get away. But instead of doing this they reported his whereabouts to the railroad special officer. Sam had had a chair set beside his cot and on it laid his six-shooter, where he could get it handy. These fellows never parted with their guns by night or day. A little later Claws came into the room with one of the McBride boys and picking the gun up handed it to the boy to look see what a fine gun it was. At that very moment the special officer was at the door. He walked in and arrested Ketchum.

On the way to the penitentiary at Santa Fe whither Ketchum was to be taken, they stopped at Cimarron to change teams in front of Lambert's Bar. Ruth Crocker Crowder, who was a child then, remembers climbing up on a wall to get a view of the bandit. He was holding his right arm with his left hand and clenching his teeth as though in pain. George Crocker was there too and says: "As they were hitching a fresh team to the spring wagon, quite a crowd gathered round. Jim Hunt was talking to Ketchum. Jim asked him what his right name was. 'Who do they think I am?' he says. Jim said, they think you are Sam Ketchum. He says, 'that's my name.' Then he went on to say he had never much harm in his life. He pointed to Pearl Claws. 'There's a meaner man than I am. If he hadn't worked it the way he did and got my gun, I'd of had his hide hanging on the fence!' " They got Sam to the penitentiary at Santa Fe, but he died four days later of blood poisoning.

Meanwhile McGinnis with two body wounds, devotedly assisted by Tom Capehart, rode two hundred and fifty miles by long rides into Lincoln county. There he stayed for a month, lying up in the hills, while his wounds were slowly healing. During all that time he never changed his bloody shirt! Meanwhile Tom, who was unwounded and less well known, tried to get work around and kept in touch with Mac. A squatter in a lonely cabin nearby let them have water from his spring and sometimes articles of food they needed. I am relying for this part of my story on the account given by my friend and neighbor, the Honorable William French of the W S ranch,* because he was in close touch with Capehart immediately subsequent to these events.

French describes at length the piece of sheer ill luck that finally led to Mac's arrest. Mac's wounds having at last stopped running, and Tom being unable to find work in the neighborhood, the two men decided to ride clear across to the extreme western edge of the state and take refuge at the W S ranch, where they had been working previous to the hold-up and where they had friends. Tom went off to get provisions for the whole trip, as it would be dangerous for Mac to show himself

*Some Recollections of a Western Ranchman: Stokes

in towns or settlements, and it was agreed that they should
meet the following morning at the squatter's hut and start from
there on their long ride. Now it happened that a sheriff and party
were out on a hunt for a band of local horse thieves. Suspecting
that the squatter was an accomplice of the band, they overpowered him and concealed themselves in his cabin, in anti-
cipation of the robbers assembling there. It happened to be the
identical morning of Mac and Tom's tryst. Mac was the first
of the two men to arrive. He got down off his horse and walked
directly in at the door of the shack to find himself face to face
with a party of armed men and every gun covering him. They
had seen him coming and believed him one of the horse stealing
gang.

Mac, on the other hand, naturally thought they were after
him for the train hold-up, and turned loose with his six-shooter
which had only two cartridges in it. He shot one man in the
wrist, threw away the gun, and started in to defend himself
with his fists. They had to beat him senseless before he could
be overpowered. Thereupon they discovered his bloody shirt
and partly healed wounds, and realized that the man they had
captured was the most advertised and badly wanted outlaw in
America, with a high reward upon his head. The sheriff had the
description of him and offer of reward in his pocket.

All this was related by the squatter to Capehart when the latter arrived at the hut a little later.

McGinnis was tried shortly after on a charge of murder at
Raton, Colfax county. People who attended the trial still describe
his gallant appearance and refined manner which won for him
the sympathy of everyone in court. Not the least among the
things that lend romance to the stories of our Western bandits
is the mystery that frequently surrounded their origin and
identity. One is certainly set to wondering about this man,
McGinnis: what was his real name; where and how was he
raised; what started him in the business of banditry. The appeal

his bearing and apparent character made to the jury seems to have affected his sentence. Instead of the death sentence which Black Jack received he was committed to the penitentiary for life, and in 1906 received a full pardon from Governor Otero.

Tom Capehart eventually escaped—along with a leading member of the gang, Butch Cassidy, who has not figured in this story—to the Argentine, where they were involved in robberies on a large scale and became notorious. Of their ultimate fate there is no information to my knowledge, except a report that Butch was killed. Even while I write this, however, Frank King, the well known Western writer, is in receipt of a letter from the widow of another bandit, George Musgrave of New Mexico, who took refuge in South America. This lady states that she was in South America with her husband, and she promises to give the public in due course much information about Butch Cassidy's career after leaving the United States. This will be welcome, since Butch was probably the most remarkable of all the Western bandits.

# 7

## Black Jack Plays a Solo Part
## and Loses

I AM giving you this story of the bandits in a rather jerky fashion, but that is the way it came to me. News did not reach us in those days on remote ranches in stream-lined dispatches. The buckboard mailcarrier brought most of it by word of mouth on his tri-weekly trips, or some cowpuncher happening by the ranch. So we will turn back now to an afternoon in August, 1899, when Tom Ketchum rode his big brown up the front street of the quiet little town of Folsom, and got off him and tied him up in front of Jim Kent's saloon. As he entered the saloon word went around speedily that it was Black Jack, the famous outlaw, and everyone wondered at his showing himself so openly only five weeks after his gang had committed a train holdup close by, followed by a severe and disastrous fight. One nervous member of the company disappeared under the table. Addicted, like many men of the day, more to gambling than drinking, Tom without much delay set himself down opposite the lone gambler of the place, who assured him that as far as stakes were concerned, the lid was off. His luck fluctuated this way and that, as the bystanders clustered around to watch the play and the afternoon wore on, but at the last a crushing run of bad cards set in, and when Tom finally rose to quit the game, the story goes that he left a thousand dollars in gold and silver coin on the table.

We can readily form some idea, from our knowledge of the circumstances and from remarks he made afterwards as a prisoner, what Tom's thoughts were as he rode out of town that evening. The holdup business was growing precarious and unprofitable. His reputation was against his starting in any legitimate business in the United States. He would break away to South America and begin life afresh. A stake was what was needed. His attempt that afternoon to secure one at the monte table had been a flop. There was nothing for it but to hold up one more train. At this point there must have confronted him the thought of his gang: one killed, one desperately wounded, all dispersed. Not much show of help from that quarter. Well, what of it? He would hold up a train anyway, and do it alone.*

Late on the evening of August sixteenth, when the Denver and Fort Worth Express, in charge of Conductor Harrington, stopped to take water at Folsom, Tom Ketchum climbed up onto it between the engine and the baggage car. After traveling thus a few miles he clambered over the coal tender and dropped quietly into the locomotive cab. With a gun stuck in his ribs he warned the engineer to stop the train when he gave the signal. Six miles south from Folsom there is a horseshoe curve and a a narrow cut on a hill. It's a wild, remote spot that has come to be known as Robber's Gap, so many holdups have been had there. Just at this point Black Jack gave the signal. The engineer stopped the train with a jolt. Tom then ordered him and his firemen to get down and cut off the engine and baggage car. The train was on a grade, making it difficult to release the lever that held the drawheads, and moreover the two men were probably stalling for time. Tom stood by with his rifle ready, Charlie Drew, the express messenger, lighting the proceedings with a lantern. About this time the mail clerk poked his head out of the window of his coach. He didn't pull it back quick enough when Tom warned him he would shoot it off. So Tom took a quick bead on him and the mail clerk disappeared, shot through the cheek.

*I am indebted for many details of the life of Tom Ketchum to George Fitzpatrick, Editor of New Mexico Magazine.

The jerk the engineer had given the train had conveyed a warning to conductor Harrington that there was trouble somewhere ahead. He hurried forward from the dining car at the rear end of the train. Entering the mail coach, he stepped past the body of Fred Bartlett, the mail clerk, who was groping on the floor moaning that he was bleeding to death, and made for the door. Now there had arisen among the traveling public great indignation at the succession of train holdups then taking place in the West, and conductor Harrington, whose train had already been held up once, had sworn that if it ever happened to him again, he was going to shoot and shoot to kill. When he stepped up to the door he had a shot gun loaded with buckshot in his hands. He opened the door just a little and by the light of Charlie Drew's lantern discerned the figure of Black Jack standing a little apart from the other three men and only a few yards away. He let drive at once.

I have remarked elsewhere on Tom's wild animal-like quickness of eye, and the instant Harrington appeared in the doorway Tom caught sight of him and drew a lightning bead on him with his high powered rifle. The conductor felt the sting of a bullet through his arm and withdrew from the door. The express messenger doused his lantern. Tom retreated into the shelter of the dark. But a blast of savage blasphemy, breaking on the night air, served notice to Harrington that his shot had taken effect.

Harrington gave orders for the train to start. The engine however had run out of steam and it was forty minutes before the engineer could get the train under way again, leaving the bandit alone with the darkness around him and forty-two slugs of buckshot in his right arm.

He had planned to make off on horseback into the country. Under a nearby cattle guard on the track they found provisions he had cached along with the dynamite to blow up the safe. But the loss of blood from his shattered arm must have rapidly so weakened him that it is doubtful whether he ever got even to where he had tied his horse. The tourniquet he had tried to apply to his arm with his left hand and teeth was only tight enough to partially check the flow of blood. The pain in the arm, too, as the night wore on became intense. He seems to have dropped down finally at a spot a few hundred yards away from the track and lain there for hours between coma and wakefulness. As day dawned the urge came on him to get help from some source. Lifting himself into a sitting position he waved with his black hat to an oncoming freight train. It stopped and the brakeman and engineer got down and came over to him. At this time all the long, long fight that had been Black Jack's life seems to have ended. He gave up his weapons readily and talked freely. True to his cowboy instinct he remembered his horse, telling them to see that someone went and got him. Presently a freight from the south pulled up; off it a man dropped, and came towards them. Tom asked who it was and was told it was Saturnino Pinard, sheriff of Union County. The sight of a peace officer stirred for a moment the old savage spirit in him. "If I had a gun," he observed, "I could shoot the son of a ——'s heart out."

"When I got word of the holdup" Sheriff Pinard writes me, "I took the first north bound freight out of Clayton. As I came up to where Black Jack was sitting, I asked him if he could walk. 'I wouldn't be here, if I could,' was his tart reply." They carried him to the train on a wire stretcher and he was taken to the hospital at Trinidad, Colorado, where the forty-two pellets were extracted from his arm. From Trinidad he went to the penitentiary at Santa Fe, for safe keeping. There his arm growing worse, Dr. Desmarais amputated it, Tom refusing to take an anesthetic. He wanted to know what they were doing when they started cutting him up. Fitzpatrick writes: Attended by a guard and a nurse, Black Jack underwent the operation without a murmur. When it was all over he smiled.

"Let me know if I can do the same for you someday, Doc," he said.

On a day in September, 1900, I was waiting at Lamy Junction for the little local train that takes one from the main Santa Fe line to the city of Santa Fe, eighteen miles distant. Everything is interesting when one is waiting for a train and my attention fell upon two peace officers and a prisoner—a heavy, powerful, one-armed man—who were pacing up and down the station platform. I was not the only one who noticed them. I found, indeed, that all eyes were centered on them and on enquiry, learned that the prisoner was the famous Black Jack Ketchum, being escorted to the penitentiary at Santa Fe. He had just been tried at Clayton, Union County. He had been convicted of "train robbery while armed," and under the statutes of the Territory condemned to be hanged. Being considered a dangerous criminal, it was decided to hold him in the penitentiary pending his execution at Clayton. The officers in charge were Saturnino Pinard, sheriff of Union County, and his deputy, Tom Gray of Clayton.

When the "local" drew in the three men climbed onto the smoking coach, and I and a few others joined them. I chose a seat near them. At close range Tom Ketchum struck me as being one of the most powerful men I've ever seen, with corresponding activity. I had a feeling he could have taken the two sheriffs and everyone else on the coach and thrown us out onto the track. Yet he was entirely free, hand and foot. I asked Tom Gray afterwards if he hadn't been afraid of his trying to escape. Gray was an experienced officer. "No," he said, "I know prisoners. I knew Tom was through."

They talked as we traveled; I observed meanwhile. Tom Ketchum's face did not impress me as being that of a particularly intelligent man; it was the face essentially of a man of action. The small black eyes were the most notable feature of it, shining and piercing, and possessed of an extraordinary alertness, like that you see in the eyes of some wild animals. This feature it was doubtless that accounted for his ability to detect, and draw a bead on, an object simultaneously. They were discussing the recent execution of some outlaw—I don't remember who—and how he had behaved at it. "Your time's yet to come, Tom," said Gray. "Yes," Tom replied, "but I believe I'll keep my nerve." He needed it. The sheriff made a grotesque miscue of releasing the trap and Tom was kept many minutes in suspense. Tom was telling us something about his life. "I've robbed a plenty of people, sure," he was saying, "but I never in my life robbed a poor man." And certainly he had the reputation of refusing to molest any women on his holdups.

The train stopped specially at the penitentiary to let them off. It was thirty-five years ago, but for some reason or other, I recall that evening as clearly as if it were yesterday. I see the bulky figure as it moved slowly between the officers through the dusk along the little pathway leading to the prison door, and the door closing on it seemed to me the closing of a desperate and adventurous career. I had wanted to ask him if it were he and his brother Sam who had camped in the Bell pasture and killed Herztein. But I didn't. I don't think he would have told me anyway.

Another record of Black Jack at this period came to me from Joe Napier of the New Mexico Mounted Rangers. Joe was quartered at my Rafter C Bar Ranch on a hunt for burnt cattle. Some Mexicans had adopted a brand closely resembling ours, and I suspected them of altering the brands on some of our cattle by means of the branding iron. We called that "burning." Joe found no burnt cattle, but he and I had some good talks. "Black Jack!" he said one day, in reply to some remarks of mine, "that's the guy give me some of the meanest moments of my career. I'll tell you how it happened. I was one of the armed guard under Sheriff Kinsell of Santa Fe that taken Tom

Ketchum from the penitentiary at Santa Fe to Clayton to be hung. We taken a heap of precautions over him; Kinsell had a guard of eight men and changed trains twice between Santa Fe and Clayton, at Glorieta and again at Las Vegas. Well we was just a-crawlin' up the heaviest grade of the Raton Pass when all of a sudden the train stopped. I run back in a hurry to the door of the coach and looked out. The train was cut. The thing flashed upon me just like that—a rescue, by God! and I don't want ever to be so scared again. A rescue by Tom Ketchum's gang wasn't goin' to be a garden party exactly. I don't reckon it was more than a few minutes till we knowed what had happened, but it seemed to me a week. As a matter of fact the train had just naturally broke in two on the steep grade and the brakeman had stopped her. They coupled her up and we got our prisoner to Clayton without anythin' further happenin'. But I believe the last thing to fade out of my memory 'll be the moment when I looked outa that train door and seen the Black Jack coach was cut off."

Black Jack paid the penalty for all his misdeeds at the Courthouse, Clayton, New Mexico, on April 26, 1901. Tom ended up his life very much as he had lived it. On his last day he was playing cards almost up to the moment of being led out to the scaffold. His sense of humor stayed with him in the face of death. When the clerk in the general store was outfitting him for his execution Tom asked him to have the shoes half a size larger than he usually wore. He said his feet would swell after death and he didn't want them to feel cramped. On the morning of the execution he expressed a wish the hanging could be held half an hour sooner. "Then," he explained, "I'd be able to have dinner in hell!" The priest came around offering his ministrations. Jack laughed as he declined them. "I'll die as I've lived, padre," he said.

I would like to have ended this story here, without entering into the details of the execution. But it seems better to throw some light on an affair which has been frequently misrepresented. The sheriff, Salome Garcia, being highly nervous over the business—as was everyone else, for hangings were an infrequent proceeding—seems to have fortified himself with several drinks. These libations appear to have unsettled his aim, because when the moment came to sever with a hatchet the rope that controlled the drop, he missed the rope entirely. The hatchet buried itself deeply in the floor of the stage, and it required several minutes before Garcia could release it and make a second attempt. Meantime Tom made good his promise to Deputy Gray about keeping his nerve at the end. He had sprung alertly up the steps of the platform at the start and carefully tested the trap door. Says Jailer Arguello: "I remember Black Jack to be game. But not boastful. 'Hurry up, boys!' I can hear him say. 'Get this over with.'"

As regards the actual mode of his death my friend Albert Shaw maintains that Tom had a dread of suffocation and that, to ensure dislocation, he gave a jump at the moment the drop was released. Such an act would have been strictly in keeping with the character of the man. This, in addition to his great weight and the (alleged) fact that the pit was eight and a half feet deep instead of the legal seven feet, was the cause, one may believe, of the outlaw's head being completely severed from his body. They found on inspection that only the black cloth stoutly pinned over it was holding it in place.

They buried Black Jack just east of the town of Clayton, where he was hanged, in an old cemetery now abandoned. I have seen a photograph of the grave, a long mound faced roughly with loose rock. We used to build range graves that way, often, to stop coyotes from digging into them. There is nothing apparently to mark whose grave it is. But at the head of it stands Tom Gray, the long-time Union County deputy sheriff, with his big sombrero off.

# 8

## I Size Up the Cowboy Bandit

In these sketches I have been giving you of Black Jack and other bandits who flourished during the years I was on the Bell Ranch and afterwards, I have offered few comments, or tried to "write up" anything that happened. Their actions and experiences have been set down and left to speak for themselves. Yet before turning away from them, I should like to see if we can form some idea of what kind of men these really were who, for a while, played so dramatic a part in Western American history. That they did play a notable part is made evident by the high rewards—French quotes a Pinkerton agent as saying that his outfit would give twenty thousand dollars for the capture of Butch Cassidy—offered for their arrest; and by the extraordinary precautions taken to prevent the rescue of Tom Ketchum when being removed for execution.

I think the first thing to do is to realize that the bandit of those times was invariably a range man. He would work until perhaps he got to be too well known—with cow outfits between raids, choosing a locality as far removed as possible from his latest scene of action, and taking a new name. I want to say that I am dealing here, not with the local cattle thief, but with the men who operated on a wide scale. That a strong sense of fellowship existed between these men and the run of cowpunchers on the ranges an incident in the taking of Sam Ketchum seems to me to illustrate. When the special officer and his guards, taking Sam to Santa Fe, were changing team at Cimarron, they left the prisoner alone in the spring wagon. The officer had inadvertently left his gun lying on the back seat of the rig and George Crocker,

THE BANDITS FIGHT IN BAD TERRAIN

seeing the bandit eyeing it, ran forward to grab it. Ketchum asked him if he was an officer and George said, no. He wanted to know then if they had caught the other men. George said they hadn't. "Then," says George, "he leaned down as if he wanted to say something confidentially. I stepped back, all I was thinking of was to keep the gun out of his reach. But after he had gone someone said to me, 'why didn't you step up there? He acted as if he wanted to tell you something.' I realized then that he had—he could tell I was a cow hand. It's my guess he wanted to send some word to his pals."

In the nature of things these men were experts in the handling of horses and cattle. No one had a better chance to know them than Captain William French, because at one time he had—entirely unknown to himself—an outfit practically composed of them, including Capehart and McGinnis. Of this outfit he says: "the way these men handled stock was a marvel." I was talking once to my friend and relative by marriage, the late J. S. (Rox) Grumbles,* pioneer cowman of Lincoln county, about Tom Ketchum, and he said to me, "Tom Ketchum was the finest cowhand I ever knew." Men of great character too, were among them. Of Jim Lowe—who under the name of Butch Cassidy was said to be wanted in almost every state and territory south of the Canadian line—French remarks that he was the best trail boss he had ever seen. Under him the outfit never got out of hand on the range, nor cut up in town. The gang these men belonged to operated over a territory a thousand miles by five or six hundred.

*Rox Grumbles was uncle of my daughter-in-law, Idelle Culley. He was a prominent early cattleman of Lincoln County, New Mexico, famous as the chief hunting ground of Billy the Kid. He came to New Mexico from Texas, whither his family had moved around 1830 from Alabama, bringing their slaves with them; the which was a common practice among Southern immigrants to Texas. As a boy Grumbles had gotten the nickname of "Rocks." He was known by no other name than Rox Grumbles during his entire life, and his ROX brand became well known.

It goes without saying that the principal characteristic of these bandits was action, rapid and independent; a characteristic clearly deriving from their cowboy training. I think an incident in Black Jack's trial before Judge Mills at Clayton affords a rather unusual yet delightfully typical illustration of this feature. Judge Mills was Chief Justice of New Mexico and the charge against the prisoner was that of train robbery while armed, a capital offence, of which he was found guilty. George Fitzpatrick gives a description of the incident.

"The court room was packed every day of the trial. Six-shooters were barred and guards scattered through the room armed for emergency. When the jury had been selected and the examination of witnesses was about to start, Black Jack suddenly got up from his chair and before his attorneys could stop him, walked up to the Bench.

"Judge Mills, astonished at this procedure and not knowing what was going to happen, drew back hurriedly. But Black Jack was merely in a confidential mood. Leaning his one arm on the bench, Black Jack asked what kind of a sentence he would get if he entered a plea of guilty. Judge Mills straightened up and became very dignified. 'Anything you have to say to this court must be through counsel,' the judge rebuked him, and motioned to two deputies to take the prisoner away."

Only men of the highest caliber were trusted to take principal part in these men's undertakings. This gave them complete confidence in each other. Tom Capehart, in describing to French the taking of McGinnis by the sheriff's party, blamed himself because he had left Mac short of cartridges. He was convinced if Mac had had ammunition he would have "cleaned up the whole bunch when he walked in on them." And with the trust went comradeship. The devotion of Capehart to Mac seems to me as fine a thing as is recorded in the annals of American life. After McGinnis' capture he made a great ride clear across New Mexico to Mogollon to seek aid from his friends there. He must have picked up fresh horses as he went, and the horse he rode in on never recovered.

These men do not seem, as a general thing, to have taken life wantonly. Only when the occasion for action arrived there was no monkey business about it. And that, to a man, they knew how to handle their weapons these stories of mine must have made clear.* Not even Sheriff Elfego Baca ever excelled the shooting Tom Capehart must have done in the fight in Turkey Canyon. There were instances of brutality and treachery on the part of the Ketchums, doubtless, and in the unsuccessful raid preceding the Turkey canyon fight the bandits breat up the express messenger, Charles Drew, who had frustrated them by emptying the safe and hiding the treasure. But such instances are rare, I believe.

Nor were they publicity hounds, posing for the mob, like our modern criminals. "What the Hell's the idea of the crowd?" was Black Jack's remark when people gathered round the hack he was in at Las Vegas, New Mexico, after his indictment there. They told him the people wanted to see him. "To Hell with them!" was Black Jack's reply, and covered up his head with the vest he wore.

I think we may believe that when these men became bandits and outlaws, they carried with them their cowboy's respect for women. There wasn't a woman in the West would have betrayed Billy the Kid. Tom Ketchum was, perhaps, the "toughest" of them all, yet I have told you he had the reputation of never allowing women to be molested. Indeed, I suspect in Tom, underlying his toughness and blasphemy, a vein of gentleness. Of the friendships he made in prison the one that seems to have meant most to him was with just a boy—young Mike, son of Governor Otero (now a district judge). Tom never seemed to tire of telling Mike stories, nor Mike of listening. Rox Grumbles, who was much of a warbler in his earlier days, says

*Black Jack's rifle is now in the collection of the Theodore Roosevelt family.

he used to have a song with a sad refrain at the end of each verse about "a prisoner for life." Ketchum was for ever getting him to sing it; sometimes several times a day. Curious, that, don't you think? "I always felt sure," says Rox, "that Tom would end his days 'a prisoner for life'!" Perhaps Tom, too, remembered that old song when he enquired, as he often did in prison, why he alone of the whole gang should get a death sentence.

These men seem to have taken up the career of bandit from various causes. I hope to tell the fine story someday of how one of them, George Musgrave of Lincoln county, New Mexico, got started on a life of crime. Emmet Dalton has told us that he and his brothers were forced into becoming outlaws, and the same is true of the Jameses. But we certainly cannot believe it was because any of these men were degenerates, as is the case with many of our present day criminals. Some of them would have liked, events suggest, to have thrown up the business. Jim Lowe's taking a foreman's job with William French is a case in point, perhaps. And Tom Ketchum's last raid seems to have been a desperate attempt to get a stake and light out to South America. But after a certain point that was difficult. And many of them, I do not doubt, were carried along by the sheer lure of the game. Well, it *was* some game, sure enough.

There are two things about these bandits that my stories have illustrated and that must interest every range man. First, their close acquaintance with immense areas of Western country. And secondly, an extraordinary faculty for traveling at high speed over difficult terrain at night. These two factors, along with the fine horses they invariably rode—Tom Ketchum's famous brown passed into the hands of Sheriff Pinard—are the main grounds for their great rides and getaways. Though their physique must be considered, too. Men like McGinnis and Tom Musgrave were models of athletic build. Every inch of Tom Ketchum's six feet, three inches, seemed to me brawn and muscle. Sam, an inch or two less, I picture vividly as the finest figure of a man in my recollection.

And if you are an admirer of the simple qualities of courage and endurance and self-reliance in men—well, these men had them. The more serious of our Western historians seem to me to take a rather smug attitude towards this bandit business. These writers, however, did not live the range life; they could not have full sympathy with the personal qualities and activities we range men admired in the bandit. But these qualities and activities were the most important things in life for us. If we ever thought about the moral aspect of the matter, we were likely to argue that our Western bandits were better people than the robber barons, like Rockefeller, who preyed upon the public in the industrial field. They did not rob widows and orphans. Be that as it might, we recognized the bandits as cow-punchers like ourselves, which they were, and we recounted by the campfire the stories of Black Jack's last one-handed hold-up; Tom O'Folliard's ride, which drew the admiration of Pat Garrett; Billy the Kid's escape from the Lincoln Jail; the Turkey Canyon fight; the taking of McGinnis. Such exploits as these, indeed, have the stuff of the great sagas and ballads in them, the hero-tales that have thrilled mankind in all ages.

I think it well that the memory of these men's deeds and character—which is all they left behind them—should be captured and recorded, before it fades entirely. Certainly there is no feature of the life of that period, for good or bad, more distinctively Western.

# 9

## A Little Grant History

I

T HE Pablo Montoya Grant, which constitutes the Bell Ranch, was made November 8, 1824, three years after Mexico achieved her independence. It is, therefore, a Mexican, not a Spanish grant. There is only the evidence of one old Mexican that Pablo Montoya himself ever occupied the property. The land comprised by it formed until 1868 part of the Comanche and other plains Indians' buffalo hunting grounds; and (writes my late friend, W. J. Lucas of Las Vegas, New Mexico, whose wide information on these subjects has been at my disposal) "that they should have tolerated an invasion of them by Pablo Montoya or any of his people, is difficult to believe."

In 1851 Fort Union was established, a powerful post thirty-one miles north of Las Vegas. The outpost of Fort Bascom, located within the actual limits of the Montoya Grant, came into existence in 1864.* Yet still—and even after 1868, when the treaty with the Indians was concluded—the Bell country remained a dangerous one. Nick Dillon, who was at one time trail boss for the famous Texas cowman, John Hittson, and who is still living near Las Vegas, went up the Goodnight Trail from central Texas to Colorado with a herd in 1872. He says the Goodnight

---

*Fort Bascom played an important part in checking westward movements of the Comanche Indians and protecting the cattle trails. It never had sufficient forces to undertake an aggressive action against the Indians. Kit Carson on one occasion gathered up all the troops in the neighborhood, including Fort Union, and undertook to make a raid from Bascom but met with more than he reckoned on and had to retreat in a hurry. Only his artillery saved his force from destruction.

Trail followed the course it did, because it was impossible to take the direct route across the Staked Plains and the Bell country at that time on account of the Indian threat. Instead, the trail drifted southwest by Abilene and the Concho (Tex.) till it struck the Pecos at Horsehead Crossing, about ninety miles south of Roswell, New Mexico; thereafter following the Pecos, north, past Fort Sumner to the Rimrock, fifteen or twenty miles from Las Vegas, and leaving the Bell Ranch well to the east. Nick relates that some years later than this, while driving a herd over the same trail, his outfit came upon Jesse Hittson (son of John) in a fight with Comanches, who ran off his horses, burned up his wagons and shot arrows into some of his cattle.

It was not till 1875, says Evetts Haley in his admirable book, *Charles Goodnight*,* that Goodnight opened a new trail which, turning east at the Cuervo (tributary of Las Conchas) and passing Tucumcari Peak, crossed the Canadian close to the Montoya Grant south line. Thereafter to follow the east side of the grant up Ute Creek, eventually entering Colorado at a crossing of the Dry Cimarron.

It seems, therefore, we may as well forego any attempt to picture Don Pablo and his family in possession of their vast and delectable grant. But I will try and give you a glimpse of life on it in the later days of the Dons—say seventy years ago. You'll have to come with me to San Lorenzo, a small settlement situated just where Las Conchas flows into the Canadian, not far from the center of the grant, and in open, rolling country.

Here was the home of Don Francisco Lopez, who bought an interest in the grant in 1867, and his son, Lorenzo. You can picture for yourself a large house of red adobe surrounding a patio, and surrounded in turn by the *casitas* of a numerous retinue of peons who carried on the various activities of the *hacienda*. The family was a prominent one—three generations

*Published by Houghton Mifflin Co.

of it contained sheriffs of San Miguel county—and lived in considerable state. When the three *señoritas*, Valeria, Epimenia and Modestita, left for the convent school at Santa Fe, or returned from their vacations, they traveled in their own coach with a mounted guard of their own retainers, as well as U. S. soldiers. In the red adobe home hospitality was extended to all comers, no questions asked, and gold—only gold (and silver) was used in those days—left in their rooms. The family had its own private chapel on the ranch. A descendent, Felipe Delgado, radio singer of Los Angeles, showed me the other day two beautiful statuettes in wood of The Virgin that stood in it. When in a dual wedding the Señoritas Modestita and Epimenia were married to brothers of the well known Delgado family of Santa Fe, the wedding ceremony in the chapel was elaborate and beautiful, the company distinguished, and the after celebration memorable and long continued. It was a gay, picturesque and—except for the threat of Indians—a carefree life.

It is, indeed, this Montoya Grant, or Bell Ranch, a property anyone might be envious to possess. One man there was who steadily entertained such feelings towards it. In 1870 Wilson Waddingham, a Connecticut New Englander transplanted to New Mexico, bought a very extensive interest in the grant from John S. Watts, an attorney of Santa Fe, who had established the title to the grant for the Pablo Montoya heirs, and who held powers of attorney from most of them. On November 22, 1872, Waddingham conveyed all the interests he had acquired to the Consolidated Land, Cattle Raising and Wool Growing Company, which had a capital of two million dollars. Of this company Stephen B. Elkins, later to become Secretary of War and an United States senator from Virginia, was one of the incorporators.

This may be considered the start of the Bell Ranch, as we know it today. Since that date this property has been used uninterruptedly for stock growing—a period of sixty-eight years;

although it was not until some years later that the entire grant came under one control. From the beginning up to 1894 Mike Slattery, who seems to have come from Denver and who became a well known local character, was Waddingham's right hand man in the field. And from an early date it seems certain that the famous Bell brand—which is made with a stamp brand in the form of a bell—was used; although the earlier shape of the bell appears to have differed slightly from the present one.

Wilson Waddingham continued to buy up all the outstanding interests in the grant; principal among them being those of the brothers Trinidad and Eugenio Romero, who had purchased the shares of two original heirs, and who ran considerable herds of sheep and cattle on the old CA ranch, in that Atarque country I've described to you so often.* I knew Don Trinidad and his charming family well. He was one of the most important Spanish-Americans of his day. Among the many public offices he held were those of United States Marshall and Delegate to Congress. Later he built a palatial family residence near Las Vegas. Finally, in 1882, Waddingham quieted title to the entire tract in the District Court of San Miguel County, and two years later a decree was rendered.

Thereafter the property underwent many transfers and changes of title, designed evidently to protect Waddingham's interest in the ranch—which he seems to have been desperately anxious not to lose—during financial crises in his affairs. In one instance the property was transferred to a trustee, William J. Mills, who was Waddingham's son-in-law, and who later became Chief Justice and Governor of the state. Waddingham seems to have been continually "on the rocks." This was due, probably, to the fact of his being a heavy speculator in land. During the time he controlled the Bell Ranch he also had

*In addition to the CA's Waddingham drew into the Bell holdings the 3P's with headquarters at Fort Bascom and the 4V's owned by Kohn Brothers on the Alamocitas, towards the north-west line of the Grant.

control of the Maxwell Grant, one of the richest and most famous of southwestern grants, situated around the historic little town of Cimarron in Colfax county, and containing almost two million acres. He had, likewise, the Armenderies grant and several others. Indeed it was talk of the time on the street that Waddingham's land holding ran up to over four million acres.

It was under one of these numerous companies, the United States Agricultural Society (they seem to have pretty near exhausted the whole gamut of appropriate titles), incorporated in 1881, that the grant is believed to have been fenced. Barbed wire was just then coming into general use in New Mexico, having been first introduced in 1877.

Eventually, however, the Bell Ranch passed completely out of Waddingham"s control, and into the hands of John Greenough, a New York financier, who conveyed it in 1894 to the Bell Ranch Land & Irrigation Company. This company, which was no friend to Waddingham, let old-timer Slattery out and employed Arthur J. Tisdall as general manager. And it was for this company that I worked.

But the elimination of Wilson Waddingham from ownership in his most highly prized ranch was not final. He still had powerful connections in the east, and in 1898 we find him in a position to form, along with Ezekiel Stoddard, a wealthy eastern capitalist, and Edward E. Bradley, a new company called the Red River Valley Company, in which he was a shareholder, and which is the concern that holds the ranch today. At this time he had arranged to bring his old mate, Slattery, back to the ranch; but, it appears, Waddingham dropped dead somewhere in the east before his plans could be carried out, and Mike Slattery never came back to the Bell's.

II

When Wilson Waddingham's control of the Bell Ranch passed in 1894 to the Bell Ranch Land and Irrigation Company, which was the name of our outfit, there was a change not only in the personnel of the ranch but in the very life of the concern. Wilson Waddingham and his general manager, Mike Slattery, were representatives of the last guard of the pioneer period of the West. That was a period, in which, if you wished to be considered a full-living and distinguished citizen, you must be tough and desperate—if not with the gun, at any rate with the poker deck, or when the boys were lined up at the brass rail. Business and professional men, cattlemen, prospective judges, senators and governors of the state, gathered at the principal hotel bar and held session for two days and nights at a stretch. The central feature of the show was the gambling table and the stakes ran high.

Ex-Governor Miguel (Gillie) Otero relates in his recent book, *My Life On The Frontier*, how Wilson Waddingham entered a poker game in Las Vegas, New Mexico, which had been fixed up for him on his return from a visit to New York. A "stacked" deck had been prepared. When he, and his friend Colonel Marcus Brunswick, had been maneuvered by means of a few good hands into betting heavily, the cards were so dealt that the two dropped thirty thousand dollars on one hand. Neither made any protest. It was an article of the code of the period that you accept success or disaster with equally unruffled front.

On the ranch a similar spirit of recklessness and bravado colored life, if one might judge by the wild stories that came to our ears about Mike Slattery and his followers. The horse herd showed a good sprinkling of horses Mike had near-killed in his desperate rides; although there was no reason, as far as we could see, for most of the rides to be desperate at all. It was just part of the tradition of the time. If you were anxious to be considered "one of the boys," it was a help to have killed a horse or two.

None of the old crowd passed on to us, except a few Mexicans and old French Joe. French Joe was one of the landmarks, and part and parcel, of the ranch. I fancy he must have been at this time in his eighties. At least I think one would have to have lived eighty years to be as battered up as old Joe was. His skin had the appearance of weather-beaten cowhide. One of his legs had been hurt and was withered and shorter than the other. One eye was bleared and blind. But in the good eye blazed all the fierce fire of the French race, the race that held Verdun; and his gait to the last was alive with French energy and *élan*—to use one of their own expressive words. Joe was by way of being very friendly to the new administration, but I think at heart he considered us mighty poor truck alongside the old gang. He lived in one of the settlements on the river and, if anything significant happened among the Mexicans, he would "mount to the top to my horse and ride over to de Bell to see Mr. Kelly!" I was Mr. Kelly. But Joe had long lived off "de Bell" in one way or another, and the real object of these visits would likely be to talk Willis Dorset into shoeing his horse or wheedle some supplies out of Henry Winn, the storekeeper. He died a few years after I left the Bell's. More and more, I used to think, there was nothing to him but an inner fire, a flame; and one day, I supposed, it just flickered out.

Then there was Manuel, the plump cook; and Juan, who could serve any turn of work; and little Tomas Romero, horse wrangler, to whom we gave the Trementina fence camp when he took to himself a comely Mexican wife.

Arthur J. Tisdall, the new manager, was an Irishman, one of an important group of men of that nationality who settled around Clarendon, Texas, in the eighties and established ranches. He had been manager for Mrs. Adair on the famous Paloduro ranch, and was one of the early members of the Texas Cattle Raiser's Association. A big, fine featured man he was. Although of an aristocratic old-country family, he was a good "mixer" with all sorts. His experience in the Panhandle of Texas, then the most advanced in range practice of any Western cattle area, had made a fine cowman of him—straight in his dealings, and possessing a comprehensive knowledge of the species, Cowpuncher.

About that time a young and attractive Scotch girl arrived in Las Vegas, with her mother, in the course of a tour of the West. Arthur Tisdall and Frances Harriott met and, after a short and romantic courtship became engaged and married. The young bride was a gifted and accomplished girl, devoted to music and literature, but the Western range and the inhabitants thereof were something entirely outside her ken. Consequently she used to make some amusing breaks. We had at the time a roan saddle horse on the place, called Mulberry, the ladies used to ride. One day Mrs. Tisdall was trying to describe him to one of the boys. I overheard her telling him that Mulberry was the color of *crushed heliotrope*. That was something of a poser for the cowboy. Heliotrope! We knew of nothing by that name in those parts—crushed or whole. Nevertheless this lady made a gallant effort to like and understand the West.

Tisdall was a man of simple tastes and, like most Britishers, was fond of flowers. He built himself a little conservatory at the south end of the long adobe dwelling house and had it gay with pots and boxes of geraniums and other flowers which he spent many hours in tending. One wonders what Mike Slattery's opinion of a conservatory on the Bell Ranch would have been! But I hardly ever knew an Englishman that did not try to have a lawn and flowers on his ranch. Perhaps to remind him of his home, which is a land of lawns and flower gardens.

After being only a few years on the Bell Ranch, Tisdall died suddenly of pneumonia, under the most unfortunate circumstances, as it is likely he could have been saved with better medical care. The nearest doctor had eighty miles to come. After his death his widow lived for several years in Trinidad, Colorado. When my eldest girl, Mary, was born Mrs. Tisdall became her godmother. Eventually she returned to Europe and has lived ever since in the South of France. Still an attractive woman, she has never remarried, remaining devoted to the memory of the man who courted and won her back in God's country where the cattle range.

### III

Tisdall's successor in the general management of the Bell Ranch was Charles M. O'Donel, another of the Clarendon, Texas, group of Irishmen, but of a somewhat different order from Arthur Tisdall. C. M. O'Donel was a slim-built man of medium height. He had served earlier in life in the British army; had known the famous English general, "Chinese" Gordon, who met a tragic death at Khartoum; and was to his last day essentially a soldier. He had, too, a good deal of British reserve and aloofness, showing but little of Tisdall's cordiality in his approach to high or low. Yet this outside coldness concealed reserves of kindliness and deep feeling.

Like many Catholic Irishmen of the period when there were no Catholic universities in Ireland, he had been educated in France and spoke French fluently. Of extraordinarily keen intellect, he was a sensitive student and critic of good literature, and master of a fine literary style. I often wondered if he was as practical a cowman and administrator as Tisdall, but he had charge of the Bell outfit for over thirty years, and that prominent position, along with his experience and high mental powers, won for him the presidency of the American Livestock Association.

Charlie and I were intimate friends. I recall paying him a visit on the ranch one time and finding a small army of Hampshire hogs—noted for the band of white around their bodies—ranging about the place. This surprised me, because I felt sure that Charlie knew but little about "hawgs," and it seemed unlikely they could be profitable stock on a ranch that bought most of its feed. But when I asked him about it, he replied gaily:

"Don't you see how handsome they look about the place with those broad white bands!" He was always a devotee of beauty, was Charlie —porcine, even!

An unfailing sense of humor, indeed, lay just underneath that reserve of his. When his first daughter was born—he was married three times and had two daughters by his second wife—he told me he called her Nuala, because that was an old Irish name used among the women of the O'Donel family for generations. The pronunciation, however, of "Nuala" proved more than the general American public could handle. So he called the next girl plain Elizabeth; and reduced that to Betty—to make sure.

Some years after coming to the Bell ranch O'Donel met with a serious accident when his horse fell with him. His life was saved by the presence of mind and heroism of a young boy, Buster Hall, son of an Englishman breaking polo ponies on the ranch at the time.But Charlie was left with a permanent injury to the head which brought on recurrent spells of intense pain for the rest of his life.

O'Donel had at one time as assistant manager, Frank Law, an Englishman who had been, I think, with the Matadors or the LIT outfit; a pleasant fellow and of high character, and a graduate of Cambridge University, England. But he died at a comparatively early age. Some day, perhaps, someone will take the trouble to trace the part the men of Great Britain and Ireland have played, alike on farm and ranch, in the development of the livestock interests of America. Those little islands in the North Sea, so productive of good stockmen, have given of their best to the job.

Charlie grew softer as the years drew in on him. He spent his last winter in that favorite resort, Tucson, Arizona; a good deal of it in company with my son, Matt Culley, director of the Santa Rita Government Reserve, and present representative of that small boy Willis Dorset and the cowboys made much of on the Bell Ranch, and who drove with me and his mother into the flooded waters of the Canadian. Only the other day Matt's wife, Idelle, was talking about Charlie, telling me how gentle, and full of gratitude for any small service, this soldier-cowman was in those last days of his.

O'Donel was succeeded in the general management of the Red River Valley Company—which is the official title of the present Bell outfit—by Albert Mitchell (in 1933). Mr. Mitchell is well qualified to carry on the tradition of ability and distinction that has prevailed in the general management of this great ranch for over forty years. In the year 1929 he served as president of that important body, the American Hereford Association, and since then he has been elected president of the American National Livestock Association, the highest distinction that can come to an American stockman. Mr. Mitchell was educated at Occidental College, Los Angeles, and took his Bachelor of Science degree from Cornell University. He made a close run in the latest election for Governor of New Mexico on the Republican ticket and has lately received the nomination of his party as United States Senator.

Albert Mitchell will be a busy man, for he has also on his hands the large range interests, as well as the famous registered Hereford herd, of his father, the late T. E. ("Ed") Mitchell. These concerns are situated on the Tequesquite Creek, almost adjoining the Bell pasture, so the far spread flats and mesas of the Montoya grant are not unfamiliar to the new manager. He is, indeed, a product of the range. Some of my readers may not know the range well, and the kind of men and women it often produces. Or they may take their sole conception of a Western cowman from the movies or the Wild West magazines. If such they be, they might feel some surprise, were they to meet the quiet-spoken, cultivated gentleman who is Albert Mitchell.

# 10

# The Men Who Rode
# the Bell Range with Me

I

**M**<small>Y</small> memories of the Bell Ranch seem to be nearing a close, yet I wouldn't want to end them without telling you something about the men I worked with down there. Like most cow outfits we kept only a small force during the winter, but some of our hands came to us every spring. Bob Bowmer was one of them; quiet, steady, bow-legged Texan; a top hand if there ever was one. Charlie Turney, jovial and ruddy, of a well known Southern New Mexico cattle family, was another. Mighty fine looking fellows, some of them, I want to tell you. You don't run onto men as handsome and well set up as Con Dennis every rainy day. Con was light complexioned (blonde as they would call it today), but Mike McQuaid was dark as night; six foot two and straight as an arrow. An intelligent fellow, Mike, and a fine hand; we gave him one of the wagons. Then there was Tom Kane, who was our range foreman; and Willis Dorset, handy man about the place.

Tom Kane was Eastern bred, I think. He had been educated for the Catholic priesthood, until he decided he was not fitted for that calling and came West. Perhaps he was right, but I used to think there were few lines of life he could not have followed successfully. Just as there was no social class he could not have entered and played his part in. He was just naturally no common sort, Tom. But he had one failing which no doubt kept him down and finally brought him to his ruin. That fault found no outlet with the Bells while I was with them. Faithful to the outfit, resourceful, capable of applying real thought to a problem, and handling several strings at the same time, as range foreman he did a high class job for us.

He was Irish to the core, and I never saw him defeated or despondent. I never saw him lose his head or his temper, though hell pops pretty frequently when you have four or five round-up wagons running side by side, as sometimes happened. He liked to put on a show. I remember once news came that the general manager was bringing out some ladies to the round-up. We were gathering our cows and calves to throw into a separate pasture. Tom kept holding them till he had five thousand in the herd. Five thousand "cailves" with their mammies; that was some show for the ladies, to be sure. It was some show for most of us. It was the largest herd of cattle I ever handled, or saw.

A strong strain of the Irish devil-may-carum spirit ran in Tom's blood, too. One time the boys came in to the ranch headquarters between round-ups and so we put them all to work of some kind around the place. There was one stable with walls about eight or nine feet high and a steep-pitched roof over that. They had just shingled it and Tom was sitting perched on the top ridge of the roof. I don't know what mad idea took him but we heard him suddenly give a cowboy's yell and shout: "Look out, fellers, watch me go," and down the roof he came a-sliding and over the eave, and when the time came to hit the ground "I was travelin' like the clatter-wheels of Hell," he told me afterwards, laughing. But he often complained thereafter of a pain in the bowel. He had hurt himself internally.

I never knew as voracious a consumer of tobacco. Always running out of it, he would rush up to you, shouting: "Got any EATIN'?" Then he would seize your plug of Climax like a hungry wolf and bite off about an inch and a half of it.

And the last I saw of Tom was one afternoon a few years after I left the Bell's. I was riding down from our summer range on the Upper Pecos waters in the Glorieta Mountains when I came on a railroad work camp. Happening in, who should be found in charge but Tom Kane. A sorry looking figure he was, compared with the husky, athletic fellow we had always known, and I asked him what ailed him. "It's the whiskey, Jack," he said. "I just can't get away from it. It's brought me lower and lower, ruined all my chances and my health. It'll kill me pretty soon." I understood it did. He was one of the few, the very few, cowpunchers I have known who allowed drink to destroy them. But I never remember feeling so keenly as I did that afternoon when Tom was telling me about himself, what Shakespeare calls "the pity of it!" For men like Tom Kane are not so easy to happen onto on the round-up of life; they don't run in bunches.

You couldn't conceive of a greater contrast to Tom Kane than Willis Dorset. Willis was one of the handiest and most helpful men on a ranch I ever saw, but I think he must have *inherited* a grudge against life. With his black beard and heavy brows overshadowing sombre eyes, he could have impersonated Shakespeare's Melancholy Jacques. A right kindly smile lighted up his face sometimes, to be sure, and he was a devoted pal to my little boy, Matt. But he was at his best when the gloom was deepest. He liked to get strung out beside a winter night's fire on some grim story of deaths and burials. One night he told me the following one.

Up in La Cinta Canyon, which lies just outside the northern fence of the Bell pasture, there lived at one time on a claim a lone woman. One summer she was taken suddenly ill and before the doctor could be brought, died. It happened that none of the two or three women living in the canyon was at home at the time, and it fell to Willis and another man to attend to the last rites. They made a coffin of rough lumber and dug a grave. They had placed the body in the coffin, arms by side, had nailed on the top, and were lowering it into the grave when Willis thought he heard a sound like something rapping on the inside of the box, and mentioned it to his companion.

But the latter pooh-poohed the idea; it was Willis' imagination; the woman had been dead for several days; and they went on with their work filling up the grave.

A month or so later some document about the woman's affairs was found missing and it was thought it might have been buried in her clothing. So it was decided to dig up the body and Willis and his companion were called upon again. It was one of those heavy dead summer days they get down there, as they started on their long task, but at length they got the earth cleared out and the coffin lifted up and set beside the grave. Then they drew the nails, and as soon as they lifted off the lid they noticed that the woman lay with one arm bent upwards and the fingers over her eyes. Willis had been right. The noise he thought he heard in the coffin had been made by a living hand.

No one had ever seen Willis Dorset ruffled or excited. One time he was helping us to drive a bunch of stock cattle across the Canadian. The river was in flood and the current swift. There was only one narrow place for a mile up or down the river for the cattle to come out on, and the calves were getting swept down below it. I was very anxious not to lose anything, so I swam my horse down below the herd to try and stop the calves drifting. In doing this I got swept down pretty far myself and it was only after a great struggle my horse succeeded in making the landing place. And as I scrambled out, thankful to have saved my skin, there was Willis standing on the top of the bank, looking down at me with a quiet smile in his sombre eyes, and all he said was: "And the next time, Jack Culley, don't—get—so—excited!" Well, Willis, we are not all built the same way, you know.

We stood guard that night together, and next morning Willis left the outfit and I've never set eyes on him since.*

---

*Since writing this I have learned from Albert Mitchell that Willis married and came to live in Fullerton, in Southern California. He was run over and killed by an automobile in some way never made quite clear.

## II

Well, here is some more about the boys that worked for the Bells, which came to me from an unexpected source.

I was all set to wind up my stories of the Bell ranch, when suddenly Frank King, who is a good friend of mine, had a letter from some man who had been with the Bells, off and on, for fifteen years and had run the wagon for seven. He asked for my address and Frank sent it to him. A few days later comes a letter from O.R. (Oat) Martine, Chief of Police of Plainview, in Western Texas. And did I get a kick out of it. Folks who have always lived in one place and carried on the same business all their life, have no idea what happens when something brings you into touch with a life which you have left behind you years ago, but which was once the whole shooting match, lock, stock and barrel, of your existence.

And that life of the range more than most others, perhaps, got hold of you, grew into your marrow. It's seventeen years since I left the range, and I've scarcely ever ridden horseback in all that time, but I remember a few years ago, their taking me out to a roundup in Arizona and giving me a horse; and just as quick as I got my leg across the saddle and rode out to the herd, I was clear back in the old days when my average ridin' ran around a thousand miles a month; just enough to carry you half around the world every year.

And, believe it or not, here's my daughter, Margaret, born and raised on a ranch, to be sure, but for fifteen years living all over the world. And she's just bought her a little car, and she and her mother are off to Arizona and New Mexico, to spend six months visiting on ranches where they'll get fewer of the comforts of life, by a jugful, than they're used to at home. Yes, the pull of the range, like the pull of the sea, is a strong and everlasting one. I remember one time visiting a friend who kept a rest home in the city for old people. One of the guests at the time was an old man who had been in the range cow business all his life. A tall powerful fellow he was, still active physically, but his mind had gone back on him and wandered continually. Every morning as I passed him at the breakfast table he would stop me and ask if I had seen his saddle horses. They had strayed off, he would say, and he had been hunting them all morning. Then he'd talk to me about the horse he was riding—a big fellow, wasn't he; must weigh twelve hundred pounds. It happened that some heavy rains came and I went out one day into the country to find the grass green and growing all over the range. Next morning as I passed the old man I said to him: "I was out over the range to the north yesterday. There's a world of good grass up there." "Yes"—and the words leapt from him instantaneously—"and I've a thousand head of steers to put on it!" In imagination the old cowman was on the range still, running cattle.

So, reading that letter of Oat Martine's was just like me and one of the old Bell boys "settin' down and whittlin'" in the shade of the bunkhouse, talkin' over all the gossip of the ranch. I'll pass some of it on to you. Oat says he went to the Bells in 1901—about three years after I left—to work for Mike McQuaid who was wagon boss at the time; with Walter Hart running the second wagon. I told you about Mike—what a tall, dark, handsome fellow he was; but it was news to me that he had married Walter's sister. Walter Hart was the sort of fellow everyone likes. Clever and even tempered. He took the first wagon in 1902 and ran it for Charlie O'Donel for a number of years. It took a man of good understanding to handle one of those outfits and keep everything running smoothly through a whole season. Those old-time cowboys were a race peculiar to themselves, and mighty independent. Then Martine took the wagon in 1913 and ran it for seven years.

It hurt me like everything to learn that Walter and Mike and Willis Dorset had all passed over to wherever it is cowboys find rest at last. But Oat gave me a good word about some of the others. Jake Munyiz is living at Logan, on the Canadian, south of the grant; where the old HOW headquarters were. Jake was the first of the Mexican settlers we got off the grant. A fine cowhand he was, and a good friend of mine. I never told you about George Kilgore. George was one of those fellows everyone calls "old," even while they are still quite young. The slow and steady sort; but there wasn't much about handling cattle he didn't know. And if there are any honester men than George in the world, they're hiding out somewhere. He has him a little cow ranch near Liberty (that's where Black Jack and his brother, Sam, robbed the store and killed the little Jew storekeeper). They tell me he lost a leg in an accident and how the heck he manages to ride a horse I can't think.

Then there was old French Joe. When I was telling you the story of him and about his death, I said I supposed "the flame of him just flickered out" one day. But it wasn't that way exactly. Let Oat tell it. He can do it better than I could. "Here is how old French Joe got killed," he writes. "Alex Street and Lee Smith, two of the Bell boys, put in a saloon at old Liberty and when the Rock Island railroad built they filed a homestead that is now Tucumcari, and moved the saloon to Tucumcari, and it was known as the Legal Tender. They were great friends of French Joe's, and he took old Barbarita and a Mexican boy and his wagon and team and went to Tucumcari to visit Alex and Lee. And coming back the boy was driving, and when they got to the Puertocito the wagon ran over a rock and threw French Joe off of the spring seat and killed him. And they took him to old La Cinta Plaza and buried him east of the Plaza and the river has caved off and French Joe has passed down the Rio Colorado." So that was the end of old Joe. But, say, folks, that was some name the two Bell boys gave to their place of business, eh? Humorous guys, those old-time punchers.

I asked Martine if he'd known Bob Bowmer, the quiet-spoken

bowlegged Texan I have told you about before, that was our top hand. He says: "I did not know Bob Bowmer. He trained two horses that were the best cowhorses I ever rode. General was a sorrel, and Chiseler, bay. They were the best cutting horses in the four hundred the Bells had." Chiseler! that's a name you hear oftener now than then. And he asks me if I remember the old 4V horse, Paddy Grant. "He lived until he was thirty-six years old."

When the company sold two hundred and fifty thousand acres to the Triggs interests, (about 1920) they got rid of the roughest country in the pasture. Oat writes: "I cleaned the part they sold and it was some job. The 74 prong of the Mule. Hell's canyon. The Dry Mule. The Bueyeros canyon. The Basin. The Atarque and Dog canyon. And I cleaned it, got all the cattle out." I rise to say, gentlemen, that anyone who can work that tract of country *clean*, is a practical cattleman. The very names of the places seem to describe it.

A few years after he took over the Bells, Charlie O'Donel decided to sell off the greater part of the range stock horses. Martine helped Mike McQuaid gather them. He writes: "It was some job." It's me that knows, Oat. I have described previously how we gathered the whole herd of stock horses in Tisdall's time and moved it up onto the Mesa Rica. In discussing wild horses at that time I said that an outlaw horse would sooner "break his neck" than submit to being driven or corraled. Those of you who thought that statement an exaggeration may find the following of Martine's interesting: "We were working the head of the Watrous (canyon) and a bunch of range horses ran out on one of the points, and seven head jumped off and killed themselves. One old paint stud laid back his ears and come out between the boys."

And at the end of his letter Oat writes: "Mr. O'Donel was one of the best men I ever knew. He was a great General Manager." I was glad to have that word about my old friend.

## II

# Charlie Goodnight's Herds Cross
# the Bell Ranch

IN a previous chapter I stated, quoting Evetts Haley in his book, *Charles Goodnight,* that the Goodnight Trail did not touch the Bell Ranch till 1875. As I went on, however, turning the pages of this fascinating work, I learned that some years earlier than this Goodnight and old John Dawson (who later with Chase owned the Mule Shoe brand on the Vermejo in Colfax county) routed a herd through the Bell country. Leaving the Pecos above Fort Sumner, they traveled due north to El Cuervo and crossed the Canadian near the mouth of La Cinta creek. This route Mr. Haley has carefully worked out in collaboration with Colonel Jack Potter, the well known New Mexico frontiersman and cattleman. It was here where La Cinta (the Ribbon or Girdle) joins the Canadian that the little settlement of La Cinta later lay, in which old French Joe lived and where they buried him; the river caving in his grave and washing his body along with its waters down towards the Mississippi.

The trail then followed up La Cinta creek some ten miles, so that they must have actually driven past the present site of the Bell headquarters, which stands on the banks of that stream; though whether there was any building there then I cannot say. Thereafter they pointed the herd north up La Cinta, climbing the big mesa I have described for you elsewhere, which divides the Lower country from the Mesa country, by a trail just outside the Bell fence. The experiences of these early trail herds become more vivid and realistic when you know intimately the ground they traversed, and it is with the idea of making them more actual for my readers that I am dwelling on those stretches of the Goodnight Trail that connect up with Bell Ranch history.

The reason Goodnight had for making this detour from his old trail, as Haley relates it, is characteristic and amusing. As long as the route lay past Las Vegas, he had no recourse but to take the Raton Pass into Colorado. That was, before the railroad became, as it is today, the principal southern gateway into that state. Now shrewd old Uncle Dick Wootton, pioneer plainsman and trader, had built a toll road over the Raton Pass and charged Goodnight ten cents a head for an entire herd. This got Charlie's goat, and he swore to get even with the old man. Resourceful as usual, he worked out, and followed, a new trail, which after mounting the Mesa, as described above, proceeded almost due north, over the rolling Palo Blanco plains where one day Senator Dorsey's Triangle Dot's and many another good brand of cattle were to range, and passing just west of the Capulin, crossed the divide into Colorado by the Trinchera Pass, a number of miles east of Wootton's road. And no toll to pay!

This Trinchera Pass thereafter displaced Wootton's famous road as the principal route for Colorado herds; a fact, says Haley, which distressed thrifty old Uncle Dick greatly. Nevertheless I am of opinion that the old man was ahead of the deal in the long run, if you consider road upkeep; even if his road house at the toll gate suffered some loss of patronage thereby. For there is nothing will knock hell out of a mountain road quicker than a trail herd.

Coming back to the Bell country, and taking up the Goodnight Trail where it turned away from the Pecos, we find good driving for cattle up to, and past, the Cuervo. Plenty of water, and sheltering mesas. Though I can't help recalling a drive I made through that country that was not so good. Boy, did she rain! That was during the period when we used to get three-day rains in New Mexico. And for three days and nights the sky fell. We were shorthanded and lost the herd every night in the pitchy dark and spent the morning gathering it again. Our beds were soaking wet. It was late fall and the rain was colder than snow. I never went to bed at all, but I had a Mexican cook along who had been a sheepherder, and, give one of those fellows a box of old-time sulphur matches, he'd start a fire at the bottom of the Atlantic Ocean. There was firewood aplenty, so we'd get a dead juniper alight some nights and squat around it trying to keep warm, when we weren't with the herd.

There is a famous spring in that district which boils up out of the middle of an open plain, known as Cabra, that is Goat, Spring, which we camped at one evening. A man kept a small store there, and I went in and asked him if he had some whiskey. No, he had no license to sell liquor; the nearest he could do for us was Hostetter's Stomach Bitters. So I bought me a bottle of that, and I want here and now to chronicle my everlasting appreciation of Mr. Hostetter. I don't know whether he stayed within the law, or strayed without it, in making up his preparation. I only know that I and my boys found out that those stomach bitters were something else beside bitter. I seem to feel them trickling through my innerds today, as I write.

From here Goodnight and his crew would very shortly hit what is now the Bell line, and a few hours drive, skirting the Mesa Rica, bring them to the Canadian. I have told you often in these sketches about that old "crick." But here's a story our friend, Oat Martine, Chief of Police of Plainview, Texas, has about it and a herd of spayed heifers. The which I will preface by remarking that a herd of spayed heifers is a lively proposition under the best conditions, if you happen not to know. And further, that the "farm" he speaks of lies in the southern portion of the grant beside the river and not far from where Old Fort

Bascom used to stand, down in the mesquite country. The Canadian here flows between lowish sandy banks, and the sides and sand-bars become mighty treacherous—death traps, indeed—when the red floods come down a-boomin'.

In the year 1904 or 1905, says Chief Martine, the Bell outfit was moving a herd of spayed heifers. We camped the night just east of the farm gap. I was standing guard with Con Dennis, and was riding Old Druggist, an old grey horse I used as circle and night horse, and the best river horse I ever rode. It was raining and the herd made several runs during the night. In one of them they mighty near overran the camp. As I rode by in the dark, the old cook came running out of his tent hollerin' to head off the herd, and I just did cut them off of the wagon. Next morning showed how badly the cattle had milled and run, for we found some with broken horns and legs.

Walter Hart was in charge of the herd and started to put them across the river. The river was up and swimming, and we put the horses in ahead of the herd. I went in with them, along with Wade Gardner and Emmett Ricks, but they got in trouble and went back to the side they started from. Meantime I made it across with a small bunch of horses and cattle. As I started to come back, two of the boys, Sherman Racy and John Putnam, came out to meet me. They made it to a sand-bar in the middle of the river, and there their horse bogged down. They got off and the horses made their way back to the bank they came from, leaving those two boys out in the middle of the river, with the river rising, and neither of them able to swim a lick. I caught up an old grey horse we called Parker Wells and led him out and got the boys off one at a time. It's a fact that during this entire time I was riding Old Druggist; and he swam the river easy and never made a bobble.—I guess old Charlie and his crews knew all about such messes as these!

And today, close by where Goodnight crossed the river, the United States Government is preparing to build, as part

of the Mississippi Basin flood control system, a dam two hundred
and thirty-four feet high, and five and a half miles long. It will
flood, when full, thirty square miles of the Grant land and
isolate thereby the northeast corner, containing forty thousand
acres, of the pasture. It is costing Uncle Sam a large sum of
money in damages, cutting up this choice domain. As for the
project itself, it will undoubtedly prove worth while, if it
succeeds in mitigating the old menace of the Canadian.

Then from the river this old trail outfit I was telling you
about must have driven over the present site of the Bell headquarters, in its red clay flat with the low juniper-clad mesas
all around it. From there to point north up La Cinta creek,
passing the spot where Black Jack and Sam Ketchum hid out
in the willow brakes, and on along to the trail up the Mesa,
just outside the Grant fence. "An elevation of some seven
hundred feet in a quarter of a mile," says Haley, describing
this trail. And I am wondering, furthermore, what manner
of lay-out it was at that time. They weren't any too good,
some of those trails, when we went over them twenty-five
years later. These early herds must have been completely road
broke long before they got this far, but, for all that, it took
cowhands to take them up that Goodnight Hill, I know.

The Mesa wall dwindles gradually, merging into the plains
to the east, and into the mountains on the west. As it happens,
this mesa lay between the Bells and my own Rafter C Bar ranch
up in the Wagon Mound country. The trail I usually took over
it, as I passed on my trips to and fro, lay a little further west
than Goodnight's—just where Canyon Largo, the Long Canyon,
joins the Canadian. I must believe the Mesa, there, is away over
seven hundred feet. At any rate it used to take me and little
CA Derby, who was a stout hill horse, three quarters of an hour
to climb the trail.

# 12

# Livestock the Company Has Run

B EFORE closing these sketches of the Bell Ranch I thought some of my readers might be interested in knowing something about the kind of livestock that has been run on the ranch during its long history, and the manner in which such stock was run.

Previous to the time when Tisdall took over the general management, (1894), and when I came to be his assistant, the livestock had been run in a rather primitive fashion, similar to that prevailing on the outside range. There was little in the way of subdivisions on the ranch, beyond a horse pasture at the headquarters and a farm enclosure at Old Fort Bascom. We fenced off a big summer pasture at the north end of the grant, the first summer. Today there are thirty-nine pastures, including eight horse pastures; although the acreage of the ranch has been reduced, by sales, to about half a million acres.

What improvement in cattle there was in 1894 in northern New Mexico was due mainly to Shorthorn blood: Durham, as it was generally called. Tisdall introduced into the Bell herd in his second year five hundred head of yearling Hereford bulls, and we followed that up with five hundred more the next year. These bulls were bought from Dick Walsh, who had succeeded Tisdall as manager for Mrs. Adair on the Palo Duro Ranch in the Texas Panhandle. They came out of the Palo Duro J J herd—distinct from the J A range herd—which had been established by Charlie Goodnight in 1883 on a Shorthorn foundation. The continuous use of the finest imported and native Hereford bulls had brought this herd to a high pitch of quality.

I fancy these were among the first Hereford bulls brought into northern New Mexico; although W. J. Tod of Maple Hill, Kansas, brought some, and very good ones, onto his Folsom, N.M. ranch of sixty thousand acres about the same period. And my old friend, Billy Parsons, who went to the Prairie Cattle Company's Cross L ranch on the Dry Cimarron in 1881, and rode for them ten years, tells me Murdo McKenzie had a herd of Herefords on that ranch some time in the '80's. But it seems clear that, generally speaking, New Mexico was a number of years behind Western Texas in the introduction of Hereford blood.

It was the common belief at one time that a continuous and exclusive use of Hereford blood in a range herd resulted in a reduction of scale and weight. Acting on this conviction, Charlie O'Donel, Tisdall's successor, used always with the Bell herd, along with Hereford bulls, a percentage of Shorthorn bulls. O'Donel believed that part of the Shorthorns' inability to stand grief was due to their being bred and raised under conditions that tended to soften them, and that they would prove hardier if accustomed to range conditions from birth. Therefore at one time he kept a herd of registered Shorthorn cows on the ranch so as to ensure a supply of range raised bulls for service with the Bell herd.

This mixture of blood resulted, naturally, in a diversity of colors and types, which is a condition that does not find favor with the modern American feeder. The present manager, Albert Mitchell, tells me that, since he took charge of the ranch, he has culled heavily cows showing Shorthorn blood; and that he sold the last four Shorthorn bulls in the fall of 1933. It is his intention to confine himself in future to straight Hereford blood. He believes that by careful selection of the bulls the scale and weight of the herd can be adequately maintained.

In my time we sold our steers as twos in the spring. At that period the northern states, Wyoming, Dakota, Montana, Nebraska, etc., were range states. The winters up there being hard on breeding stock, it had become a general practice to bring up southern steers and run them to four or five years old. Fine gains could be made on the northern grasses. It was found unsafe to ship cattle from the south up there younger than coming two years. Our steers went to different buyers in the states mentioned. One year I recall our selling to Richards and Comstock, a firm running seventy thousand head of cattle in Nebraska. Mr. Richards came down to take delivery; a very pleasant, youngish fellow, as I remember. We cut them into herds of about seventeen hundred, which is large enough for cattle in the spring of the year. How clearly it all comes back to me today, counting out those herds; tallying off the hundreds with knots in my saddle rope!

O'Donel shipped his steers mostly as yearlings, generally feeding them out in the corn states. Mitchell tells me he intends from now on to conform to the prevailing range practice and ship out everything as weaner calves. In passing I may say that at the turn of the century the Bell herd numbered probably around twenty-five thousand head. Since the reduction in acreage of the pasture fifteen thousand should be a good estimate.

The company ran some sheep for a while on Government claims owned by it on the Canadian, south of the grant. This was discontinued in 1912, and most of the land sold.

The principal stockholders in the Red River Valley Co., which owns the Bell ranch, are the Stoddards, a well known eastern family. J. A. McNaughton, vice president and manager of the Los Angeles Union Stockyards and an original member of the California State Racing Commission, has described to me their sumptuous home estate on Long Island, where he visited them. The Stoddards are inveterate horsemen. Louis Stoddard, now vice-president of the company, is the famous international polo player of a generation ago. And a year or two ago we find his son, Louis Jr., riding a horse in the great English steeplechase, the Grand National. Young Louis did not succeed in completing the four and one-half mile course, with its thirty jumps—only one American, little Pete Bostwick, the polo player, riding his own horse, was among the ten out of thirty-four starters who did that—but the fact that he rode in the race at all is proof that he is a fine and daring horseman. This young fellow represents actually the third generation of Stoddards owning interest in the Bell ranch. It was doubtless due to Louis Stoddard's influence that an attempt was made at an early period to raise polo ponies on the ranch. One carload of ponies was shipped east and some of them tried out. But the venture was clearly not successful.

The range horse stock on the ranch in our day ran pretty small, owing to the use by Slattery, the previous manager, of small thoroughbred stallions. The offspring of these, were often models of symmetry. What a picture was Sonny, that used to be in Charlie Turney's string! But they were not robust and rugged enough for general cattle usage, and we found most of them too hot blooded for work in a herd.

Mr. Mitchell tells me the horse stock still runs quite small, owing to further use of small, light thoroughbred and Arabian studs, with an eye to getting polo ponies, and he is trying to increase the size. He is using two half Steeldust, half thorough-bred stallions, as well as one U. S. thoroughbred remount stallion, Lord Martin, and one of mixed breeding. He is primarily interested in breeding good cow horses; secondarily, polo ponies. The original horse herd of eleven hundred head was greatly reduced by O'Donel, who sold the greater part of them. Oat Martine, who helped gather them, says they brought three dollars and fifty cents each!

The U. S. Government has lately established a Conservancy District, containing ten thousand acres of irrigable land, on the Canadian, not far from the center of the grant, and is constructing a dam to provide water for the project. The company has the privilege of using as much of this water as they desire at the ordinary rates. This project may well mean a fundamental change in the working system of the Bell ranch, which has always been far removed from any considerable original sources of feed supply.

THE BELL RANCH TODAY

# 13
## I Revisit the Bells and Look Back

I
F you were to visit the Bell country today you would find
many things different from what they were when I went
there. At that time I could have ridden out at one of the north
gates of the pasture and made my way to the line of Canada without striking anything in the way of a fence except a horse pasture
or a drift fence. From a south gate the same, to El Paso. On the
east not so far, because a good deal of Texas was fenced up
earlier. But westwards you could have traversed three states
clear to the Pacific Ocean. To ride over a country like that
is to promote your chest expansion.

There was no railroad town nearer the ranch than eighty
miles; we traded at Las Vegas on the Santa Fe, and shipped our
cattle from Clayton on the Colorado and Southern. To see a
railroad train was to us an adventure. If any of the boys happened to be in a town when a passenger train pulled in, the
thing to do was to march in chaps and spurs through the chair
coach and tourist sleepers. Those cars were considered to contain all the pretty girls. The homely ones in our judgment rode
the Pullmans.

But a number of years after I left the Bells, I went to pay
Charlie O'Donel a visit on the ranch, and what should I find
but a great transcontinental railroad—the Rock Island—a few
miles from the southwest corner of the pasture. And, stretching
out from that at Tucumcari, a little one-horse line running
north just inside, and along, the east line of the grant, through
that Atarque country I've told you about. This track ran up
to the railroad company's coal mines at Dawson, in Colfax
county. I traveled over it to get to the ranch.

It was certainly a great advantage to the Bells, having these railroads. They cut out an eighty-mile horseback or buggy ride to the ranch, which wasn't any too pleasant in zero weather. And an eighty-mile cattle drive to Clayton in the spring that had always been a mean business. For cattle and cowhorses alike were poor, and when you left the lower country and mounted onto the Mesa, you struck a sharper climate which stock were in no condition to stand. Many a good horse on those drives, unsaddled, sweating, in the evening, failed to show up when the horse wrangler rounded up his cavayard in the morning.

Yes, I thought, as I traveled over the little branch line towards Campana, the ranch station—*campana* is Spanish for "bell," and is the name the ranch is known by among the Mexicans—these railroads are a big help all right to these folk. Yet, somehow, as the dinky engine snorted up the steep grades where little Derby used to pack me so surely among the loose rock; and when it scurried over the flats where old Smoky invariably would get his head down and run like hell; a sort of sadness crept through me. And in a day dream I saw that old Atarque country just as it used to be before we ever thought of a railroad; and me ridin' the fence line with old man Turner, or swingin' out on circle with the boys.

But worse far was to come. For when I got outside the Bell fence, out onto the wide rolling grazing lands where the H O W's and the S Bar T's used to range at will in their thousands, lo and behold, the whole country, as far as you traveled, cut up into little two-by-four compartments, with a two-wire fence around each. And, worse than all, the sod—that good sod that in wet seasons or dry was always there, ready—broke up and GONE! converted into dust that will drift, and Russian thistle that will roll, till Judgment Day. And I said to myself, it's fortunate there are some tracts like the Bell pasture that can be, and have been kept clean for the cattle.

. . . And that, my friends, is the end of my story of the Bell Ranch. I have always lived so much in the present; life from day to day has always been so engrossing to me; that these records of past episodes, personal and historical, have never been related by me hitherto—hardly even by word of mouth. So that it has been odd for me to dig back into the past and try to relive the events. For, in order to write about a thing, you have to LIVE it.

Yet I have enjoyed doing it. And thinking so much about it all has carried me far away from life in a great city (in which I live), where the clatter of street cars takes the place of the lowing of herds, and the stench of automobile exhausts supplants the clean scents of the prairie. And I have enjoyed it all the more when I was talking about the Bell country, which I liked better than any western range I ever rode over.

It's been a bit sad at times, of course; so many of those I was writing about had passed along. Tisdall and O'Donel; and Mike McQuaid and Willis Dorset and some others. And only about a month ago I wrote to a friend in Las Vegas, New Mexico, enquiring where I could find Con Dennis. And my friend wrote back: "Con Dennis took the last trail two years ago." It doesn't seem possible. It's true that I knew Con a number of years after he left the Bells; up to a time when, I dare say, he was growing greyish and developing a bit of a window-front. But that's not the Con Dennis I'm remembering. The one I'm remembering was a young Greek god that rode with the Bell wagon!

What I say above in relation to the Bell Ranch applies equally well to all the varied happenings, personal, technical and general, recorded throughout this volume about horses, cattle and men. Indeed I picked up the thread of these things after a longish period devoted to far removed interests and pursuits.

I think I have felt in the main throughout it all that I was writing as a cowman, for cowmen, even though some "higher education" I had the misfortune to receive in my youth sometimes makes it hard for me to write in the simple, direct style in which we cowmen talk. At the same time I have kept in mind those readers who may have had no experience of range life, and I have tried to recreate for them something of the atmosphere of the great ranches, and of this grand old Bell Ranch in particular; as well as to carry to them a bit of the flavor, the aroma of the earlier days.

But first and last I know that I am writing for that unchartered brotherhood of men and women who feel that just to ride out on a crisp morning on a good horse, across the flats, and along the draws, is the best thing life has had to offer. And it makes no difference whether it was Arizona, or Wyoming, or Western Texas, or my own New Mexico.

# II
## Horses

# I

# I Learn to Ride

I

I HAD a Western novel dedicated to me once by a good
Western writer, who had worked the range with me in
earlier times. The inscription (in part) ran like this:

TO
JOHN H. CULLEY
THE FINEST RIDER I HAVE KNOWN-
IN A LAND OF FINE RIDERS—
IN MEMORY OF OLD DAYS

That is a pleasant thing to happen to one. But it looks sort of
swanky putting it at the top of one of my own chapters; as
though I wanted to toot my own horn. Well, it isn't intended
in that way at all, at all. Only inasmuch as I was planning to
write a few stories for you about horses I've known, good and
bad, I thought I'd "declare myself" at the start, so you would
know I wasn't just gassing, like some of those windy guys every
range man has suffered from; but that I had handled and ridden
an old plug or two at one time or another in my life.

As a matter of fact I learned to ride early. Although not
reared in the West, I came from the northern part of England,
where the tradition is still strong that calls for a man to know
how to ride and shoot. I can't remember when I first rode my
pony, Shelty. He ran in a small field with a shed at one end,
and no one ever handled or rode him but myself.

My father generally kept about five horses. Two for carriage
work, and the rest for road riding or for riding with foxhounds,

of which there were several "packs" in the neighborhood. Keeping horses in England is an expensive business. We kept two grooms, and I used to hang around the stables helping them curry and feed and bed, till my clothes smelled so strong of ammonia that the folks wouldn't allow me in the house. Horses were a passion with me. Years after, when I was living on a Western ranch and would keep up a couple of winter horses, I'd go out of nights and fool around the stable rather than sit in the house. As I look back on the horses I have owned or ridden, they come back to me more clearly than the men and women I have known: Tinker, and Smoky, and LD Maud . . .

When I had grown up a bit, my father told me I could ride a real horse and go to a fox hunt on him. He put me on Titmouse, an old stager and perfect hunter. I recall clearly today the first jump we took: a low fence, but Titmouse always jumped steep and high. And how far up in the air I flew, and how I managed to renew my connection with Titmouse on my way back I never could tell for sure.

I think one may say that there are two kinds of jumpers in England. First, there's the horse that takes his fences galloping fast, like a steeplechaser—running, as we say in the West. He takes off a long ways from the fence and lands a long ways from it on the other side, forming a sort of graduated arc. Such horses are not generally hard to sit, unless they fall or stumble. This is the style that prevails in America. And there is the up-and-down jumper, who has been trained in what they call a "cramped" country, where the fences are crowded. He can go up to a high rail fence at little more than a walk, "raise up" almost perpendicularly and drop down at the same angle on the other side. The best up-and-down fencer I ever rode was Paddy, a grey Irish horse. As you may know, the finest hunters in England are Irish, raised on the rich limestone pastures of county Meath, which gives them their bone. I have taken Paddy many a time right out of a dense mob of riders, at a slow jog, at a high rail fence only a few yards away. I never knew him to refuse, or touch a bar.

Well, when you've ridden one of these up-and-down jumpers for a while and got used to their action, it isn't such a tremendous remove to riding a pitching horse.

Eventually my father bought me a hunter for my very own, a beautiful little brown thoroughbred, with grey stripes across his tail, and called Silvertail. Visiting my home many years after, I was pleased to find that all my contemporaries of the hunting field still remembered little Silvertail.

He wasn't what you would term a model hunter, by a jugful, but he provided good practice for a young rider. In the first place he had been raced, and once he got to running, it was useless even trying to stop him. That wouldn't have been so bad, if you had known what he was going to do when you got to a fence. But that depended on Silvertail's mood at the moment. He always gave you the impression he was going to take the thing in his stride. But I remember once especially, coming up to a wide water jump, full speed and with complete assurance; and the suddenness with which Silvertail stopped on the edge of that ditch would have put to shame a top cutting horse. I managed not to take a bath, but the position I occupied on Silvertail's neck for a few moments was a sort of precarious one.

Once the hounds went off full cry and I thought I'd follow the same line across the country an experienced, older rider was taking. I saw him jump a short high section of five-rail fence set in a line of blackthorn hedge just in front of me without so much as grazing a bar. As he did so, Silvertail got his eye on him, and straightway took the bit in his teeth. And away he went, hell bent for election, up to the fence, and past it, and headed full bust for the next one. But it occurred to me my horse hadn't risen much at the fence, so I looked back. There wasn't one rail left standing. He had never risen at all; just run plumb *through* the damn thing.

Although Silvertail showed no sign of it outwardly, he was blind in one eye. That didn't make matters any easier, because it caused him sometimes to swerve unexpectedly in the middle of a jump. Up in the hill regions of that country they have dry stone walls between the pastures. When we came up to one of these in the hunt, we would usually look for a gap some other horse had made in the top of the wall, jumping it. One day Silvertail and I went at one of these gaps at our usual headlong speed. Just as he rose at the wall he gave one of his sudden squirms to one side. My toe caught in the edge of the gap and I took three somersets on my own account into the next field, while Silvertail continued the chase alone, on *his* own account. (Though that wasn't so bad as another fellow I knew, who caught his foot in a similar gap. He did not come off, but when he looked down at his foot, the toes were where the heel had been. His leg had broken and the foot turned completely around.)

Almost every winter my old-time friend, Mat McCallister, who owns the Arrowhead spread on Sweetwater, out from Springer, New Mexico, comes with his wife to spend a few months in Southern California. When he comes we sure have a foregathering. Last winter we were chinning away as usual and Mat said, kind of reminiscently: "I never can forgit"—Mat comes from Texas, and says "forgit"—"the first ever I seen you, Jack, was the time you ridden that bronc for George Crocker— do you-all remember?—on the roundup at the head of the Escondida." I laughed, and then went on to tell him just about what I've been telling you in this sketch. "So that's the way"

MY ENGLISH HOME

Mat said, when I finished, "that's the way you learned to ride, was it?"

## II

Having given you already a glimpse of my background in England, it might not be out of place to bring you into closer touch with that Border country where my ancestors lived so many centuries and where I learned to ride and shoot. Indeed it is no flight of fancy that recognizes some similarity between the early border country as I shall describe it and the western range country that is the subject of this book. I will center my description upon my old home, Coupland Castle, (pronounced Copeland) where my youth was spent, and where Silvertail lived and died.

I may say in starting, for the benefit of students of livestock history, that my family came into possession of Coupland Castle through marriage of my great-grandfather, Mathew Culley, with Elizabeth Bates, a first cousin of the famous Shorthorn breeder, Thomas Bates.

The estate of Coupland lies in the extreme north of England, only a few miles from the border of Scotland. Before the Union of Scotland and England was accomplished continual fighting used to go on between the English and Scotch along the border. It is almost six hundred years since Sir John de Copeland in a battle between the two peoples greatly distinguished himself by his courage, and took the Scottish King, David Bruce, prisoner. He refused to surrender his royal prisoner to the English King until he could strike a bargain with the latter that he be made a Knight and be awarded a pension of five hundred pounds a year. That was the kind of folk these north country Englishmen were: hardy fighters and keen bargainers. And such they remain today!

For centuries constant depredations were carried on from both sides of the border. The Scotch would come over to the

English side and drive off some cattle and the English would go over to the Scotch side and bring back some Scotch cattle. It was an early form of trade reciprocity. In 1580 Queen Elizabeth of England ordered a line of forts or castles built all along the English side to protect it from the Scotch raids. Coupland was one of them. The two square towers to the left of the Great Gateway date back to this time. The other part was added, in excellent Elizabethan style of architecture, about a hundred and twenty-five years ago. They consider that pretty new in England.

The outer walls of the older part are immensely thick—six to seven feet. The present windows have been developed from the original narrow loopholes through which much of the shooting was done when the castle was attacked. Up on the fine battlements of the towers, some of the defenders would gather and drop such destructive objects as molten lead and rocks on the heads of the assailants. Inside the towers are ascended by means of a remarkable stone corkscrew staircase that grows narrower and steeper as you climb it. The door of the old tower has long disappeared, but the huge iron hinges that remain imbedded in the masonry are witness to how big and massive it must have been. And into the great domed hall on the ground floor, which we used as a kitchen, the bunch of home cattle used to be driven for safekeeping when marauders put in an appearance.

Even after the union of England and Scotland, when the two peoples had assumed friendly relations, and long after the rest of England had become peaceful and orderly, this tradition of lawlessness pervaded the north country. Bands of marauders occupying debatable lands sallied forth from them to drive off cattle and sheep and horses, burn down houses and barns, rob and often murder wayfarers. Even the more reputable citizens, having no more Scotchmen to fight, practiced on each other

in the course of numerous feuds they maintained. A hard drinking, hard riding, fighting crowd they were. And many a desperate fight without the old walls of Coupland and many a wild
scene within, must have taken place in those long centuries.
The ghost that made her headquarters in the haunted room of
the Great Tower might have had some strange stories to tell
of them. But she never communicated with the people she
appeared to; only scared them. I well remember how the house
maids going up to their bedrooms in the tower at night would
band together and scurry past the haunted room door. And
when wild winds off the North Sea battered the old castle walls
you could hear odd rappings all about the place there was no
accounting for.

But the newer part of the house was light and cheerful, with
a wonderful library lined with books where I spent many
hours of my youth and got most of my education; with the
family portraits hanging in the red-papered dining room, and
old furniture filling the spacious apartments—some of which
(with the portraits) is in our present home in Los Angeles.
And the rooms looked out onto park lands dotted with ornamental oaks and elms and ashes and copper beeches, and across
pleasant gardens and lawns to the Cheviot Hills where they,
grow the Cheviot wool, which used to be so popular in America.
A mountain trout stream ran clear through the estate, small
game of all kinds abounded in the fields and woods, so that
I learned almost as a child to be an expert shot. Equally early I
learned to ride with surrounding packs of foxhounds. Then
there were dances and tennis tournaments and house parties.
Returning in recent years and occupying the old home with
my family I used sometimes to wonder whether today with
its automobiles, and telephones and movies and electric lights
and all, life is better worth living than when I was a boy. At
any rate we grew up a race of hardy, resourceful men and women.

If you pass through the Great Gateway in the finely embattled wall you find yourself in a courtyard around which were
the dairy, where stoneware crocks of milk and cream were
ranged on cool stone shelves; and beyond that the huge laundry
and the coachman's house. Another smaller gateway led into a
second court. Here were stables for about a dozen horses and
a coach house where we could enclose five cars, I found; and
many other outbuildings.

The estate itself consisted of some three thousand acres, part
hill land where the Cheviot sheep grew pretty wild and often
dropped their lambs in the snow. The remainder was good
farming land, planted to diversified crops, and in grass. They
are resourceful farmers these folks, who use a scientific rotation
of crops. Some cattle are fed, but chiefly to secure fertilizer—the
feeder cattle coming mainly from Ireland. But sheep are the
principal stock. The Border Leicester, which was originated
by my own ancestors about one hundred and fifty years ago,
is well suited for the lowlands. A race of expert sheepmen cross
them for mutton with Cheviots, and Oxford and Suffolk Downs.
They use the wild moorland Blackface breed too. Chris Culley,
my brother and erstwhile New Mexico partner, used to breed
and win prizes with them. They made him a judge at the great
Perth (Scotland) sheep show—the only Englishman, they say,
ever permitted to judge sheep in Scotland! Weekly auction
marts are held at which the lambs you can often see offered
would be hard to beat anywhere in the world. Keen is the competition among their breeders and shepherds to top the market.

Our estate, like most others in England, was let out to well-
to-do tenant farmers. But by the time one has met all the taxes
and upkeep of the extensive improvements, there is little left
for the landlord, and most of the old properties have passed,
like ours, into the hands of the new rich, who have independent
means to maintain them. None the less, that old English border
castle and estate where my ancestors lived and wrought and

I grew up still ranks equally in my tenderest remembrance with the Western range country in which so much of my more mature life was lived, and whose history I am trying to deal with in this volume.

### III

The English are undoubtedly the most humane people on earth as regards domestic animals. It was in England the Society For Prevention of Cruelty to Animals originated. The Blue Cross, too, which aims to relieve suffering of horses engaged on war fronts. I believe the British had a Blue Cross organization on every allied front in the World War. Then they have a society that concerns itself with the humane slaughter of cattle; and I don't know how many others. If you own a horse over there you may be sure there's a special officer of some kind snooping around to see if you're treating it kindly. Indeed, when I was living there I used to think they paid more attention to their horses and dogs than to their children.

I had a cousin who belonged to all these humane societies for animals, and was mighty keen on the subject. When we would start out on a trip into the country in the car, she would say to the chauffeur; "Now, Davis, be very careful not to run over any dogs!" And I would add; "Yes, Davis, be very careful about the dogs. It doesn't matter if you kill a few old women or children!"

But, joking apart, it's a fine thing; and nowhere in the world will you find the horses so slick and well fed as in Great Britain. I used to say it was an exception to come across a work horse without a nosebag on it.

Some of the other peoples show up differently in this respect. The Latins, for instance: the French, Spanish, Italians. No one is prouder of his *caballo* than the Mexican. Yet he doesn't seem to mind riding him when he is thin and weak. And saddle sores and collar galls don't appear to worry him as they do people of the Anglo-Saxon race, in which category I include the American.

One year, long ago—around 1890, I believe—my sister May, came out from England to spend a summer with me on my ranch in New Mexico. I had some good saddle horses and we took a lot of rides together. May was a fine and fearless horse-woman, having ridden with foxhounds all her life. About this time considerable attention was being given by the range men of Wyoming and other northern states to the breeding up of their horse stock. With improved blood they were producing on those northern grasses a strong-boned animal, and some of their geldings were being shipped to England to be sold as hunters. It was not unusual those days, I was told, to see west-ern American brands on the English hunting field. The horses, however, were not overly well broken, and my sister had topped off a number of them for the English dealers. The which enabled an animal to be advertised as "ridden by a lady." (It seems as though old Dave Harum hadn't much on the British horse trader.) But May had never seen colts handled by the rough and often cruel appearing methods we used on the range. Moreover, she, too was a member of S.P.C.A., and woe betide anyone she caught maltreating a horse.

I was living at this time on the Escondida. That is a beautiful arroyo lying southeast from Wagon Mound, fed by springs its whole length, and with gradual, softly broken slopes rising on both sides, over which it was a sheer joy, I still recall, to see cattle grazing out as they left the water. A few miles below our house the arroyo drops into the abrupt malpais canyon of the Mora river which threads twenty miles of wild country before it joins the Canadian, some ten miles north of the great Bell pasture.

The Wagon Mound Cattle pool was working the range at the time and one evening made camp at the head of our arroyo. Next morning my friend, George Crocker, sent word to me that he had a bad horse in his mount, and would I come over and ride him for him.

It is a great mistake, as Frank King has pointed out somewhere, to suppose that every cowpuncher was continually hungering and thirsting for bad horses to ride. George Crocker had worked cattle since babyhood, but he wasn't any more anxious than most of the other boys, to run risks with a dangerous horse when he could get someone else to top him off for him. Moreover, it should be understood that although all the boys could ride, not all could "stay with" a hard pitching horse. (I use the word "pitch." I don't recall ever hearing the term "buck" used in a cow camp in those times, except in the phrase "bucking strap.") Generally speaking, in the big outfits each man would be assigned on the summer work one or more of the colts just off the bronco buster's hands. He would saddle him up after noon when they would be branding calves or such like and there wasn't much riding to be done. Thus the horse got gradually broken to the work.

Well, after dinner I rode up with my sister to the camp and told the boys to catch their horse and saddle him up. He acted pretty mean when they led him out of the cavayard, but a horse don't stand much show with a bunch of cowpunchers handling him. I don't know why it is so, but I recall quite clearly that as I lifted my foot to the stirrup, the colt raised straight up on his hind legs and his fore part never touched the ground again till the horn of the saddle hit the prairie. I mention this, I guess, because it is one of the things a horse does that never failed to terrify me.

Well, as quick as I crawled him he went to snorting and bawling, and considering he was just a youngster—it takes age and experience to make a real bad'un—the bronc did some pretty lively pitching. And the boys all gathered around and hollered "Let *me* ride 'im!" and "quirt 'im down the laig!" and such other jocosities as cowboys of those days affected when a fellow was riding a raw one in camp. Although I used to "ride 'em slick"—most all the fellows on that range used a "bucking strap"—I was no fancy buster, pulling show stunts. But following George's instructions, I gave that colt the works, and when I got off him half an hour later, a lady could have ridden him.

And a lady it was that showed up at that moment and gave me the works. For when my sister came up and saw the colt sweating and "gaunted," and the bloody foam gathered on his lips and flecking his chest and forelegs, she up and told me what she thought of a coward and brute that would treat a horse like that. If it had been England, she said, the S.P.C.A. would have had me arrested on the spot.

And I thought to myself, yes, it's a fine thing to have someone stand up for our dumb animals and all that, but what seems to me to be wanted here is a society to protect us guys who get our backs broke and our guts twisted up forkin' these here goddam broncs. But I said nothing, for my sister, May, is a grand good sort, and I felt sure she'd see things differently once she got cooled off.

# 2

## Bronco Breaking

For a while during my early days in New Mexico, I made most of my living by breaking horses. By that I don't mean that I undertook to bust strings of broncs for big outfits. That would not have interested me at all. The process in such cases consisted largely in knocking hell out of a colt for three days and then turning him over as broke. And, provided you took the colt right off the bronco buster's hands and continued riding him regularly from then on, the results were wonderfully good. If, however, you let up on riding him for a day or two, a surprise might be awaiting you. Most colts seemed to use the interval in meditating mischief for the next ride; and when that took place it was distinctively a case of "Beware!"

But I took on horses that people wanted more carefully gentled, and taught something, and never more than two or three at a time. My system was a sort of compound of many other systems, but it differed considerably from most that were used on the ranges. I thought it might interest some of my readers to know something about it, and perhaps it can best be illustrated by describing a particular case.

My brother, Tom, who had come over from Australia, was staying with me one time on the ranch. He decided he wanted to make me a present, so he told me to go to any of the surrounding horse herds and pick me out a colt. That suited me very nicely, as we were short of horses at the time and had a lot of riding to do. I selected the AI Bar outfit, because I knew their stock well and the ranch was handy. It lay just across the Mora river, which in that district runs at the bottom of a perpendicular malpais canyon, crossed by steep and rocky trails. My old friend, Gus Mayhan, was in charge of the stock at the time. Gus and I had worked together for "Cap" Brunton on the Rail Twelve ranch at Cherry Valley, years before.

So I rode over to the picturesque AI Bar ranch, and Gus and I ran in a bunch of broncos. I looked them over and chose a powerful three-year-old roan colt and laid my line on him. As soon as we had choked him down I made a simple hackamore or halter out of the end of my rope, putting the noose loop of it fairly well down on the colt's nose, and tying it with a piece of string to his forelock, so as to keep it in place. This done, we let him up. "Now," said I, "I'll teach him to lead, so I can take him across the canyon tomorrow." Gus offered to help me, and came in behind the colt with a gunny sack. I said to him, "Gus, old man! there's only one way in the world you can help me, and that's by getting out of this corral and staying out of it till I say I want you!"

You see, my idea of a horse leading is not that you should have to pull him, but that he should FOLLOW you. Therefore when he is learning to lead, his attention must be centered on the person in front of him, not on someone in his rear, flourishing a gunny sack or even a buggy whip. I'm willing to bet there has been more profanity expended during the history of the cattle business over horses that wouldn't lead than over any other single thing. Any horse I broke would lead at any pace from a walk to a high lope at the barest touch of the rope. Indeed my stake horses would come running up to the pin as soon as I went to it and took the stake rope in my hand.

Well, I guess Gus thought I was crazy, but he finally consented to pull out altogether. We had already turned the rest of the horses out of the corral, and I was left alone with my bronc. Nothin' in the wide world but the corral sides and the sky—and me and him! That is the first requirement. To fix the colt's attention on one object: the man that's breaking him. He'll never forget you—for weal or for woe—as long as he lives.

The noose on his nose being pretty low down enabled me to jerk him to one side or the other whenever he tried to run, and it was not long before his nose began to get a bit sore and I could pull him around either way easily. Only you must be careful not to let him get his tail towards you endwise, or he'll pull you. Then little by little I got nearer and nearer to him, till finally his head was close to me. Then is the moment, my friends, NOT to put your hand out or make any gesture. Let him do the investigating. Pretty soon he will stretch out that tremulous, sensitive nose, or upper lip, of his, by which through the sense of touch he judges everything—as a dog judges by sense of smell—towards you. Once he has touched you with that nose and found that you don't flinch or react from it, the colt is yours. It won't be long before, if anything scares him, he'll run up and bury his nose in your stomach. And remember: be careful not to jump, then. If you don't, he won't.

After a while he would let me touch his nose, and when I did, I would move the noose of the hackamore off the sore spot and rub it a little. That felt good to him, and I would repeat it over and over. And before long, whenever I pulled on the rope, he would run up to have me loosen the noose on his nose. (Only be careful never to pull hard enough to make him rear or fight.) Gus did not come back to the corral that evening, but, if he had, he would have found the roan colt following me around like a dog, and from time to time making little nervous rushes at me and burying his nose in my vest.

I lived only a few miles away, so I went home that night, leaving the bronc trailing his rope in the corral. Next morning bright and early I rode back across the river to get my horse. The trails down to the river on both sides were bad ones even for a gentle horse, and I thought I would bring Gus along in case anything went wrong. One thing in my favor was that the colt was used to rough country.

But I never needed Gus at all, although he wanted to come behind the colt with his saddle rope. Several times the bronco would stop and balk at an extra bad place. Then I would pull on the rope till it tightened the hackamore on his nose, and in a moment or two he would give a plunge to where I was, to have me loosen it. And so with a little patience the colt and I got down the trail and across the river and up the other side. Meantime Gus sat at the top of the rim rock where we started from, watching us. And the last remark I heard him make was: "Well, I'll be damned! I never seen nuthin' like that before!"

Well, it was all just as easy, of course—as I have shown you— as rollin' off a log. But Gus thought I was a magician.

[The colt I have been telling you about, and using as an example of my system of breaking, I called Melbourne, from the city in Australia where my brother, Tom, had lived. He turned out one of the best horses I ever owned. Perfectly kind, but you could never use quirt or spur on him. He was stolen from me later by the well known Mexican outlaw, Jesus Romero, whose career was, I believe, shortly afterwards abruptly and effectually closed by Frank King's old-time peace-officer friend, June Hunt, of Colfax County.

We recovered Melbourne, however, and in a curious way. My brother Chris at this time was working down on the Rio Grande about two hundred miles south of our ranch. Recuperating from an attack of malaria, he went up to a resort in the Sandia Mountains, which lie out from Albuquerque a few miles to the north. There was an old half-breed at the resort who kept saddle horses for rent and Chris feeling peppy enough to ride, ordered a horse to be sent up to him. A boy came with it. "I pretty nearly dropped dead," Chris told me afterwards, "when I saw that the horse was your roan colt, Melbourne!"

Chris said nothing but went back to Albuquerque and took out replevin papers for the horse. Tom Hubbell, the famous Bernalillo County Sheriff, wasn't able to go with him but sent his brother Felix, who Chris says was only a little fellow but "cold nerve clear through" (and I may say the same for brother Chris.) They found the horse had been removed from the resort and they had to track him to a ranch belonging to Jesus Romero far up in the mountains where after something of a scrap they got him. It was often the case that stolen horses were ridden down and ruined. They had burned up the roan's AI brand pretty badly, but I was rejoiced to find him the same good horse.]

## II

I was telling you about halter-breaking a colt. As a matter of fact I didn't always begin with that. Indeed, I came to believe that the sooner you mounted a bronc, the better the results. My schedule generally ran: 1. Pick your colt out of the band (that was always good fun). 2. Rope and throw him, and fix the hackamore. 3. Blind and saddle him; and (4) crawl him, pull up the blind and—let her rip! In nine cases out of ten the colt just ran; and he stopped when he was tired—too tired to cut up. Only it had to be done in the open. I never mounted a bronc in the corral, or allowed him to pitch with the saddle. County forty minutes in all from the first move, and you were back at the corral with a one-third broken horse. For in three saddles—magical number! a range horse was considered gentle. Though personally, I liked to handle them several weeks.

Of course you need a good man with a stout horse to pilot you. I broke broncs for Arthur Isaacs on the old AI Bar ranch, where there was only a narrow strip of prairie outside the corral between the canyon side and a rocky arroyo. It was worse than "riding off" at polo, holding a bronc on that strip of land.

As a rule a red "bandanny" handkerchief was used for a blind. It was not very convenient: hard to pull up and impossible to let down from the saddle. I used a strip of pliable harness leather, perhaps sixteen inches long by four broad; the exact dimensions escape me. At each end I made two holes, one above the other. Through these holes ran, snugly enough not to slip, a soft quarter inch cord, which passed over the colt's head just behind the ears and then under the jaw, and was tied snug but not tight. On this cord the leather blind worked up and down as on a hinge, flat on the front, and bent over the sides, of the colt's forehead. The rider, leaning forward in the saddle, had no difficulty in pulling it over, or off, the animal's eyes.

Now for the hackamore—and a little comment, in passing—on the word itself. The compilers of our dictionaries are for the most part easterners, who still incline to highhat the West. They have for some years given "hackamore (U. S. Western)" in their dictionaries, but it is only recently that they have deigned to offer a derivation. Most of our Western range terms came to us from the Mexicans along with range practice, and hackamore is clearly the Spanish "jaquima": the "j" pronounced like an "h"; the "qu" as "k"; the accent on the first syllable and the word itself universally used by Spanish-Americans to indicate a halter.

I just made my riding hackamore out of the rope I caught the colt with. With the usual half-hitch I fixed the loop around its neck so it wouldn't run. Then I measured back about ten or twelve feet of rope and doubled it. I slipped a single half-hitch around the colt's nose, knotting it under the chin with the doubled part of the rope. The doubled end in this way formed a loop to be used as lines, while the remaining single end served to trail, or lead the colt by. It remained only to tie the front of of the nose noose with a piece of string to the colt's forelock to keep it in place. There I was with a hackamore, lead rope and reins complete, made almost at one stroke within about three minutes time.

I rode with the hackamore alone till the colt's nose got a bit sore and I could pull his head around and guide and stop him readily with it. The next step was to put on a bridle and let him get used to the feel of the bit in his mouth, though being careful not to bring it into play. Only as I pulled on the rope to turn him to one side or the other, I would let the bridle rein press lightly on the opposite side of his neck. In this way he learned to turn—as, of course, all cow horses turn—by the simple pressure of the rein on the neck. Under this system the bit is never brought into play while the colt is learning to turn. Consequently the animal rarely learns to fight the bit in turning, as so many horses do. I'd ride the colt quite a while with both hackamore and bridle together, before discarding the hackamore.

When my family and I were living in England—which we did, largely, between 1921 and 1931—our first home was in the country. There was much horseback riding around us, so we bought ourselves a saddle animal. A fine little mare, indeed, she was, that had been driven and also regularly ridden by a lady. Considerable was my surprise on first mounting her to find she had been trained to turn only by a direct pull on the bit with the line on the side one wished to turn her to—as in driving. This seems to be the usual custom in England with all saddle horses, except polo ponies. Now it is obvious that under such a system both hands are required in turning your horse. It doesn't seem to be quite clear when the method of turning horses by pressure on the neck—"the indirect rein," as it is called—which I have described above and which is used universally on the range and at polo was adopted. But it enables the rider to turn his horse with one hand; and it is obvious that the idea of its adoption arose from the need of having one hand free, for some independent purpose.

The modern system of horsemanship dates only from the 16th century, but I have sometimes wondered about the Knights of the Middle Ages. They are generally represented as laying about them in battle with their weapons with vast energy and adroitness and in all directions. To be able to do this, they must have had one hand free and must surely have "guided" their chargers "by the neck." The cowboy, who was their logical successor, in that he operated on horseback and because, as with the knights, certain essentials of his life and character were inseparably associated with the horse, adopted their method of reining, so as to have a hand free to manipulate his rope, and do various things.

An additional advantage of guiding by the neck is, of course, that it tends to lift over the whole forefront of the horse in turning, instead of just turning his neck and head. As a matter of fact, in *haute ecole*, or high school, riding proper both reins of the curb are employed together in turning. The one to give pressure on the neck, the other to stabilize the bit and maintain uninterrupted the essential relation between the rider's hand and the horse's mouth. But if you had made mention of the *haute ecole* to an old-time cowpuncher, he might have thought you were calling him foul names, and have "drawed" a gun on you. I personally did practice up a few *haute ecole* stunts and try them out on the old range cow. I don't know whether she felt flattered or offended by them, but I thought they enabled me to work her out of a herd a little quicker than otherwise. I'll tell you some more about it presently.

III

In telling you about the early stages of breaking a colt, as I practised it, I described the blind and hackamore, and how I used them. But it is rather an odd thing that I got nothing of all this from New Mexico. I never saw a hackamore used in breaking in my district (though they were doubtless in use elsewhere in the state), nor anything in the way of a blind except an old "bandanny." My patent, leather blind and my quick-change hackamore and manner of using it came to me from the Mexican bronco riders of California. It happened this way.

When I first hit the West, I stayed for a while with a relative, William Pinkerton, near Wagon Mound, in northern New Mexico. Pinkerton had bought the west half of what was known as the Nolan Grant, which had been granted by the Mexican government to Gervacio Nolan of Taos. This Nolan, by the way, had owned likewise a grant in Colorado, an interest in which came into the hands of Charlie Goodnight, when he was ranching in that state. Pinkerton had previously owned another large block of land, the well-known Pleyto Ranch in Monterey County, California, now a part of the great ·Hearst ranch. On moving to New Mexico he had conveyed the Pleyto property to his son, William, Jr., and William Jr. came to pay his first visit at his father's New Mexico ranch just after I arrived there. I am frank to say I have never known two men possessing so profound and complete a practical knowledge of livestock husbandry from all angles as William Pinkerton and his son. It had been gathered in many countries: England, Australia, New Zealand and America.

I was handling a young horse at the time for a daughter of my host, Mrs. Steavenson. A fine young bay colt he was, I may recall in passing, which had a short time previously thrown and killed Mrs Steavenson's only son, Frank. Pinkerton, Jr., always interested in what was going on and seeing me with the colt, got to telling me how his Mexicans handled his colts on the Pleyto.

The large California *haciendas*, which are now worked chiefly by Americans, at that time employed Mexican hands.* Very expert hands they were. The Mexican is a natural horseman; and as for the lariat, these fellows grew up roping chickens and hogs and everything else on the place from the time they could walk. There is, of course, only one way to catch broncs, and that is

---

*In many parts of California the early cowhands, literally, were Spanish-speaking Indians. These grew to be very expert in all branches of range work.

by the forelegs (in a round corral). But you must be dead sure on the job to do it. Otherwise it may mean catching a colt by one foreleg and him trailing a rope till you can catch him by the neck and take it off him. I am of the opinion that real skill in roping by the feet—like the cowboy's yell!—must be acquired in childhood. At any rate, hard as I tried to learn—and I got to be a pretty useful roper in a general way—I rarely trusted myself to forefoot. (And I wasn't much more successful with the yell.) These California Mexican *vaqueros*, Pinkerton said, could catch 'em any way you wanted without any effort whatever. And I recall what a pretty sight it was to see 'Suz Ruiz, a crack hand from Old Mexico I used to have, send them spinning heels over head. Nor was Moyses Romero who used to bust the Bell broncs in my day and is still with that outfit—the best man, Manager Albert Mitchell says, he has ever had with a day herd—any slouch when it came to tripping up their front end.

However, although I adopted much of the system young Pinkerton described and demonstrated to me, not all my knowledge of bronco breaking and training came to me from the California Mexican. For some of it I went back to a man who lived a hundred years ago, to Baucher, the Frenchman, famous exponent of the *haute ecole*, or high school, for horses. If you have ever watched a range stallion rounding up his *manada* of mares, you'll have noticed how easily and freely he moves. His head moves back and forth on his neck as though it were working on a well oiled hinge. Stopping, starting, or traveling, his action is smooth and in balance. Now break him and put a bit on him: he sticks out his head stiffly; moves either behind the bit or ahead of it; most of his elasticity and balance have disappeared.

Well, Baucher—as many of my readers know—tried to remedy this by teaching the horse to relax his jaw and flex the neck under the action of the bit, thereby suppling up every other part of the body; and at the same time, by use of the spur or leg, bringing

up his hind end, so that the entire action should be brought
into equilibrium—"collected," as the term goes. I didn't see why
this should not help a cowhorse. So, as I have said before, I tried
out part of the system on the young horses I rode. I think it
made them more supple, easier to turn. You could stop them
quicker and with less jar, which is a help over a long day of
work around a herd.

Of course the high school horse is generally a showy animal;
he carries his head and tail high, and has plenty of action.
I didn't want that. That's the sort of thing the Mexicans like,
often carried to an extreme degree and secured by methods of
their own with use of a heavy spade bit. Mention of this brings
to my mind my good friend and one-time neighbor, Blas
Romero. Don Blas Romero came from Old Mexico, of a notable
family. A very distinguished looking and courtly *caballero* he
was, and an accomplished horseman. As became a person of his
standing, he always rode a fine horse, carefully trained along
Mexican lines. I remember his coming to a roundup of mine
one time. As every cowman knows, it is the custom for the
boss of the roundup to invite all attending cowmen one by one
to go into the herd and cut out their cattle, if any there be.
In due course I told Blas to go in and get out his stuff. So Don
Blas made entry into the herd, his bay horse going on its hind
legs, shaking his head and champing the bit. There is no doubt
whatever the Señor Romero felt that he and his *caballo* were
making a great impression upon all the spectators. They were
making a great impression upon the herd, certainly, for before
they had been in there five minutes, they had the whole business
milling, like the music in the popular song, " 'round and around,"
till the only way you could have gotten an animal out of that
herd was to have roped it and dragged it out on the horn of
the saddle.

No, the high-headed, up-acting horse is splendid on the road
or in the park, but his place is not in a herd of cattle. I might

not be far wrong in saying that a cowman prefers a cutting horse on the plain and lazy side, if anything. One that, as he grows older, may get a bit foxy and let a cow slip past him once in a while, and you have to work him over with your quirt to show him you mean business. At any rate I believe all old hands will agree with me that the most desirable characteristic in a cut horse, next to cow sense and quickness on his feet, is that he cause as little disturbance in a herd as possible. I've known old timers that could be cutting, and cutting fast, yet so smoothly you'd hardly notice there was any work being done in the herd at all.

## IV

I have been giving you some description of the earlier methods of breaking colts—"busting" them, as we termed it, and really that term expresses pretty well what we did to them. Today these methods are largely things of the past. The vast majority of colts are handled and gentled long before they are ready to be ridden. And the colts themselves have generally a much diluted mixture of the blood that made them bawl and pitch.

But if there are any youngsters who still have to handle and ride regular broncos, they may find some interest in my experience and ideas. And in the first place I'd say, don't be discouraged if you find the prospect of riding a "bad" one scares you. I know in my own case, in spite of considerable familiarity with dangerous horses and a good deal of luck in riding them, I never got rid of some nervousness. A horse falling back always scared me. Even their bawling unnerved me a bit sometimes! I recall one time undertaking for a friend to ride a saddle horse that had been running out and got to eating loco weed. We thought we'd try him out in the corral first to see how bad a dose of the weed he had gotten. He removed all doubt on that point the instant we had the saddle on him. Actually screaming like some maniac human thing, and pitching furiously, he made a bee line across the big corral, never turning to right or left till he crashed head on into the poles at the opposite side and fell in a limp and tangled mass on the ground. I felt discouraged.

But I give you my word I never pulled my saddle off. I rode 'em somehow. But not, I fear, with that gaiety and nonchalance that was so admirable in some riders. Out from the long years comes to me the memory of Frank Ortega, handsomest of young Mexicans, who came to us on the old AI Bar ranch on the Escondida one year, to help with the broncs. What a headline Hollywood type Frank would have made today with his dark skin and teasing eyes! I can still picture him as clearly as if it were yesterday, whenever a horse went off pitching with him, looking back over his shoulder at us, laughing and showing his white teeth. . . .

But when it came to handling horses on the ground, I had practically no fear of them; and that's the attitude, with reservations, I recommend to young breakers. I remember once a man taking me to look at some pretty wild stuff he was starting to break. He had three of them tied together in one stall and I started to go in between them to handle them. As soon as he saw my intention he shouted out, "For God's sake, man come outa there! Those horses'll kill you!" But I went right on, crowding in between them without a vestige of hesitation, and they took no more notice of me than if they had been old gentle mounts. It's not the horse, it's the man, that's scared oftenest.

In illustration of which statement I propose to relate to you the tragic story of Ed Taylor who used to ride for the Bells when I was with them. A stocky built, florid-faced fellow Ed was; a good hand, but a trifle excitable. It was the custom of the Bell ranch, as on most big outfits, to turn over to each of the boys on the summer work one or two broncs just off the buster's hands. The fellows would saddle them up after dinner when not much was doing, and thus the colts would gradually learn to work with cattle. One day we were camped at the Huerfano Mesa and were going to brand calves in the corral there after dinner. So Ed and I thought we'd saddle up our broncs. Ed usually took numerous precautions with his and I was surprised to see him on this occasion saddle and mount him just as though he was an old horse. And the colt never made a move. But no sooner was Ed in the saddle than he suddenly hollered: "By God, fellers, I plumb forgot this was a bronc! I'll be durned if I ever even cheeked him when I got on him!" And there he sat on his horse actually scared stiff at the thought of what that bronc might have done to him—and didn't!

Of course one must use discretion. Avoid all sudden movements. You will recall the roan colt, Melbourne, I told you about. He was an animal without a trace of viciousness, but I came in behind him unexpectedly one day and he lashed out at me. A powerful beast, he caught me fair and square just above the kneecap, paralysing the nerves and muscles of the leg and almost turning my stomach. It must have been a good half hour before I could drag myself down to the house fifty yards away. You have to take some chances, but it's well to remember that a colt's mean actions are the result much more often of sudden nervous reactions than of any vicious intent. Moreover, as for the kick, it is the horse's natural method of self-defence when he thinks he is threatened. So unless you want to convert a temporary lapse into a confirmed habit, don't go after your colt with the pitchfork when he kicks you. And if you find you can't control your temper under such provocations, you better be looking out for some other vocation than horse breaking.

I used to take considerable pains to make my colts unafraid of the rope in contact with any part of their anatomy. This was not the usual practise on the range, however. Most men liked their horses tetchy about the rope around their legs and tail. It made them leery about stepping into the slack of the lariat when roping, or getting otherwise mixed up in it. Then the corrals in which we caught our horses on a roundup usually consisted of ropes stretched on iron stakes. Wariness of the rope kept the horses from crowding up against the sides and breaking them down. And finally a touch of "snuffiness" in a cowhorse was generally favored as being in keeping with the spirit of the West.

Whether you are going to break broncs or train high school horses, you will want to be a good rider. To that end constant horseback riding is, of course, the first requirement. But if you are to be a finished horseman, I suggest some exercises to increase your flexibility about the waist. That will help you to realize the twin objective you will always keep before you: complete rhythmic unity with the movement of your horse and (from the waist up) complete independence of it. These requirements seem at first thought to contradict each other. Nevertheless the combination of them is the basis of all good horsemanship. Through it alone you can acquire that magic quality of "hands," whereby you communicate your will to your horse, and establish a *rapport*, an infinitely delicate understanding between yourself and him; as though some psychic current came and went between you along the lines.

And here I am going to relate to you a little personal happening, not in the least to glorify my own horsemanship which is very defective at several points, but to illustrate for young horsemen the practical value of good "hands." Years ago, just two weeks before I left the old country to try my luck in the West, I accepted an invitation to a New Year's house party in one of the great English country houses. My host was Master, as it is called, of the principal north country pack of foxhounds. As such he kept a large number of good hunters to mount the staff that conducts the hunt in the field, and he offered to many of his forty guests a mount for the New Year's Day hunt to be held at the Castle. These meets of hounds are a charming and animated spectacle, with their well kept horses, their red coated riders, and the large pack of carefully bred-to-type foxhounds. You can picture all this with a background of English lawns and gardens, surrounding some stately mansion. The mount they chose and led out for me was a six-year-old mare about 15.3 hands in height, of that type which combines beauty with considerable power. She was usually ridden by Lyons, the huntsman of the hounds, a heavy, big-fisted fellow, and they told me how high strung she was, and that she always came near wearing Lyons out with her fractiousness and excitability. We started several foxes during the course of the day and had some good runs. I found my mare free and fast, a smooth and finished and big-hearted fencer, with a perfect mouth. She carried me from morning to night without ever a shake of her head or a pull on the bit, and at the end of the day my host remarked to me on the change wrought in his mare. Yes, I remember saying to myself, if I could only *own* this brown mare, I'd stay on here in England and just chase foxes.*

That visit dates back a good long way, my friends, but believe it or not, just two or three years ago the present lady of that great house happened to pass through Los Angeles and, learning that my family and I lived here, she paid us a visit, bringing with her her two young daughters, Elizabeth and Diana, grand-daughters of my old-time host. True north country sports girls these proved to be, whose principal interest is horses. Their excitement was great when I told them I had punched cows and ridden broncos on western ranches, and I gave to each of them an original drawing by Katherine Field which delighted them as they delight all who know cows and horses. And you may bet I didn't forget to tell them the story of the brown mare.

And a year or two later, to complete my tale, I saw by the papers that Elizabeth was married to a young man who belongs

*I suppose all this is suspended during the war.

to a distinguished Scottish family and who is known the world over as the "fighting Marquis," by reason of having been, a few years since, perhaps the finest living amateur pugilist. I sent the young couple a copy of the magazine in which this story came out and received a pleasant acknowledgement from Elizabeth, now Marchioness of Clydesdale.

# 3
# How Cowboys Rode: Cowboy v. Polo Player

EVERY school and style of equitation or horsemanship, has at least one main feature distinguishing it from other styles or schools. If you were to ask me what was the distinctive feature of Western range horsemanship, I should answer without hesitation: the loose rein. The cowboy less than any other class of rider I know of, used the bit to control or direct his horse. In training a cutting horse his plan, as far as he had a plan, was to teach him to follow a cow, interfering meanwhile as little as possible with his mouth. He certainly never attempted any manipulation with the bit. Indeed it wasn't always easy to switch a good cowhorse off a cow at all. As to my own cowhorses, as I've told you elsewhere, I worked on with their mouths quite a bit and generally aimed to keep them "in hand" when they were working in a herd. There were times when this proved itself of value.

One afternoon on our Rafter C Bar ranch in New Mexico I and John Hinde, (long time foreman and now part owner and manager of that old established outfit,) had to cut some cows out of a small herd I was holding for shipment. We had only one man, the dayherder, to help us, so we threw the bunch inside the deep entrance wing of our large main corral. This wing swung out from a corner gate and then curved back towards the corral side, forming an enclosure except for the open end. This free end our day-herder "held up," while we cut the cattle through it into the open.

I was riding Tinker, a ganglin' sorrel, little more perhaps than an average good cowhorse, but bridlewise in a high degree.

John had caught up his top mount, Silver, a powerful little half-Chihuahua horse, silver white from tip to tail, and the finest all-around cowhorse I ever owned, rode or, I believe, saw. The wing on one side and the corral fence on the other crowded the cattle greatly and left but little room for our horses to work in. Consequently I would keep switching Tinker away from his cow and make him cut her off short against the fence instead of just following her as a horse would do on the outside, and as Silver seemed to be doing. By these means Tinker and I cut three head of cattle to John and Silver's two all that afternoon. At least that's how I had it figured out, though I hope John won't see this statement because, if he does, the next time we meet he may go get him his big .45 and bore a hole or two in me with it. He's tetchy, John, about that old cowhorse.

So much for the use of bit and bridle in Western riding. But it would be impossible to leave that phase of my subject without remarking that if the cowboy used the rein comparatively little, he used the leg and spur a lot, in the handling of his mount. And that brings us to the question of the seat. I have frequently remarked in these chapters that most of our range practice was derived from the Mexicans, who were already ranging cattle in the Southwest when the Americans moved in on the scene. In the light of this one may wonder why the American cowboy seat should differ so pronouncedly from that of the Mexican; for you can distinguish an American horseman from a Mexican as far as the eye reaches. The Mexican "sits" in the saddle, using what is known as the "chair seat." This is undoubtedly a seat well adapted to the gait he chiefly affects, namely, the canter or as we called it on the range, the "lope," (a word perhaps adopted from the Spanish *galope*\*(*gah-lo-pay*). I think perhaps the most characteristic memory one has of Spanish-American life is the vision of the Mexican horseman

*However the Standard Dictionary says the word is an American one, derived from an Anglo-Saxon word meaning to "leap." I wonder!

hitting it across the prairie at a high lope, his usually jaded mount rising and dropping, rising and dropping to the furthest horizon, while the rider sat back easily in the saddle. Old Narciso Castro, foreman on that California Pleyto ranch I told you about, when he was training young Will Pinkerton, the owner's son, to ride, would push him down in the saddle whenever he saw him rise from it. Narciso sat close himself, and never moving in the saddle would rope calves for a whole day, in front or rear, or on either side of his horse, by fore or hind feet, neck or figure eight, for ten flankers, without ever boggling a shot.

The American, on the other hand, rode on the stirrup with a straight leg, deep and straight in the saddle. He did not often use the lope except where his horse, in the course of working cattle, broke into that gait as a modified form of the gallop, or run (to use the Western term). In traveling he used the jog-trot, either sitting straight in the saddle or sideways; in the latter case often throwing his weight first on one stirrup, then on the other, as a means of getting relief. When he wanted to travel faster he usually put his horse to a trot, standing in the stirrups and leaning forward slightly over the horn of the saddle. He used this position too in roping or doing other work. Our idea in general seemed to be to make the riding position conform as nearly as possible to the natural standing position when on foot. And this still seems to me the most logical position where you have, as we had, many functions to perform from the back of your horse.

This straight-legged seat with long stirrups may be said to be the typical American seat, well adapted to the smooth-gaited horses—single-footers, pacers, etc.—which have from earliest times been so popular in America and Canada. Of late years it has become considerably modified through the wide intro-duction of the English saddle. The "muley," as the boys used to call it, was a rare sight in the early days. With it we get the shorter stirrup, the rider sitting far back on the cantle of his saddle, with his knees extending far out in front of him; using the "chair seat," in fact. This style of riding has even made its way into polo. It is claimed for it there that the fact of the rider's weight being carried on the hindquarter of the horse relieves the jar on the tendons of the forelegs when stopping or turning, of which there is as much in playing polo as in working cattle, and very similar. Some even make the mallet stroke from this position. But the usual American play seems to be to sit back in the saddle until the moment of making the stroke and then stand in the stirrup while making the stroke itself. Standing on such a short stirrup raises the rider's seat far above the pommel of the saddle, though this is corrected to some extent by not altogether straightening the knee. Even so, it is difficult to see how the position lends itself to security of seat, or control of either horse or "stick." But I take it that the increased leverage from the stirrup thus obtained does create power in the stroke, and the principal object in American polo is to "belt" the ball, our American players being the hardest hitters in the world. It also enables the player to get the mallet to the ball sooner.

There is the further objection to this sitting back in the saddle that the rider's full weight falls upon the loin, the least protectable part of his mount, either unrelieved, or in a series of bumps, as may occur when a rough horse is checked on the run in a hurry. I have seen the posterior part of a two-hundred-pounder thumping up and down with great violence on the loin of a never too large pony. It must tend to "bucket" or knock the wind out of them, surely. And certainly when it comes to appearance, this style in general compares unfavorably with the easy seat of the cowboy, poised in the center of gravity of his mount.

Indeed the latter seat differs but little from the polo seat as described by Colonel F. W. Ramsay of the British Army in *Polo Pony Training*. "The rider should be balanced from his feet up, and each part of his body should rest on that which is immediately below it. If his seat is on the saddle, pressure should be vertical through seat bones, but I prefer to raise the seat slightly off the saddle and lean a little forward and press on the stirrups." I think this might serve, as it stands, for a description of the cowboy's seat. It suggests the way, too, in which the late "Pat" Roark, the Irish ex-British Army Captain, and famous polo player, rode. I'd go a long ways, any day, to watch that nine goaler, reckoned the finest horseman in the British Empire, handle his mount. And it hits off according to my observation the style of all the polo players who hail from the range countries: the Argentine, Australia and our own West. Possibly it may not lend itself specially to power in the mallet, but it gives surely the right position for handling the horse and maneuvering the ball.

It is true that the more intricate plays in polo have been largely supplanted by the long drive and hefty "riding off" of the modern game, but those of us who have watched Louis Lacey, who breeds and trains his polo ponies in the pampas of the Argentine, weaving his way with the ball with perfect poise and rhythm through a charging melee; or the four Ashton brothers who breed and train their ponies in the back country of Australia, "following up" among themselves like easy-working part of a machine; or Cecil Smith, Texas cowboy ten-goaler, hitting the ball on either side his horse with all the mastery and freedom the western style of riding gives; must surely give the preference to the seat these riders use. Furthermore, Henry Lacey, Louis' brother and an expert critic, says the recent defeat of the champion American Greentree team by the Argentines was due to the Argentines being better horsemen and their ponies consequently better schooled. And if I should need any further testimony to the value of the seat that became so familiar and proved so serviceable to me during many years on the range, I could draw on the greatest No. 4 the game of polo has ever known: Devereux Milburn. Milburn advocates standing in the stirrups to make the mallet stroke. He compares that with a man making a golf stroke standing on the ground, and that position on a horse, you may remember, I have previously described as being the one it was the principal aim of the cowboy to maintain, I thought.

The cowpuncher's attitude towards horsemanship was curiously similar to that of the Englishman. As in the case of the Englishman, it would have been difficult to interest him in any scientific or theoretical system. He preferred to work things out along practical lines. The English, who have been, among the civilized peoples, the most active horsemen in the world, and under whom most of the principal breeds of horses used under the saddle either originated or were developed, were never greatly interested in the French system of high school education of the horse. What they wanted in their saddle horses was "handiness" and activity, rather than form or show. And the cowboy was actuated by the same motives. His cowhorse, either roping, cutting or driving stock, was allowed to act naturally, and largely on his own initiative; and on the whole, I think, became as practical a factor in the general work of the range as could well have been produced. And that I think stands true also for his rider.

There was one feature, however, in Western riding, typical and, as far as I know, unique, which I never adopted, or fully understood. I mean the action of the arms. Going at high speed the cowpuncher's hands were held high above the horn of the saddle and the arms from the wrist to the shoulder swung loosely up and down, up clear above the shoulder and back down to the ribs. Says Langworthy-Taylor in *The Saddle Horse*: "The cowboy flapping his arms like wings as he gallops along and using them chiefly as a ropewalker uses his pole or parasol, is the exemplar of all that the school rider should not be." My own belief is that this action of the arms was used (unconsciously) by the cowpuncher, not as Mr. Taylor implies, to secure balance, but as a means of taking up, absorbing the shock and jar of the horse's movements. It didn't interfere with the rider's use of the lines, because it hardly affected the hands at all, the movement taking place almost entirely from the wrist to the shoulder. However I never could see the need for it. I'm thinking of asking my good friend, Frank Gyberg of Cornville, Arizona, if he can tell us. For besides being a practised rider, Frank is given to digging out the philosophy of things; and I suppose he has been flapping his arms like that all his life, himself, as he rode around these old prairies. I'll write him about. it. It might draw one of his humorous letters out of him.

# 4
## The Story of the Cowhorse:
## Thoroughbreds on the Range

### I

I HAVE taken no part in the discussion that has been raging in
the Western Livestock Journal of Los Angeles lately, over the
character and breeding of the western cow horse. But now
that the shooting seems to have slackened up, I thought I would
sit down and take a quiet and perhaps rather wider survey of the
situation. Dealing with it from the point of view of one who has
no cow horses for sale, who is not breeding polo ponies, or race-
horses, or Morgans or Quarter-horses; but who nevertheless lived
most of his earlier life on the back of a horse. One who furthermore during a number of years studied and struggled with the
problem of producing a horse suitable for ranch purposes.

To begin with then, I am a bit puzzled as to what people mean
when they talk about the "old-time cowhorse." One writer refers
to them as "knotty-headed runts"; another calls them "snorty
little old rusty misfits"; yet another terms them "mustangs" and
bestows upon them all the colors of the rainbow. Such descriptions as these are picturesque and incisive but they bear little
relation to the horses in use on the Western roundups, say in
1880 and the immediately succeeding decades which constituted
the real period of the range cattle business.

When I first landed in the West I was naturally much interested in the character of the horse stock. I had of course been
used to good horses all my life: fine harness horses and hacks,
Thoroughbred and Irish heavy-weight hunters. And I remember that these range horses did not strike me as being knotty
headed runts. While their colors, as I recall, corresponded
largely to those I was used to in the English hunting field and

the "Row" in London. Moreover I thought them unexpectedly uniform, as well as adapted to the work they had to do. Paste the last half of that sentence up on the wall where you'll see it often and easily.

Leaving out of consideration small and inferior Mexican and Indian stock in use in sundry wild and remote parts of the range, I imagine the average of these horses would weigh from 850 to 900 pounds. We didn't measure horses by height in those days, but these might run around 14 hands. I know a 15-hand horse was a tall one in the West then. They showed not much refinement, but were well formed, sturdy and well chested. Their stride was short, which made them slow travelers on the road but enabled them to stop and dodge and "jump off" readily, as well as handle themselves in rough terrain. Altogether lacking "style," their endurance was thereby the greater by having no stylized action to maintain: they used up no superfluous energy. Some of them, which we used for running in broncs, were long winded and had a fair turn of speed. Outside of a tendency to buck when rested, they were good dispositioned and teachable. Their colors ran largely to bay, black, brown and different shades of chestnut, with some greys and whites, and a scattering of buckskins. There were few Palominos or paints.

Now consider the multitude of these horses coming into use more or less suddenly at the climax of the range business. Where did they come from? I think we may assume that the bulk of them, including mare stock, came from Texas, along with the cowboy and the vast herds of cattle. What other state had so many horses, and of that character, to supply? Indeed one authority (quoted by Osgood: *The Day of the Cattleman*) asserts that a million horses went out of Texas during the range cattle period. And how were these horses bred?

There are few records to throw light on that: the early Texans were not given to keeping records, being generally short on education;* but there are sundry facts from which we can draw deductions. A great majority of Texans hailed from the South. Now everybody knows that the men of the Southern states were our greatest horse breeders. In their hands the American Thoroughbred developed into such horses as Gallant Fox and Lexington. And long before the first Thoroughbred set foot in America they had developed types of excellent light horses. We know when they migrated to Texas they brought good stock with them, and as their herds of cattle grew, bringing increased need of cow horses, we may be sure they would use their good stallions on the native Spanish mares running all around them, which in their native state were undersized for cow work. And there is no doubt they did. Here is a statement on this point from W. B. Mitchell, the well-known Texas cattleman, whose family moved from southern Texas to their present location in the Marfa district in 1884. "We brought with us," says Mr. Mitchell, "a brood of mares that had quite a bit of good breeding in them. This was also true of a good many ranchmen moving into this country in '84 to '86. There was quite a bit of the Quarter stock in these horses." And then he adds that they had likewise a good measure of Spanish blood, and "this mixed with the Quarter horse gave us a very desirable cow horse."

Now the Quarter horse, though not a distinct breed, is a strong and early type of American horse, for running 80 rods, or less, was a favorite pastime in America well over a hundred years ago. And the Texans seem to have specialized in these "short horses." It can be taken for granted that they carried the best running blood of the required type that American breeders had developed, along with considerable infiltration of Thoroughbred blood. And here we may well bring into the picture the Mor-

---

*Mrs. Lona Shawver, a clever Texas writer, took me to task once for making this remark. However, Frank King says when he was a boy in Texas, anyone who could count up to one hundred could qualify for a school teacher.

gan. For horses with Morgan blood had been used in considerable numbers before the Civil War by Tennesseans, some of whom, migrating to Texas, would take Morgans along with them. Mrs. Lona Shawver tells me how her family crossed the Red River into Texas as early as 1869 from Virginia bringing with them a "large number of Morgan (and part Steeldust) mares which met with a ready sale." Not the least part of the reputation of Justin Morgan himself, who, though declared mainly Thoroughbred on both sides, was a type all his own, rested on his never having been beaten in a short running dash. It was inevitable that men so keen on this class of race as the Texans were, would use Morgan blood in breeding their Quarter horses and other horse stock. For Justin Morgan's blood, dispersed and weakened as it came to be, was extraordinarily potent. It would be curious, too, if some of the good blood of the trotters and saddlers in which the South abounded did not go into these Texan horses. And certainly the range men of the other states, as the cow business developed, introduced into their horse herds stallions carrying some of the Texas cow horse blood.

Here we may add to our picture Missouri. For the West was heavily peopled from that state, and Missouri became at an early date light horse minded. Some of the early settlers from there brought good stock with them, including stallions that would produce stock from the native mares.

Something along the above lines, then, we may fairly accept as one side of our range cow horse, and the other side would be Spanish. We are apt to regard the Mexican mustang as scrub stock, and it is true it had deteriorated in size and quality through inbreeding and neglect over several centuries. Moreover the horses brought by the Conquistadores to North America were not in the main so uniform and pure in blood as that memorable bunch they left in the Argentine. Nevertheless our mustang stock was undoubtedly largely of that Libyan or Asian (later more widely known as Arabian) blood which has been the most potent and enduring equine blood of record, and which has been in existence since before the dawn of history.

And it has a bearing on the subject to reflect that numbers of these Spanish explorers were intelligent and accomplished horsemen. Cortez brought only sixteen horses with his expedition, but a list of them has come down to us, in which each is carefully described. Most of them had the notation: "de buena carrera," good at running or racing. "Gonzales Dominguez," runs the list made by the old chronicler, Bernal Diaz, who himself loved a horse, "a very consummate horseman; a dark chestnut horse, very good and a grand runner." Or, "Moron: a dappled horse with white forelegs, *muy revuelto*—lively, very easy to turn." Cortez would have them exhibit their horses, galloping and turning, in order to impress the natives, who had never seen a horse. Pedro de Alvarado's sorrel mare was swift enough so Pedro could run onto a deer and spear it. Later Spanish invaders and settlers brought further supplies of this Spanish stock to the Americas.

I think these mustangs largely shared with the Quarter horse the ability to "jump off," which to my mind is an indispensable quality in a cow horse. The story goes that the "Denton Mare" which won so much money for her owner, the notorious Sam Bass, in quarter races (which depend so greatly on the quick start) in Texas, was caught up off the range out of a band of straight "broomtails." I broke a string of these mares straight off the range in Chihuahua. Although they were definitely undersized and never lost a certain wildness of spirit, I found them marvellous animals under the saddle or to light rig, and the easiest to gentle and teach of any horses I ever handled.

Such then, judging by the facts we know, was the background in breeding of the horses, the "knotty headed runts" and "little old misfits," which our range cowmen and cowhands rode after cattle about the '80's and '90's. To sum up briefly and in a general way, that stock may be said to have been straight Libyan-Spanish, top-crossed with stock that knew no pedigree, but generally carried excellent American blood. It's hardly surprising that we found the run of them good.

But satisfactory as we found them, there was plenty of room for improvement. And we took steps to that end, without any clear purpose, generally; chiefly in the direction of increasing size and weight. The draft sire was used a good deal, the British bringing over their own breeds, Shires and Clydes; more of us using Percheron and Percheron grades. I used half-bred Percheron stallions for a number of years in an effort to get a general purpose ranch horse, for work and saddle, with a degree of success, and was on the verge one time of trying a Suffolk. This breed is more of a farm work horse than a drafter. Nimbler on his feet, too, by reason probably of an early infusion of Thoroughbred blood. Yet the draft horse is designed to pull, and though his get were tractable and intelligent, their action was inclined to be draggy, and tiring to a rider, and without much "pickup," to adopt an automotive expression. Some tried the coach horse: the British the Cleveland Bay, others the French coach, which had more style and quality. And my friend Sam Freeman of Dillon, Mont. tells me of an Englishman who imported an English "hunter" stallion to that district. "He was much larger than the ordinary Thoroughbred," says Sam, "but had plenty speed and action. Crossed on a bunch of keen little cayuses he got some very fine stock horses." This hunter stallion would undoubtedly be largely Thoroughbred, with a strain of Draft or Coach.

The Standardbred was employed to a considerable extent at one period, especially in Wyoming. The action in this breed being highly specialized is apt to interfere, in my experience, with the variety and kind of movement cow work calls for. The Morgan in the last half of last century lost such identity as it had, though Asst. Professor John A. Gorman of the University of Wyoming, who is an authority on the Western horse, tells me that some Wyoming stockmen bred the Morgan to type with considerable care, and the last forty years have done much to establish the type and bloodlines, generally. The semi-legendary Steeldust or Quarter horse, appearing to be more a type than a family or breed, was a byword throughout the range always. An effort is now being made by John Casement of Whitewater, Colorado to organize this type into a breed.* But on the whole John Clay's dictum—and he knew the range from A to Z—that we have failed to establish any general organized improvement of the original cow horse, holds good today. In fact, one must agree with Gorman's comment that, with notable exceptions, our present range horse stock presents to a critical eye a hotchpotch of every known breed of horses.

No mention has been made of the Thoroughbred. That's the one that makes some of our old-time cowmen gnash their teeth. I will try, following this, to describe the part that has been and is today being played on Western ranges by that great breed, whose blood has been an essential factor in every modern breed of light horses, harness or saddle.

II

Among the earliest range outfits to use the Thoroughbred sire on its stock mares was the Bell Ranch. Already in the '80's Manager Mike Slattery put out some light thoroughbred stallions. Their get were as lovely and symmetrical animals as I ever set eyes on, but the boys found them too easily "het up," working in a herd. Perhaps the cowhands of those days were rougher than they are now. They were plenty rough, certainly, alike with cattle and horses. But there were always men like Bob Bowmer of the Bells, who were patient and intelligent with their mounts and it was to such as these that outfits owed their top cow horses. Anyhow in the '80's we replaced the Thoroughbreds with some useful range bred studs from the JA ranch in Texas. But the principal owner of the Bell Ranch, Louis Stoddard, was a

*Since writing this a strong and representative organization has been formed to promote this breed.

famous polo player and more interested in polo than the cattle business, and for the last forty years they have used small Thoroughbred and Arabian stallions. The result has been a loss in size which Manager Albert Mitchell tells me he is trying to rectify. He is now using two Thoroughbred-Steeldust horses, one U.S. Army remount Thoroughbred and one of mixed blood. His aim is to get, first, good cow horses; after that, polo ponies.

It may be remarked that Thoroughbreds were brought into the range country, chiefly Wyoming, in the early '80's by some of the wealthy British cattlemen, but more, one can believe, with a sporting than a practical purpose.

The Swenson Land Cattle Company at Stamford, Texas, is one of the early and most famous outfits in the Southwest. They have for many years been using Morgan stallions almost exclusively, part of their mares being registered Morgans, brought from the Richard Selmon herd at San Saba. Their Morgans have been found good for all kinds of cow work, sure footed and with lots of stamina. Since 1931, however, the Company has been using an Army Remount Arabian sire. "We believe," writes W. G. (Bill) Swenson, "this Arabian cross on our Morgan mares has produced one of the best types of cow horses we have ever had." In addition to the Arabian they use Thoroughbred Remount stallions. Their get also make good cowhorses, says Mr. Swenson, but the Arabian colts seem to show more intelligence and sense.

Everybody knows the great Scottish outfit, the Matador Land and Cattle Company, shrunk today from its former stature but still after close on sixty years, running over fifty thousand head of cattle on its two Western Texas ranches. In early days Murdo MacKenzie used Cleveland Bays and Standardbred stallions on the part Spanish stock mares. For the past thirty-five or forty years they have kept Morgan, Standardbred, Thoroughbred and Quarter horse (or Steeldust) sires. "We have found," writes Murdo's son, John, now managing the company, "by crossing a Morgan stallion with a Thoroughbred type mare we bring up the size and bone structure, whereas if Thoroughbreds are bred too closely on the range they lose size. We usually raise," continues John, "around two hundred colts a year which supplies our needs at both Texas ranches, and any surplus is sold either to the U.S. Army or in the case of Palominos, as pleasure horses, for which there is a great demand. The average weight of our cow horse is 950 to 1050 pounds and while they are not gaited horses, such as single-footers, most of them have an easy fox-trot, or running walk, particularly suited for range work.

In the days when people went from place to place on horseback it might have taken you ten days fair good riding from the Matador (Tascosa) ranch, crossing the Staked Plains and bearing off a little towards the Big Bend of the Rio Grande, to get to Marfa. That is the town whose Fair and annual feeder cattle sales, under the organization of W. B. Mitchell and his fours sons, have grown into a feature of the South-west. It has long been a great breeding country, that. In a previous chapter I told you how settlers from Southern Texas came there in the early '80's, bringing a stock of good cowhorses with them, bred up with Quarter horse stallions from the Spanish mares. They continued breeding horses along these lines for twenty or twenty-five years, supplying many a range outfit with good horses, till the stock became too numerous and a nuisance, and they disposed of them.

Let Mitchell take up the story in his own words. "Some eight or ten years ago," he says, "the stockmen began to engage in the business again and the horses produced now are more of the Thoroughbred together with more of the Quarter stock, and the combination makes a very desirable horse that can be used for the Army type; also as polo pony or cow horse. These horses range in height from 14.3 to 15.2 and will weigh from 950 to 1150 pounds. We ourselves have been producing and promoting the Palomino color horse, and our Palomino stallions have been of the type mentioned above: Thoroughbred and Quarter stock. These horses are very desirable and we have a good demand for them from all over the country."

To get to the origin of the Reynolds Cattle Company you have to drift back into the dim beginnings of the Western range cattle business. As early as 1876 this firm bought registered Hereford bulls to put on their native Texas cows. At one time, says Alvin Sanders in his history of the Herefords, their herds ran as high as 50,000. Today they are kept at about 8000, with a calf branding of from 5000 to 6000. Their mare herd consists of 50 animals, produce of years of breeding to blooded sires. They are using three stallions at present: two Thoroughbred and one "Mexican." The ranch is situated mainly in the Davis Mountains which lie to the north of Marfa, and certain parts of which are so rough that the cattle cannot be gotten out and remain outlaws. I will quote here from an interesting letter sent me by Ted Garner, who runs cattle and sheep on the ranch and who is a finished horseman. Says friend Ted: "The horses from these mares and the Spanish horse make better cow horses and for general use than the higher bred animals. This is due to the fact that they are better able to take care of themselves in this rough country. Then too the blooded animals must be handled very carefully until they are four or five years old. The average cowboy is not capable of this, therefore ruins them." Some of the colts from the Thoroughbred sires are sold as polo ponies. Palominos and Paints cater to the public taste for pleasure riding.

It is my wish to make this brief review of Western horses as comprehensive as possible, so we will hop across from Texas to Southern Arizona where my good friend J. C. (Jack) Kinney, who has played a distinguished part as stockman and in public life in several western states, is president of La Osa Livestock Company out from Tucson and runs a large herd of high class horses. Kinney has at one time or another used Thoroughbred or Standardbred stallions but for some years has specialized in Morgans, mostly registered. It has become possible of recent years to secure registered stock carrying a fair concentration of the original Justin Morgan blood. From these he raises cowhorses and a number of fancy saddle horses many of which are carefully trained for show and circus. Of the cowhorses he says that they have as much cow sense as it is possible to get. "But the problem is how to keep them at that point. They must go one way or another. Consequently I am looking for my kind of a horse, which is a first class stallion on the Steeldust order, with the muscle, the head and the feet of the Steeldust. I am having a hard time locating just what I want."

Now let's take a glimpse at the northern ranges. It's getting on for sixty years since the Wyoming Hereford Ranch, was established on Crow Creek, just east of that most famous of all cow towns, Cheyenne. Robt. W. (Bob) Lazear who runs the ranch writes telling me about their horse breeding operations. He says they have never paid any attention to the production of fancy saddle horses or polo ponies, but try almost altogether for a good horse to use with the cattle. Having the opportunity to break out quite a number of horses from year to year, those that show real cow sense they retain for their own use, and the others, if they show breeding, are readily taken up by the Army buyers. I think the experience and conclusions of this master breeder, who produces the WHW Domino Herefords, will interest every stockman.

"We used a Morgan stallion for a number of years," he says, "in cross with our mares that were one-half to five-eighths Thoroughbred. We were not at all satisfied with the colts of our Morgan horse, and so we have now gone back to a Thoroughbred stallion. I understand, in talking with other ranch men in this vicinity, that some of them had considerable success in using Morgan stallions, producing a horse of a little more quiet disposition than the Thoroughbred. I think this question of gentleness and disposition rests more with the stallion himself, and with the

mares in the herd, than just the question of breed. Our experience
with our Morgan horse shows that his colts have been much more
difficult to break out than were the colts sired by the thoroughbred stallion that preceded him, and certainly the horse we are
using now. He is exceptionally gentle and we anticipate no
trouble with his colts at all."

There you have a brief and very general review of the use
made of the Thoroughbred on the western ranges. I will now try
to deal with some of the arguments we hear about the Thoroughbred as a range horse, for and against.

### III

Perhaps the most serious dead weight expense on a cow ranch
was the horse herd. During summer and fall roundups, and if you
had hay to put up, a considerable number of horses were required. But throughout many months of the year there was only
use for a few, even on the large ranches. The remainder eat their
heads off on pasture—for horses graze a range closer than sheep.

I think it was not till the late '90's that many range men became
aware of such a thing as the game of polo. Scouts from Colorado
Springs took to dropping around on the lookout for polo pony
prospects. I call to mind when Garrett Eckerson, foreman of the
ZH's that had moved in onto the Mora Grant in New Mexico
from No Man's Land, sold his private cowhorse for $400 or $500
for a polo pony. From that moment everybody who had a cow
horse that was handy and could run a quarter at a decent clip,
lived in hopes of someone from Colorado Springs taking him off
his hands at a cool $1000. The polo pony of those days was not
required to be as large or as speedy as he is now. I suggest that
Foxhall Keene and the other aristocrats of the polo field were
originally responsible for the interest in the Thoroughbred
among range men. A few high priced polo ponies would serve
to balance up the horse account very nicely. Much later on came
the U.S. Government with its Remount stallions.

I propose now to try and deal briefly with some of the arguments set up by cowmen for and against the Thoroughbred on the range. We'll call the disputants the pro's and the anti's. Let's handle the anti first. He is apt to be found among the old-time cowmen, and to see red at the mere mention of the crazy, high-headed, ring-tailed, limber-necked, stargazing, tree-topping proposition known as the Thoroughbred horse. When he cools off —I mean the cowman, not the horse—and gets down to argument, the principal one he uses is that the Thoroughbred has been bred for centuries for one purpose only: to race. Consequently he can only transmit that tendency to his get, and it isn't one the cow horse needs. The argument looks like a good one, but it's not as good as it looks. What weakens it is the fact the the Thoroughbred has been used in the improvement of *every* breed of modern light horse. This for the reason that there is no other breed can transmit so certainly some qualities he possesses: speed, refinement with size, high spirit, density of bone. And this again for the reason that there is no other breed whose blood has been so long and so rigidly protected, or that has been subjected individually to such drastic tests of performance.

Another reason for this wide serviceability of the Thoroughbred in cross breeding is that his gaits are in the main natural ones, with nothing of the highly specialized or stylized action that might make the trotter or hackney transmit undesired characteristics to his get. The Thoroughbred stride is long, which is against him as a cow horse, but it can be modified with time and careful training. To see the late Pat Roark lope his blooded pony across the polo field between periods was a study in slow rhythm. And he can be trained to turn on his heels.

Next let us consider the charge of hot headedness and bad temper. The anti has a better case here. It is absurd to maintain, as some ardent defenders do that the Thoroughbred is not sometimes excitable and errratic. The essence of his success on the turf lies largely in his high, fighting spirit. But it is easy

to exaggerate this point. In the first place there is a wide variation
in the disposition of individuals: contrast War Admiral whose
aim on the track sometimes seems to be to break up the starting
gate, with Seabiscuit, who takes every race as it comes, and who
is as fond of dropping off to sleep as Joe Louis. The reader may
recall Robert Lazear's remarks, previously quoted, on this point.

Then the conditions attending the start of a race, recurring
time after time, are enough to set up ill-temper in any animal,
and the horse is often savagely beaten in the race. Nor are the
jockeys usually horsemen in any real sense, and, if they were,
they could not help much, perched precariously on top of a
1½-pound saddle. It must be considered too that the racer is
kept at a high and unnatural pitch of condition. Men who handle
Thoroughbreds off the race track declare most of them to be
pleasant in temper, but they need time and patience in handling;
they won't stand rough usage or jagging around.

The argument that the Thoroughbred is not stout built enough
for some of the rougher side of cow work seems well enough
taken. It is, of course, a fact that the ability of a horse to carry
weight out of proportion to his own poundage is dependent
on the amount of Thoroughbred (or Arabian) blood he has
in his veins. Nevertheless the racer is built light and narrowish
in front, for several good reasons. (This is likewise true of the
Arabian.) He has also a tendency to "buckle over" in his forelegs, which I absolutely never saw in an old-time cow horse.
Now every old cowhand knows that a sturdy fore-end in a
horse is a great comfort when a 1000-pound steer is running
on the rope.

Next let us take up the pro's; one of whose main arguments
is that the Thoroughbred must be good for cow work because
they use him for polo, which much resembles cow work.
That's another argument that's not quite as good as it looks.
Let me give you the three main qualities called for in a polo
pony: (1) Speed. He must do the quarter in 24 seconds. When

the polo players took to smiting the ball to such vast distances, fifty yards at a clip, it became necessary to get to where the ball was as speedily as possible. But your opponent aimed to get there too, before you did, so the next requirement was that your horse have (2) ambition, the natural desire to beat the other horse to it, for the polo player is busy with his mallet and cannot find time to belabor his mount. And when both of you have made the run, the ball may be returned to another remote part of the field and you have to start back again full split, which brings us to requirement No. 3: one must have a horse that can go at top speed the entire 7 ½ minutes of the polo period. Well, there was nothing in the world could do all these things except the Thoroughbred. And that's why the polo players use the Thoroughbred. "There's no other reason" remarked Pat Roark to a friend of mine in conversation a short while before his recent death on the polo field. "Except for that I'd get just as much fun playing the game on an old cab horse." The Quarter horse, which was largely used at one time, has the speed but cannot stay the course.

And if you should argue that the fact the Thoroughbred is used for polo is proof that he has intelligence enough to be a cowhorse, I should have to draw on you my friend, Lionel Pedley, the well-known professional polo player and trainer of polo ponies; brother of the famous international player, Eric Pedley. Quoth Lionel: The reason we don't like the cow pony for polo is that he's too smart. The first thing you know, he is learning to follow the ball, or something. We don't want that. All we want of a pony is to do *as we direct*, and this part the Thoroughbred is quite content to play. Again, one of the principal plays in polo is to "ride off" your opponent, crowd him with the point of your own horse's shoulder. This is often a painful process for your horse and after a few attempts we find the cow pony inclined to get wise and refuse to repeat. Here the Thoroughbred comes in again. Though often badly hurt in charging, he comes right back at it every time without flinching. As we polo fellows put it: The cow pony has a small heart and a big brain. The Thoroughbred has a little brain and a big heart. In short, the cow horse learns his business largely by his own *intelligence*. The Thoroughbred has to be taught over a period of years by *habit*. It takes years, as the polo saying goes, to make a polo pony, and an hour or two, with a dunce up, to spoil him.

There is one feature the blooded horse has that is equally good for the polo player and cowhand. He goes on the run with his head low, out of the way of mallet or rope. They are breeding the Morgan today to have a longer neck and more upstanding crest. That looks very handsome, to be sure, but it only gets in the way if you have any work to do on the back of your horse.

Well, there I have given you briefly, and as fairly as I know how, the straight of the argument for and against the Thoroughbred as a cow horse. Previously I described the use the breed has been and is being put to on the range, with ranchmen's comments thereon. Our informants on both sides were representative and experienced men. Their evidence, like most evidence, conflicts, but for anyone studying it a few points seem fairly well demonstrated. 1. The use of Thoroughbred blood on the range today is very general, and generally accepted as desirable; 2. The Thoroughbred strain under range conditions, is the better for some infusion of cold blood. This would tally with the practice of the breeders of English and Irish hunters, which have to stand some rough work, and are rarely straight thoroughbred; 3. Different types are indicated for different classes of country. An animal that may fill the bill in the rolling benches of the North and South Platte may be of little use in the wild terrain of the Mogollons or Davis Mountains; 4. Much of the success of the Thoroughbred cross depends on the temperament of the individual stallion used; 5. Finally, leaving aside the question of range use, the Thoroughbred cross has created a great supply of high-class pleasure horses for the public at large, raised under healthy and economical conditions.

# 5
## Some "Bad" Ones I Knew

I HAVE explained on an earlier page (for the benefit of inexperienced readers) what really constituted an outlaw animal on the range. Certain horses or cow brutes by dint of managing a number of times to escape being corraled or caught, contracted a violent objection to having their freedom interfered with in any manner whatsoever. They'd break their own necks sooner than enter a corral. I've told you how we broke La Vaqueta's heart, the brown mare that ran so long on the Bell range, by roping and throwing her; and how the old outlaw longhorn steer out of the Atarque brakes, after we had caught him and dehorned him, went off into the creek and drowned himself. And I've given you Oat Martine's story about the bunch of bronco mares the boys ran onto a rocky point in Hell Canyon, and that jumped off and killed themselves. I am inclined to think that the career of the animal outlaw, like that of the human one, usually ended in disaster.

There weren't very many such animals, certainly. We didn't encourage them because they had the effect of spoiling other gentle stock they got with. I can't tell you how Black Jack, the AI Bar bald-faced black I have in mind, got spoiled, for the AI Bar horse herd in which he was raised was a mighty gentle one and well handled. But he was naturally a high-headed, wild-eyed brute, who single-footed, and horses with natural saddle gaits usually have a touch of eccentricity about them. Anyhow Black Jack got out of the AI Bar pastures and was heard of all over the range, keeping carefully shut of anything that looked like an enclosure or saddle rope. So I was surprised when Old Man Turner's boy, Allie, offered to sell him to me one day, saddle and bridle broke. It appeared that Allie and his cousin Bud had spotted the horse running on the Cerro Pelon, or Bald Mountain, that lies just west of the Turkey Mountains, and had bought him on the range. There's a long fence on the Cerro Pelon and into an angle of it the boys managed to work Black Jack and get one throw at him. It wasn't long before they had him in a corral and saddled. I gave Allie twenty-five dollars for him.

He turned out a free and easy gaited saddle horse, mighty tough, and gentle enough if you gave him plenty of riding. I took him for a while as my own mount. Eventually, as I was leaving the ranch for the winter, John Hinde, ranch foreman, took him over for a winter horse on account of his easy gaits.

But John and Black Jack didn't hit it off. Now you expect a range horse to cut up a bit when he comes up fat and rested at the beginning of the summer work. But it's a different matter when one insists on staging a private rodeo show every frosty morning. One day Black Jack put on an extra scandalous performance. The bald-faced black was long in the legs and John's are short, and nothing approaching a contact was possible. In cases like this some men react in one way, some in another. I've known men content to let loose a flow of pure profanity which may or may not have impressed the horse. John is not like that. He wastes no words in emergencies. He walked back to the house, some fifty yards away, and when he returned to the corral he had with him his big .45 Colt's revolver, and he applied it to that part of Black Jack's anatomy where it puts 'em to sleep soonest. He described the whole affair to me when I got back to the ranch and remarked to him that I didn't notice Black Jack anywhere around.

I have suggested in some other place that this outlaw spirit, this dislike of restraint or confinement, is congenital in all animals, human included. Nevertheless it may well be that it is stronger in some cases than others. It's hard to believe that the instinct of escape isn't more pronounced, for instance, in the mustang than in the more domestically bred horse. I happen to have handled some pure mustangs straight off the range in Chihuahua. They broke perfectly gentle and indeed I found them particularly tractable. But one day after they were thoroughly accustomed to life on the ranch they got away from the gentle horse herd, and off by themselves on the open range. No sooner did they find themselves free than they hit it for the Ocate Mesa, a steep and rugged bluff three or four miles distant. We never had a show to stop or turn them. Once there they climbed up under the rim rock, and I have a particularly clear remembrance of those little wild creatures running along the rocky mesa side, looking down at us as they ran. Deer couldn't have appeared wilder or have shown a sharper instinct of escape.

Mighty persistent was this wild blood. Some of these Chihuahua mares were bred to a half-bred Percheron—or Norman, as we called it in those days. I bought one of their colts and made a cowhorse out of him—the best I ever owned or rode. Although he never got over a strong propensity to pitch, he showed up just like an average cowhorse. I found him just as teachable as the original mares. And perhaps it wouldn't hurt if I were to break into my narrative here to give you a brief description of the little horse, for I think he was a remarkable one, and it may help my readers to kind of picture him to themselves as my story of him runs along.

Silver—he was silver white from head to heels—was what you call a big-little horse. He stood barely fourteen hands, I believe. He had the perfect conformation of the Percheron; the power and substance. But through these ran all the litheness and spring of the Arab. He was a living example of controlled energy. He could stop dead short going at top speed without giving you a suspicion of a jar. This is not an invariable rule with even the best of cow horses: some stop hard and are difficult to sit, turning. When an obstacle suddenly confronts a horse running in rough ground, it breaks up his stride, often making the rider feel as though he were being torn into several pieces. You experienced nothing of this kind with Silver. He would simply change his lead, slipping into another gait or combination of gaits, selected by himself out of his vast repertory of paces. This mixing and sliding in and out of gaits is one of the pet aversions of the show ring judges, who judge horses according to show standards; but in actual practise the horse himself knows best. Silver would, by a clever manipulation of stride, bring you down a rocky hillside after a cow as easy as running on the level.

He was the only cowhorse I ever rode that could be in more than one place at the same moment. In corraling a bunch of cattle he would crowd both ends and the center simultaneously. Or so it seemed. You never needed to touch a line; he would take complete charge, and woe to the animal that tried to break back past him; Silver's teeth were sharp.

It was this combination in him of power and agility that made him the best horse for roping in the open of my experience. Every cowhand knows that in this operation the "jump off" is the most important thing. If you can get on top of an animal before he begins to dodge and twist, roping is a simple enough business. Silver was plumb on top the first jump. It was a lovely thing to put this little horse to catch a calf running loose on the outside. He did everything except throw the rope.

On the road it was his habit to pass from one easy gait to another to suit his own sweet fancy, like a musician trying out different tunes on his instrument. Full of energy as he was, with saddle on and the bridle dropped I could depend on his staying in any place I left him till the cows came home. Once he was through with his after breakfast highjinks, a lady could ride him. I remember a picture of him with my wife in the

saddle and her baby on her lap. A thoroughly tame and domesticated example of mustang blood, I hear the reader remark.
But wait.

One day I rode him in to our little town of Wagon Mound
five miles away. Having a good deal of business I pulled off
his saddle and bridle and turned him loose in storekeeper
Adler's corral. It happened someone left the gate open and Silver
slipped out onto the street. I at once borrowed a saddle horse,
thinking to have no trouble in putting him back into the pen.
But the only sight I got of Silver was him sailing over the
nearby hill top in the direction of the Piedra Alumbre, a wild
mesa lying east of town. During the next few days I saw him
and made several attempts to get him back inside our fence,
but the instant he'd catch sight of me he'd start off with mane
and tail flying, looking back over his shoulder at me as though
he were mocking me. He made a fine sight. Three centuries
of unbridled liberty were in that stride of his. I have always
maintained that the movement of an unbitted range bronc had
an element of freedom in it the most highly finished show bench
animal doesn't exhibit. Finally he disappeared altogether and I
heard no more of him till after many weeks Dolf Harmon
who rode for the Red River Cattle Company wrote me that
he was running over towards their pasture on Red River, (which
is what in those days we called the upper Canadian.)

So over to Dolf's camp in the Red River brakes I went one
evening and that night we planned to take out Dolf's mount
of saddle horses and try and get Silver to join in with them
and so get him into the corral. Sure enough next morning there
was Silver all by himself out on a high point of the Piedra
Alumbre. We turned Dick's remuda loose and hid ourselves.
Mighty circumspectly Mister Silver circled around for a while
and finally joined it. Then, having allowed him a spell to get
on terms with his new mates, we, likewise mighty circum-

spectly, rounded the bunch up, greatly tickled to find that Silver showed little signs of wanting to break away. Indeed he acted as though he were tired of being alone and was glad of companionship. Very shortly we had him in Dolf's corral. He was hog fat and evidently plenty salty. Dolf seemed to be looking forward to his putting on a show when we saddled him up, but I gave him very little chance to act up, although, believe me, a feller needed to be greased lightning, mounting, when that little white horse was feeling like that.

We kept Silver till he died a number of years later, but he never got a chance to make another breakaway.

II

One of the principal reasons why it was an advantage for a range man to be a good rider was that he was able sometimes thus to pick up an extra good horse at a low price because the owner was afraid of him and wanted to get rid of him. This happened several times in my case. Among the instances was a horse I bought from my old friend, W. H. Willcox, who ran the WHW brand in the early range days and carried on with it after most of the range men had gone out of business. Willcox was not much of a horseman. Actually he did most of his traveling around as a land surveyor in a buggy. He had bought him a big, powerful horse and was driving him. He was, however, a mean tempered brute and W.H.W. was pretty scared of him; and indeed, if he had ever started to cut up I don't believe there would have been very much left of Willcox or his outfit. One day he offered him to me. My brother Chris and I were running the remnant of the WHW cattle on a shares basis on our Escondida and Salt Lake ranches. As we hadn't a rod of fencing on either ranch there was plenty of hard riding to do. I thought I saw a heap of work in the big bay, if he didn't break my neck. I bought him, and so began a partnership, long

but unmarked by any affection on either side. I always felt he
would just as lief have killed me at one time or in one manner
as another.

He came pretty near doing it one fine morning within
a few feet of our back door. My wife and I with our baby
were holding down a claim on the head spring of the Escondida
at that time. Close beside our two-room "dobe" we had
run up a log shanty to keep odds and ends in. It had been
made in a hurry and the top log at one corner had been
left protruding several feet. Right here I used to saddle up
every morning. One morning the big bay broke away the
instant I climbed him, pitching violently. I saw him heading for
the protruding pole, but you can't check or deflect a bucking
horse. He carried me full bust against it, striking my chest and
knocking me from the saddle to the ground, while he passed
on underneath it. My wife was standing close beside us and
came and picked up what she could find of me. This horse had
not been trained for a saddle horse and would run off if ever
you let him get loose with the saddle, and in my many solo
rides the dread used to haunt me lest he get back to the ranch
where my wife was, with only the saddle on. It's a scary business, a horse showing up riderless. We named him The Rogue.

I believe we may say that the most important distinction
between the native Indian-Mexican horses and the American
stock of the '80's lay in the fact that the latter were greatly
better built and sturdier. Practically all the native stock I ever
saw were narrow and inclined to be "wobbly" under the saddle.
In the wilder and more remote districts of the range country
the Americans had no option but to ride this class of stock.
My good friend, Sam Freeman, whose family came to western
Montana in 1881, writes interestingly about it. "This part of
Montana," says Sam, "is very mountainous with rather small
valleys. This is the reason for a number of small stockmen
rather than a very few large outfits. Around here the holdings

run from a few hundreds up to seven thousand, which is the largest. In the early '80's there was a great number of 'Indian ponies.' No one, not even the Indians, knew much about their breeding. One reason for this arose from the fact that the Indians did not practise castrating. I have bought many saddle ponies from the Indians and had to trim them up myself. The Indians had no mercy on them. Rode them in the hunt for antelope till they were wringing wet and kicked them out in zero weather to rustle." Under such conditions no growth or development was possible. Nor did the average Mexican show much more care or consideration. "Many of these ponies," continues Sam, "were picked up by horse outfits and "bred up" into larger horses, which still retained the Indian pony qualities of hardiness and endurance. The result of this cross we called a 'genuine cayuse.' One could not afford to put much "stylish" breeding in a cowpony and raise him and break him and train him and then get around twenty-five or thirty dollars for him from the big outfits. This is about all the kind of cowhorses that were used here for many years."

But in the more rolling country of eastern Montana and Wyoming, where the larger outfits held sway, and all along the main trail and traffic lanes of the West, generally, improvement of horse stock was much more rapid. Excellent stallions of various breeds were introduced. I have before me an early (1888) copy of the *Stockman*, published in the small but important cattle town of Springer in northeastern New Mexico, in which is featured an "ad" of a French Coach stallion that shows much English Thoroughbred and pure Arab blood in its published pedigree. I remember well taking a good mare of mine over to the beautiful ranch of Don Jesus Abreu on the Rayado to breed her to this horse. A grand animal he was, showing the style and quality the French Coach often had; I spent the whole afternoon admiring him! Then there is a notice of an imported Percheron whose dam is shown to be by Brilliant, considered the greatest sire of the breed of all time; and alongside it a cross-bred horse, half Norman, half Kentucky saddlehorse, which is making the season at the well known Taylor Maulding ranch out from Wagon Mound. I have already told you elsewhere how the big cow ranches, such as the Bell, the Matadors, etc., ran Thoroughbred, Standardbred, Coach stallions with their range mares in the '80's. In addition to all this there is no doubt that great numbers of Texas horses, already considerably bred up, were distributed over the range country from Texas along with the vast herds of cattle that flowed from that great state. So that before the middle '80's the main American cattle outfits were supplied with horses, not usually showing much quality, but well-looking and in particular, as I said above, well built and sturdy. And of all these well built, sturdy horses I ever rode or saw, about the best built and sturdiest was The Rogue.

He was a brightish bay with black points. Had been left to run a stud for several years; consequently was too heavy in front to start off or dodge quickly. Nor could I ever flex him up satisfactorily. For these reasons he was of little use for cutting cattle in a herd or for fast rope work in the open. Indeed there were just two points I valued him for: he was a grand horse roping heavy cattle in a corral, and for ease and comfort on an all-day trip I never rode his equal.

Let's take the road angle first. I have told you elsewhere that whereas the Mexican invariably used the lope for traveling, the American cowboy, generally speaking, went at the trot on the road, or on "circle." I myself used the lope more than most cowpunchers (chiefly because it amused me to develop gaits in horses.) Now the lope, (or canter) depending as it does on the horse being able to maintain a perfect balance between his fore and hind end, an even see-saw motion, is the most tiring gait, for himself, a horse can travel at. He must gather and hold the stride on the hind quarters and legs and drop lightly on the forehand. When the muscles of his hind end tire and he begins to drop heavily in front, the action becomes distressing alike to horse and rider. I had managed to put a good enough mouth on The Rogue to keep his action "collected." His good withers and well placed shoulders kept the saddle in perfect position on a short saddleback. No exertion ever seemed to tire a powerful loin and iron-muscled thighs, and thus impair the easy armchair motion. I used to ride over to our county seat at Mora quite often, a distance of fifty miles, in a day. It is my firm belief, if the character of the terrain had permitted, that The Rogue, without ever so much as a suspicion of flagging or lost rhythm, could have gone the entire distance at the lope. I don't remember any other horse I could even imagine that of. And I may add that neither quirt nor spur would have been needed.

Then I said he was a good rope horse. During the first years we owned him we had nothing whatever in the way of chutes or squeezers on the Rafter C ranch. Everything had to be roped and thrown, and The Rogue did a good share of the work. He wouldn't have taken a prize at a roping contest, for he never learned to "set back" in the orthodox way. He never seemed to think it necessary. And indeed, although The Rogue and I tied to some pretty heavy stuff first and last, I never knew him jerked off his stance nor felt myself the least bit jolted. To tie to The Rogue was the same as tying to a tree.

I remember one July bringing a bunch of cows to the ranch from the JJ pure-bred Hereford herd belonging to the famous JA ranch in the Texas Panhandle. As it happened, we had to brand them in our Escondida corral, a big awkward-shaped rock corral with some outcroppings of rock scattered here and there inside it. There was no one but John Hinde and me to do the work. Now branding grown cattle with just two men is something of a chore, what with the fire and irons to tend, and the holding down and burning the cattle, and the simplest plan, if the stock is fresh and rollicky (which these were), is to rope 'em on the run and jerk 'em down. And that's what we were trying to do. There was one extra big fine cow in the bunch. She was coming past me on the dead run when I wrapped my 7/16-inch hard-twist twine around her horns. The Rogue stopped and stiffened, and Mrs. Cow turned over on her back with a resounding smack. We jumped off our horses and ran to hold her down. But it served no purpose, for she never moved an inch. The Rogue had broken our top JJ cow's neck.

> But he grew old and blood grew weak,
>    'Twas nature, all men said;
> Better than stand and watch him die
>    To shoot him through the head.

Well, that's the way I dealt with all my old horses, with the single exception, I believe of The Rogue. Somehow this big bay horse and I never got to be real friends. In the end he got so he didn't keep in good shape on pasture, and one day—on a hasty impulse—I traded him off to a passing band of Gipsies for a rattling chestnut-sorrel gelding with an easy rolling walk, that took my fancy greatly. (The idea of trading horses with a Gipsy!) But on sooner had I made the trade than thoughts began to haunt me of the long hard rides The Rogue and I had taken together, and the big bulls we'd stretched out, over so many years. You know the man and the horse were so much actually one in that life and at that time. It didn't help me much, worrying over how his present owners might be using him, to hear that he had gotten into a Mexican's hands, but I felt a genuine relief when they told me not long after that he was dead. He was the last and only old servant and mate of the horse kind I ever sold or traded off.

And the handsome chestnut-sorrel with the rolling walk, what of him? Shortly after he came into my hands it happened that I had to make one of my fifty-mile trips to Mora, and it seemed a good chance to try out my new road horse. The chestnut-sorrel rolled along merrily the first twenty miles. At that point he gave out, and I had to ply quirt and spur to get him to Mora! (You may bet there's always something wrong with a Gipsy's trading horse. This fine animal had been badly ridden down at some time or other in his life.)

### III

I've told you elsewhere, I think, that our system of trading, buying and selling stock and other commodities, in early days was a pretty casual one. We took a good many chances and few, if any, precautions. Yet, and although as far as stock was concerned there was a world of stealing going on everywhere, it was surprising how seldom we found ourselves chiseled. Horses were probably the most popular thing for the thief to handle, being so easy both to get hold of and move. Yet I think it was the exception to ask for or offer a bill of sale for one. Later on, after brands came to be registered and bills of sale and record of brands had to be produced in order to show title, we grew to be more careful. But I've bought and traded for numbers of horses from fellows drifting through the country and wondered frankly, sometimes, how they came by them.

I remember one time their sending me word from town that some fellows had a bunch of good saddle horses in Aguilar's corral. So I rode over to look-see. Though I was no horse trader, indeed, I liked to try my luck once in a while with a new mount.

Well, it turned out that this outfit came from southwest Texas. They had a lot of fair good saddle horses, as I recall them, but what struck my fancy most was a white mule, mighty well built and in good condition, weighing around 850 pounds perhaps. I'd often had a fancy for a saddle mule to use in the roughest part of the range; no other saddle animal is so sure-footed. They're stout for their size too. "How about your white mule, boys?" says I. "Why, he's broke gentle to the saddle 'n' all. Yu kin try 'im, if yu've a mind to." And in less than five minutes we had my saddle on him and me on his back.

Now due southeast of Aguilar's corral gate rises the Wagon Mound, a bluff crowning as ragged a group of malpais hills as you may want to climb. I had hardly gotten my leg across the saddle when the mule was off like a flash up and into this country. Dead southeast by the sun. That mule was set on getting back to Texas by the shortest route. At a high lope or one might say, a handgallop which he never varied, he carried me over the crest of the first slope into a steep and rocky canyon, traveling the broken ground as easily as if it had been a race track. That was all very well, but when we reached the bottom there suddenly confronted us a wide and deep wash-out, whose walls had been washed perfectly perpendicular by the floods. Supposing the mule capable at all of making the jump before him, there wasn't six inches of footing, I noticed, between the bottom of the hill and the edge of the chasm for him to take off on. That was one of the moments in my life when I thought I faced death. It seemed inevitable that the two of us should jump into the wash-out and break our necks against the opposite side. I drew my feet far out of the stir-rups—I always kept a look-out for being dragged—and sat tight waiting for the next development. A fellow feels no fear facing a crisis like this; he is too busy preparing for it.

I shall never cease to wonder how that mule gathered himself up on six inches of level land to make the big leap. What I recall most clearly is that it didn't seem to cost him an effort and that in a second we were over and hitting it bang straight up the opposite slope; over the crest of that and down the long broken decline to the prairie. That brought us shortly to the main road leading back along the mesa foot to Wagon Mound, and here I made a tremendous effort to stop or turn my mount. But he paid no more attention to the pulling and jerking of my lines, than if they had been strands of wool yarn, never so much as checking his steady running gait, and pointing always dead southeast across the bare plain. He was bent on returning to Texas, that white mule. As we got down near the Vermejo creek at the foot of the plain I looked back and saw a rider evidently following us. He caught up with us presently and asked me where we were going. "I'm not running this show," I rejoined. "I'm under the impression we're on our way to Texas." The upshot of it was that he put his saddle rope around the mule's neck and led him (and me) back to town.

Arrived at the Aguilar corral I discontinued negotiations with the Texans for the white mule. My desire to ride a mule seemed to have been temporarily satisfied. I like my riding stock to have a mouth, and I saw no prospect of flexing this mule's jaw short of using a blacksmith's hammer on it. But what a mount for one of those fellows who make these all-around-the-world trips. He could have made a non-stop flight on him.

As for the Mexican who came after us and took us back, I never knew his name nor where he came from, for I never saw him again. I fancy he belonged to the Texan's outfit. Nevertheless I hope still to meet him some time and take him to the corner place on Front street and buy him a drink. That seems the least I could do for one to whom I feel I owe nothing less than my present general freedom of whereabouts. For I am quite convinced that if that fellow hadn't come and got us when he did, I and that white mule would still be on our way to Texas.

I TURN MY MOUNT LOOSE

# 6

## The Horses We Loved Best

O F all the subjects I write about the one that seems most to interest my readers is horses. Almost always letters I receive call for more about them. Anything about them; even from the historical or technical angle; wild horses and gentle ones; high-bred and scrub. Perhaps the "bad" horse generally gets the limelight, being more spectacular, and likewise easier to "write up." But as I look back I think the gentle, good-tempered ones come most readily into my thoughts and give me the greatest pleasure to remember. I've been telling you about some mean stuff lately, so for a change here goes for a little gossip of some of the kind, lovable horses I've owned or known. It's a curious feature, perhaps, of range life that a fellow grew just as attached to horses that belonged to the outfit he was working for as to horses he owned himself. That was because, after all, it was the *work* a horse did for a cowhand, and his way of doing it, that won his rider's good opinion and regard. If a cattle boss wanted a hand to hate him, all he had to do was to take away his top mount. I took one away once, I needed badly. I hope Bob Bowmer—he was our top hand—has forgotten it. I haven't, Bob, though it's so many long years ago.

There has been a plenty of rot talked and written about the cowboy and his horse. Bill Hart and his Paint, (Tom Mix is a real cowboy) and others of like ilk have put the situation in a false light. Whatever the cowpuncher may have felt, I never saw one show what you'd call affection towards a horse. Indeed, we often treated 'em rough, all right. Cow work is pretty hard on the temper at times. "Cowmen loved their horses," says John

M. Hendrix, the well known cowman and fine writer from Sweetwater, Texas, "but loved them as horses not as a horse." And a good Arizona friend of mine, who is full of ideas and experience of cow horses and cowboys, writes: "A cowboy sat on a horse so constantly that when he turned him loose it was generally with a playful snap of the reins and then he wanted to forget about him. . . but who under heaven ever heard a cowboy or cowman say anything about his horse except 'That's a dam good horse. I wouldn't take $200 for him.' Or 'That's a tough bastard. If I want to be sure to get back I generally take him.' " It may of course be argued that this is a typical American trait not confined to cowpunchers. It is certain that the average American horseman treats his race or show horse as a purely commercial asset out of which to make as much money in as short a time as possible, often wrecking the animal in the process. The American polo pony, too, is sacrificed quite mercilessly by many of our top players in the sheer determination to win the game.* However this may be, I think the horses that came nearest to getting something like real affection on the range were the plumb gentle ones, if only because the women folks and kids about the ranch, if such there were, made much of them.

Take for instance Nigger Babe. Nigger Babe was one of a carload of Abreu broncs from the well known Rayado ranch, which H. M. Porter had bought to ship to his V+T ranch on the Gila river in Western New Mexico. He sent them down to his Red River ranch till he got ready to ship them. There was a black horse among them that Jeff Towner, the Red River foreman, took a fancy to and held back when he shipped the rest to the Gila. George Crocker was working for Jeff, and his little girl Ruth, who was to grow into a fine horsewoman, became greatly attached to Nigger Babe, as they had called the horse.

---

*It has been remarked that the Texas players, the like of Cecil Smith, although among the hardest riders at the game, are the most careful of their ponies.

So when George left the Red River company he traded a horse to Porter for the black and took him with him to Cimarron.

Nigger Babe had turned out very gentle and fond of George's children. It was a favorite habit of his to go down the pasture on hot days and stand for long stretches asleep, or reflecting. Ruth and her little brothers and sisters would go and lie down under him to get the shade, and fall asleep. When the Babe got ready he would move off, carefully lifting his feet over the children's bodies as they lay, so as not to hurt them.

George came of English stock and for that reason perhaps made a good deal of his horses. He generally had a good one or two around. At one time he owned a three-year-old sorrel mare called Uno. She had a lot of Steeldust blood in her and he was training her for the track. The first time she ever ran was in a matched race at 300 yards. George tells the story. "I had gone up to the end of the track where they started from, but decided to go back to the outcome; thinking I could get there before they started. I was on foot and had got no more than half way down the track when they got off. I was on the same side of the track the mare was on. She was winning easily but when she came opposite to me she turned out of the track and ran up to me and stopped. The race was matched for $50, with some side bets."

As for our own horses, one of the earliest brother Chris and I ever owned was old Ginger. He was a dark sorrel, bald-faced, and must have been pretty near mustang with his stubby mane and broom-tail which Chris would never trim. Deep-bodied and everlastingly tough. Chris happened to be dragged by a horse one time and badly broken up. It had him in bed for several weeks. I should tell you we had no fence of any kind around our house on the Escondida in those days; our bunch of saddle and work horses ran loose on the range. Horses do not stay long in the hollows or creek beds like that in which our house stood. They come down to water at the creek and then light out for the high open ground. But from the day Chris was taken down Ginger separated from the rest of the remuda and established himself alone close to the house. He would stand for long stretches with his bald face close to Chris' window. Occasionally he would graze off a little and then come back. So he continued to act till Chris was up and about again, when he went off as usual with his mates to graze. I'd like to say here that I am no booster for the hyper-intelligence of horses. I am merely giving you some facts about a few I've known.

Then there was Dick. Dick had a good strain of Standardbred blood in him that gave him quality and spirit. A big-hearted one indeed he was. We used to use some of our saddle horses in harness, buggy or wagon. None of them probably weighed more than 900 pounds. But it's matter for pure amazement how much courage in a horse can take the place of weight and size in pulling at a pinch. I fancy it depends on the traces of Thoroughbred in their veins. The crossing of the Escondida arroyo just below our house was, like most ranch crossings, generally rough and always steep. One day I remember a team got stuck in it starting from the ranch with a load. There was a bunch of Mexicans working on the ranch, but with all of them at the wheels they couldn't get it started.

I happened to be riding by on Dick. "Let's have your horse," said one of the boys. So we hitched him up in place of the near horse and I took the lines. It wasn't altogether healthy to use the whip to Dick, but I spoke to him and let him feel the bit. And straightaway with a series of short leaps and bucks, and digging his toes into the side of the hill, in about two minutes, singlehanded, he had the wagon rolling, up and over the crest and away onto the level, while the Mexicans stood around and cheered. It takes something to make fellows cheer on those silent range plains.

A call came from a doctor about midnight one night at the ranch. The nearest one was at Wagon Mound, 18 miles away.

Chris was awaked and, saddling up Dick, started out in the dark. He wasn't more than half awake, I suspect, for before he had gotten well into the rough lands of the Megotes he happened to lean over to one side and his saddle, evidently loose, turned over with him. He had no sooner hit the ground than he found that his foot was caught up in the stirrup. Now it's not surprising that a horse gets badly scared when he finds himself dragging an object on the ground behind him. Probably to his excited mind it is some creature rushing madly after him to catch him by the heels. Dick naturally went off full bust with Chris dangling and bumping between his hind feet. If you've ever seen a man dragged you'll remember that men in such position use terrible, although essentially futile, language. Chris I guess was no exception, but he remained able to take some observations and he told us afterwards he noticed Dick gradually slackening his pace and turning his head slightly. And little by little he eased up till at length he came to a standstill. Thereupon he twisted his neck and head clear down and around till his nose touched Chris' foot. This investigation apparently satisfied him that the terrifying object he was dragging was nothing but brother Chris in an unaccustomed situation. He stood stock still while Chris disengaged his foot from the stirrup, got up, and replaced the saddle, and they went on their way.

We Americans did not use many Mexican cow horses. This was partly because they ran too small; partly because most of them had been more or less over-ridden and ruined. Nor did we generally speaking like their way of working with cattle. When they should have been attending strictly to business they were apt to be dancing around on their hindlegs. A few natives, however, who had worked with American outfits learned to be good cow hands and to handle horses satisfactorily. Among these was my good friend, Modesto Aragon, a man of unusual intelligence who worked for me a lot in his early days and who became an excellent sheepman, cow hand and horseman. So when he offered me a young cowhorse he'd been riding I bought him. He'd called him Ruby and this little black horse turned out as handy an animal about the herd and gentle around the ranch as you could wish for. When the dry farmers came in and cut down our range we had to sell some of our horses. Little Ruby went to a farmer who had taken up a claim out on the high flats north of Wagon Mound. A year or so later riding past this farmer's place I stopped to pass the time of day with him. I asked him if they still had Ruby and how they liked him. "O, yes," says the farmer, "we wouldn't part with Ruby. The only thing is that we don't have enough work for him here, so every once in a while he rounds up the milk cows down in the pasture on his own hook and brings 'em up and puts 'em in the corral in the middle of the afternoon."

## II

When you meet in with a horse that is well shaped and a good color; that's high spirited yet as kind as can be; that you can bank on under all circumstances because you know he has a big heart; that's the kind of a horse to tie to. The above description fits in all particulars Bay Nelly, who was for many years a habitant of Dr. Pring's farm in Cherry Valley, that pleasant little irrigated section on Mora river, situated a short way above where the Mora drops into the black malpais canyon that conducts it to the great Canadian thirty miles away.

Bay Nelly was known the whole valley over and far beyond. She was but a small mare but a glance would tell you she had plenty fine blood back of her somewhere. She was chiefly used for heavy harness and her fame rested on the fact that she had never been known to refuse to pull. Whatever Nelly could move she would pull, as the saying went. At very long last, when my friend Dr. Pring sold the farm, I managed to secure her for twenty-five dollars. I thought I might get one colt from her before her end came. I bred her to our Percheron-Standardbred stallion, Glen, that got so many fine colts for us on the Rafter C Bar ranch. And sure enough next spring she produced a fine black filly. It was her last effort in the breeding line; she died that winter.

But the filly grew and prospered. In every respect but color and size—she must have been several hundred pounds heavier—a replica of her mother. I called her Nettle. She never needed breaking; we just hitched her up at three years old and she seemed as if she had naturally succeeded to all the qualities and attainments of her mother. I gave her to Francisco Chavez, one of my best machine men, to drive at haying time, but our vega had numbers of deep potholes in it and one day Nettle got a hindleg into one of them. The hock joint broke open and started to run. I brought her down to the house to treat her and did it long and patiently. But there is nothing you can do for open joint, the lubricating oil just keeps slowly oozing out. I had to shoot her in the end. But only those who have bred good livestock know what a wrench it is to see the last of a highly treasured line of horses pass away.

I am writing now about the horse one got attached to, and lost. It may make things clearer to some of my readers if I point out that in early range times our connection with most of our horses was not overly close. The bulk of them we never saw from late fall till late spring, or summer; they were running out on the range or in pasture. When we took them up for the year's range work we were apt to be looking for someone to "top 'em off" for us. But as ranches became fenced up and ranching, so to speak, more domesticated, the ties with certain of one's horses grew closer. And perhaps under these conditions, too, mares came to be used more frequently than formerly. You couldn't use mares in a working range remuda. But the mare, when available, is smarter and sweeter to handle than the gelding. It was in these later times and under these conditions that Nettle lived her short life.

Then there was Caprice. Years ago—longer than I like to admit remembering—a traveling salesman named Goldammer came from somewhere in what we called in a general way "the East" and bought a claim some miles out from Wagon Mound, bringing to it his wife in the hope that the pure dry air of the high plains might cure her of lung trouble. I don't know what state they came from but they brought with them a few good milk cows and several horses. Among the horses was a mouse-colored mare, trim and breedy looking, and an easy mover. From this mare, which later fell into my sister, Mrs. Ethel Martin's hands, descended a number of foals, all possessing the pleasing qualities of old Mouser. When Mrs. Martin left the country I secured from her one yearling filly, got by my stallion, Glen, out of one of the old mare's daughters.

As I watched her grow out in the pasture I made up my mind to keep her for my own use. At three years Blas Romero broke her carefully to the saddle and I took her over and prepared to make a finished ranch saddle horse of her. She was grey with a faint tinge of iron. From as smooth and well placed a shoulder as you often find—reminding me somewhat of the Steeldust—rose at a practical angle a clean neck, connected with the head by a cleanly articulated crest and throat, supple but not limber. There was nothing of the peacock about her frontal arrangements: the peacocky animal has no place on a working ranch. A level walking gait was readily developed into a lively flat-footed walk. I was a busy man, but most of my work was on horseback; well, to be on a horse was always the thing I liked best. I got to take a delight in the prospect of riding for years to come this dapper grey mare. Along with her sensible disposition there ran a light vein of waywardness. I called her Caprice.

Then one day I noticed her coughing, or perhaps choking over some object in her throat. I worked on it, massaging her gullet and giving her food that might take the obstruction along with it, but all to no purpose. I don't suppose there was a capable veterinarian nearer than Denver, two hundred and fifty miles away. As I worked with her day by day in stable or corral we got to know each other thoroughly. I used to teach my young mounts tricks; they would nuzzle me and shake hands, etc.: it helped, I thought, to establish our understanding of each other. But as far as Caprice's ailment, whatever it might be, was concerned, nothing seemed to bring any relief. I saw no prospect of ever riding her again. I got out my little .41 Smith and Wesson and shot her through the head.

A few miles from my old home in the north of England lay a pleasant estate belonging to a man called George Grey. He did general farming on the land, but his principal interest was breeding hunters, and training them to hounds. His hunters were among the best bred and he himself was considered the finest horseman in the British Isles. Hundreds of times have I followed and studied him in the hunting field; with those wonderful hands of his he could get more out of a raw colt than most of us out of a finished hunter.

As the years closed in on him his eyesight began to fail him, growing at last so bad that he could not see his way about alone. He refused, however, to give up his favorite pastime of hunting, and the job of training his young hunters. He thought him up a plan. He mounted one of his grooms on a good horse. Across his black hunting coat he made him wear diagonally a white pipe-clayed belt and bade him follow the hounds. The old man could see the white belt flashing in front of him on the dullest day, and where the white belt went George Grey followed. There aren't many men so devoted to horses and horseback riding as that. I've heard him say how he believed implicitly in an after life: a place where he could meet and ride his horses again. Lucifer, his famous stallion, and all the good hunter colts and fillies of his the old horseman had broken and sold, often, for fancy prices in the fashionable hunts of midland England.

That—the meeting up at some future time—is an angle of horse concern we cowmen never considered; mainly, I think, because I don't recall a cowman or cowboy who took any interest in religion or such a question as the future life. We had our own simple code of behaviour and ethics which I believe we observed as well as any class of men I ever consorted with. But outside of the few larger towns there were no churches except the scattering Catholic ones and only Mexicans attended these. I remember my brother, the late Monsignor Culley, coming out from England to visit me at the ranch. He was a strict Catholic priest and gave the white Catholics hell in general for not attending the masses he held in some of the local Spanish churches.

Certainly there was old man Sydes, manager of the HOW outfit, whose range lay alongside the Bells and S-T's on the Canadian, who was an active church member, but when I knew him in the toils of religion he had already gotten out of the cow business. And over in the Texas panhandle good Methodist Middle West farmers set up a highly pious and respectable community at Clarendon under the very shadow of the toughest town in the southwest, Tascosa. But the cowboys referred to it as "Saint's Roost" and had but scant dealing with the Saints.

They were shrewd enough fellows, most of the range men, and could have put up a good talk for their own point of view. Some of my New Mexico readers may have known Taylor Maulding, old-time cowman who had an interest in the OK ranch near Wagon Mound and was partner of old John Dawson who ran the Horseshoe brand (inverted) on the Vermejo, and had been in still earlier days trail partner of Charlie Goodnight. I remember Taylor closing up a discussion about religion and the existence of a god with the query: "They say God made the world. Well, who made God?" We had no answer to give the old cowman. And I think that, by and large, expressed the range man's attitude towards matters religious.

There were other ways in which you could lose a favorite horse than by his death. Indeed the majority of our horses did not belong to us at all, but to the outfit a fellow was working for; and we just lost them by separation when in the course of events we changed outfits, as many men constantly did. I wonder, as I think back, whether I ever had a horse I was more attached to or remember more affectionately, than old Smoky, who was a straight Bell bred and Bell owned horse. Indeed, I never got him till he was an old horse. He had good blood and some speed and had been used in his earlier days for running in broncs off the range. And to his dying day it was useless to try and stop him when he once got running. All his teeth and jaw on one side had been broken up by the boys jerking at the bit. But he and I between us worked up a flat-footed walk of our own contrivance and traveled many a hundred miles together at it to our complete satisfaction. No fancy affair at all, that gait. I kept his head low, stretching the neck over with side pressure of the rein so as to lengthen and flatten out the stride, to the point where it just didn't break. I wish I could get a ride on him today!

Smoky! I wonder how many "Smokys" there have been on the range since cattle days began. We hear people say there are no more cow horses, but there'll be cow horses as long as there are range cattle, and there'll be horses called "Smoky" as long as there are grey horses.

Only lately—as I mentioned previously—I got a letter from W. G. (Bill) Swenson, assistant manager of the old and famous SMS ranch at Stamford, Texas, telling me about the kind of cow horses their outfit is breeding today. Their best success has been with an Arabian cross on their Morgan mares, the result being a cow horse easier to handle and showing better cow sense than any other they have had. He writes: "John Selmon, foreman of our Flat Top ranch, is now riding one of these horses he calls Smoky and this horse is John's pet horse. John does all types of cow work on him and he is one of the best cutting horses in this part of the country. He turns so fast that it takes a good cowboy to 'set on' him."

All right, John, here's wishing good luck to you and your Arabian Smoky. If I ever manage to get back to that good West Texas country I'll look you and him up. Mebbe you'll let me ride into the herd on Smoky. But you better not set him to cutting cattle with me or he'll sure throw me off!

# 7
## V8 v. "Hoss"

THE principal qualification for writing on any given subject, these days, seems to be to know as little as possible about it. On questions on which you are informed you are apt to be cautious about expressing an opinion. But let the subject be one on which you have a comfortable and pervasive ignorance, and you can turn yourself loose. On these grounds I feel prompted to discuss the subject of the Modern Cow Horse, because I have hardly been on the back of a cow horse, ancient or modern, since the day I quit the cow business a number of years ago.

That ought to give me an opportunity to unburden myself with complete freedom. For what's the use, I say, of all these finicky pains one takes to verify statements when we get letters like the following: "I hope," writes a lady, referring to some remarks I had made about some relative of hers in a recent magazine article, "if you continue to write for publication, you will confine yourself to the facts."

There has been an interesting and lively discussion in the *Western Livestock Journal* within recent months about cow horses, dealing with the virtues of the old kind, and methods of breeding the new. The late Jack Zurich wrote from New Mexico in praise of the old-timers that would carry a man a hundred miles a day, but had "no pedigrees nor nuthin'." Jack was an old friend of my brother-in-law Stan McKellar's, and Stan says he was a wonderful hand with horses, as well as being a successful handler of them in a business way. Then Thos. Adams of Montana and others spoke up for the fancy bred kind. These old-time cowmen usually don't leave you in any doubt as to where they stand. But what no one discussed in any detail was what are the requirements of the modern cow horse, as compared with those of earlier days, and I thought I would take a long shot at this angle of the question myself.

Well then, to start off with, it will be well to remember that in the '80's and '90's almost all travel on the range was done on horseback. It was the only way most fellows had of getting from one place to another. Even if you had a rig, roads were often bad, as well as circuitous. That last is some word for a cowpuncher to use in describing a road, but what I am getting at is that when I was working for the Bells, for instance, their headquarters was a hundred miles away from my own ranch by road, but you could make it in fifty on horseback, taking the trails across the brakes of the Canadian. So I went horseback.

You could make our county seat at Mora from Wagon Mound in like manner by way of the Turkey Mountain trails. I'd ride the 50 miles over there and attend to my business one day and back the next. We often had to ride our horses, too, fifteen or twenty miles and back just to shut a gate or do some such other chore. It needed horses with stamina for all this riding that wouldn't get jaded or leg-weary on you. But today I hear them talking about slipping over to Mora and back between breakfast and lunch in their V8's. Albert Mitchell of the Bells uses his private plane. And when you do have a job of work in the saddle, you carry your five-gaited Kentucky saddler to the scene of action in a trailer behind you and, after ambling around on him a while, haul him carefully home. Why trouble your head about breeding horses that have stamina?

Rope horses? When I and brother Chris first started running cattle we had one big corral with no divisions in it, much less a chute. Everything had to be roped and thrown. As we had no pastures, if we wanted to wean calves we had to blab them, oftenest catching them in the open. Suitable horses were needed for these jobs: stout ones for holding the big stock, and quick ones to catch the young stuff. But, bless your soul, long before I gave up running cattle I did all my handling in chutes and squeezers; even separating our young calves for branding into small pens where the boys caught them afoot. Why bother with rope horses anymore?

Flesh is the commodity on a cow-brute that brings the dough on the market. Is it not foolish to wear it off the animal, running after him on a horse? An up-to-date cow outfit can train its cattle, as I did mine, to run through chutes and separating gates, if they are properly contrived, as quietly and readily as a herd of sheep. Who wants a cut horse today?

I have been studying lately the influence of the horse on mankind, more especially with reference to the cowman and cowpuncher. One finds that the horse has always been associated with ideas of aristocracy and dignity. From the days of good King Arthur down kings have always been attended by the choicest of their subjects on horseback. Great military leaders like Xerxes, Alexander, Hannibal, Gustavus Adolphus, regarded their mounted troops as the flower of their forces, and for many centuries cavalry carried all before it in battle. Thus arose among horsemen a complex of superiority, an aristocratic tradition. The folks who rode horseback set up standards of their own and came to regard with disdain the ordinary run of mankind, whether soldier or civilian, who did their jobs on foot. This condition reached its climax in the middle ages when the knights under the feudal system with their chargers and accouterments rode about the country, lance or sword in hand, lopping off people's heads, and rescuing damsels from imaginary difficulties.

Now it has been the custom with the story books and movies, so it seems to me, to depict the cowboy as a sort of cross between a rough-neck and a half-wit on horseback. And certainly the cowpuncher was of a simple turn of mind, and on occasion did stir things up. But Mr. Cowpuncher, all the same, was something of an aristocrat. His manner had a measure of dignity and reserve. Like the knights of old he had certain standards which he observed, and like them he looked down on people—such as grangers, and others—who carried out their jobs afoot; he himself like the knights, generally disdaining to engage in any occupation not conducted on horseback. He wore gloves always, of leather or buckskin, often with gauntlets, and took them off when shaking hands or apologized for wearing them. He never wore the blue denim pants the cowboy of today wears; they were considered to be the mark of the Mexican peon. He did not stoop to eat "sheep meat." Now if it is true that these pleasing characteristics in the cowpuncher are the result of his constant association with his horse, what I want to know is, if he takes to doing his work in a V8 instead of on horseback, what is to prevent him descending to the level of ordinary "civilians"—which is the term one cowboy I know used to apply to the general public that doesn't punch cows? And that would be the real passing of the cowboy!

But there's the physical side of the matter too. It was all that tough horseback riding that made the cowman the lean and sinewy chap he usually is. I once suggested to Katherine Field, the gifted Western artist, that she change the slim figures of her cowboys sometimes, and put in a good round-bellied one. But she never has. She couldn't find one, I guess. But as sure as sun-up, if the cowman continues to convoy his spare form from place to place on the easy cushions of a modern automobile, he will shortly become undistinguishable from the tub-shaped city business man whom we see around us everywhere. That will indeed be the windup of the Western cowman.

He will be then nothing more than a cattle dealer. All that he or his boys will require in a horse will be an easy gait. Well, he can go buy him one of those beautiful animals we see pictured in the livestock journals. Even so, I am wondering whether his Rex McDonald-Bourbon King mount will be better riding than LD Maud, little chestnut sorrel that was in my string when I rode with the Bells in the '90's. But then LD Maud had no pedigree nor nuthin, gol-durn 'im!

# III
## Cattle and Men

# I

## Real Rodeos

IN all that I have writen about the range you will find but little mention of the everyday working of a ranch, or manner in which a roundup was conducted. This is for the reason that I have generally felt I was writing for cowmen to whom such particulars were too familiar to be of any interest. Yet as a matter of fact, of all the ways of living ever existant among mankind perhaps the one that most excites the interest of the average person is that of the early western American range folk. And I don't except the career of the Crusader or Medieval Knight who likewise owed his effectiveness as a figure to an inveterate use of the horse, as well as to exclusive and somewhat similar social habits.

So I haven't written much descriptive detail of range operations, and for the reason given above. But all of a sudden one fine day a letter arrived from George L. Branham, written from Plainview, Texas, in which place he lives. Living there he knows well Sheriff Oat Martine whom I've told you about many times, who used to run the Bell wagon.

But the point of George's letter was that he had been reading and enjoying some stories of mine somewhere. Only he didn't understand why I didn't write more about the everyday life, and how the work was carried out on the roundups and so on. The fact is George has been indulging in an operation and while recuperating in Kansas City, he found, he says, that everyone he ran up against, hearing that he was an old cattleman, wanted to know something about cattle life on the range. "I thought," he writes, "it would be very interesting if you would write in

A HARD WINTER, BREAKING ICE

some detail how the work was carried on on a ranch like the Bells, for instance."

To begin with then, there were different sorts of ranches and ranch work; the former more especially in early days when settlers took up land claims and lived alone on them. Few old-timers there are but have put in some lonesome months in for-lorn places with no neighbors for miles around. I remember stopping one long hard winter on the Cerro Pelon, west of Turkey Mountains, alone in a wild camp whose accommo-dations consisted of one structure seven feet by eight feet, of open lumber lined only with muslin. They brought me chuck and firewood and water every month. Once they failed me and I had to pack water in a five-gallon keg on my shoulder a mile on foot, my horse being gone. And what beautiful water it was! After straining it three times through my pockethandkerchief it still retained a rich supply of live animal matter. I'd like to offer some of this kind of beverage to some of our fancy high-school youths who swill out of marble fountains with celluloid cups. But we fellows never bothered our heads about it; it had a true flavor of cow and helped to thicken up the Arbuckle.

Some of these lone ranches had a nice log hut or two, and a bunch of horses and a rig, whereby one could make one's way, twenty miles perhaps, to town every Saturday and get mail, and white flour for hot biscuit, and sowbelly, and black strap. My very good friend, Freeland Latourette, lived like that near me on one of the pleasant benches of the Mora River, approach-able only by horseback, and very nice it was. Then other cow-men were married and put up decent log or "dobe" houses, and some even *milked a cow*, if my memory is correct: (I must write and ask my friend George Crocker about this; he is my walking Early West Encyclopedia.)

And it was in such times as these my wife and I, with three-month-old baby, had occasion to occupy for a while an adobe shack of two rooms with a Mexican dirt roof that didn't hold water; and when it rained heavily we had to keep moving the baby from one spot where the water was pouring in on him to some other spot where it was dry. That was Matt, now of the U.S. Forest Service, with fourteen months duty overseas. All of us living well or evilly; brothers and sisters of one great family reaching from Canada to the Rio Grande.

Then the work varied a lot. In early days the first work of the year was "spring work." At this time the one-year steers were gathered and shipped north. But when it was found that yearlings could not stand the sudden change from southern parts to Montana, Dakota, Idaho, Wyoming, etc., so early in the year they took to shipping two-year olds. Even so it was mean driving, neither cattle nor horses being in fit condition for the trip, and grass being scarce. Only a few top horses would be fed grain and I've told elsewhere how horses chilled at night, failed to make the remuda ground next day. Well I recall driving the Bell "twos" over to Clayton to ship; a cold rain set in and for three days we never got a fire lit.

But before this and thereabouts came the routine work of breaking ice, and "pulling bog" when the frost began to leave the ground. I had the bog-pulling job to look after and organize over sixty miles, both sides, of the Canadian, admitted to be the most treacherous watercourse in the West. That was on the Bell ranch when the pasture with its one hundred and twenty miles of riverbank had but one division fence. Now it has thirty-five, so the bog business is easily taken care of. And on our own Rafter C Bar Ranch I used to ride from nine to twelve hours a day in spring, and pull out fifteen to twenty cows. That's what's causing these cricks in my back, now. I was glad whenever John Hinde had time to help me. He would bring Mac, a black horse John had trained to do whatever a cow horse is expected to do. A good bog-pulling horse must never hesitate; he must just hit her from the word "go." Mac wasn't a large horse, but it was a sight to see him snake 'em out.

Before I pass from this subject I may point out that after you had pulled the old cow out, you had to "tail her up." As soon as that was done she'd put down her head and come after you. Then being stiff in the knees, she'd fall down again, and you'd tail her up again and make a swift dash for your horse. O, it was a sweet business pulling bog in the Spring!

The kinds of roundup outfits, too, were different. Firstly came the purely professional one which handled trail herds and the herds of the big cattle owners, occupying their own range and running outfits of their own. Such outfits generally contained Texans not a few. There probably wasn't a cow outfit in the range country that didn't have a Texan in it. They taught us the cow business just as the Colonial Spanish had originally taught them. The Texans inclined to handle cattle roughly, but they knew how.

Alongside these came the "pool" outfits. The pools were organizations of private cattle owners, possessing water rights and homesteads within certain given districts. Turning their cattle loose on this land, from which they excluded outsiders by refusing to work their cattle, they pooled all operations and expenses. A number of regular cowhands worked on these roundups, but they were also attended by some of the private owners. Of the latter some were cattlemen and rode their own cattle. Others knew little or nothing about the business and caused some entertainment among the older hands. Many of them were given the chance to learn the art of capturing snipes at midnight with the aid of a sack and a lantern. To be sure, they found snipes scarce on those dry plains!

There was one young fellow belonging to an eastern city, as I recall it, who bought cattle and joined the Wagon Mound pool. This pool was a section of the Northern New Mexico Stockgrower's Association which was powerful and extensive enough to embrace the Long H's, the Cross L's, the Bells, the 101's, the Red River Company, the ZH's—in all two hundred and eighty-four outfits. The young fellow may have been an expert in his own line, which I believe was jewelry, but his ignorance of handling cattle was complete. F. J. Maldaner was his name, and he ran the nifty little brand, Y Rail. However he liked to play the cowboy and ride out with the boys. One year my kid brother-in-law, Stan McKellar, was wrangling horses for the Wagon Mound roundup. Maldaner asked him to catch and saddle a horse for him. This he did and they started off together. Presently Maldaner's horse got going pretty fast, and he shouted out excitedly to Stan to help him stop him. "Can't you see" he exclaimed, "the bit's fallen out of his *face!*" Fortunately it didn't take Stanley long to stop the runaway and replace the bit in his "face."

I've known of odd things on roundups. In a certain district a young Southerner—whom we will call Leslie—ran a considerable bunch of cattle in a local pool. He was a man of good position and family, owning besides the cattle property in his home state. An unusually handsome fellow and a glib talker, his favorite source of conversation, as is frequent with Southerners, being their women folk; how beautiful they were, how virtuous, and in what high respect they were held. All of which was well and true, no doubt; but when it came to our western ranch girls his attitude was different. He showed them no respect: indeed it was known he had taken advantage of more than one of them. Tom Porter and I used to discuss him with disfavor. Tom was a fine clean fellow, just newly married, like myself, about this time.

Well, the day's work on a summer roundup was over and we were all gathered around the camp fire down on Tipton Flats that lie just east and at the foot of the Turkey Mountains. I might say here that the cowboy was no more particular about his language or choice of subjects than other classes of men who live with little or no association with women. Indeed we were a pretty coarse mouthed bunch generally speaking, if the truth be known. Tonight, Leslie, who was a good singer had started on a long song that was as realistically bawdy as they make 'em. Everybody seemed to be absorbed in the entertainment when suddenly from the corner where Tom Porter was leaning on his bed roll, came a voice quiet but perfectly clear: "Say, fellers, suppose we cut out this here dirt."

Gentlemen, I want to say that for a few moments following this remark that cow camp was the silentest place I was ever in in my life. The song had stopped abruptly and it was some moments before any conversation opened up again. Tom told me afterwards: "You know, Jack," he said, "I'm no Sunday school man. I get a kick out of a smutty song once in a while. But to see that double-acting bastard settin' up there givin' us stuff like that, and me and you with our good young wives at home—I just busted up."

That is not a very remarkable story, I suppose; but all the same I am willing to bet that no other bunch of cattlemen in the history of cowpunching ever had a similar experience. It was just one of those things that come out of the void and drop back as suddenly into it.

I will try now to describe a day on a Bell Ranch roundup.

## II

Chuck! A good sound that, generally; but sometimes not so good.

If you talk to New Mexico fans, who I will say are unusually ardent, they will tell you there is no sun like New Mexico's— here they may quote D. H. Lawrence; there are no colors so rare as those of New Mexico's mountains and plains; and above all—and here I agree—no skies as deep as New Mexico's night skies. How many a night have I lain on my camp bed and gazed into them, learning, as I thought, something of the mystery of things. The deadest part of the night, as all night birds know, is the hour that comes just before the dawn. If you have been standing guard in the earlier hours you are apt to be sleeping heavily then, and in that period the word "chuck!" breaking sharp upon your ears is NOT so good. But everybody in camp rolls out of bed at once. A remarkable feature of roundup life was that in spite of the bare show of authority the rules and duties of the work were freely accepted and carried out by every cowhand.

Food varied little from day to day and meal to meal: fried beef, hot biscuit, stewed prunes or raisins, perhaps, and gravy, good thick gravy. But at that dead hour half the boys had no appetite, took only a cup of coffee, dipping their tin cups into the big pot. I don't know who the Arbuckles were, but they should have a monument erected in their honor somewhere on the High Plains. For many years they were the principal standby of the range cow business.

By this time the horse wrangler had his horses inside the rope corral, and just as soon as it was light enough the men went out with their saddle ropes to get their horses. Some bosses let each man rope his own horse. Tom Kane of the Bells was fond of roping and caught all the horses himself as men called for them. When the rope flies the horses run and rampage around the rope corral, which is supported by iron stakes or held up by the men, but the instant one feels the noose around his neck he stands and leads out of the bunch quite quietly, that side of the ropes having been lowered to the ground to let him pass over. Sometimes a horse would pitch (buck) when mounted and give the camp some fun. "Let *me* ride 'im," they'd all holler, while the rider as a usual thing held onto the bucking strap. That was a stout strap fastened around the fork of the saddle which the rider gripped, bracing himself with arm rigid. Some of us, however, used no bucking strap. That was called "ridin' 'em slick" or they would say, "So-and-So rides 'em all alike." As a matter of fact it meant using balance as against sheer strength.

And then off on circle! It's a summer work we're taking part in, so branding calves is the order of the day. Our camp is on the Conchas river, close to where the huge diversion dam on the Canadian is being built today by the Government. A beautiful rolling-broken country to work over, reaching on one side up towards the Mesa Rica, the Rich Mesa, turquoise blue in the distance, and on another across the Canadian and the little Mexican plaza of La Cinta towards the timbered mesa where the Bell headquarters ranch lies. Some old-time cowboy writers, in reaction against the fake romanticism of most modern western literature, try to make out that there was really no romance in the cowboy's life; that it was all humdrum drudgery. So it was, mostly. Towards the end of a long day it got pretty monotonous. Yet always for me, to ride forth from camp on a fresh horse on a clear New Mexico morning— and what is true of New Mexico is true of most all the high Plains—swinging out to hunt the draws and breaks, and heading off the startled cattle as they break away before us—that never failed to stir something in me. And of all the things I have done in a long life that is the one I like best to recall. Nor do I doubt that secretly this held good for the tough old cowhand who had never done anything but punch cows since childhood.

So then behold Tom Kane sending his men out on circle. The boys used to laugh at his arms whirling like the arms of a windmill, as he pointed out the line for each circuit leader to follow. When all the cattle that have been found are brought in and gathered in a bunch near camp the fellows change horses and "work the herd." Some cattle would be cut out and joined with the day herd, which was carried along with the camp; the cows and young calves held back for branding, later to be turned loose again on the range.

Then dinner and a Bull Durham "cigareet," hand-made with brown paper—I never saw a "tailor made" on the range—and catch fresh horses and off to brand the calves. One or two of the top hands rope the calves, five or six flank and brand and tend the fire and carry the irons; and the rest hold up the herd.

Holding up the herd! That was a job, like most apparently simple jobs, that needed experience. Sometimes there would be a number of cuts or bunches being held up at the same time, cattle being cut into each from the main or central herd. That meant the bunches being held up at the edges, just tight enough but not too tight, else the cattle would break away. When an animal broke away a cowboy would take after it, trying to circle around it and so steer it back into the herd. A new hand beholding him would sometimes light out on the opposite side of the cow, thinking to employ the "pincer" process on her, or on the principle, as brother-in-law Harry McKellar, expert cowhand, used to say, that "if one couldn't catch her, two could!" The result being that Mrs. Cow, seeing no opening to get back into the herd, lit out for the tall grass.

And here I feel like telling you about the very first herd I ever held up. It was on the flats of the Sweetwater, Colfax County, New Mexico, a small creek whose waters later form part of the great Canadian. As far as I remember, Nick Cooke, a well known cattleman of that district, who ran the 3 Cross brand, shoulder, side and hip, was in charge of the roundup. He was roping calves in the open and I was doing my untutored best to help hold up the herd. Now most cattlemen know that they are apt to have days off, roping, and that when calves have been missed once or twice they become amazingly wise about dodging the rope. The which is apt to make the roper see red. This is how it was with Nick that day; and looking around and beholding a "furriner" galloping about the herd somewhat indiscriminately, Nick thought well to vent his wrath on him. As he came near the edge of the herd he suddenly shouted at me: "What the goddam hell d'you think you're doin'?" I was no prude, but I remember feeling that his remark might have been couched in politer terms. However, it wasn't long before I learned to hold up a herd and to rope a calf myself—as well as to command a complete line of profanity.

Then there was the cook. He was the most important person in camp. I never cease to wonder why someone has never written a history of roundup cooks. They were often pretty cranky, but it was a tough job cooking for a full outfit; getting your breakfast things cleaned up, the bed rolls loaded on the chuck wagon, and drive your four mules to the next camp over what was generally an excuse for a road, in time to get dinner. Some of my readers will remember "Maverick" Thompson who cooked for the Wagon Mound outfit a number of years. He was a long-legged fellow, perfectly good natured. He had a ranch in the breaks around where the Mora and Canadian rivers join; a broken timbered country excellently adapted to the harboring of stray cows. It was said that Thompson was an expert at weaning calves from their mothers, and that his little herd of cattle showed an unusual percentage of increase.

Down in the Lower Country we used sometimes Mexican cooks. Old Manuel was one of them, half Indian, plump and placid, a walking epitome of silence, whereof the memory refreshes. But Mexican cooking is greasy and the biscuit not so light. Old man Garvey was American, probably around fifty years of age and a typical roundup cook with a kick on hand for most occasions. When I first joined the Bells I was for a short time on a diet. The old man would say to the boys: "That new Manager man says he's sick and can't eat. Then he comes over here and cleans up everything in camp." But he was at bottom a decent old fellow. He lived, when he wasn't with the wagon, a solitary life on what was known as the Farm, lying down on the flats of the Canadian, twenty-five miles from the ranch headquarters. Finally growing weary of life alone, and the nearest single white woman being fifty or one hundred miles away, he subscribed to a matrimonial paper. In due course he got in touch with a spinster who declared herself eager to become the mate of a western man and share the life of a ranch. It was all agreed upon that he should meet her at Clayton, the nearest station. The old man put on his store clothes and Sunday hat, and started for Clayton, some eighty miles distant, with a pair of the chuckwagon mules in one of the farm wagons. He met the train, but there was no spinster. He waited for the next day's train, but still no spinster. I think that all of us fellows on the ranch were just as sorry as we were amused when our cook came back to the farm with his broken dream of connubial bliss—only I don't suppose he referred to it in such flowery language as that.

As for the calf roping—to return to our roundup—Tom Kane did most of it, with our top hand, Bob Bowmer, the best cowhand from every angle I ever knew, helping. And sometimes I'd ride in myself and show the boys my own particular style of catching calves. I believe the original and natural method of roping was to swing the loop up over the left shoulder, twirl around the head, and then deliver from the right; and this method is still used in catching running animals from horseback. A man roping a running animal throws his rope at the moment when he sees an opening, and this method enables him to keep his rope in action in the air, ready to seize such opening; also maintaining the momentum to overcome the resistance of the air. I don't know when the fashion of throwing the rope "in reverse" came in, a kind of backwards stroke, as one might say, everywhere prevalent. In using this throw on foot the loop is laid on the ground a little to left of roper; then swept across to the right side and thrown thence with a reverse action; or sometimes, and especially perhaps in Mexico, carried on in reverse around the head and delivered from above the left shoulder. Both are pretty throws and create little disturbance among stock.

But I could never handle either satisfactorily. With standing

or slow moving animals, roping horseback, I used to ride my
horse always to the right of the animal, more or less, holding
the loop low down on the off side of the horse; then with one
quick arching sweep across the saddle, leaning the weight on
the left stirrup, I was able to throw a 30-foot rope (over the
left side of the horse) the full length of the lariat. It was an
interesting shot, requiring strong and supple wrist and fingers,
to project and manipulate. The main advantage of it was that
the animal had no suspicion of the rope till it was over him.

Branding finished, the boys may have an hour before supper,
catching and staking out their night horses or perhaps a couple
of them are out to rope a yearling heifer to kill for beef. Supper,
and unroll your bed.

> "Day ends; come glinting campfires;
>     Tonight not a wind is stirred;
>   You can hear the boys on guard, if you listen,
>     Singing to the herd."

# 2

# A Cowboy of the '70's

## I

IF you were to take your idea of range life around the 80's from most of the books that are daily pouring forth from the press about the Old West, you would imagine every round-up outfit to consist of a gang of wild Texans, raised to ride and rope and shoot. That might be true of the '60's and '70's, but it would be a false picture of the '80's.

The recovery of the United States from the panic of 1873 was marked by a gradual increase of livestock in the West which reached its peak in the great boom of the early and middle '80's. From 1880 to 1886 the numbers of cattle in the seventeen Western range states are estimated to have risen from 12,000,000 to 21,000,000. Cattle companies such as the Prairie Cattle Company or the Swan Land & Cattle Company, ran well over 100,000 head, with the "Syndicate" claiming 150,000. Alongside such as these were the herds of innumerable smaller owners, all eager to get in on this unparalleled bonanza of the range cow business; till by 1886 the entire West had become one vast cattle ground. All these cattle (though receiving scant enough attention during winter) had in the fall and summer months to be worked: gathered, branded, shipped, returned to their own range. It called for a heap of men.

The principal sources of supply of practised cowhands at this period were Texas and California. The *vaqueros* of California, however, were in the main what are known now as Spanish-Americans or California Spanish. We called them Mexicans and, generally speaking, no Mexicans were employed with the cow outfits of the plains country. Texas, herself, from earliest days a cattle state and the cradle of the range business, had heavy demands of her own to supply. And although she sent out her cowhands to every range state, vast additional numbers of hands were required to man the innumerable outfits the cattle boom had called into being. Where did these hands come from?

Well, they came from every corner of the United States and, I might add, the British Empire; and were of every character and condition. When I first came to Wagon Mound, New Mexico, the Wagon Mound Cattle pool controlled the cattlemen and their herds in that district. Perhaps by describing a few of them I can best give you an idea of the curious motley of men who composed their roundup outfit. Visiting their wagon you would have found Len Leech, socialite of Philadelphia, riding side by side with old man Marshall, English ex-sailor and New Zealand farmer. Dave Colville, who had run sheep in Australia, would be sharing a teepee with Freeland Latourette, son of an American Army chaplain, and graduate of a swanky New York "prep" school. These men and others like them—Jim Elzea who hailed from the middle states and Ollie Fairchild who had been a traveling salesman—were small owners, riding their own brands. Compensating their comparative lack of experience and cow knowledge you'd have found Sam Kail, old cowhand, who ran the wagon, and such top range men as young George and Frank Crocker, who had grown up, under English parents, in the historic little cow town of Cimarron. Such a medley of men as this could be matched in scores of districts on the plains. I used to amuse myself sometimes trying to trace the background of the men I worked with.

So it interested me when one day lately my old friend Billy Parsons, who lives in an adjoining town to mine, where I like to visit him from time to time and chew the rag, started to tell me how it was he took to cowpunching.

Billy's father was a lawyer practising in Kansas City. One day in the year 1875 a friend of his, Mr. Evans of the livestock commission firm of Hunter and Evans, asked him as a favor if he could give a few days' board and room to a customer of the firm.* Lawyer Parsons out of friendliness agreed to Evan's request, and the upshot of it was that Mr. (Sim) Holstine, of the firm of Holstine and McCoy of Gonzales County, Texas, made his headquarters at the Parsons home for a year. This incident proved the turning point in Billy's life. Doubtless thousands of other riders on the range were pointed in that direction by a happening just as casual.

A drama lay behind this one, though it was a drama common enough in those times. Sim Holstine, who operated in cattle on a large scale, was engaged in shipping steers to New Orleans in partnership with a man known as Doughboy Taylor. On one occasion a difficulty arose about a shipment of steers Sim made in spite of a strong objection from his partner. Just as soon as Holstine got back from the shipment, Doughboy presented himself at his boarding-house and asked to see him. Taylor was a man who came of bad stock; his two brothers both died in their boots. When Holstine came to the door, he said to him: "Sim, you gave me a dirty deal, and I've come to kill you." Holstine wanted no trouble around the boarding-house, so he persuaded his partner to walk out a way with him under the pretext of talking the matter over. Sim was a powerful man, weighing over two hundred pounds, and afraid of nothing. Suddenly he grappled with Doughboy, wrested his gun from him and shot and killed him with it. Following a fracas of this kind, at that period, it was quite common for no arrests to be made nor any legal action whatever taken, but it was understood that the surviving party leave the country. Sim Holstine pulled up stakes and went north to Kansas City.

At this time Billy Parsons was around twenty, and studying

*This firm, I may say in passing, has a place in range history as having bought, according to Evetts Haley, a total of no less than 50,000 head of cattle from old John Chisum's Jinglebobs on the lower Pecos.

telegraphy—just about to qualify, indeed, as an operator. But
the climate of that region had affected his lungs and he suffered
continually from coughs and colds. One fine day Mr. Holstine
suggested to him that the outdoor life of the range might benefit
him. He offered to take him on as a hand. To the which Billy
finally agreed, and just sixty-four years ago he joined the ranks
of the men who rode the wide silent ranges, under sun and
Dipper, in the rain and snow, and the everlasting west wind.

II

Sim Holstine handled cattle on a considerable scale and was
bringing up herds from Texas right along. In Billy's second year
he brought one up to Dodge City and Parsons joined it there
and helped graze the cattle across the broad, sweeping plains of
Western Kansas and Eastern Colorado. They pulled up finally
at Horse Creek, a creek which heads northeast of Colorado
Springs and joins the Arkansas river not far from Rocky Ford.
That was the place you'd hear the boys talk about mostly, says
Billy. But the savory cantaloup long since displaced the romance
of cow camp and cowboy as the source of Rocky Ford's fame.

There they wintered the herd. All this serves to show that
even up to a year or two before the great boom with its hopeless overstocking and subsequent near-destruction of the range,
cattlemen could still drift around with their herds in search of
unoccupied ranges. Sometimes lighting upon one where the
stand of buffalo and grama was so plentiful and fresh that cattle
turned loose on it in the fall could be gathered up within a radius
of a few miles in the spring. It starts a cowman of today a-
dreamin' dreams just to read about it.

Not far south from where Holstine's boys held their herd
on Horse Creek, the Apishapa, heading in the Spanish Peaks
to the southwest, flows into the Arkansas on its opposite bank.
In its canyon just nine years before this (1867) Charlie Goodnight had established the first important cattle ranch in Colorado.

And there, the same year, the famous northern cattleman, J.W. Iliff, bought one of the Goodnight herds and drove it up to Cheyenne, the first Texas herd, according to Osgood, to enter Wyoming ranges.

Billy's baptism into the cow business became complete in his second year when Sim took him down to Gonzales County, Texas, and Billy came up the long trail with a herd of cattle, crossing the Colorado five miles above Austin and proceeding thence past old Camp Supply in the Nation, to Dodge City. Summering the cattle on Smoky River, they shipped out part of them in the fall, and drove what was left to winter on the South Beaver. And there Billy had his first experience of a big snowstorm. It was not possible, of course, to even loose herd these herds in winter time. What the riders did was to "line ride" or "cut trail" on them, trying to keep them back within certain limits. Naturally the Texas cattle inclined to drift south to get back to their own range, and there was nothing in God's wide world to stop them except the line riders.

One day Sim sent Billy and another fellow out to cut trail on the Beaver herd. A heavy snowstorm overtook them, quickly covering up their tracks, while the dense snowfall obscured any natural objects, leaving nothing to guide them but the direction of the wind. It wasn't long before they realized they were lost. That realization—that you are lost in a snowstorm—is always a disturbing one. I've known men to get desperate and curse the elements themselves. But Billy, though a young hand and city-bred, did not lose his head. "If we just keep goin' north, we're bound to strike the Republican," he said. And that was true enough, for the Republican River skirts the entire northern line of Kansas to the point where it turns southeast to join the old Kaw about the longitudinal center of the state.

So they rode north all day by the wind, which fortunately remained constant, and when dark fell on them, they found themselves in timbered brakes. They had a pack horse along and tearing down boughs they laid their bed on them and lighting a big fire, waited for morning. And sure enough, when day broke, there below them lay the Republican, black in the surrounding snow, and on the far side a lone shack which proved to be the camp of a fellow line-rider who made them welcome to whatever he had.

In 1880 and 1881 the Scottish Prairie Cattle Company was established, one of the most famous cattle concerns in history. It was formed in three divisions: the JJ on the Picketwire, representing the holdings of the Jones brothers and controlling the southeast corner of Colorado. The LIT, which comprised the Littlefield interests, among the earliest in the Texas panhandle, centering around the famous, or infamous, little town of Tascosa; and the Cross L, acquired from Hall Brothers. This division controlled sixty miles of the upper waters of the Dry Cimarron, or Cimarron Seco, running along the northern boundary of New Mexico to the line of No-Man's-Land. As it happened, Sim Holstine was put in charge of the Cross L in 1881 and took Billy Parsons with him.*

A wonderful place for cattle that Cimarron canyon. The flat at bottom not very wide, but the sides gradually spreading out as they rise to the level of the mesa country lying north and south more than a thousand feet above the creek bed. Canyons cleave its side walls, deep and rugged in their upper portions, where cattle were hard to reach, and many a steer grew to be an outlaw. Once in a while the boys would happen on one of these old renegades and run him into the day herd. There they'd throw him and put a bell on him so the fellows on night-guard

---

*On leaving the Cross L's Holstine moved to southwest New Mexico, where he established a ranch on the Mimbres river. At his death (about 1910) his ranch passed among others to Dave Pryor, son of the well known Texas cowman, Ike Pryor, and eventually to John T. McElroy whose widow now owns it. It has become one of the show places of the Southwest, but of the old ranch not a vestige remains. Even the cotton trees around the house have been removed.

would know in case he tried to slip out of the herd under cover of the dark. How they hated to lose their freedom, those old boys!

Further down the river in No-Man's-Land, or the Strip, as it was called (now the panhandle of Oklahoma) were other famous outfits: the OX, the IOI, the Pitchforks, the VI's. Of these the last three worked the range together. The OX outfit is memorable in that one of its owners was Charles Gudgell, who brought to the ranch, in 1879, from Kansas City, nine bulls bought at the first public sale of registered Herefords held west of the Missouri River. The younger generation may need to be reminded that Charles Gudgell was the originator and developer of what is known as the "Anxiety strain" of Hereford cattle; a strain whose domination of its own breed, almost complete today, is without parallel, I believe, in the records of cattle breeding. From this strain the Dominos derive.

One of the early managers of the Prairie Cattle Company was my good friend, Colonel R. G. (Dick) Head, the well known Texan. It was during his term of management—around the middle '80's—that the company contracted 5000 of its long yearling heifers to go to central New Mexico. Dick moved them in two bunches, 2500 being Cross L's, and 2500, LIT's. Henry Miller was in charge, who later froze to death in the Sierra Grande with one of Dick's own herds in the great November snowstorm of 1889. Billy was with the Cross L herd. He says he never remembers a worse job than they had the first two or three days, getting those heifers to string out. But once road broke, they traveled nicely till they struck the Staked Plains. Before they had that waterless tract crossed things got fierce enough. Billy seems still to picture vividly the staring coats and hollowed flanks of the cattle; their eyes sunk deep in their heads. That distressful low moaning parched cattle make can still sound in his ears. There were times when the herds were strung out for five miles, the men scattered along their flanks. Then when the Pecos loomed up in front of them and the heifers sniffed water, every last man in either outfit was ahead of his herd and you could pretty near have thrown a rock across the cattle as they jammed and jostled each other to break loose to the river. Many and many a hundred head of good trail cattle, since Goodnight first broke the trail, had met death crowding down those steep banks of the Pecos.

The place of delivery was on the Hondo, about ten miles out from old Fort Stanton, right close to the Capitan mountains, and there the job of branding faced them. There was no chute and the boys had to rope and throw the entire herd of 5000. You'll agree with Billy that was some job.

He's a quiet-talking sort of fellow, this Billy Parsons. He makes his descriptions interesting because he is clear-minded and you feel they're true; but he doesn't ever try to "tell 'em scary." When he reached this point in his story he went on to say, without any change in his voice: "We were makin' delivery of the cattle to a man—you may have heard of him —"

"Tell me what his name was, Billy," I said feeling interested.

And Billy directed a quiet glance at me as he replied, "Pat Garrett!"

(I take it most all who read these lines know that Pat Garrett was the famous New Mexico sheriff who closed up the Lincoln County war and killed Billy the Kid.)

III

You may wonder why in a time like ours when one has to be in the headlines in order to count, I have given so much time to describing William Parsons, who certainly never got into the big type. My principal reason for doing so is that Billy's early experiences take us back to the most interesting period and phase of Western range history. Moreover his long employment with a famous company brought him into personal touch with a series of remarkable men, whose lives I shall presently deal with. I employed Billy at a time when my company was losing cattle heavily by stealing and he did good work for me over several years. Later on, he tells me, he lost his grip for a while and things went badly with him. Today at 84 he is living a quiet useful life in Southern California with his daughter, Carrie, a very competent and attractive young married woman.

I remember, too, in those days when Billy was riding for the Rafter C's often thinking that he was in many ways a typical cowboy. He is a little fellow, to be sure, never weighing more than 130 pounds, but his small stature showed to no disadvantage on horseback. Riding standing in his stirrups with straight leg, he had a peculiarly easy seat; and I don't recall a smoother worker in a herd. His grey eyes have to this day the steady gaze that comes into eyes that day by day have scanned the ever receding, far horizons of the prairie, and searched for stray brands in countless herds. One of his bronzed hollow cheeks shows a blue scar where a pistol bullet ripped through it. You can add to all this the quiet dignity and reserve, and the dry speech, that were elemental in that life of the range. Yes, I think that Billy Parsons, as I knew him, might stand for a type, not of the screen, but of the real, cowboy of the range days.

He had had a wide experience, too, had Billy. From Gonzales County, Texas, which is further south than Houston, he had worked across Texas and Oklahoma and Kansas to the line of Nebraska, up along the Beavers and the Republican; and from there across the broad plains of Colorado to the Rockies. Up north in Wyoming he knew the Laramie plateau, had driven team out of Rawlins, and made camp in the high regions of the Snake River around the Colorado line. Turning south again, those wide plains that divide the Arkansas from the Cimarron were familiar ground to him. He knew every inch of the mesa

regions from the Corrumpa to the Canadian, and had trailed
cattle across the Staked Plains, over the alkali flats of the Pecos
to the Capitans. It was a big country, and a stock country, over
which Billy learned the stock business.

It was part of the range system for every considerable cattle
unit to have one of its men riding with outlying wagons. His
function was to look out generally for his employer's stock,
brand up calves and carry along all cattle in the brand; eventually returning them to their own range. This was a responsible
job, as well as an interesting one: a fellow learned a heap of
country and met a lot of men. Billy Parsons was outside man
for the Cross L's for ten years.

After a man had ridden a number of years for one outfit he
got to know their horse herd pretty thoroughly. And if his
standing were good, he could probably pick him out a mount
to suit himself. Billy's string of horses was admitted to be the
best of any rider's in that country. His top horse was Cross A
Johnny. Cross A Johnny had been Dick Head's cut horse when
that well known cowman was running the Prairie outfit. Billy
says he could show Johnny a cow in a herd of three thousand,
throw the reins down on his neck, and Johnny would take her
out without ever a bobble. "And once," Billy continues with
rising voice, "once Johnny had her outside, there wasn't no
way in the world for that cow to get back into the herd, only
over or under him!"

Many of the large outfits at the time I'm writing of would
keep what was called a "floating outfit" of five or six men and
a cook, riding the range during the winter months. Its business
was to brand up late calves and such as had escaped the earlier
roundups. And later in the spring "pull bog" perhaps. The
creeks were apt to get pretty bad about the time the frost came
out of the ground. Billy was out with a Cross L floating outfit
one time when they made camp on an evening at Buffalo

Springs. These springs lie in the northwestern corner of Texas and were claimed at that time by the Prairie Company but later came within the XIT pasture.

They weren't more than settled down in camp when who should breeze in but a bunch of the ZH boys, from the Muscatine (Iowa) Cattle Company's ranch in the Neutral Strip, out on a similar hunt. It wasn't often two outfits met up like that on a winter work and you may be sure the boys chewed the rag till long after midnight. It was a bitter cold night and in the morning as quick as the cook had the fire started in the little rock hut, Billy ran over to wash and warm up. There was a bench standing just outside the hut and in his hurry, and half asleep, he stumbled over it, and as he fell his six-shooter jerked loose out of his hip pocket and went off, the ball passing through Billy's cheek and grazing the bone. It was a close shave but the wound proved only a flesh one and Billy tied a handkerchief around his head and started out for the ranch. "That was a bitter cold, and a long, ride," he'll tell you, "that sixty miles in the day to the Cross L headquarters, and before I got there I like to played out, bein' weak. I got off my horse and laid down a while once, but I made it to the ranch that night." That was how Billy got his bullet wound in the cheek; not in a gun fight as you may have supposed.

Indeed Billy doesn't seem to have had a great deal of luck with his gun. In his very first year he and another fellow were going with a trainload of Holstine's cattle from Kit Carson, Colorado, to Kansas City. At Topeka they were getting a cup of coffee at the eating house when the train started off on them. They ran and grabbed the first car and climbed on top. Livestock travel in those days of link and pin and short cars and unballasted roadbeds was not the de luxe affair it is today, and the top of a stock car, at its best, can do as many unexpected things as anything I know of, so as Billy essayed to jump from one car to another on his journey back to the caboose, he stumbled and his six-shooter jumped out and went off, cracking the bone of his leg and laying him up for a month at his home in Kansas City.

Billy will tell you a little coyly that he took a whirl at the sheep one time. Coming out of hospital at Laramie, Wyoming, after an operation, he struck the first person he met for a job. It happened to be a big sheepman, Bill Dailey. He asked Billy if he'd ever branded sheep and Billy said no, but he'd branded a world of cattle. So Dailey took him on and sent him over to his ranch near Rawlins. There they handed him a stamp brand and a pot of paint, and "I branded twenty thousand head of sheep runnin' through those chutes," he tells you. Nor would I swear that there isn't a ring of pride behind the words. After all, twenty thousand's a heap of sheep to brand.

When that was over Dailey gave him a team with a wagon and trailer loaded with supplies and Billy took them up one hundred miles into the mountain country around the upper Snake River to await the coming of the summer herds and take charge of the commissariat. That was the lonesomest time he ever put in in his whole life, he tell you, waiting for those sheep to arrive. "There'd be days on end I'd never see a living soul. I come pretty near believin' sometimes the only things in the world was me and those old mountains." Billy put in two years in Wyoming.

Theodore Luce is a name you often hear on Parsons' lips. Luce came from Lockhart, Texas, and he and Billy were partners in a bunch of cattle. He was foreman of the Cross L's and later on ran the OX wagon; a capable man and, to use Billy's favorite phrase, "afraid of nuthin'." One day in conversation with Billy I made mention of the Canadian River. Billy gave a little laugh. "O, the Old Canadian!" he said. Every old timer laughs and says that when you mention that notorious stream. "I remember once," he went on, "two Cross L wagons were workin' the north and south sides of the river. They wanted to send a message from one outfit to the other, but the Canadian was bank-high and a-bilin', and no one would take the message across. Luce, he swam the river with it, hisself. He was afraid of nuthin'."

Billy paused and then went on. "But he lost his life thataway later on. He was takin' an OX herd to Wyoming. When they got to the North Platte they found her in flood. Luce throwed the cattle in, but they started to drift down with the current. He wanted to try and stop them drifting so he jumped his horse off the high bank into the river. Both of 'em went down and out of sight. They come up presently and the boys throwed their ropes to Luce, but Luce, he never tried to get aholt of them. He acted kinda dazed like—the fellows thought his horse must have kicked him on the head when they went down the first time. The next time he went under he never come up. No, they never found his body."

In these simple, direct words Billy tells the story of his partner's death. And I believe he'd like me to hand on to you this tragedy of one of the old rivers they had to cross their herds over so often in those trail days, and which took so heavy a toll of their men. That phrase, too, Billy applies to Luce, "he was afraid of nuthin'," might well stand for Billy's epitaph for his long-dead friend. Because what it expresses—fearlessness in the face of danger—was the thing one cowboy demanded of another above all else. "God hates a coward," they used to say.

IV

During Billy Parson's long stay with the Prairie Cattle Company he worked under and knew well a number of general managers who were remarkable men. First among them comes to mind Murdo McKenzie. It is doubtful if any man ever lived who organized and administered cattle concerns on as comprehensive and successful a scale as this bluff-spoken, bearded Scot. After a short stay with the Prairie people he went, in 1891, to

the Matadors, another famous British company, operating in
Texas, Colorado, The Dakotas and Canada, and still in business
today with fifty-three thousand head of cattle in the panhandle
of Texas.

McKenzie came of that solid middle class to which belong
in the main the farmers and stockmen of Great Britain. Men
these are, with good general education and brought up to a
businesslike outlook upon life. Of this class, too, were W. J.
Tod, John Tod and John Clay, three other Scotsmen who were
associated with western cattle in a large way.* It is interesting
to contrast such men with some of the aristocratic youths who
engaged in ranching during the same period, more especially
in Wyoming. These young patricians, many of them raised
without any thought of depending on their own resources,
invested in the range cattle business because it was believed to
offer an easy road to a fortune, as well as providing opportunity
for sport: riding, big-game hunting; and such other outdoor
avocations as became a gentleman. I well remember in my
Oxford days how we under-graduates would discuss with
excited interest cattle ranching in Wyoming, and when I finally
decided to come out West, I told the girl I left behind me to
wait just a year or two till I'd made my fortune. She's waiting
still, I guess.

You could scarcely find a better example of this type of
Englishman than the Honorable George Montagu Bennet, son
of the Earl of Tankerville, who went out to Wyoming in the
early '80's. Handsome, splendidly built, trained in all outdoor
sports and considered one of the finest big-game shots in the
world, ex-officer of the British Army as well as Navy—here
was a figure to fit the atmosphere of adventure and romance
the world associated with Western range life. Yet, however

*They were big men physically, as well as in a business way, nearly all these
Scotsmen. My friend, the late T. R. Field of Denver, wrote me: I remember
once meeting Murdo McKenzie, John Clay and Donald McKie, walking down
17th. street together; and they took up the entire ten-foot sidewalk!

ornamental they may have been, neither he nor most of his class, I believe, contributed much to the real advance of the West. Perhaps their most useful work was the introduction of English Stallions—Cleveland Bays and others—to cross upon the northern range mares. There were, of course, many notable exceptions to this generalization: the Moncrieffs, old schoolmates of mine, still very much in business in Wyoming; Captain E. G. Austin and the Honorable William French in New Mexico; Colin Cameron in Arizona; the Rowe brothers in Texas and others one could readily name.

When the bubble of the cattle boom burst the Honorable George Montagu found himself at a loose end. He joined a circus and otherwise made a precarious living as a waiter in restaurants and by the use of a fine trained tenor voice. But his principal claim to distinction lies in his romantic pursuit across the entire States of a beautiful New York debutante whom he finally captured and made his wife. This charming lady, when her husband succeeded to the earldom, became the Countess of Tankerville, mistress of a famous medieval castle where my family and I, and other Americans, were always made welcome. This was Chillingham Castle, in whose spacious parklands runs a remarkable herd of original wild white cattle.

Thrifty Scot though Murdo McKenzie was, he was as prodigal of money for the improvement of the herds under him as Charlie Goodnight ever was. He was one of the earliest and staunchest supporters of the Hereford for the range, especially the Anxiety strains, and his Matador whiteface steers had a reputation over the entire west and Canada. The maximum cattle holdings of the company were about seventy thousand head.

But this solid Scot did not find sufficient scope for his ambitions in America. In 1911 he undertook the organization and management of a British company in Brazil. There his job was to stock with cattle a ten million acre pasture of a high grazing order, as well as establish a packing plant. Following his policy of breed improvement, he imported large numbers of Herefords, one of his shipments, containing five hundred animals, being the largest single exportation of registered cattle from America on record. Most of these cattle were bought from the famous million acre King ranch in southeastern Texas, in hopes of securing fever-proof cattle. But in spite of this and further immunization at the Texas Experiment Station, great losses were suffered. The Brazil fever tick is of a different species from our little Texas friend.

My sister-in-law, Mrs. Stanley McKellar (born Agnes Persefield at Goodnight, Texas, and a frequent childhood visitor in the Charles Goodnight home there) tells me how Murdo invited her to go out and take charge of his headquarters household at San Paulo. It was a generous offer he made her and Agnes was all for taking him up, but her father disliked her going away so far. Murdo happened in on Billy Parsons in a Denver restaurant one day and suggested his joining him, but Billy didn't. He took along with him, however, that handsome Irishman, Dick Walsh, who had done such fine work for Mrs. Adair on the famous Paloduro Ranch. But Dick didn't stay long in South America. He moved on to South Africa to organize and run, in Rhodesia, yet another vast British cattle concern. World adventurers, these British; organizing and civilizing as they go! Dick is dead a number of years ago. Murdo McKenzie passed away in Denver, in 1939, at the age of eighty-six. The Brazilian concern he organized is still in business with a hundred and fifty thousand head of cattle. And Murdo's son, John, holds forth at the head of the Matador office in Denver.

Another early general manager of the Prairie Cattle Company was "Colonel" R. G. (Dick) Head, Texan; perhaps the best known western range man of his day and reckoned the finest cowman. The legend of what the company paid him as salary was long recounted around every campfire in the West. It was reputed to be more than our United States Presidents then received; and that, in those simple times when big business was still young, was considered quite colossal. In spite of this, I don't believe the Prairie Cattle Company was open to the charge of reckless extravagance made against some of the early big companies. The JJ's had, perhaps, more buildings on the Picketwire than was needed, and Billy recalls that the checks the Cross L boys received their pay on were of as fine a material as a bank note and contained, each one, pictures of little Etta and Margaret, Dick's two baby girls. But they didn't employ more than a dozen men or so at the Cross L during winter, and around fifty on summer and fall work, which does not appear excessive for a company running a hundred and twenty-five thousand head of cattle.

A distinguished looking man was Dick Head with his square beard—growing grey when I knew him some years later. Tall, spare and straight backed; and possessed of as dry and ready a wit as ever I ran up against. After giving up his position with the Prairie people he ran cattle of his own in Union County. It was a herd of his, being shaped up for shipment, that was turned loose on the slopes of the Sierra Grande in the great November snowstorm of 1889, when Henry Miller, the herd boss, and Johnny Martin froze to death, and Charley Weir lost all his fingers but the thumb and fore-finger of one hand.

Some years later Head bought the Phoenix ranch near the little town of Watrous, twenty miles north of Las Vegas, New Mexico, on the Mora river. A charming property that, containing broken pasture lands on one side, and in the river flats wide irrigated alfalfa fields, beyond whose vivid green one could sight the Rocky Mountains, turquoise blue at forty miles distance. In the midst, beside a lake stocked with fish, stood the roomy, square home. Here the Colonel and his good lady, very much assisted by Etta and Margaret, now grown into elegant young ladies, product of an eastern girl's school, dispensed hospitality that had a touch of the South in it. I've spent some pleasant hours there. Dick was a busy, ambitious fellow, forever buying and selling stock on a large scale between New Mexico and another ranch he had in Kansas. But what had come freely, had gone freely, and like most of the pioneer cattlemen, Goodnight, Maxwell and the rest, he had little to leave his family when he died. Yet Dick left them his record: that of being a first-class cowman, and a straight-dealer. And that's a lot.

It's difficult to believe sometimes, as Billy and I sit and whittle, that the events he describes with such freshness took place, the earliest of them, sixty-four years ago. Even then Billy was twenty. That makes him eighty-four today. But I'll swear I can't see him changed a particle since he used to ride for me thirty-five years ago. And he says the same of me. That's a queer thing about cowpunchers, you know, and I have a theory regarding it, which is that the sun and the wind and dust after a certain time sort of pickles us fellers, so that from then on no further change comes about. What takes place when the final call comes to "shuffle off this mortal coil," has never been known with any certainty. My own belief is we just dry up and blow away.

# 3

## A Many-sided Gunman

I

STUART Lake divides the men who used the gun to kill, into two classes: the gun-fighter, and the gunman. But the thing is not so simple as all that. Several types existed. There was the bona fide peace officer, for whom a killing was an unavoidable proceeding incurred in the carrying out of his duty. Of this class Pat Garrett was a perfect example. There was the "killer," pure and simple; a psychopathic case, egocentric; unable to see anything but himself in the spotlight; such as Joe Fowler of Socorro, who could rip open a stranger's bowels because he refused to drink with him. A third class were perfectly good citizens when sober, but became dangerous when intoxicated. And alongside of all these came the gun-toter who brought imagination to bear upon his performances. For whom a gunplay or a killing was the accompaniment of a show, staged for the benefit of himself and the public. These were the humorists, the artists, of the gun, and by far the most remarkable I know anything about was Clay Allison of Colfax county, New Mexico, probably the most bestoried man in western annals.

There have been so many highly colored descriptions put forth of Allison's personal appearance that I am going to start in by telling you, as near as I can, what he really looked like. He was unusually tall, rather slim built and weighing around a hundred and seventy-five pounds. Though not what could be called handsome, he had strongly marked aquiline features and a great mass of black hair. Albert Shaw describes him as being active as a cat in spite of one leg shortened by a misadventure so that only the toes touched the ground. Stuart Lake paints him a great dandy, but Governor Otero tells me he was not particular about his dress; indeed, when drinking, he would get very slovenly, sometimes taking off his coat and vest and shirt. He seems to have enjoyed fighting whether with firearms or fists, and in either case the speed and accuracy of his hand and eye were phenomenal.

As for the short leg the legend ran—according to Governor Miguel Otero: *My Life on the Frontier*—that Clay had a deadly quarrel with an old friend back in the panhandle of Texas where his previous home and cattle ranch had been. It was agreed—on Allison's suggestion, one feels sure—that they dig a grave of the usual dimensions; that they sit down in it at opposite ends; and that at a given signal they attack each other with knives. The survivor to shovel the soil over the dead body of his opponent in the grave. Clay conquered and duly buried his rival, but he received a deep wound in the leg which left him crippled for the rest of his life. After this fight he moved away from Texas and established a new home and cattle ranch on the upper Canadian (or Red River) in Colfax County, New Mexico, about twelve miles out from Cimarron City.

Allison belongs also in the third class of gunmen I described. An attractive and reasonable fellow when sober, under the influence of liquor he became mean, as well as possessed with an utter recklessness and indifference to human life. His best friends at such times gave him the widest berth possible. The saloon keepers of several states were apt to close their doors when Allison on his black horse came down their front street on the run, letting out one of his famous war whoops at intervals.

The most famous and characteristic story that is told about him concerns the killing of "Chunk" Cooper, a notorious desperado with eleven notches on his gun, and sworn, some say, to "get" Clay Allison. The two met at a horse race in Clifton, New Mexico, got to drinking and quarreled. They agreed to fight it out on horseback. Dinner time, however, intervened and Chunk suggested they eat first, as he hated to send anyone to Hell with an empty stomach. Entering the dining room of the Clifton House they sat down opposite each other before bowls of soup, each with his six-shooter on his knees. No one really knows how the shooting started, but when it did start and Chunk raised his gun to fire, it hit on the edge of the table and the bullet went wild. That gave Allison all the chance he wanted; in the following instant he shot Chunk between the eyes. The dead man's head fell forward into his soup and Allison went on quietly eating his. When he had finished a full meal, relates Otero, "he arose and, taking the dinner bell from the shelf, went to the door and began to ring it vigorously, announcing: "Gentlemen, the proposed horse duel is now declared off, owing to an incident to one of the principals!' "

Probably the next most famous affair of Allison's was his killing of Pancho Griego, as tough and dangerous a man as the West could show even in that wild period of the '70's, in Lambert's bar in Cimarron. The versions given of it have been as numerous as inaccurate, so I am just going to hand you the story as I have it from my friend, George Crocker, who was raised in Cimarron and is the principal living authority on northeast New Mexico history. The episode is part of a larger story I intend to relate later on, so I will merely premise here, that in that fall of 1875 Pancho and Allison had each good reason to wish the other out of his path.

"Pancho started drinking then (says Crocker) and making threats against Allison. Not long after this Allison came in to Cimarron with a load of beef. Drove to Donahue's house, who lived on the southeast side of town and put up his team. Pancho lived near Donahue's.

"Allison started up town. It was just about sun down when he got almost in front of our house. He saw Pancho coming on his way home. Pancho had two men with him and one of them was supposed to be tough. Pancho was carrying a Winchester rifle as well as his six-shooter. As soon as Allison got close enough to recognize Pancho he threw his right hand on his six-shooter and put his left hand up and told Pancho to stop. He said, 'Pancho, you are better armed than I. You have the best of me.' All this time Allison had been edging towards a bank. Pancho said, 'Hold on there, Allison; I am not going to hurt you. Don't be afraid of me!' With these words Pancho threw the Winchester on the ground, walked up to Allison and they shook hands. As I have said, they met in front of our house and my father and mother stood on the porch.

"After they shook hands Pancho turned and told the two men that were with him to take the gun and go to his (Pancho's) house. Allison and Pancho started up town. When they got to Henry Lambert's saloon, there was no one in the barroom.* Lambert was in the kitchen getting supper. He served meals and did most of his own cooking. He heard someone come in the barroom and went in; Allison and Pancho were standing by the bar. They called for drinks and he waited on them. When they finished drinking Pancho said, 'Come here, Allison, I want to have a talk with you.' Pancho started across the room with Allison following. Lambert returned to the kitchen, and Allison followed Pancho, drawing his gun. When Pancho turned to speak Allison must have shot him through the temple, then went out the front door. Lambert heard the shot and rushed into the barroom and locked the front door. It was just about dark but he had not lighted the barroom yet. Pancho had slumped down behind the billiard table and Lambert did not see him until the next morning when he went to open up.

"That night mobs of armed Mexicans put in the night look-

*This Henry Lambert was a Frenchman, widely known as the proprietor of the famous Lambert Hotel and bar in Cimarron.

ing for Pancho. Allison made his way out of town on foot, maybe catching the stage which would take him past his brother, John's, ranch on the nearby Vermejo."

It is an almost invariable rule with Western biographers to paint their hero with all the virtues and no faults. In whatever situation he is placed, he is made to appear in the right; to be invariably successful and above all, brave. Sometimes the hero himself was adept at planning his "affairs" with this purpose in view. Allison was one such. In nine out of ten of his innumerable scraps and killings the generally accepted version gives him the best of the story. Take the case of Pancho. Almost all accounts, including Otero's, describe Allison as detecting Pancho maneuvering to get the drop on him behind a large sombrero with which he was fanning himself; whereupon Allison shot and killed him. Crocker's authentic story shows how far from the truth a popular version of an occurrence may be. Then again, practically all the stories I ever heard of the Chunk fight show Chunk trying to get a sudden advantage of Clay, and Clay shooting in self-defense. But Chunk was a man without fear. He had killed a tough nut, Charlie Morris, only a short while before in Cimarron and had taken no advantage of him, though he was in a position to do so. And Abe Severs, an ex-sheriff of Colfax County, who was a neighbor of Allison and had run with his gang, says there was but one witness present in the Clifton House dining room, a stranger, and that Allison took him home and gave him a job on his cow ranch. "These are some of the reasons I have," says George Crocker, "for believing that Allison killed Chunk and Pancho, not in self-defense, but because he was afraid of them. And few old timers will maintain that Allison had the iron nerve of men like Mace Bowman or Pete Burleson, who were sheriffs of that district and period; or for that matter, of Pancho himself. If Pancho had been sober,

more than likely it would have been Allison they carried out
of Lambert's saloon heels first, not Pancho!"

But nerve or no nerve, he laid 'em out, this Clay Allison.
No man ever pretended seriously to say how many men he
had killed. They were generally estimated at anywhere from
fourteen to twenty-one; "six of them frontier Marshals or
sheriffs," to quote one writer. A bad man from Bitter Creek,
all right. And yet of the considerable numbers of men and
women of my acquaintance who were his neighbors or who
knew him, I don't recall one who was not "to his faults a
little blind, and to his virtues very kind." Otero who knew
him well writes me about him: "I do not believe he ever
killed a man that didn't deserve it. Allison was a very likeable
fellow, and the public all liked him." And George Crocker
who criticizes him so severely on some points, ends by saying:
"I consider him one of the greatest characters that ever came
to New Mexico."

Clay Allison's character was a highly complex one. I will
try now and describe for you some circumstances that throw
interesting light on it.

II

Along in the '70's Colfax County, New Mexico, which is
the district I am writing about now, and Lincoln County,
became the resort of the most desperate characters of the
Southwest. It was probably Elizabethtown with her gold mines
that did most to attract them to Colfax county. Though Cimarron itself was tough, too. The cowboys of the district had a
standing difficulty with the townspeople. M. W. Mills says that
eleven men were killed in one saloon in one month. To make
matters worse the whole state of New Mexico was in the grip
of a powerful and unscrupulous political organization which
ran the elections and the courts to further their own selfish
ends and keep themselves in power. This organization was

known as the Santa Fe Ring and was supposed to be headed by Tom Catron, a transplanted Missouri lawyer; one of the ablest, most energetic and grasping public men in Western history. Historian Twitchell says of Catron: "He entirely controlled the Republican party in New Mexico; framed its policies, wrote its platforms, controlled its conventions, for nearly half a century." And during the early part of that period, I may add, dominated the courts.

There were, however, influential people who resisted the Ring and its evil doings and among the most fearless and aggressive of them in Colfax county was the Rev. F. J. Tolby, a Methodist minister serving a large district from Cimarron. On September 15, 1875, the Rev. Tolby was found dead with two bullet holes in his back on the mail road from Cimarron to Elizabethtown. The murder caused general indignation. It was universally held to have been planned and paid for by members of the Ring. Even the Governor of the state, S. B. Axtell, was suspected of being implicated. But the elected sheriff of the county had just resigned, and Sheriff Rinehart who had been appointed by the Governor was in sympathy with the Ring; and it became clear that the forces which engineered the murder were powerful enough, and determined, to prevent prosecution of the two actual assassins, whose identity seems to have been perfectly well known from the start.

At this point the Rev. O. P. McMains, who had succeeded Tolby in the ministry at Cimarron got Clay Allison interested in the case. Allison gathered up a few neighbors. They went and got Cruz Vega, one of the two assassins, who had carried the Elizabethtown mail on the day of the murder, took a confession from him and hanged him to a tree. Then a warrant was sworn out for Manuel Cardenas, the other suspected culprit, and Allison, appointed a deputy, served it on him at Taos, and brought him to Cimarron to be tried before a Justice of the Peace. The story goes that Allison attended the trial, but shortly before the case closed was noticed to have left the courtroom. It was already dark when Charlie Hunt and another deputy started to conduct the prisoner from the courthouse back to the jail. They hadn't gone far when there arose from somewhere, directly in their path, a tall man. He drew a pistol and shot the prisoner between the eyes. It was not possible in the dark to identify his features, but his height and lameness left little doubt as to who it was. At this point my friend George Crocker, whose account of the affair I am following closely, offers a comment on the situation. "The people of Colfax County," he says, "should have erected a monument to the memory of Clay Allison."

Allison was no respecter of persons. Having settled with the two paid culprits in the case, as well as—as I have previously recounted—Pancho Griego, who seems also to have been implicated, he turned his attention to the higher-ups. At daybreak one fine morning he rode into Cimarron at the head of about twenty extra well armed men. They were looking for Dr. Longwill, a well known physician, who was supposed to have handled the money in the case, and for Mills and Donahue who had the handling of the mail carriers on the mail route. The doctor had fled and Allison, pursuing him alone, caught up with him near Fort Union, attended by a body guard of United States soldiers. What took place between the two is not known, but the upshot was that the doctor turned back headed for Santa Fe, and Clay returned to Cimarron. What might have happened if Clay had caught up with the doctor before he secured his Ft. Union escort can only be conjectured.

This activity on Allison's part, however, brought reprisals. It is said that a reward of five hundred dollars was offered for him, dead or alive. However this may have been, the Governor provided a detachment of U. S. soldiers to help Sheriff Rinehart arrest him at his ranch on Red River. Surrounding the ranch they took him and brought him to Cimarron where he was bound over to the Grand Jury in Taos, court having been moved there on account of the turbulent condition of Cimarron. When court time came they tell how Allison, journeying to Taos, accompanied by a little band of his friends, was overtaken by Sheriff Rinehart, thither also bound, driving in a sulky and wearing a hard-boiled hat. That was the sort of situation Allison knew how to make the most of. He stopped Rinehart and said: "Mr. Sheriff, I was your prisoner a few weeks ago, now you are mine!" Then he made Rinehart mount his, Allison's, horse while he got into the sulky, wearing the Sheriff's hard-boiled hat. And so they traveled, Clay laughing and joshing the while, till they got near to Taos. The jury found a true bill against Allison, but he being surrounded by his friends, and Rinehart not having his troops, there was no show to make an arrest. Allison came home an outlaw, and an outlaw in fact he remained for the rest of his life. But no further effort to arrest him was ever made and within a few years he moved to another part of the state.

An old friend of my family, Mrs. Annie Crocker Kingman of Topeka, Kansas, writes me at this point as follows. "When the Rev. Tolby was murdered my mother, Mrs. Crocker, brought Mrs. Tolby and her two children to our home in Cimarron, and kept them till they went East. Allison sent word he wanted to come and see Mrs. Tolby. She was timid about facing the famous gunman and asked my mother to go into the room with her. My mother said Allison was 'kind and gentlemanly as could be,' asked Mrs. Tolby if he could help her financially. He gave her a roll of bills; I don't remember how much it was. Told her he would do all he could for her and not to hesitate to call on him."

Allison had come to Texas from the deep South and un-doubtedly brought with him that Southern respect for women which the Western cowboy was to inherit. My friend, Albert Shaw, describes a cowboy dance they gave at Raton, which he and his wife attended. Clay was there. He was a man of good address and manners and Shaw brought him up to where his wife was and presented him. Later on Mrs. Shaw remarked to her husband: "Who was that nervous man you introduced me to a while ago. He actually blushed when I spoke to him and was far too shy to talk to me. Who on earth was it?" "Oh, that fellow?" queried Shaw, "that was Clay Allison. He's killed fourteen men!"

But, along the lines of his relations with women, I like best of all the story Otero tells about how this "killer" went back to his old home in Louisiana and married his childhood sweetheart and brought her to New Mexico; to the new ranch on Blackwater in the lower Pecos Valley, to which he had moved shortly after the above described events. And how from that time on Clay became a changed man, indulging in no more drunks or escapades or gunplays. Otero entertained the bridal couple as they passed through Las Vegas on their way to the ranch.

It is interesting to chronicle that the repercussions from the murder of this Methodist minister were so powerful that Governor Axtell was removed from office by President Hayes. The territorial Governors and other Presidential appointees of those days were not generally selected for any reasons of fitness, but to reward political services. Governor Axtell was an Ohian, who had previously acted as Governor of Utah and as a member of the legislature of California. A sort of political carpetbagger, it would seem. It is said that as he left New Mexico on his removal as Governor he traveled in a Government ambulance and crossed the Cimarron river at the old Holbrook crossing, thereby avoiding Cimarron City by eighteen miles. And when the news of his removal finally reached Cimarron, the inhabitants of the little burg celebrated the entire night.

It is no more than justice to Governor Axtell to record that four years after this he was returned to New Mexico as Chief Justice of the northern district. In this capacity he proved himself a man of indomitable courage and high integrity. When Judge Axtell held session Mr. Tom Catron no longer controlled the court.

### III

I sometimes wonder why western writers have not concerned themselves oftener with that famous tract of northeastern New Mexico land known as the Maxwell Grant, within whose spacious area of two million acres most of the events I have been lately describing took place. Undoubtedly it is the finest body of land, if you consider its wealth of grazing, its endless supply of water, its mines and timber, in the entire Southwest. This is not the place to dwell at length upon the interest and romance of its history. Granted by the Mexican Government jointly to Guadalupe Miranda and Carlos Beaubien, it came into sole possession of Lucien Maxwell, the famous frontiersman, who married Beaubien's daughter, Luz, and bought out all the interests. Maxwell was a simple, rough-and-ready fellow, an incurable lover of the plains and mountains, but with the great wealth which poured in on him from his flocks and herds and gold mines, he built himself a sumptuous home on the Cimarron, around which the town of Cimarron was later built. There he lived in royal style. Places were laid daily for over two dozen guests, who sometimes ate off solid silver plate. There came to visit him all the notables of the West. He had his own race course, stables to accommodate seventy-five horses and corrals, with solid adobe walls eight feet high, that held several thousand head of cattle.

Maxwell sold his grant in 1871 to a group of men of whom one was Wilson Waddingham, long owner of the equally famous Montoya Grant, better known as the Bell Ranch, lying some eighty-five miles, as the crow flies, to the southeast. After a short while the Maxwell passed to an English company and later to a Dutch one.

I never knew a Spanish grant that was not infested by squatters. Before the Court of Private Land Claims was set up by the Government in Denver in 1891 neither were the titles of most grants confirmed nor their boundaries definitely established. Agitators too there always were to induce land-hungry people to contest the claims of the grant owners, and to preach the inherent right of every American citizen to settle on any piece of ground he found not completely occupied. Far up in the northeast corner of the Maxwell Grant, near the Colorado line, lie some rich lands around Sugarite Creek, and there in the fall of 1874 a band of farmers from the Middle West moved in and established farms. Possibly with a view to driving these trespassers away, the grant owners rented the land to Fine Ernest, a wealthy cowman who owned and ran a string of brands around Deer Trail in Colorado, between the Kansas Pacific Railroad and the South Platte.* The three thousand head of cattle Ernest turned loose on the Grant played havoc with the settlers' young crops in the spring. The latter defended themselves by dogging the cattle and finally turning their shot guns on them. This incensed Fine and he swore out warrants against twenty-five of them to appear in court at Cimarron. The settlers duly appeared. The Prosecuting Attorney was Tom Catron, whose court tactics were notorious. The case was deferred day after day, the settlers meantime fretting over their families left at the mercy of raiding Indians, and unused to Western life.

At this juncture Clay Allison became interested. Although a big cowman himself, and renting pasture from the grant, and although, it may be remarked, the cattlemen at this period

*I am indebted for much information about brands to my friend Lamar Moore of Clovis, N. M. who has compiled an interesting and authentic record of early brands over the entire range country.

were riding on the crest of the wave and running things generally with a high hand, he seems to have decided that the settlers and their families were not getting a fair deal. When the second Saturday came around and no release for them, he visited their camp and told them to pack up and get ready to start for their homes on the following Monday.* He offered no explanation. Later in the day, however, he met Fine Ernest and sauntering up remonstrated with him on the injustice being done to the settlers by the repeated postponent of their trial. He received no satisfaction from the cowman, whereupon he drew his gun, rapped Fine over the head with it, and after a little appropriate profanity remarked, "now, take my advice, you dirty cur, and don't let the sun go down on you in this town. Sabe?" That was Saturday. On Monday morning the settlers were summoned to the courtroom, put under bond to appear in court later, and released to go back to their lands and families.

And there is another story that illustrates at one stroke a whole group of Allison's characteristics. In those early range days, before movies came and when there were but few theatres, the principal evening entertainment was dancing, and dances were quite frequent. One night Clay and his brother John, presented themselves at a dance in Los Animas, a town in Colorado on the Arkansas, and got gloriously drunk. They insisted at the point of their pistols on making everybody dance and otherwise disturbing the proceedings. An appeal for help was sent out and Sheriff John Spear hastened to the scene with his deputy, Charlie Faber. Immediately on opening the door of the hall, Faber, who was in the lead, started shooting and wounded John Allison. The instant Clay saw his brother fall he opened up with his 45, his first shot killing Faber. At this point Spear seems to have retired. "Then,"

*I am following here the account of this affair given by George W. Coe, who was an eye-witness, in his *Frontier Fighter* (Houghton Mifflin Co.).

to quote Governor Otero, "Clay walked to the door where the body of Faber lay and, taking the dead man by the hair, dragged him to where his brother John lay wounded on the floor, remarking, 'John, this is the damned son of a ———— who shot you. I got him all right; so don't worry. You'll get well soon.'" Then he knelt down beside John and the bystanders remarked that as he bent over his brother's body, this gun-toter, who had just added another sheriff to his long list of killings, was crying like a child.

Allison was always putting on a "show" of some kind, and doubtless in those days when the horse played so great a part in Western life, his favorite horse had a share in catching the imagination of the people. Jet black and very shapely he was, and Otero, to whose father's store in the little town of Los Animas Clay would often come, says he never tied him up when he went into a saloon, just turned him loose to graze. When he wanted him he would go out onto the stoop and whistle, and the black horse would come running.

But it would never do to overlook the part that Allison's perennial sense of humor played in tempering the public's opinion of him. I am convinced it covered a multitude of his sins. No better illustration of it to my mind, can be found than Otero's epic of Allison and the doctor's hat. Good Dr. Menger, who held forth in Moro, affected a stovepipe hat. Now it seems there was nothing in the world that irritated Allison more than the sight of a stovepipe hat. So he loaded up a sawed-off gun with birdshot and as the Doctor passed the saloon he was in one day he rushed out and, holding the muzzle of the gun close to the offending hat, blew it to pieces. Then, he took the Doctor to a store and bought him a good Stetson.

I cannot recall my authority for the tale that Allison rode his horse one day into the courtroom of a judge and ordered the judge to adjourn court till he got out of town and that the judge complied. Or for the legend that he was once made foreman of a grand jury and that he kept the whole jury drunk for days, transacting meanwhile no business of any kind and paying for the liquor out of the county funds. His practical jokes were callous enough, sometimes, as when a dentist pulled the wrong tooth for him. He went back to his office, tied him down and extracted six of the dentist's teeth. I like better the one about the Cimarron *News and Press*. That sheet had published something Clay disapproved of, so he and some of his gang visited the office, broke up the press and threw it into the Cimarron river. It turned out to be a sacrilegious act because the press was none other than the one good Padre Martinez had brought to Taos in 1873, the first printing press to enter New Mexico. But the best part of the story is that these roysterers, discovering the latest issues of the *News*, took possession of them and went around town selling them at twenty-five cents apiece.

The fact that Clay knew how to take his own medicine helped him too with the public. One time in Trinidad Frank Cattlin, then just a boy, happening into the saloon where Allison was drinking, Clay made him dance at the point of the gun till he was played out. A little later Clay was surprised to find the boy at his side again, this time with a gun. Frank stuck the gun into Allison's ribs. "Now," he said, "*you* dance!" And Allison did, till his poor game leg gave out altogether. But he got the joke and, laughing, declared the boy had taught him a lesson. And I will close my line of humorous instances with a very brief one which Albert Shaw tells with great gusto about the occasion when the Government sent a detachment of colored soldiers to Cimarron to help suppress some disturbance or other. Shaw relates that as soon as Allison heard about it, he came over from his ranch and ran the whole detachment out of town. He said they were interfering with the authority of the sheriff.

Allison moved from the Maxwell Grant and settled near Roswell in the southeastern part of New Mexico, a few years before his marriage. One day he was hauling out a load of lumber from Roswell to his ranch. Going down a steep grade, his lame leg missed the brake, the brake shot loose, and the heavy wagon ran onto the horses. Clay was pitched off and run over by the wheels of the wagon and killed.

And yet even here in the very hour of his death, legend, that had ever been busy with his adventurous career, steps in again. Legend, which is the expression of what the people, the "folks" think and say of a man or woman, whether Greek Ulysses, or English Robin Hood, or Joan of Arc in France, or Clay Allison of our own American Southwest. The following story appeared in print about the time of Allison's death, and Joe Nash, a well known cowman of that district repeated it long after to George Crocker, so it clearly had currency. It relates that Allison left Roswell one day in a buggy and overtook an old man driving a four-horse team with a heavy load of lumber. Stopping him, he said to the old man, "Look here! You're too old to be driving that heavy load. Let me drive your team and do you get into my buggy." So the old man got into the buggy and Allison took the team, and the team ran off going down a hill and Allison was pitched off, the heavy wagon running over him.

The old man came up as quickly as possible to where Allison lay, mortally hurt; and when he got up to him, Clay said to him, "Old man, pull off my boots!" And the old man pulled them off. Then Allison exclaimed, "Ha, Ha! my enemies always prophesied I would die in my boots. But I have fooled them!" And with that he died.

And that is the legend, the folk-story, of the death of Clay Allison.

# 4
## Grama and Buffalo Grass in Colorado

THERE have been endless books written in late years about
the men who handled cattle in the early days of the West,
but the saga of the sheepman is still unwritten, as far as I
know. I take it that this popularity of the cow business over
the sheep business in modern literature is primarily due to the
fact that the cowboy carries on his business on horseback,
whereas the sheepherder goes afoot. So in old times the knight
and his charger got all the press notices and the favors from
the ladies, while the pikemen, who operated on foot, remained
unnoticed (and did the solid work.) Even to this day the caval-
ryman gets the plums: witness General John J. Pershing.

Yet in past periods from time immemorial the shepherd has
been a principal theme of story and song. The *Eclogues* of Greek
Theocritus and Roman Virgil, telling of shepherds and shepherdesses and their loves, were but expansions of Greek folk-
songs that originated in primeval times. Since the days of the
*Eclogues,* and framed along their lines, pastoral poems and romances have flourished in Europe periodically and been highly
popular, the subject, always, the shepherd tending his flock—
and looking out for the shepherdesses. While the cattleman,
until the recent eczema of western cowboy romances, has seldom
figured in poem, play or story.

I think it will be generally admitted that the breeding and
handling of this combination wool-mutton machine which we
term a sheep, calls for greater intelligence and observation than
the raising of cattle. Certainly some of the most intelligent men
I ever knew were shepherds, especially those from Scotland.

In Australia and New Zealand the sheep owner is IT in the public imagination. And as for romance, the New Mexico sheep herders who drove their herds from Albuquerque to the fair at Chihuahua a hundred and fifty years ago, or who grazed them in the '70's clear across to the Paloduro Canyon in Texas, faced dangers from flood and bandit and Indian as great as any cattle drover. Some of the old sheep *mayor-domos* I have known were men of great character, resourcefulness and courage. Yet, as I said before, the saga of the Western sheepman remains unwritten.

Certainly the prejudice against sheep among cattlemen in early days was very strong. I think it came to us from the Texans, from whom we derived our range practice and much of our tradition. The Texan associated sheep with Mexicans, and from the day of the Alamo for many years nothing Mexican looked good to the Texan. Furthermore, with the exception of certain localities controlled at an earlier date by Spanish-Americans who owned large herds of sheep, and the Mormon territory, practically the whole range country owed its early permanent settlement and development to the cowman. E. S. Osgood has shown how his trail, roundup and brand systems, voluntary at first, but gradually settling into the legal framework of the land, represented the first bona fide politico-social systematic organization effected within territories whose governmental set-up was weak, corrupt and almost wholly self-seeking. The cowman felt he had a right to call the country a cattle country and to regard the sheepmen as intruders. Irritation was increased by the fact that just when the cattlemen could believe their long continued efforts had succeeded in stabilizing the livestock business of the range country, sheep from California and Oregon were poured in on them in hordes. It spelled chaos—and war.

Of course today the prejudice against sheep has largely passed and numbers of cattle owners also run sheep. But even well before the present century opened the prejudice was not so great as to prevent some cattlemen all over the West from adopting sheep in whole or part. One of these was F. D. Wight, whose Cross F (connected) DW brand was known far and wide in northeastern New Mexico. As widely known as his brand was old F. D. W. himself. He declared he went into the sheep business "in self defense." Certain it is that the range where his cattle ran became a great stronghold for sheep: the Californians, Otto and Schleter, alone ran fifty thousand head from Clayton to the Sierra Grande.

A notable "character" was old man Wight. Mighty rough-tongued, even for those days; but my brother-in-law, Stanley McKellar, who night-herded his remuda for him for two years and got to know him well, calls him kind-hearted, and good to anyone he took a fancy to or who served him aright. His most widely known characteristic, however, was his tight-fistedness. Everyone around Folsom knew his buckskin horse, Hyena, with black mane and tail, which the boys would leave tied up to a hitching post in town so the old man could ride out to the ranch and not have to hire a rig, the times he came in on the train from his home in Trinidad. These visits were pretty frequent, for he could never be brought to put any trust in his men. As familiar as Hyena was the figure of F. D. W. himself crouched on the store steps over a lunch of sardines and crackers that saved buying a twenty-five-cent meal at the restaurant. He kept all his hands, cattle and sheep alike, on scanty rations. One time a deputation from his roundup wagon came to see him and tell him the boys would like to have some prunes in camp. "Prunes!" exploded the old man, "What the Hell do you want with prunes? Don't I kill my own beef for you, and give you white flour and beans and sowbelly? And you ask for prunes! To Hell with ye, ye high-headed, cigareet-smoking sons of ——!" And the old man got away with it. The boys got no prunes.

He never made any bones about it. He'd say to Stan, to whom he used to confide sometimes: "You know, Stan, my boy, there's nuthin' on earth I enjoy so much as savin' a dollar." He saved them to the tune of a million or so, they relate. It is related, further, that his boys to whom he left most of it, got as big a kick out of spending it as the old man had gotten out of saving it. It's not often in life things work out as satisfactorily as that.

There were other reasons besides self-defense for switching over from cattle to sheep. The lure of the "golden hoof" was one of them. By and large, sheep made more money for the range man than cattle. Take the case of T. P. James of Clayton, New Mexico. James was a native of Texas, and by virtue of that and the grace of God—which in Texas are the same thing—a cattleman and a Democrat. He ran the well known Flying A brand, made with an open A, the wings extending outwards, right and left, from the tips of the A. A right pretty brand and easily made, one would have hated to give up using.

But James was no sentimentalist. On coming to New Mexico he announced that he was in the stock business for whatever money there was in it; and reaching the conclusion there was more of it in sheep than in cattle, he switched over quite cheerfully to the wooly boys. Those were the days when our two great political parties were playing the game of shuttlecock with the tariff. When the Republicans got in they put on heavy tariffs, while the Democrats tried to get elected by promising to take them off. Wool was the focal point in tariff legislation for the Westerner. Carrying the principles which had guided him in the matter of business into the sphere of politics, James let it be known that, Texas or no Texas, whatever party put an import duty on wool was his party. This implied becoming a good Republican, and boosting McKinley and Roosevelt and Taft, who successively represented in the White House during that era the Party of Prosperity. This James did with a will, and truth compels me to relate that these proceedings resulted successfully. His sheep made him money, and with them, some remaining cattle, and other interests he became one of the important men of northeastern New Mexico.

It would be difficult, indeed, to find a lovelier home or one more typical of the western range country, than his headquarters ranch at Willow Springs. This cluster of springs forms the source of the Corrumpa Creek, which, fringed with willows and cottonwoods, wends its way through a wonderful shortgrass country eastwards to Oklahoma. Here James lived, faithful, at any rate, to one time-honored Texas custom to the last. The latch-string of his house hung ever outside, and every guest, neighbor or stranger, was made to feel as if it were his own home.

Charlie Springer of Cimarron was another cowman of a pioneer family who took up the sheep business, in partnership with A. A. Jones, lawyer of Las Vegas, and later distinguished U. S. Senator from New Mexico, running twenty thousand head around Turkey Canyon and the Corrumpa in Union County, New Mexico. Both good men, these; I knew them well. Across the Colorado line on the wide range lying between the Cimarron Seco and the Arkansas River, Stinson Brothers, who ran the horseshoe nail brand, shifted over to the woolies on a big scale.

## II

I'm going to tell you something about that great stretch of country lying between the Arkansas River and the Cimarron, and about some of the folks that had stock there thirty or forty years ago. For there wasn't, probably, a grander piece of grazing land in the west. As my story runs along, you'll likely find me mentioning pretty frequently my brother-in-law and old friend, Stanley McKellar, whose big frame occupied some fifteen cubic feet of the scenery of that region for twenty-two years. So partly for that reason, and because Stan is a nice sort of fellow for anybody to know, I'm going to introduce him to you at once by telling you how come he was ever in those parts, not being native thereto.

Stan left his mother's ranch near Wagon Mound, New Mexico as a kid of eighteen, to work for that pioneer cattleman, the late Ed Mitchell, whose herd of registered Herefords on the Tequesquite is known throughout the west. Ed's son and successor, Albert Mitchell, is now general manager of the great Bell Ranch, about which I've told you so much in previous pages, as well as being past president of the American Stockgrowers Association. At the time I'm writing of, Ed terminated a land lease he had with one Fred Burch, and Burch had to move his cattle. He started north with them, pointing for East Waterhole which is at the head of Coldwater Creek in No Man's Land, now the panhandle of Oklahoma, grazing them all the way through, over the whole summer. Stan went with them and continued working for Burch. One day he drifted into Kenton, which is the most westerly town in No Man's Land, and close to the corners of New Mexico and Colorado; and there on the front and only street of that city he achieved fame throughout those regions at a single stroke. As he rode along he noticed fifteen dollars lying on the ground. He got off and picked it up and, being an honest lad, turned it in to the hotel clerk, thinking its owner might call for it. And sure enough, a few days after, in walked that well known Texas cowman, Jack Potter, who ran cattle in those parts then, enquiring if anyone had seen fifteen dollars he had dropped. The clerk told him about Stan, and as he took over the dollars, Jack remarked that he'd like to know from what part of the country that young feller come; "because" he added, "he sure don't belong around here!"

The stretch of country I'm writing about reaches from Trinidad, Colorado to the line of Kansas, a distance of about one hundred and twenty-five miles. The creeks in it that run north into the Arkansas, after you leave the Picketwire canyon, flow pretty near the surface of the surrounding plains, but I have described elsewhere how those that flow south grow into deep and rugged ravines where they break through the caprock of the Dry Cimarron, affording fine shelter for stock. Above this caprock several long mesas stretch: the Mesa de Maio, Tecolote Mesa and Carrizo, (Spanish names these, which signify in English the month of "May," "owl," and "reed grass.") from whose northern base the reader may picture a seemingly endless sweep of prairie, without break of any kind at the Kansas end, but, towards Trinidad, threaded by a strip of Juniper breaks known as "the Cedars." Rich stands of buffalo and grama thirty years ago covered the entire tract except for a strip of sandhills along the south edge of the plains where out of a close sod rose sand-grass tall enough so you could pass your fingers through the tips of it a-horseback. Not an early grass this, but strong growing, and mighty useful feed, especially in heavy snows. Sounds altogether like a good stock country, don't you think?

As for the cattle on it, it was JJ and all JJ,* ranging out from their headquarters ranch on the Picketwire Creek which started north of the Cedars and joined the Arkansas at Fort Lyons. The original cattle which the Prairie Cattle Company had bought from the Jones Brothers had already been improved by those pioneer cattlemen by the use of Shorthorn bulls in the '70's; but as the country stocked up, it was found impracticable under the open range system to continue grading up, so the JJ's went into steers. A further reason alleged for this change was the skill and activity with the short rope of the neighboring No Man's Landers, the which had a depressing effect upon the calf brandings of the company. Indeed the OU canyon of those parts got its name from the fact that a gentleman who lived in it conceived the bright idea of con-

*The actual brand of this outfit was JJ "up and down." JJ inverted on left side, and JJ erect on left hip.

verting the JJ into OU (try it!) and was five hundred head
of cattle to the good before the company caught on.

With forty to fifty thousand four and five year old steers
ramping around, it was impracticable for anyone to run breeding cows in that district, and cattlemen either got out or went
over to sheep. Among the latter were the Stinson brothers,
John and James, originally from Harrington, Texas.* They
bought forty-five thousand head of good sheep from Macintosh
Brothers, Scotsmen and real sheepmen, whose headquarters
ranch was on the Carrizo, above the main springs which the
Prairie Cattle Company owned. Stanley McKellar, experienced
sheepman as well as cowboy, went to take charge.

The Stinson brothers ran the Horseshoe Nail brand. In case
you should want to know how that brand is made, I will
explain that it consists of a horseshoe with the heels downwards,
and a short bar sticking out half way up either side at right
angles, connected, which represents the nails. These brothers
had the Texas habit of thought and action. There was an FDW
puncher of the name of Sam Collins had started a little bunch
of sheep on his ranch about twenty miles away from the Stinson headquarters where Jimmy, who handled the range end of
the partnership, lived. Jimmy wanted a herd of sheep sent
over to run Sam out. Stan told him the first herder who tried
to crowd Sam, or anyone else, off his own range, would get
his time. "Well, well," said Jimmy, "run things your own
way!" They were good sorts, both those two big Texans, says
Stan.

Progressive fellows, too. Where the saving Scots they had
bought out, used five or six windmills to supplement their
natural watering places, the Stinsons had over forty. They were

*Jim Stinson was a pioneer cowman. In 1883 he had trailed a big herd from
the plains of Texas past historic Fort Sumner to the rolling mesas of the
Estancia valley in central New Mexico. The Stinson Trail was taken up and
continued across the Rio Grande through the tough town of Magdalena into
Arizona by the Slaughter Brothers, widely known Texas cattlemen.

WOLVES AND THEIR PREY

probably the first, as well, in that district to introduce the mutton cross on their eight pound Rambouillet ewes.

The coyote pest on these ranges at that time was a serious one. Although the grey, or lobo, wolf is infinitely more destructive to cattle than the coyote, the latter, by and large, can do more damage among sheep than any wild beast I know. Of wolves there were but few, but McKellar, who was an experienced hunter, killed two hundred and fifty coyotes in his first two or three months with Stinson. He and his brother, Harry, had had packs of dogs over in Union County, New Mexico when Stan was running the Springer and Jones sheep and Harry, the Otto and Schleter outfit. Stan had picked his best seven dogs out of thirty, to bring with him to Colorado. The boys' hunts, apart from their practical use, had been very popular with outsiders. Townspeople from Clayton and Folsom would come out on Sundays and attend them. The Colorado and Southern Railroad big shots took up the tune and would bring out a dining car and a string of dogs from Trinidad to try and beat the range fellows, the latter providing them with horses. People who have never taken part in a horseback hunt wonder where folks find all the excitement. But I may point out that the "chase" is one of the oldest forms of sport. Early art extant portrays hounds pursuing wild animals, accompanied by hunters. All the medieval kings had their royal forests for hunting the wild boar or stag with horse and hound. And today in England the fox-hunt is still a national sport.

There was a cowpuncher around those parts called Dudley Walker, who was kind of pernickety about his cowhorses. One afternoon he happened past just as Stanley was starting on a hunt alone, and Stan asked him to come along. "Ner," Dudley replied; "I got sumthin' better to do than chouse my horses after them dam kyotes!" However he followed along and presently the dogs sprung a coyote. Stan was too busy to notice his companion at first, but after a while he glanced back, and "there come Dudley just a 'foggin', bent over the horn of his saddle, and wrapping his quirt around his top cutting horse every time his hoofs hit the prairie!" After killing their prey they rode on a while quietly. Finally, Dudley sidled up to Stan: "Say, Stan," he said, "was you thinkin' of tryin' for another o' them kyotes this evenin'?"

The breeding of those dogs was an interesting problem. A cross between the greyhound and the staghound was the most usual method. The greyhound supplied the speed, the "stag" the "guts." But out of around two hundred dogs raised by the McKellar boys, two only could run down an antelope. Once "Queeny" or "Fly" got good and ready, Stan says, either of them could jump onto an antelope as if he was standing still, stringing him by the ham and then going for the neck. Stan agrees with me he has never known a horse could run onto an antelope. My old friend, Joe Holbrook, fiery little ex-Indian scout, used to tell me about his horse, Spider. If ever Spider got within a hundred yards of an antelope, that antelope was my meat, he'd declare. Well, I was in the habit of believing what Joe told me, but I will remark that Spider must have been a good horse. My own top horses used to look pretty good till I started to get down my rope. About that time the antelope would invariably give two good jumps and bring the proceedings to a close by disappearing over the nearest horizon.

Voracious appetites these hounds had. I recall one purebred greyhound we had on our own ranch, Bracelet by name, and as elegant and innocent looking a little lady as you ever set eyes on. One day my wife was entertaining a number of friends to dinner and had a big roast prepared for them. She set it on the dining table and stepped out to bring in her guests. But on returning with them to the room, lo, the platter! but no roast. Neither it nor Bracelet were anywhere to be seen.

One day some of Stan's dogs on the Carrizo ate up a number of eggs and chickens belonging to a neighbor. The next time he passed the neighbor's house, the good lady came out at him with all sails set. Stan, however, is not the sort of fellow it's easy to get a rise out of. Riding by without stopping he called out: "That's nothing to worry about, Mrs. MacArthur! The dogs eat up our eggs and chickens all the time, too. But" he added cheerfully, "I never known it do them a particle of harm!"

The experience of most livestock breeders that any success in breeding they may have had was due mainly to one animal or strain of blood, was repeated in the case of these plains dogs. The foundation of the McKellar pack was old "Vic," who had been brought up by Bob Miller from somewhere in Texas. Not only was her progeny successful, but she herself ran true for many years. When she began to get old and felt herself too stiff to run, she used to raise herself up and look around, note where the coyote was heading for—and cut across!

### III

If I wanted to mention to some old-timer from that Dry Cimarron country a man he'd be sure to have known, I'd never hesitate in naming Alec McKenzie. Alec was a brother of Murdo, the well known Scottish-born cattleman, and started life in the West riding for the Cross L division of the Prairie Cattle Company, which Murdo managed. Then he got staked—probably by Murdo—with ten thousand head of sheep, which he ran from a ranch on the Cimarron. His was one of the best ranches on the river. He took out a ditch and had a hundred acres of fine alfalfa.

Alec McKenzie was a man of fine appearance, six foot two in height and powerfully built. He was an easier man than his brother, Murdo, to meet, less bluff and direct, and had a world of friends. Open house was the daily order at his ranch, Mrs. Gross, Irish wife of John Gross who worked so long for

McKenzie, catering for his guests, a full table day in and day out. Indeed, this good lady became as widely known as Alec himself. A right kind-hearted soul she was, but of a free mode of speech that sometimes startled strangers. They tell how one evening a gentleman of considerable standing from the East, traveling through the country, found himself benighted at Alec's ranch. Approaching the house and seeing a woman—who happened to be Mrs. Gross—at the door, he came up to her and enquired in his politest eastern tones: "Madame, could I stay the night here?" And the good lady replied cordially and without hesitation: "Why, yes, I guess you can! Every other son of a ——— in the country does!"

But this unlimited hospitality no doubt played its part in bringing about Alec McKenzie's gradual financial ruin. He had but little of a good stake left when at the end of thirty-five years on the Cimarron he sent for his old friend and one time foreman, Stan McKellar, and told him he had only a few hours more to live.

I have just told you how McKellar took over the charge of the Stinson sheep outfit. Well, after he had been running that for a number of years he decided he'd make a break on his own account. He contracted with a neighboring sheepman, Creed Davis, to take over seven thousand head of ewes, hand picked out of nine thousand good eight pound shearers. It was to be a cash proposition: thirty-five cents per head per annum Stan was to pay in rent and meet all expenses; returning ewe for ewe at the end of three years. Davis provided the range. It looked like a good proposition for Stan, didn't it?

Now Creed was an old-timer and when he first came to southeastern Colorado thirty years before this time, he had practically the whole country to pick from. Looking over it he became so smitten with the wealth of grama and buffalo

grass on the high plains out north from the Cimarron breaks
that he settled there, locating his ranch at Cat Creek, northwest of Springfield, now capital of Baca county. A grand
summer range it was, but, alack, not a stick of shelter, nor any
tall grass or browse for winter storms.

They finished shaping up the sheep McKellar was to take
over, on October twenty-second. "On October the twenty-
third," says Stan, "it began to snow, and it snowed till June
the twenty-third of the next year!" Stan has a kind of inclusive
way of describing things. Now they have lots of delightful
winters in that part of the world, but I may point out to those
readers who are used to countries where snow doesn't appear,
or lie long, that when the snow falls early and deep on those
level northern plains, the sun with its "winter arches" makes
no impression on it. The native short grasses remain blanketed
for months at a stretch, while the snow slowly packs down.
(On this occasion they didn't sight bare ground till March
sixteenth.) Meantime winds that may have come over a thousand miles of frozen snow slip endlessly over the level surface
with a biting edge, while fresh blizzards recur frequently. One
wonders a living thing survives.

Stan didn't spare himself. He took the sheep out poaching
on the neighbors' sandhills till the sand-grass played out. He
hauled broom-corn fifteen miles, a poor feed at that. But what
the sheep did best on—would you believe it—was the notorious
Russian thistle, digging down to it with their tough forefeet.
"That was the one good turn the dry farmers ever done me!"
says Stan.

It didn't befall him as it did Cameron Brothers, who lost a
whole herd of seventeen hundred sheep buried in one drift
on Cat Creek; he just kept on skinning steadily all winter. In
May he lambed: seven hundred lambs. That was ten percent
of his original ewe herd. June is usually summer time with
them up there, but from June seventeenth to the twenty-second,

that year, it snowed and hailed continuously, and when it was all over Stan counted his stuff and found he had forty-one hundred ewes and three hundred and fifty lambs!

Stanley went to Creed and said: "Creed, you better take back your sheep. I owe you two thousand, four hundred and fifty dollars for rent and around eleven thousand dollars on account of the ewe herd. You'll have to give me time to pay out."

To this Creed replied as follows: "Look here, Stan, I been studyin' this thing over already and I tell you what I'll do. You turn me in what sheep are left and pay me one thousand, one hundred dollars in cash, and we'll call it quits." Then he added, "If I'd been handlin' the sheep myself, I'd of lost the whole dam caboodle!"

I fancy some of my readers may exclaim that that was a generous act of Creed Davis'. But I want to say I don't believe there was anything unusual about it, coming from one of our early-day range men. Whatever you think about those old fellows—and there were features of their social code I never could agree to—it's pretty safe to say that few of them had much of the Shylock about them. They didn't go after their pound of flesh. When some fellow's luck went back on him and he was in a tight place, they were a lot likelier to help him out the way Creed did than to skin him. This was the result, I think, of a certain largeness and scope that attached to life in those days in that part of the world, a sense of there being room for all. Why, men staked a herd of cattle, or a hundred thousand acre grant of land, on the turn of a card. The idea of social existence for these folk was a kind of general, loose cooperation, rather than the cut-throat competition of today. The word "neighbor" had a wider application, geographically, while its inner spirit was a more real thing.

It must be admitted that their code of ethics, the way in which, that is, to treat your fellow-men, was open to a rather broad construction. The big British and Eastern cattle com-

panies, seem to have been considered as scarcely coming within
its pale at all. No limit, for instance, apparently was placed on
the number of times a herd sold to one of them might be
counted round and round a hill. Nor did it injure a man's
character seriously to kill an XIT beef. Skinning Uncle Sam
on weights of hay or beeves was permissible. And always the
calves of stray cows had a curious way of disappearing. But
as far as their code did go, it had more moral force than any
code we have today. I remember my old friend, Joe Holbrook,
and me closing up a deal one time that involved signing some
deeds. Joe was an old Indian Scout who had served with Kit
Carson. As we proceeded Joe remarked, "There's a hell of a lot
of papers to this thing! You know, Jack," he went on, "in old
days we never used none of these here contracts, or promissory
notes, or such like. A man's *word* was all we wanted!" And the
fiery little fighter's eyes flashed defiance of the new-fangled
style of doing business. Haley relates that in the historic contract between Charlie Goodnight and Jimmy Love, which
resulted in opening up the cattle trade between Texas and the
northern range states, they had nothing but a verbal understanding. In all our multitudinous horse deals we rarely bothered
with a bill of sale..

I am very far from being a "praiser of times past," but I
do believe we range folk—I speak of them rather than for the
lawyer people and politicians and such like—of the earlier days
moved in a freer, ampler atmosphere than any that exists today.
And I'm certain Creed Davis would not have wanted any
greater praise for the way he handled the Stan McKellar deal,
than Stan's own comment that "Creed was a pretty decent old
feller!"

IV

I was trying in that last section to lay my line on some of
the more intimate characteristics of the earlier range people,
their attitude towards each other and life in general. Trying,

small as my effort might be, to do this before, under the barrage of claptrap about the West that storms our bookstalls and the screen, the real character of early range life and of the men and women who lived it, be lost sight of altogether, so that future historians searching for the truth about it, shall have no means of finding it. For this period of Western history from, say, 1867, when cattle ranching began to spread over the range, till the early 1900's, when the dry farmers swarmed over it like a plague of locusts, is the most interesting and dramatic period of American history.

I have said how, by and large, a helpful, cooperative spirit prevailing throughout the range, I thought; and that the rules of conduct were lived up to in many respects, but were open to considerable exception. Indeed, the code, to be frank, was fundamentally a crude one, and had features a man brought up in more advanced centers could not agree to.

Yet that it was the natural outgrowth of prevailing deep-rooted tradition the following little episode may serve to prove. When that good boy and excellent cowhand, 'Dolf Harmon, who rode so long for the Red River Cattle Company, was shot and killed by Gabriel Gonzales in the barroom of the old Springer House in Springer, New Mexico, his brother, Albert, never let up in his purpose of reprisal till he succeeded in killing the Mexican, himself getting a shot in the face during the fracas that shattered his jaw. Now to my mind Albert's own character and reputation were not such as to warrant his assuming the functions of sheriff, judge and jury, not to mention executioner, in this or any other case, and I expressed this view of the matter to a cowpuncher friend who though raised in the West, came of parents who had certainly grown up under more enlightened principles. But my friend surprised me considerably by replying instantly. "Well, what would you have done, Jack, if a man had killed your brother?" I saw no use in answering, for the words made it evident that the primitive code of "an eye for an eye," relic of times before laws and courts were available, had become implanted firmly in my friend in one generation. Yet there were law officers and courts and jails, etc., and it took Albert a number of years and about all he had to get clear of them. It didn't make very good sense. It was only one step from this to killing any man who seriously got in your way, or whom you might have any difference with. And that tended to be the prevailing condition.

The situation was perhaps aggravated by the fact that during and following the era of the six-shooter, the fist fight, as a means of settling personal differences, seemed to offer little satisfaction to the Westerner, and was quite uncommon. Nor were such fights as did occur governed by any code I ever heard of. Certainly the Marquis of Queensberry's rules were not observed. Combatants availed themselves cheerfully of such breaks as the good Lord provided, and when they got an opponent down, planned to fix him as far as possible, for keeps. Take, for instance, the famous fist fight between Tom Tipton and Sam Kail, which took place on a New Mexico roundup in the late '80's. Tom and Sam were the roundup "captains," respectively of the Watrous and Wagon Mound cattle pools, which were branches of the powerful Northern New Mexico Stockgrowers' Association of Springer. The wagons were working side by side and friction between the two culminated in the bosses clashing. That was a fight of Titans. Either man was well over six feet in height, weighing around two hundred pounds, and of unusually powerful build. But Tipton had the edge on skill. He got Sam down and proceeded, to the cheers of the Watrousites, to put him *hors de combat,* as the Frenchmen call it.

Now my friend and neighbor, Freeland Latourette, who ran the SU brand, was riding with the Wagon Mound outfit. He was, as I have previously told you, son of an Episcopalian Army chaplain and had been educated at a swell New York "prep" school. There, I suppose, and equally around the army, Freeland had learned the British rules governing the fist fight, and it seemed improper to him that Tom should continue to lambast Sam after he had him down. But when he interposed to drag Tom off him, the Watrous boys objected vigorously. This idea of depriving a man of the full fruits of victory was something they just didn't get.

In the case of the pistol, however, there was an established code, and a fine one, I think; strongly Anglo-Saxon in character. So well established, indeed, that the courts were governed by it. It was not considered justifiable to shoot an unarmed man, and any man, on trial in a case of killing, proved to have done so, was apt to be convicted of murder. But in cases where both men were armed it was correspondingly impossible to obtain a conviction for murder, whatever the circumstances. Harvey Fergusson in his book, *Rio Grande*, quotes Neil B. Field, the well known Albuquerque lawyer, as saying that this was practically the invariable practice of the courts. Field had court experience in his young days in Socorro, when that town was the toughest place in New Mexico.

This was tantamount to a determination by the courts that when a man armed himself, he undertook his own self-defense and, by implication, waived any claim on the courts for protection. One may perhaps assume that the courts took this stand to escape responsibility for establishing guilt in the innumerable killings that were apt to occur, and did occur, in the period of the six-shooter. It is a little difficult for us to realize the prevalence of the gun at that time. But Twitchell relates how Chief Justice Axtell held court in Santa Fe on one occasion when feeling over a case ran dangerously high. As soon as the court was in session, the judge ordered the sheriff to search all court attendants and spectators present. This the sheriff did and piled up the six-shooters on a table—forty-two in number! But about 1884, in New Mexico, it became illegal to carry firearms on a roundup. The boys had to pack them in their beds.

As we proceed with our survey of the code of the six-shooter, I think we cannot fail to observe how few men seem to have been shot from ambush, and I don't recall an important case of a man shot from behind. Peace officers were expected to act on the principles I am trying to describe for you, and usually did. There were even those who blamed Pat Garrett for shooting as desperate an outlaw as Billy the Kid without giving him warning. And on the occasion when Clay Allison, the Colfax county gunman, killed the Mexican peace officer, Pancho Griego, in Lambert's bar in Cimarron, there is grave suspicion that Allison took his opponent at a disadvantage. But he took care not to shoot him from behind: Pancho was found shot in the temple.

Linked, too, I think, with this observance of a manly six-shooter code is the noticeable absence of the "feud." Sundry "wars" there were—the Johnson county, Lincoln county, etc.,—generally based on some solid ground of contention. And fights between sheep and cattle men a-plenty. Differences would come up between cattle owners or companies, the cowboys on either side always loyal to their employer's cause. But aside, perhaps, from parts of Texas which belonged more to the South than the West, the feud arising from some ancient grievance and perpetuated indefinitely without any reason, was extremely rare, I believe.

I think there are some grounds for the theory that the "feud" prevails in mountain countries where families and communities live in valleys more or less segregated from each other: such places as the Kentucky mountains and the Highlands of Scotland. But among the earlier dwellers in the Western range country, taken as a whole, with its wide horizons and spaces, there was no feeling of separation. Your next-door neighbor might live fifty miles away, but it was a simple matter to saddle up and singlefoot it to his door. When I started running cattle, there wasn't a vestige of a fence around the house I lived in. Straight from my very doorstep ran the open road to Arizona or Montana, Texas or Nevada or Wyoming. Your cattle, too, might stray off to a point a thousand miles away from their home range, but there were means there, through brand books and a system of advertising, to restore them to you or dispose of them for you. The occupants of the vast range country during the range cattle period constituted a kind of fraternity, loose but cooperative in certain important purposes of life, on a scale such as the world had never seen, and may never see again. This mutual help principle, indeed, was inherent in the running of range cattle, and was descendent from the early Texan range days when Americans first turned their cattle loose and united in periodical "cowhunts" which were the forerunners of the roundup.

v

I was telling you a while back about that great tract of Colorado country that lies between the Arkansas and the Cimarron Seco, when I got switched off about the codes of conduct and such like that prevailed on the range at large. If I resume my story of that tract—and the tract indeed extended on east clear into western Kansas and Oklahoma, a hundred miles beyond the Colorado line, over ranges like the Anchor D's, where the Stonebreakers had twenty-eight thousand head of cattle and forty-seven windmills around Meade, Kansas; the IOI's (not the Miller Brothers show outfit, which was in the Cherokee Strip); the T. E. Owen Cattle Company which owned the Pitchfork brand; the Z. H.'s from Muscatine, Iowa, run by big A. J. Streeter and eventually shifted bodily to the Mora country of New Mexico—if I should tell you a little more about all this, it is because this country is now the head and front of the "dust bowl," and what one writes of it may have the interest which a record of something passed and gone has. It was only a month ago I was talking to a man who had left that region around Springfield, to try and make a living in California, and I asked him what there was there today in that district where one hundred thousand head of cattle and half a million sheep used to grow fat in a good season—what stock or crops; and the man used one word to answer my query:—

"Nuthin' "!

It's a tragic pity, for it was not merely a fine piece of stock country but, as far as the Colorado section of it was concerned, the life of its inhabitants would serve very well to illustrate what I wrote about the range country at large: its spirit of cooperation and neighborliness. Some of my readers may know Jack O'Neal who runs sheep up there. He and Stan McKellar arranged lines one time between their ranges, neither to graze their sheep across them. Almost immediately Jack's sheep were found on Stan's side. Stan is not an easy fellow to get change out of. He never said a word to Jack, but took a band of sheep and plumped it right down at O'Neal's headquarters ranch. Now, that sort of thing would make bad blood in some parts. But what happened here was that O'Neal at once ceased trespassing on Stan's range, whereupon Stan withdrew his herd from O'Neal's place. And when they met a short while after, Jack comes up to Stan and shakes hands with him. "Say, Stan," he says, laughing, "another time just camp in my house!" That was something of the spirit of the people, and you couldn't go near a man's place without his hollerin' to you to "git down offa your horse" and "come on in 'n' eat!"

As for McKellar, after his sad experience with Davis' sheep on the plains, his cry became, "Me for the breaks!" He betook himself and his wife Agnes over to a ranch on Mustang Creek at the end of those cedar breaks I have elsewhere described to you as running out east from Trinidad. Here he had a nice pasture, fenced in by natural bluffs with wire across the bottoms of the canyons, and started to breed up a bunch of pure-bred Herefords. Jimmy Stinson gave him seven hundred head of steers to take to the Mustang and run on the range outside the pasture, which was fine for Stan. There was no man handy to help him drive the steers to his new range, and Stinson enquired of him afterwards how in hell he'd ever got them over there. "Oh," says Stanley, "that was simple. I drove the cattle and Agnes, she drove the wagon and done the cookin'!" One man driving seven hundred steers alone on the trail was something of a novelty to the Texan, but that's the way Stan is. Here on the Mustang he put in eight good years, building up a fine herd of Herefords and running a thousand head of steers for Jimmy Stinson. He stayed there till the dry farmers ran him out.

But I think this couple must have had a strain of Gipsy blood in them, for every once in a while they'd pull up stakes and hit the trail. One time Stan took a notion he could make some money out of Navajo sheep, which could be bought cheap on the Reservation. So he and his wife Agnes took their wagon and team, and trekked three hundred miles southwest across New Mexico to Albuquerque. There they turned northwest, heading for Mesa Prieta which lies in a big bend of the Rio Puerco, a tributary of the Rio Grande. Here the Indians run many sheep. It's high bleak bunch grass country, with mighty little water. What with chasing from bunch to bunch of grass and from one waterhole to the next one, these sheep develop great length and strength of leg; nor are they over-weighted with wool, the Indian not being a devotee of breed improvement. Stan bought him a bunch of ewes and started home with them, he doing the herding and Agnes driving the team and attending to the camp business. Stanley says he never knew anything that could walk like those Navajo sheep. But he stayed with 'em and they throve under his care and grew so fat and slick that when they got to Albuquerque a sheep buyer made him an offer on the bunch he hadn't the strength of mind to turn down. Thus they got back home to Colorado without any sheep after all. But McKellar says that adventure taught him he had mistaken his profession in life. He was clearly cut out, he considers, to be a sheepherder.

Another time they hit it overland for Southern California. As they passed through Bakersfield Stan got an offer to take charge of the sheep department of the Miller and Lux outfit at Button Willow, thirty miles west of Bakersfield on the canal that leads from Buena Vista Lake. This concern, perhaps the most extensive ever engaged in stock raising and agriculture, ran its business along liberal lines. Food was plentiful and of the best. The foremen of the various departments—cattle, sheep, hogs, farm—ate their meals in their own dining hall, apart from the men. All stock was number one quality, the Rambouillet ewes being bred to high class types of the mutton breeds. Stan says the best lambs came from the Dorset cross. He lambed two bunches of these on wheat and barley stubble in October, getting 187% of lambs, and when he put them on the market at Christmas they weighed a hundred and eight pounds. Now then, folks, come along with your lamb stories!

Generally speaking, we people of America are too much in a hurry to observe things, much less reflect upon them. Yet life for the stockman was only occasionally urgent, and he had long hours in which he could think things over. That is why the cattleman, as I see him, is usually steadier in his vision and more independent in his judgment than many other Americans, and a satisfactory sort of companion. I don't know anyone I'd sooner sit down and listen to than my big friend Stan McKellar, when he is in a reminiscent mood. So much of his talk reveals quiet observation. "The run of young fellers in those days," he'll say, "didn't cotton much to the job of horse herdin'; but I got a big kick out of it, studyin' the habits of horses. The

FDW roundup outfit that I wrangled for didn't hobble their horses of nights, you know. They nightherded 'em, and I had the job two seasons. Cowhorses at night, I used to notice, graze till around eleven o'clock, then go to sleep, layin' down or standin', till about two. I'd get off my horse and lay down with my slicker over me those three hours or so. About two the horses'd start to nicker and wake me up. Whenever some outside man joined the outfit his string of horses would want to break back to their home range all the time. Some bunches would get broke in a week, others take a long while. I was wise to whatever direction every new bunch of horses came from and would lay down on that side of the remuda. If I heard some of 'em nickerin' when I woke, I'd be sure some of their mates had pulled out and they were nickerin' for 'em, and I'd know to light out after them."

Here Stanley may pause, shovel about four ounces of cut-plug into one cheek, and continue thoughtfully: "I liked to compare the boys, too, how they acted towards their mounts. Did you ever know Buck Miller, Jack? There was a man was good to his horses. He run the Schleter cattle outfit. Schleter was a sheepman, but most all those big sheepmen run cattle as well. Buck was a little bit of a fellow, too, but he sure could handle a bronco horse. His own brand was 7XL, all connected. A neat brand, that, and some fine horses in it. Mebbe you know Lloyd Miller who has a cow ranch near Santa Fe. He's Buck's boy. Then there was Alec Like. He run the IL brand of cattle and horses on the Carrizo in Colorado; his IL colts were reckoned the best in that section. Alec lost his wife and was badly cut up over it. Someone was sympathisin' with him one day about it. 'Yes,' says Alec, 'it sure went hard with me, that did. I'd sooner of lost one of me best hosses than me wife!' "

Stan doesn't live on the plains any more. His home is in the coast range of northern California, which is a good country for raising trees, but not so much for livestock. Indeed Stan says he is a native son, having been born in Santa Rosa when his mother was living there after she first came from New Zealand. But you'll find he's a range man at heart still, if you happen in on his little cottage beside the Redwood Highway, seven miles north of Willits, where he lives alone, having lost his good helpmeet and companion, Agnes. For he'll come out to the door and holler to you to "get down offa your horse"—although it's more likely to be an automobile—"and come on in 'n' eat!" And before you know where you are he'll have a fire lit in the wood stove and fix up a meal for you. And I'm telling you Stan's biscuits is tops.

# 5
## No Man's Land

CORNERWISE and closely connected with this southeastern region of Colorado of which I have been writing, lies the Panhandle of Oklahoma, commonly known as No Man's Land. This tract was the only part of the State of Oklahoma that was not acquired under the Louisiana Purchase. It was originally part of Texas, and in 1850, Texas having entered the Union as a slave state, it was "ceded" to the United States, as being north of the Missouri Compromise line. From then until 1890, when it became part of the Territory of Oklahoma, it was United States public domain, not included in any state or territory. Hence its name of No Man's Land.

Now the pioneer population of the entire Southwest, that region's warmest admirers must admit, was liberally sprinkled with individuals who had come there bringing no credentials with them. It is an old joke to say that the ancestor of every native-born Texan left his original home state for that state's good. Certainly long before, and still more following, the Civil War countless men with desperate records betook themselves to Texas either to make a fresh start in life or to carry on their chosen mode of life where peace officers were scarcer. In the '70's, Twitchell says, New Mexico took the place of Texas as the principal asylum for the worst characters of the Southwest. Colfax and Lincoln counties to the east, and the Mogollon district to the west, being specially well supplied. The Chisum herds of "Jinglebob" cattle attracted multitudes of such men to the Lower Pecos country, where John's herds ranged at large to an estimated number of sixty to eighty thou-

sand head over five thousand square miles of sparsely settled
territory. It was held by those who didn't bring New England
consciences with them, to be easier and quicker to build up
a herd of cattle with a short rope and Jingle-bob "long rail"
calves than to breed one.

But I greatly doubt if any district harbored more desperate
cases than No Man's Land. A man could settle there with
small fear of arrest and none of extradition, since there was
no organized government. Nor were conditions surrounding
it much more propitious. Immediately to the east lay the Cherokee Outlet or Strip, granted to the Cherokee Indians as an
outlet to their western hunting grounds, but controlled solely
by an association of cattlemen, the most powerful of its kind
that ever existed, who ran things with a high hand till finally
the Government expelled them. Through the Outlet, too, and
through the east end of No Man's Land, passed the great cattle
trails to the north, attracting large numbers of desperate men
who preyed upon the early trail herds along the neighboring
Kansas line. Immediately south of the Outlet and cornering
with No Man's Land, were other areas of the Indian Territory,
some occupied by tribes of Plains Indians, the most uncivilized
of all the Indian tribes, and some by American cattlemen who
ran their herds there without leave or license, and kept bringing
them back as often as the United States troops would drive
them out. You can add to this description of lawlessness the
fact that during the whole of one year, 1890, the entire state
of Oklahoma, newly formed, was without any government
of any kind.

Such conditions of disorder and unrest in and around No
Man's Land did not tend to attract to it homeseekers of wholly
peaceful bent. And indeed I am frank to say that this strip
of country contained, along with the men of the big cattle
companies and other good citizens, a number of families as
wholly without appreciation of the rights of private property

and as reckless as regards human life, their own or anyone's else, as ever went to form an English-speaking community—if community it could be called. I have told you already how their depredations helped to drive the JJ's out of the breeding business, and there was plenty of petty stealing besides. They packed their guns everywhere; even to dances, which were frequent and generally ended in a fight. And when the shooting began at these affairs, do you suppose the women ran for the doors? Not on your life. They crowded around to watch the fun, laughing with excitement and delight as the bullets flew and this or that body dropped. Perhaps the best way to convey an idea of the life and nature of these people would be to give some description of one notorious family.

All Californians, and many on the outside, are aware of the case of the Brite boys, John and Coke, who lay for some years awaiting execution in Folsom Prison, the last to receive a sentence of death by hanging in California. Their crime was the killing of a Yreka deputy sheriff and constable, and a civilian volunteer, in Siskiyou county, in December, 1936, while resisting arrest on a charge of murder. They had killed a man in a dispute over a mine. After the killing of the three possemen the boys escaped and hid out. This is not a hard matter in that densely timbered region, and the search for them continued for several weeks and aroused great interest over the whole Pacific coast. Their trial was held in Yreka in an atmosphere of intense hostility. The evidence seemed to show that the boys had been found asleep and in that state assaulted and beaten up by the posse, whereupon they started shooting. And old Ma Brite will tell you, if you talk to her, as she pierces you with those burning old eyes of hers, that her boys "never got no justice." "I wanted to die with 'em," she'll say.

These fellows belonged to Kenton, a little town in No Man's

*The newspapers recently report a reprieve from the Governor of the state.

Land I've told you about before, lying just one mile from the line of New Mexico and the same from Colorado. A close friend of mine who served as deputy sheriff there knew them well. They were not in themselves bad boys, but they came of a crowd of men it's better not to attack unless you're prepared for a scrap, and who weren't greatly concerned as to who got killed in the scrap, themselves or their opponents. It was all part of the game.

The Brite family itself was an excellent one: old grandmother Brite a fine old woman. Still these Brite boys would fight anything, always. One time when Coke was riding for the Cross L wagon, he had a disagreement with another of the boys. They came to blows and Coke received a good licking. Later in the day they were riding along side by side and Coke said: "By God, I been studyin' over this thing. I orter to be able to whip you. Let's try 'er agin!" So they got down off their horses and Coke got another good pasting. Even then he wasn't satisfied and wanted more. That was what the Brite boys—and many others in No Man's Land—were like: they liked fighting, and bore no malice.

If there was any real "bad" strain in these boys it came from the mother's side. No one ever denied that the Hoods were tough. Two of the mother's brothers and one sister died in their boots. The story of Annie Hood is known in every household in No Man's Land. Annie had had trouble with a neighbor and had killed him. When the officers came to arrest her on the charge of murder, they found she had left her home and taken refuge in a wood. This they surrounded, and when she refused to give herself up, they started shooting. But Annie had provided herself with guns and ammunition and proceeded to return the fire. And they relate how high above the racket of her own and the posse's fusilade, she could be heard laughing and laughing as the fight waxed fiercer. She was having the grand time of her life, this Annie Hood of No Man's Land!

Finally her shots ceased and the officers ventured into the wood, where they found her dead.

Then there was brother Tom. A cow belonging to a neighboring range cattleman had got into a farmer's crop and the farmer held it in his corral, claiming damages. These the cowman refused to pay and not being able to recover his cow he went to Tom Hood and said: "Look here, Tom, this dam farmer has my cow in his corral. Do you go get her for me!" And Tom just rode over to the farm and took the cow away, the farmer offering no resistance. A while later the farmer and Tom happened to find themselves face to face at a poker table in a local saloon. Some difficulty arose over the game and the granger, already mad at Tom about the cow, and now irritated still further, exclaimed, "By God, Tom, if I had a gun I'd kill you!" "If that's all the trouble," returns Tom, "here y'are!" and he reached back and pulled out his six-shooter, and threw it across the table to the farmer. But the farmer never made a move to get it.

As for old man Hood, the father, he disappeared suddenly one day and has never been seen or heard of since.

Those of you who read this brief account of No Man's Land will probably come to the conclusion that the people it describes are not what one would call desirable citizens or satisfactory neighbors. Nevertheless that quality of contempt of death which they are seen to have possessed so conspicuously is to my mind the most notable among the qualities which accompanied our winning and making of the West.

# 6

## A Sporting Cowman

IHAVE described in past pages some events that took place in Colfax County. Few sections of New Mexico have produced more interesting characters. And few, perhaps, of its citizens were better known for a while, and led a more colorful life, than Albert Shaw, who ran a large herd of cattle on the Raton range along in the '80's. Everyone who has traveled over the Santa Fe railroad knows Raton on the Continental Divide.

Albert Shaw is an Ulsterman, born and raised in Belfast. He was a friend and schoolmate of James Alexander Craig, now Viscount Craigavon of Stormont, and Premier of Northern Ireland. Coming to the country with a good stake, he bought a ranch near Raton, and cattle, and all went merrily for a while. Few of the cattlemen of those days ever entertained any doubts about the future of the range cattle business. There was nothing to do, to their mind, but just let your herd grow and live in clover off the increase; while your water rights advanced to incredible values. Alas, for human dreams! Delano and Dwyer threw ten thousand Mexican dogies on the Raton range. A disastrous winter followed. And Albert Shaw found himself, along with many another cowman of that period, broke. "I lost three thousand cows in two winters," he'll tell you. And you can see it hurts him still to tell it.

Nevertheless, while the going was good, Albert cut a wide swath; kept open house on his ranch near Raton and took a hand in every activity of the district. Like most Irishmen, he was a keen sportsman. Horse racing was his favorite game, and he owned some fine horses. His thoroughbred mare, Bright

Eyes, was never beaten in New Mexico. He matched her with Jim Lynch's Nightshade at Las Vegas for a thousand dollars, the best out of three races. His mare won, but Lynch's check was not certified and when Shaw came to cash it, there was nothing doing. Indeed, the mare was too good to get races in New Mexico, so he sold her to go back east, where she won eleven consecutive races. And eventually she went to England for breeding purposes.

There were seven or eight fellows in that Raton neighborhood who owned race horses of sorts, and who had tried to "work" Shaw on several occasions. Finally, he decided to try and get even with them. He had bought, for a song, an old race horse, and renamed him Bronco Jim. The horse had run a nail into his foot at one time and had a hollow hoof. This hoof was always kept shod, with the other hoofs bare, and when the horse traveled the shoe went clip, clop, Albert says, so you could hear it a quarter of a mile away. He was a raw-boned looking cuss at best, and Albert let him run out in the pasture all the year round. One spring he was shed off all over except for one big bunch of hair on his rump that wouldn't come off. Shaw says he was surely a horrible looking sight with that bunch of hair sticking straight up in the air like a bale of hay.

Well, he told the boys he would run any, or all, of them a mile with his horse, Bronco Jim. When the fellows got sight of the old horse they thought they had the world by the tail and let loose with all the money they could lay hold of. Shaw decided to have a lad he employed at the ranch ride the horse in place of himself. On the day of the race he gave the boy careful instructions to keep his mount well in hand, and to be sure and win—*but by not more than a length or so.* He had further plans for the old steed later on, you see. But before the race was half run, he saw to his dismay that Bronco Jim was out of hand and running away with his jockey, and the end of it was that he beat the next horse by seventeen lengths and ran a mile afterwards. "I wished I'd ridden him meself," says Albert.

It was for Albert Shaw that Ed Cain was working, when he had the duel with Jeff Dale, in which both men were killed. Shaw was living in Catskill at that time, a little mountain town about thirty-five miles from Raton. Cain was taking care of his race horses. One afternoon he remembers asking Ed if the horses had been fed, and Ed said, yes, and that he was going over to the saloon, which was just across the street from the house. A few minutes later there were several shots. Shaw hurried over. Jeff Dale and Ed had met, it appeared, just as Ed had' got across to the saloon and the two men had opened fire on each other at once. When Albert got there, Dale was lying at the foot of the back steps, wounded. Cain was inside, running towards the door. He kept on shooting. Just as he got to the top of the steps, the blood started suddenly to gush from his mouth, and he pitched forward on his face. Shaw and Joe Fowler, the bartender, lifted him up and carried him to a billiard table. He had just strength to whisper in Fowler's ear; "Joe, if I didn't get him, *you* get him!"

They opened up his shirt and could see nothing, but after a careful search discovered a tiny place like a pimple on the left breast. He had been shot with a .22 rifle through the heart. It seems that when Dale had arrived in Catskill that morning and heard that Cain was there, he had hunted the whole place trying to buy a gun, and this little .22 was all he could find.

Ed lived long enough for them to tell him, as he lay on the billiard table, that Jeff was dead. Albert says, when he heard that, a smile lit up his dying eyes.

These two men, Ed Cain and Jeff Dale, had had trouble, according to Shaw, over a woman eight years before. When they met after all those years, they shot and killed each other on sight. It was a bloody code, that old code of those days. Yet there is something in it one feels admiration for. For, if most of the men of that time were reckless of the lives of others, they were equally indifferent as regards their own.

So there they were with two dead men in Catskill. A meeting was held and it was decided that it wouldn't do to bury the two bodies at the same time. So they trudged out to the graveyard, which was three quarters of a mile from town, with Ed, first. Catskill had just organized a town band, with Shaw in it. The musicians were not what you'd call experts, and they had only one hymn tune on their list: "Nearer, My God, to Thee," and they didn't know that very well. And all the way out with Ed they played "Nearer, My God, to Thee." Then they came back and got Jeff, and played "Nearer, My God, to Thee" all the way out with him. "It was lucky" says Albert, "that both men were dead, so they couldn't hear that music!"

Shaw knew and admired Clay Allison, the great fighting gunman. He had no objection to a scrap himself. When ———— ———— was running for sheriff of the county, Shaw opposed him, telling people about a dirty deal ———— had given him. So ———— comes up to him one day and tells him if he says anything more against him, he'd shoot him. And it's worth the price of a ringside seat to see the Irish in the old man's eye as he describes how "I stuck my nose plumb up against his, and I says, 'Blaze away!'" "I'd have hit him before ever he could draw," he explains, demonstrating how he would have used his left. Shaw attended the trial of the cowboy-bandit, McGinnis. His description of him helped me to get the vivid impression I have of that romantic figure. And he was present at the trial of Black Jack Ketchum at Clayton, and can tell you some stories of the Turkey Canyon fight. He was actively interested in the organization of the Catskill schools.

If you should want to see Albert Shaw today, you'd have to come to this city where I live. I will take you to a tiny house set way back on a lot not far from the foot of the Hollywood hills. All in front of the house is a garden of flowers. Here the old sporting cattleman will show you some of his water color sketches, or read you a poem of his own composition, or thrill or set you laughing with some tale of the old range days. On the way out to the street you will pass through his garden. Every plant in it is of Albert's own planting. "I work two hours in it every day to keep meself fit," he says. And as he points out this or that flower, he will gather a bouquet of the prettiest that are in bloom and, if your wife is with you, present it to her with a manner that reminds you of something we seem to have lost in these modern days.

# 7

## Tex Austin Takes the West to London

I'VE remarked elsewhere in these chronicles that only those who radically alter their whereabouts and kind of business, can ever feel the thrill one gets from being suddenly brought into touch with some familiar long-past association. One of the men who was a means of giving me a most effective experience of this kind, was so well known over the world that his own unexpected appearance in any place need not have caused anyone any surprise. The man was Texas Austin. There were few great cities of any continent where Tex' handsome face and great and shapely figure were not known. Certainly there was no one in the length and breadth of London and New York who was not familiar with his big open car with its six-foot long-horns riding out across the front of the radiator.

It was in a place rather smaller than either of these cities that I first met Austin, when he set up his first rodeo in Las Vegas, New Mexico. Right primitive were the arrangements for carrying out the Las Vegas show. There may have been a grandstand, though I have no recollection of one, nor of any means adopted for shutting the outside public from an un-limited view of the show, except perhaps a barb wire fence.

There didn't exist at that time such a being as a professional rodeo performer; but the surrounding cow country supplied a good number of competent contestants, riders, ropers, bull-doggers, etc. In the horse line too the range afforded of real "bad 'uns" an adequate number. I remember Harry Johnson at the barber's shop the morning after the bronco riding dis-cussing the matter with Frenchie, the barber. "O yes," says

Frenchie, "Tom Rogers gave Possum a good ride all right, but I'll swear he pulled leather on him."

"Pulled leather, do I hear you say?" Harry cries. "Ef I'd bin a-ridin' that hawss I'd of pulled off the whole front of the saddle!"

But it was a far-removed and very different rodeo that administered the "thrill" I started to tell you about. The scene was in London. Now English people love anything connected with livestock. Indeed the actual Western-American cattle range— of which this was a representation—had been largely built up by British stockmen and with British stock and capital. Almost everyone in London stood ready to flood the great plus-100,000 capacity stadium at Wembley. I took it into my head a few days before the opening of the show to run over and look up Tex Austin who was putting it on.

I found my way to the clerk's quarters. Sure enough every boy in attendance there was a cowpuncher. "Hello, you chaps, can you tell me where I can find Tex Austin?" No, he was somewhere out in the yards attending to the men. But one of the fellows asked me for my name so as to give it to Tex when he came in. I called out good and loud: "John H. Culley!" The place was crowded with desks and from the very back among them suddenly came clear and emphatic to my ear the words: "IS-THAT-JACK-CULLEY?" and up to the counter sprung Butch Jones who had been a pal of mine years and years in New Mexico. "When I left America on this trip," says Butch, "I told them I only knew one American in England and that was Jack Culley!"

Well, I hunted around till I found Tex. He began at once to tell me all his troubles. "You know, Jack, when I put on my late show in New York City I said I wanted to put up some temporary chutes and corrals; and the Polo ground folks told me to get me what lumber I needed and go ahead. I and the boys had them built in no time. And pulled down again. But when I got to this here burg—by which I mean London—and began to talk about chutes and pens they told me I'd have to have a special permit from a department of the London County Council for each and every structure. And all the work must be done by Union Labor men, who (as you know) work by the minute; and done in strict accordance with blue prints prepared by the Council architects. Now, I ask you, Jack, did you ever build a cow corral to a blue print! Two days more" he went on "till the show opens and the chutes not up! Any time an inspector comes around and finds a post half an inch too deep in the ground the whole thing has to be tore up and planted over again. They're sure devoted to accuracy and permanence, this here people!"

But Tex' troubles had only just begun. I've told you previously, I think, about the Royal Society for Prevention of Cruelty to Animals and what a powerful and officious concern it is. It cast critical eyes upon the Austin rodeo, taking special exception to the heavy steer roping. Tex told me the whole story of the thing. In the States he had secured a bunch of light, wild, long-horn steers which at the last moment could not be delivered. He was therefore obliged to bring over a band of Angus cattle bought in Canada just before leaving. These were fat and slow and heavy and the boys had to give them a hard run and a heavy jerk to throw them. The which resulted in many injuries to the cattle and in one of them eventually having its neck broken. Thereupon furious indignation on the part of the R. S. P. C. A. and suit by it in court to render the throwing of heavy steers in the rodeo illegal. The court gave judgment against Austin, making it difficult for him to continue the show and make any profit.

Now it is currently known that if anything goes wrong with any person in England the proper course for him to take is to address a letter to the London *Times* newspaper. This I did, being irritated by the attack on the Austin show, as well as

being an old-time cowman. I made a copy of it and took it to
Tex. It's too long ago to remember the exact words, but they
ran somewhat as follows: "Dear Editor: I am writing about
the case brought by R. S. P. C. A. against Texas Austin on the
grounds of cruelty perpetrated on animals in his rodeo. I should
like to point out that the British people have long practiced
forms of sport painfully cruel. It is hard to imagine anything
more inhuman than fox-hunting, coursing, stag chasing, etc.
To all of which R. S. P. C. A. has offered but little objection.
Yet in comparison with these British sports the performance
of the American rodeo, which I have just attended, seems to me
to resemble a RSPCA short course in kindness to animals."
I remember Tex laughing at this last break.

I received a nice reply from the editor of the *Times* in which
he said that his paper was not permitted to comment on cases
before the court.

All these *débâcles* (that being the French word for mishaps,
as you will understand if you have ever been to Paris.) deprived
the show of much of its interest. Nevertheless the attendance
continued great, the favorite remaining form of entertainment
being the promiscuous riding of broncos by amateurs, whereby
considerable injuries were caused and a number of necks
(human) came near being broken.

Well, Tex, old friend, we shall not ride together any more
along the flats of the Gallinas; nor discuss rodeo matters in Bob
Ross' office—Bob had run the Cross Bar brand around La Cinta
in the Lower Country and gone busted like the rest of us, but
what a hell-fired good fellow he was! Much less will you
organize mammoth rodeos to stage in faraway places, equipping
them with men, old friends of mine who will recognize me and
call me by name. . . .*

*This was written before I knew of Texas' death at Santa Fe late in 1939. This
occurred under unhappy conditions. He had lost all the considerable accumu-
lations of his life in an unlucky venture. They tell me too he was in dread of
becoming blind.

# 8

## The Great Snowstorm of '89

### I

Outside of the boys who got off about wild horses they had ridden there were no worse windbags on the range than the "hard winter" bunch. Indeed pretty nearly all of us had at least one bad storm we'd been through and liked to tell about. I remember a bunch of cowpunchers sitting whittlin' on the MacArthur store steps in Wagon Mound one afternoon, and me breezes up. "A dandy bunch of cow thieves!" was my greeting to them. "Always room for another!" comes back Mat McCallister, little Texan, who could be relied on at any moment for what the literary guys called a repartee. Well, they were telling about the big snowstorms they'd been through and as the talk went on the snow seemed to be getting deeper and deeper and the thermometer lower—though to tell the truth we didn't know much about thermometers in those days. Just about then who should come drifting along what we called the sidewalk but old Charlie Fraker? Charlie was an old Santa Fe freighter of the '60's. He had dried up then and stayed dried up ever since, in the flesh and in the spirit. He listened awhile to our talk in his usual attentive silence. Finally in a pause in the conversation he cleared his throat and remarked in his dry nasal voice to no one in particular: "I remember in the winter of 186— comin' over the Glorieta Pass with a mule train. There'd been a lot of heavy snow storms that year. The snow was so deep where we passed that when you wanted to light a fire all you had to do was to strike a match and set fire to the tops of the pines!" Then without another word and with a defiant glance at the group in general the old man drifted on.

He seemed to have settled the snow question. There was an interval of silence and then someone opened up a new subject.

Although the winters in our northeastern corner of New Mexico were nothing like so hard as in the more northern states, we did have some bad storms and it came into my head to tell you about some of them today.

Probably the worst was the one that happened on October 31, 1889. It was the early winter and the late spring storms that were the most dangerous, because they caught us unprepared. The cattle might be on their summer pastures, and a lot of such land was high-lying and cold. The 1889 storm was exceptionally long continued and heavy. When it quit snowing it was said that three feet of snow lay on the ground on the level in Union county. It was marked by severe cold and peculiarly blinding blizzards. It wasn't safe to venture out into it at all. Three hundred head of cattle drifted off the Johnson Mesa near Raton before the storm and were totally destroyed. Twelve herds of beef cattle from southern New Mexico, headed for the Colorado and Southern R.R., were caught up in it and scattered. Trying to hold a herd in such weather merely resulted in splitting it up. The only thing to do was to turn the cattle loose. That was what Henry Miller did with Dick Head's beef herd, which got caught high up on the western slope of the Sierra Grande.

I've told you before about Dick Head, one of the great early cowmen, who for a while ran the Prairie Cattle Company. After giving up that position Dick had started a ranch of his own not far from the Cross L ranch on the Dry Cimarron. He took with him Henry Miller who had been his wagon boss on the Cross L division of the Prarie Cattle Company. I was over a hundred miles away from that district when the great storm broke, so in order to get the story of it, as concerns the Head outfit, as near straight as possible I am going to give it just as I have had it from my friend, Billy Parsons. Billy, as I've told you elsewhere, had ridden a long time as ouside man for the Cross L's, but left when Miller left, to work for Head. This fall Dick was gathering all his cattle to sell out, so Billy seeing there would be no job for him there, hired out to Phlem Humphrey to take charge of his race horses and livery stable in Folsom. But Billy was cutting cattle for Head in a roundup on the Corrumpaw just the day before the boys got caught in the storm, so while he wasn't actually with them then, he probably came as close to the affair as anyone living today. Fred Jolly who was one of the survivors of the outfit is dead since then, but if Charley Weir who was another, is still alive, I'd be awfully glad to hear from him.

Dick Head's outfit, Billy tells me, consisted of Henry Miller, in charge, Charley Weir, Johnny Martin and Fred Jolly, the cook and horse wrangler, and four outside men. They were holding the herd pretty high up on the west side of the Sierra Grande, maybe 8000 feet up. When night came Miller made two guards. The first stood till 12 o'clock. They were the outside men and when they were relieved they got back all of them to camp and woke up Miller and the three men I mentioned by name, who took the second guard. As time went on Henry saw he couldn't hold the herd as the snow had started coming down in gusts or whirligigs—what the Mexicans call *revoleon*—and it was impossible to see anything. So he turned the cattle loose. When the boys started back to camp they couldn't find it. There was nothing to do but sit on their horses till daylight came. When daylight did come, still failing to find camp, they made a try to get to the headquarters ranch but the snow kept on falling thick and steady, and the ground was covered deep with snow, a condition that seems to disguise the whole face of the country, so it wasn't long till they knew they were lost completely.

You can't ride but mighty slow in snow as deep as that; moreover, settlements in those days were widely scattered; the boys rode all day without getting anywhere. Finally along towards night they found themselves in a small draw where the snow had drifted deep, and there, turning their horses loose, they stamped around till they had two hollow places worked out in the drift, into which they crawled, Henry and Johnny into one, and the other two into the other. The storm never let up a moment, the cold getting worse for them hour by hour, for of course they had neither food nor fire nor cover to keep up any heat in their bodies. The partition between their two little dugouts was thin enough so they could talk to one another through it. When dawn of the next day broke Jolly and Martin heard Henry telling them that Johnny was in bad shape and not likely to hold out much longer. Johnny was a young powerful fellow and one is at a loss to know why he should have been the first to succumb. Anyhow it wasnt long till Henry hollered out to them again to say that Johnny was dead. Shortly after that the day seemed to be opening up clear, and Fred and Charley made their way out of their dug-out. The first thing they saw was Henry Miller sitting clear out on the open frozen snow. He was "weavin' back and forth" they said, in what must have been his death throes.

The day came so clear that the two surviving fellows thought they could find their way to the ranch. When, however, they tried to start Weir couldn't get onto his horse. (It seems the horses must have stayed around.) Jolly who was a powerful hardy chap, made his way to where an old couple lived who chafed his hands with snow and so prevented their becoming frozen. Meantime a sheepherder happened to drift past the spot where Charley was and putting him onto his burro carried him to a hut where two men lived. These men got him to Raton where he could get medical care. He lost all his fingers but the thumb and forefinger of one hand.

There is however another version of this tragedy. George Crocker tells me that Henry Wilson, having with all his men got back to camp, left with his whole outfit on horseback in search of a ranch. Getting nowhere they finally stopped and turned their horses loose. They tried to make a shelter out of their saddle blankets. Charley Weir, a member of the party, saying that if they stayed there they would all die, started out on foot with one other man. They ran onto a sheepherder and started for his camp, but in spite of Charley's and the herder's assistance this other man played out. He died where they left him.

Meantime Henry Wilson and the four or five men remaining with him stayed where they had stopped and died in a bunch. Will Temple, a well known cowman of those parts, took George to the spot where they died. Will had helped to dig the bodies out of the snow. It was just on the north side of the Palo Blanco peaks. While Parson's account is circumstantial, George's tallies, as to the number of men who perished, with the story as I heard it at the time. I always understood that six or seven men were frozen to death. As for Jolly, he survived, but George does not remember when he left Wilson's party and how he managed to escape death.

The story of the Head herd spread over the whole country rapidly. It was often much exaggerated. We were told that the herd had been driven off a bluff by the storm and lost. But that apparently wasn't so. The cattle, after being turned loose, scattered and were gathered as the snow went off. I do not think the storm caused much general loss of livestock.

I was caught in it myself, leaving the Puerto de Luna country a hundred and thirty miles south, as the crow flies, of the Sierra Grande, on the morning of the storm, for my ranch in Turkey Mountains sixty-five miles away, on horseback alone. My adventure was not anyways so tragic as that which befell the Head boys, but it was curious and interesting enough to be worth relating, I think.

SNOW STORM

## II

On that October 31, 1889, when the great snowstorm started I was on my way up from the Puerto de Luna country to our ranch in Turkey Mountains, sixty-five miles away, on horseback and alone. I aimed to make the trip in the day, though you have to keep ridin' to do sixty-five miles in one of those early winter days. But Dick, I was riding, was a stout and willing horse, with a long trot. Puerto de Luna lies in what we called the Lower Country. I think I've told you before about the high steep mesa wall that runs across northeastern New Mexico, dividing it into two separate countries, differing in their plant life and climate. A cold dark land atop; a warm sweet one below. It must have been around noon that I reached and clomb the steep high trail of the mesa, and after I had ridden on a piece the snow began to fall. It fell as thick as I've ever seen snow fall, but it was soft and warm and I paid no heed to it. I didn't know it was going to continue that way for three days and nights. I was riding by direction, as we often did in those days before the fences were put up. You could sight the Turkey Mountains a long ways off, and I knew the time of day and the points of the compass by the sun almost as well as an Indian or Mexican. But when both sun and view were completely shut off by the snow there was nothing left to guide one but the wind, which was very light, though it remained constant. Still this bit of country was strange to me and it wasn't long before I realized I was lost. There was nothing to do but travel northeast as near as I could, hoping for the best.

It's not much fun being lost in snow, as many of my readers must know. Of course you can be lost a hundred yards from home, but in the middle of the prairie far from human habitations, it's a bit terrifying, I'd say. For although the mind is busy figuring out what would be the best thing to do, none the less stories you've read and heard about people lost in storms come crowding in on it. I remember one morning leaving my ranch on the Escondida to go to our trading town of Wagon Mound, eighteen miles away. There was about a foot of snow on the ground and the air was full of brilliant sunshine. I was driving a good team to a Bain lumber wagon. Just as we got to what is known as the point of the Megotes the snow began to fall. Within a few minutes it had become a blizzard—a *revoleon*, in the expressive Spanish term—in which the wind has no one direction but eddies around and around in circles. You can seldom see more than twenty yards. It was quickly evident it would be hopeless to try and make Wagon Mound; moreover we were still only three or four miles from the ranch. I turned my horses' heads and gave them the rein; they would know the road home.

Adolph Bandelier, the well known explorer, writing about traveling on the prairie, says: "It is a constant fact that anyone lost on the plains inclines to the right and finally describes a circle." I don't know how that may be, but that is what I believe we did. It's my belief the team under pressure of the storm, which was driving furiously and with a biting edge, bore off their course to the right. At any rate it wasn't long before I became aware by close observation that we were going in a circle. I gave up all idea then of reaching our ranch, nor were there any others for miles around. But all along to the south of us about three or four miles away stretched the brakes of the Mora River. If I can hit them, I said, I can get shelter and build a fire. So I whipped up my team and we drove hard through the blinding snow, I hoping our direction was the right one. But no timber loomed up. I remember beginning to feel a little desperate.

And then all of a sudden a miracle happened. A kind of brightness lightened up the dense masses of the storm. A moment more, the snow ceased falling. Thereupon the dense masses themselves broke up and rolled away on all sides. And lo and behold this here Jack Culley, New Mexico ranchman, sitting in his Bain wagon amid the wide sunshine, with the landscape all around him as clear as crystal to the furthest horizon, exactly as things had been when he left the ranch a couple of hours before. Was it all just a dream, an illusion? Had there really not been a blizzard at all? It took me several minutes to locate our position. We had been traveling southwest instead of southeast, the direction of the ranch, and were only a few miles from home. Clearly the team had had the direction in their heads and had been beaten off it by the strength of the storm. It was a marvel we had not hit one of the sundry outcroppings of jagged rock that lay in our course. That would have meant likely the loss of the team and certainly the wreck of the wagon. As I turned Dick and Black Bess's heads to the ranch I thought I'd never before felt so well contented.

This has been a long detour, to use one of their automobile expressions, and I must hurry back to where I broke away from my original story. In view of the storm I determined to try and make only for the little town of Watrous, which lay not far out from my homeward road. Things were beginning to look unfavorable, as I didn't seem able to reach any country I recognized. The chances of Dick and me spending the night out-of-doors seemed pretty good. It was while I was going down a long narrow draw sheltered by broken bluffs on both sides, that I rode right onto a ranch. It consisted mainly of an excellent house and barn, though no living thing seemed to be about. The door of the house was unlocked, as ranch-house doors always were in those days. I went in and looked around to see if I could locate some grub, but nary a scrap was visible. That was a blow. However the barn, which had excellent horse stalls, contained several tons of good baled alfalfa. And at the kitchen door was a pile of grand split firewood. I remember thinking how fine a fire of that good wood would feel when night came on, and how well fixed Dick would be. If I had know then what we know now, that alfalfa makes good food for man as well as beast, I'd have stayed, I think. As it was, I debated long. Probably hunger cast the deciding vote, for I hadn't eaten since early morning. I swung my leg across Dick and we sallied forth again to try our luck in the storm, which showed no signs of abating. It's a curious thing but to this day I don't know whose ranch that was. (Perhaps it was the TW.)

Well, we traveled along I don't know how far or how long exactly, but it was beginning to get dusk when we turned into a rocky draw. Within a few minutes I recognized it as the head of a long draw that leads from Cherry Valley and Boone Valley plumb down into the town of Watrous. No fear of missing the road now. I guess I was probably singing as Dick and I went down that draw in the dusk.

All that night it snowed and the next day and the next night and another day, so thick and heavy that I didn't dare to leave Watrous. On the third day I lit out in clear sunshine for our Turkey Mountain ranch, twelve miles away. It takes all day to ride twelve miles in twenty-six inches of snow. Dick's forelegs soon were bleeding where the surface crust of snow was cutting them. Deep washouts, eight and ten feet deep, alongside the road, filled up level with snow made riding dangerous. I got home to find brother Chris cutting down pines to feed the stock. But as I remember, that storm did not cause much loss.

But there were winters in which men lost pretty near all it had taken them twenty years to get together. Such was the winter of 1905-'06 (as I recall the date.) There was no one great storm, but a succession of snows and thaws during a long winter, following a poor grass summer, wore down the condition of the cattle. However with plenty of hay and hard work I had come through without too heavy a loss, and the spring was opening up nicely with prospects of early grass. Already some of our cattle had been turned into open summer pastures. So things stood on April 27th when, as we sat down to our Easter Sunday dinner, a light snow started to fall. In a few minutes it had become a blizzard. Taking thought for some poor cattle that were without shelter in a nearby pasture I got up from my meal, saddled a horse and taking with me W. who was the only man on the place that day, we rode up there and started to try and move the cattle into a more sheltered pasture. But the storm was growing fiercer, and the cold intenser, every moment, and the cattle acted crazily, scattering on us in all directions so we could neither bunch nor drive them. It was so cold, indeed, that W. who wasn't a regular hand, gave out. I sent him home and remained to handle the stock alone. Giving up all idea now of getting them to another pasture, I thought to put them in a board corral there was, where at least they would get some slight protection from that crucifying wind.

And then followed one of the most curious things I ever saw in all my long experience handling cattle. The ends of the bunch, as I said, instead of closing in kept scattering. I saw one old cow drift off to the side by herself, meander away into the storm, and drop to the ground in what struck me as a rather unnatural way. I rode over to where she lay to try and get her up. But she was stone dead. I was riding like the devil all this time, though with little result. I started back to turn in the opposite flank. The cattle there too were acting in the same crazy way. I saw one of them stagger off by herself and drop. She was stiff and stark when I got up to her. There was something weird and gruesome, I remember feeling, these cows acting so queerly and dropping stone dead around me in the storm. I asked a medical man afterwards what had caused their sudden death. He said it might be shock, or pneumonia. Finally I got fifteen cows in the corral. Twelve of them were dead in the morning. And in another larger open pasture I found the cattle had drifted five miles before the storm. I tracked them by the dead carcases. There were a hundred of them.

And if, by any chance, any of my readers should ask how about the human end of the concern on these occasions, I think most experienced stockmen will agree with me in saying that in one such year a man lived ten.

# 9
## Arizona

THE main objection I hold against my home state of California is that I can't see far enough in it. You can climb to the top of Mt. Lowe, which should command a vast view of land and sea, and I'll be doggoned if you can sight the ocean twenty--five miles away.

That's so different from the real range country where I used to live. You know in earlier days there, when even the main roads consisted of little more than a couple of wheel tracks and a high center, and there wasn't a signpost from El Paso to Calgary, you had nothing to guide you on a long trip but natural objects of the landscape. They'd tell you: You must keep the Bald Mountain on your left all the time; or, you must head right along for the Huerfano Mesa. And you would travel day after day singling out that object two hundred miles away, perhaps, in that clear atmosphere.

Then the forms and contours of the mountains there are striking, and the sunsets, especially in Arizona, full of brilliant color. I must say I never found cowpunchers much interested in the scenery. Yet I remember one time on a roundup one of the fellows describing the Pintada valley, which lies down towards the center of New Mexico, in Guadalupe county. "That Pintada country" I recall him saying, "is the doggonest sorriest looking layout I ever set eyes on. It ain't so much that there's no feed down there. That wouldn't figure a great deal. A cow raised in New Mexico gets used to doin' without much to eat. But down in that Pintada country there ain't even nuthin' for an old cow to look at!" "I kinda believe," he continued meditatively, "that it sorta helps an old cow when she's hungry, to have somethin' to look at!" And perhaps the boys, too, got some satisfaction looking at the scenery around them.

I know I did. That's why every now and again I roll up my bed and hit the trail for Tucson, Arizona, where I can enjoy the sunsets, and see a long ways.

The little city of Tucson, although a winter resort, which is agin' it, is the center of a real cow country. Real cowmen can be seen on the street with weather beaten Stetsons, and the sheriff, Ed. Echols, is an old IOI man. And while I was there lately they held a stock show that was a genuine range cattle show. No sheep, or hogs, or chickens, or truck of that kind. Not even Jersey or Holstein cattle. Just Herefords—and some saddle horses. The distinguished visitors attending were not of the baby-kissing order. I didn't even see the Governor. But Albert Mitchell of the Bell Ranch was there; and Bob Lazear, from the old, old cow town of Cheyenne; and two brothers of the Boyce name, which is known by cowmen from the Panhandle to the Pacific; and Frank King. And the spectators around the sales ring and the sheds were cow folk who didn't ask you any fool questions about the cattle. I never got a bigger kick out of a stock show.

Then just after that the U. S. Forest Service held a conference under the only Fred Winn, who directs the scattered empire of the Coronado, extending eastwards to the line of New Mexico. They met at the U. S. Range Experiment Station in Santa Rita mountains and Matt Culley, who is in charge of that outfit, took me out to it.

A beautiful layout they have up there. Built at the mouth of a canyon emerging from mountains that rise, fold upon fold, with extraordinary abruptness to a height of 9000 feet. On either side the canyon the mountains open and decline gradually to the foothills, disclosing a vista of desert plain that stretches away towards far distant mountain ranges, range behind range,

to the West. And when the sun is setting, these ranges are trans-
figured into magic regions of subtly changing color and texture.
The buildings at the station have been designed and placed with
artistry, each one on an area hewn out of the mountain side,
so that they appear to be a part of it.

I attended several of their conference meetings which dealt
with modern methods of fire control. They gave a practical
field demonstration of their portable radiophone by which a
ranger at the scene of a fire and the supervisor at his desk can
communicate with each other. It's an up-to-date organization,
this U. S. Forest Service. The spirit of Teddy Roosevelt and
Gifford Pinchot still animates it.

Driving over some of the experiment Station pastures, I found
grass and near-fat cattle. The only instances of either I saw on
Arizona spring ranges. These cattle are privately owned but are
run under limitations prescribed by the Forest Service; strict
record of handling and finance being kept. They have made
money, and good money, for the owner. All of which started
me thinking that if the research department of the Forest
Service could come into closer touch with our stockmen the
latter could get great help in making the handling of their stock
more profitable, as well as in establishing means to restore
depleted pasture.

Another day in this Arizona pilgrimage of mine, we drove
out to visit Jack Kinney. Welcoming us at his own door the
well known cowman told us entertainingly about his coming
to Arizona. How the shadow of the granger had haunted him
all his life, driving him from state to state. First from the Texas
Panhandle; then from Wyoming in the fierce days of the Jackson county war. Moving to the Tucumcari region of New
Mexico, the farmers from Iowa closed in on him there; and
now he is being squeezed out of his final place of refuge in semi-
desert Arizona by settlers who are clearing out the greasewood
to plant cotton!

Kinney showed us his Johnson grass pastures, created out of unproductive flats, on which he pastured fifteen hundred head of cattle for three months of last year. The natural floods of the Santa Cruz valley irrigate them. But what interested us most was the story of his horse herd. Starting eighteen years ago with California native mares, to which were added over one hundred pure Morgans, he has crossed with Thoroughbreds, Standard-bred and Morgan stallions. But for a number of years he has used only registered Morgans, that have produced for him some first class cowhorses, along with fine saddlers. But the problem of maintaining the standard of "cow-sense" in a herd he finds to be one requiring much study.

This big Texan with all his knowledge and experience has a deferential manner which is very charming. He offers you his opinions, doesn't ram them down your throat. I'd like to have talked all afternoon with him. And as he waved us a courteous goodbye with his broad-brimmed Stetson and we drove away, I said to the lady at my side: "You see, one doesn't have to go outside the range country to find a thoroughbred gentleman!"

Then, after lunch at the Montezuma, we took the back track along 84, stopping at Marana to visit my friend Frank Herron who runs a dandy bunch of Herefords just across the railroad track from that hamlet. Frank had read a story of mine about Albert Shaw of New Mexico, and being as he is kin to James Craig, who is mentioned therein, and who is now Lord Craigavon and Premier of Northern Ireland, an own brother of Frank's being named for the distinguished statesman, he wrote me a letter. Frank's house is an old adobe stage of the coaching days, deftly remodeled, with a charming kitchen and a sleeping porch that is a place to dream in. There are bullet holes in the high ceiling beams, recalling some old-time brawl, and the Mexicans declare the place haunted. But friend Herron doesn't seem to take much stock in the ghost. The spick-and-span order of the place must be ascribed to Mrs. Martha Prince, his sister, a pleasant lady who comes from Seattle every year to spend the winter with him. As for Frank, he has ridden after cattle ever since he was big enough to be put on a horse in eastern Washington. His friendly eyes are Irish grey, and he rolls, continuously, Bull Durham "cigareets" in brown papers—the which tickled me exceedingly, recalling old times.

Then, a wonderful day drawing to a close, in the crisp western twilight we wended our way home to Tucson. Yes, I like Arizona.

II

It is in few livestock shows that you feel the atmosphere of the range so sharply as at that which is held annually at Tucson. I try to attend it regularly. It brings me into touch, living as I do now in a big city, with the life of the range, which is the best life in the world, as well as giving one a chance to meet up with genuine cowmen, who are, as far as I am concerned, the best people in the world. Tucson lies in a cow country pure and simple. In keeping with this the horses exhibited at the annual stock show have an equal flavor of the range with the cattle, and the horse breeders of the district direct their chief efforts towards producing good stock horses; horses that can be ridden over all kinds of terrain and hold up under it; and horses that can do any kind of work a cow horse is called on to do.

Conspicuous along this line are men like Melville H. Haskell and J. C. Kinney who are doing genuine constructive work in horse breeding in place of the hit-or-miss practice long and widely prevalent in the West. These men are using mainly Thoroughbred, Steeldust or Quarter horse and Morgan mares and sires, crossing and crossing back as seems indicated in the course of establishing the type in mind. Haskell is using an unusually fine Thoroughbred, Bayard II, Irish bred and imported by Colonel Bradley, the celebrated Kentucky racing man. He is a big powerful animal of even build throughout. Haskell mates him with Steeldust or native mares in breeding for stock horses. As for Kinney's operations, anything that Jack Kinney does along the horse or cattle breeding line is of interest and importance. He has brought his horse herd, deeply bred in Morgan blood, to what he thinks as fine a point as possible. To keep it there and head off any over-refinement, he tells me has contracted with Jack Casement of Colorado, through Jack's father, for a first class Steeldust stud.

Another fine stallion, which won the stallion championship at the latest show, is Master Bunting, belonging to Rukin Jelks who has a picturesque cow ranch some miles out from Tucson. This horse is beautifully built all over, combining power with activity. But by far his most remarkable feature is his temperament and intelligence. On the Jelks *hacienda* where Master Bunting does his regular all-around job of cow work, the footing is rough, the brush thick, the cattle hard to catch if, and when, you find them. Master Bunting is a shining proof of the assertion that Thoroughbreds can be found to handle themselves in rough country and take life quietly. Thoroughbreds of the type shown at Tucson, should, mated with sound substantial cool-blooded mares, produce useful range horses.

But I am quite sure that what stole the present year's show at Tucson were the Steeldusts or Quarter horses. This type of horse was represented by several unusually brilliant specimens. W. D. Wear of Willcox, Arizona, brought forward Tony and Red Cloud, chestnuts, of extremely compact and muscular build and showing plenty of quiet style. While another Steeldust stallion was Billy Byrne who stood second throughout to Tony and is owned by J. E. Browning of Willcox. He is of considerably more refined type than the rest—might, but for his head, pass for a Thoroughbred—and was shown in something like racing condition. I am frank to say that in all my experience of horses I hardly recall one whose conformation was harder to fault than this horse's. The judge, Albert Mitchell of New Mexico, placed him second to Tony. He may have preferred the latter's power and substance. But Mr. Browning is wisely awake to this ultra refinement of his horse and plans to mate him with mares having plenty of substance. Dulce, a roan two-year-old filly of his get, shown along with her sire, is an animal of the sweetest disposition, and promises to develop into a lovely general saddle type. I wish I could figure out some good excuse for trying to become her owner! Other breeders, among them my good friend, "Dink" Parker, representative range cattleman, if there is one, show good horses of this type.

Most of these horses perform nicely in the reining classes. Red Cloud only did not compete this year. But this horse gave a private showing of how he works for the benefit of Mr. G. W. Wiggett of Ventura, California, who ended by buying him for use on Palomino mares over in his own state. I am no show horse man and I know nothing about rodeo rules, but Red Cloud ridden by his owner handled himself in just the way a practical hand likes a cow horse to do, working around cattle. Absolutely adequate, without a shred of fuss.

And as if to add a touch of drama to a great exhibition what should happen but that Mr. Dan Casement himself should breeze in, clad in sporting tweeds and a red tartan waistcoat, from his large farm at Manhattan, Kansas. Do you believe the boys who owned these Quarter horses got a thrill when the man who is more responsible for the present existence of this type of horse than any one else in America was brought up by Postmaster Collins to pass an opinion on their stallions. His son Jack, now living at the family homestead at Whitewater, Colorado, bred both Billy Byrne and Red Cloud, and Casement had not set eyes on Billy since he was nine months old. Both Red Cloud and Billy Byrne are by Ballamoney; he by Dan Casement's most famous sire, Concho Colonel.

These Steeldusts are indeed a remarkable type of horse. In

spite of their vague, legendary origin and the promiscuous way in which they have been bred without organization or records, they adhere to type more closely than many well established breeds. I have known them ever since I struck the West. Short above and long below, always. Powerful shoulder and arm; quarters square but not overloaded, trim and perfect, growing clear from the ground up. An unfailing quality seems to be the muscular loin and back. And a remarkable feature is the strong Roman nose, appearing even in the most refined types, like Billy Byrne. I asked Dan where it came from: "There's no means of knowing," he replied, with one of his merry flashing smiles. It's one of the mysteries that surround this interesting type of horse. They run from 14.2 to 14.3 hands in height, which is on the small order and one would imagine they should be so mated as to increase their size and weight somewhat, if they are fully to fill their place on the range. The cow hand usually likes a good sized horse, though I myself could never see the desirability of it. Jack Casement is now planning to establish a breed and pedigree registry, to be based solely on performance. Any horse will qualify that can run the quarter from a standing start in a given time, to be determined. It would be somewhere around 23 seconds, doubtless.*

The Steeldust has mighty short gaits. It would be like old times going places on one of these chaps. But they'd fit nicely into a trailer! and the short gait is what is needed in their business. Their movement is without a vestige of stylization but is full of a subtle spring and rhythm that is a result doubtless of a perfect balance of every part, with consequent coordination. He is cool and steady, and takes to all forms of cow work instinctively. Back of their quiet disposition lies a light streak of devilment. "Nothing vicious, you know," laughs Dan, "they just enjoy cutting up a little on a frosty morning!"

*Since this was written a powerful and representative organization has been formed to promote this breed.

A distinguished man is Dan Casement, and intimate friend of distinguished men who built up the West: Murdo MacKenzie, W. J. Tod of Maple Hill, Kansas, Charlie O'Donel, long manager of the Bell Ranch in New Mexico, and many others. He is himself a cultured, polished gentleman, who can tell a good story and make a perfect speech. He has filled a large place in American agriculture, his car load lots of fed cattle having topped many a great show. But a succession of disastrous years has overtaken his district of Kansas. The section of land he owns, perhaps as rich as any in the world, which used to return him $150,000 annually, last year could do no better than $35,000. With a host of interests to fill his life, nearest his heart always, I feel sure, lie his Steeldusts, and he was a proud man as he witnessed these brilliant specimens of his own breeding heading the classes at Tucson. Dan Casement was one of a group of those men of distinctive bearing and character who have appeared in our Western range country always, present at this Tucson show.

It's a range show this, and as clean and open as the range on which it takes place. Here are no side shows that have to be hid, admission charges, or rackets. The commissary is in the hands of the "Aggies" of the University, any profit made going to help build up their Aggie Club. The boys don't have what you'd call an up-to-the-minute restaurant, but you get a helping of beans and bread and coffee for fifteen cents that led one to reflect upon the high cost of living at other larger shows we have all attended.

# 10

# The Humble Sheep

I SUPPOSE that in what purposes to be a record of the western
ranges, I ought to have devoted more space to sheep.

I have remarked before how little general interest is shown
in the United States in sheep, and how small the amount of
literature dealing with them, in contrast with the wide romantic appeal of the range cattle. There is one delicious book about
range sheep, called *Sheep*, by Archer B. Gilfillan, which everyone who handles sheep should possess. If the experiences the
writer describes do not duplicate the reader's own, and make
him laugh, then he cannot be a sheepman at all, or he was
born lacking the blessed gift of humor. *Sheep*, however,
deals with the northern ranges where they use a house wagon
in which the herder cooks, eats and sleeps. The system I am
thinking of had no such luxurious appointments. It was the
system that had prevailed on the Rio Grande in New Mexico
for several past centuries. The herders were Mexican peons;
they slept on sheepskins in a tepee tent; and their transportation problem was cared for by the patient New Mexico burro,
which could live off a thistle for a week, and which at that
time constituted a chief part of the general transportation
system of the Territory.

Whatever knowledge I myself had of sheep came to me
through William Pinkerton of Wagon Mound with whom I
lived a while when I first came West. He was then handling
mainly sheep, and could tell you more about them in half a
day than anyone else I ever knew in a year. Years later, when
the dry farmers crowded our cattle off the range, I put sheep

on some outlying claims and my knowledge of them came in handy.

I said the herders were Mexicans, and considering the generations of experience they had had, it was astonishing what poor sheepmen they were. One of my clearest early recollections is of old Mr. Pinkerton ramping up and down his sheep pens trying to explain to his herders in wholly inadequate Spanish how to handle the sheep through the lanes and gates. Pinkerton had learned the business in Australia where the real range sheepmen are to be found. They work their sheep in the yards always from the head—somewhat as you point a herd of cattle. If you keep your front sheep moving, the rest will follow, whate'er betide. Sheep, enclosed, have an inclination always to *pass* you. The Mexican idea was, everybody get in behind the bunch with gunny sacks and pebble-loaded tin cans, crowding and rushing, with the result that the sheep piled up on each other or else broke back, while those in front advanced not at all. I think I never knew but one Mexican, my good friend, Modesto Aragon, who got completely free from the "crowd 'em from behind" complex in a corral. Well, all their early experience had been with native Mexican sheep which were of practically no commercial value—the only market being Chihuahua, six hundred miles away—and indeed little better than a species of gregarious wild animal.

Lambing is of course the most critical time in the sheepman's life. It is easy going, maybe, on a farm, with ewes in good condition, on good feed, sufficiently sheltered. But out on the range it often happens ewes are thin, there is no grass, and scant shelter from the weather. You find yourself with lots of lambless mothers and motherless lambs, which means much adjusting to be done. Now there is one principle envolved in this mother and child question in the domestic animal world, on which a great deal hinges. When a ewe lambs and loses her lamb at birth, it is for three days, and three days only, that her desire to possess a young one persists. Immediately after that period the maternal instinct in her dies completely. When a lamb turned up in my lambing corrals without a mother I would give it to a newly lambed ewe that had lost her lamb. If she did not take it within three days of her own parturition, I'd wait till another newly lambed ewe lost her lamb, and give it to her. But during the first three days the average ewe that has milk will take ANY lamb, if you give her a chance. After that you are wasting a lot of time trying to get her to take one at all.

This principle applies equally to weaning, and to cattle. When I was weaning calves I would separate them from their mothers in a corral and drive them away to some place. Then I would turn the cows out and let them run around the corral for three days. They would go off and graze and come back to the pen to bawl, alternately, during that time. On the morning of the fourth day I would drive them back to their usual range, turn them loose and never give them another thought. I never knew one to look back or return to the corral for her calf. It's just not done.

The magic number, three! I sometimes wonder about it. Three days for a cow or ewe to forget her young one. Three saddles, and a bronc was broke—provided you went on riding it steady. And three drinks and 'Sus Ruiz, my Old Mexico cowboy, would knock hell out of any horse you'd put a saddle onto. Range life ran in treys, it looked like.

Most of us old-time cowmen despised sheep, and had some good reasons for doing so, and some not so good. *None the less, the range sheep business with its wool-and-mutton complex is an interesting one. I fancy I was the first in New Mexico

*One of the good reasons was that range cattle will not graze where sheep have been. Just when one had got a bunch of cattle settled on a tract of range, a sheep herd would come in and run over it and every last cow would pull out. Nor would they return till a rain or snow had removed the smell of the sheep.

to try the Southdown on range Merino ewes, the result being as choice feeder lambs as ever left the state. I did not want to retain any of this cross in our breeding herd, as Southdown wool runs very light in that dry climate, nor did I want to run an extra herd at bucking time; so I adopted a device used by the shepherds on the Cheviot Hills on the borders of England and Scotland. I ran the Rambouillet and Southdown rams together in the corral with the ewes, but I painted the Southdowns with red paint on the brisket. The red paint enabled me to know which ewes had been attended to by the Southdowns and I'd put a mark on them to last till lambing. I thus used the plan so as to distinguish two classes of lambs. The Cheviot shepherd used it to enable him to remove, as is their custom, each ewe as she has shewn to have had service. But actually in my case it proved superfluous; you could distinguish the Southdown cross a hundred yards away.

I have said our Mexican sheepherders were poor sheepmen; and that is true. But I should like to put on record what a cheerful bunch they were to work alongside of under all circumstances. It was a gay scene around the campfire at shearing or lambing time. We are apt to think the Mexican peon dumb, but his apprehension of some things is keener than our own. Although often illiterate, their conversational give-and-take is surprisingly bright and ready; and in the evenings they would sometimes organize plays or mock legal trials in which the command of their own language they displayed would have put to shame most educated Americans. Many times I have sat beside the campfire under the stars and listened while a couple of them sang in parts what Robert Louis Stevenson calls "those heart-broken songs" of theirs. Gay ones too they had, sung with a style and animation no Anglo-Saxon of any class can attain. The warm sensuous Spanish strain predominates in the much mixed blood of these people.

The life of a sheepherder was one of year-long exposure.

Not so dangerous but fully as hard as that of the cowpuncher. Indeed the coldest I ever came to feel was one time working with sheep. It was at the end of one of the heaviest snow storms we ever had in that country that Eliseo Vigil came in to report his herd cut in the storm and a large bunch of them missing. The snow had already stopped falling and bright and early next day I saddled up a horse and went out to hunt for them. I found them comfortably ensconced on one of the timbered beaches of the Mora river, that sloped pleasantly to the south. How to get them back to the ranch on the Escondida through two miles of snow two feet deep became the immediate problem. There seemed no solution but to make a trail with cattle. Numbers of range cattle had drifted onto the benches in the storm and I rounded up a bunch and drove them from where the sheep were across the open plain of snow to the ranch. But drive as I might, I could not get them to make a trail wider than single file. You can't push cattle much in snow; they'll play out on you.

So much done, Eliseo and I started in to get the sheep to take the trail. But they didn't want to leave their pleasant camp. Hour after hour we worked on with them, sparing no effort and trying every device, and at the end of six hours they were at the exact spot where they were when we began. The hot sun made the deep snow as wet as water, and I was presently sopping wet up to the waist, chaps and all, clear down to the skin. And so I guess was Eliseo. It was many hours after sundown when, at long last and suddenly, the sheep started to take the trail, traveling slowly but steadily, single file; mechanically, as though activated by a single motor unit, through the narrow snow-walled corridor beaten by the cattle's hoofs, their grey bodies small and weird seeming in the pallid glitter which in a setting of snow plain and starlit sky that rare air of the high plains takes on. The early sunset had been followed by bitter cold. Just half way between the river benches and the Escondida lies a deep dry lake, through which my trail passed. As the lead ewe reached it we decided to stop the herd and bed them down for the night. At that moment the last of the column was just leaving the river bench a mile away. We rode back and forth alongside it, as one rides along the flanks of a trail herd of cattle. If you stood in the lake, it was odd to watch each sheep arrive and join quietly the gradually increasing band there. Once started, they never paused or hesitated in their long march; indeed, I don't believe you could have stopped those sheep coming then.

It must have been near midnight when we got the last of them bedded down, and ourselves rode in to the ranch. As quick as we were in the warm house I made the discovery that six hours of freezing temperature had frozen everything I had on, clear from my chaps to my underwear, stiff and solid to my skin. I don't remember anything like it before or since. It would doubtless have felt severely uncomfortable, if I could have felt at all. But I don't believe I did.

Next morning we found our herd complete and unharmed in the lake. They were now eager for the ranch, and threading their way through the remainder of the trail were shortly in their home corral.

# II

## Hereford Cattle, Past and Present

### I

Iᴛ seems pretty plain sailing in the registered Hereford field
in these times; sales well attended, demand brisk, and prices
that should return a profit to the breeders. But you don't
have to be so frightfully old to remember when conditions
were very different; when breeders were struggling for a chance
to introduce the comparatively new breed of cattle—to dem-
onstrate, indeed, its superiority as a range animal to the "Durham" with its old established, world wide circulation.

This was perhaps harder than might seem likely today, for
the Hereford of those times was inclined to be coarse in the
shoulder, from generations of use as a work ox in the old
country, and rough and peaked in the hind quarters, and in
the effort to get them evener, American breeders were running
to the small, smooth, light-boned type whose get were already
showing up small and light-boned on the range. So much so
that some range men were fain to renew an original Shorthorn
cross, in order to maintain the scale and weight.

The majority of range cattlemen in those days, while well
qualified to handle cattle along various lines, were not close
judges of fine stock or highly finished cattle. A slick fat animal
was apt to take their eye. I remember well one time visiting
Emporia, Kansas, to look at C. A. Stannard's Sunnyslope herd
of Herefords. Stannard had brought out Mrs. Kate W. Cross'
outfit after her husband's tragic death. Like Charles Gudgell
of the Gudgell and Simpson firm he had started by breeding
Aberdeen Angus, till that breed was shown to be unsuited for
the range. Stannard's best bull at Sunnyslope was Wild Tom,

a son of the great Anxiety 4th. bull, Beau Real, a bull who had something of the square quarter and rugged charater of the Anxiety 4th—North Pole cattle, then first appearing on the horizon and later practically to sweep the entire Hereford field. But Stannard had a selection of fat pretty little bulls for sale as well. I was telling him how I thought these little "quality" bulls were lowering the size of the range cattle, and that range bulls needed scale and bone to maintain weight. "Yes," he responded, "that's what all the cowmen say when they come to look at my bulls. But they all buy the fat ones!"

There's a moral in this story for our present day breeders, perhaps, so I may as well go on with the rest of it. As soon as I got home I sent a little account of my Sunnyslope visit to Clay, Robinson & Company's *Weekly Livestock Report.* I related our conversation about the bulls and then continued somewhat as follows: "The famous 18th Century English wit, Sidney Smith, once said of a hot day that it was the kind of day on which you would like to take off your flesh and sit in your bones. I could not help thinking as I looked at these fashionable bovines that if they were to take off their flesh and sit in their bones, there wouldn't be much of them."

Some time after this I had occasion to go to Ed. Mitchell's ranch on Tequesquite in New Mexico to see about some bulls. Ed.'s first remark to me was, "I want to show you my new herd bull and see what you think of him." He then told me he had read my little story in the *Report* and been so much impressed with it that he went off and bought him a herd bull which he thought would put range and bone into his cattle.

That's getting on for forty years ago but I like to think that my ideas influenced the foundational stages of what is today one of the oldest and largest registered Hereford herds in the world.

Hereford cattle are much evener than they used to be, but we had some heavy fleshed cattle in those days. One of the good bulls Stannard had was Java, an extraordinary thickly fleshed animal with a deep dimple, or tie, in the middle of his spine. I could never see why this should be regarded as a blemish in the show-ring. It descended to Java from the great imported bull, Tregrehan, belonging to Fowler and Van Natta, through his 2800 pound son, Fowler. When people objected to it in Fowler Van Natta would say: "If he didn't have that great load of beef on his back, he wouldn't have the dimple!" Stannard and I were discussing the question whether it was legitimate to cut the ligament that causes this tie, and Stannard went on to tell me how a well known exhibitor had lately been detected operating on a cow to correct a showyard blemish. She was a famous show and breeding cow whose name in various forms appears in many Herefords of today. One show-bench fault, however, she had: she was a trifle hollow from the tail bone to the hook or hip bone, and her owners had conceived the plan of filling up this depression by pumping good United States air into the part. The judges, however, discountenanced the move.

Incidentally, I happened lately to relate this bygone occurrence of the illicit operation to a well known present-day livestock judge; and the only comment he made was: "Oh, so they started that game as long ago as that, did they?" Ahem!

Speaking of cowmen being easily deceived by high condition in bulls, I may say that it needs a shrewd judge to size up a thin animal. No one of record was more expert at it than "Governor" Simpson of the great firm of Gudgell & Simpson. His selection of Dowager 6th in England is an historical instance. Dowager 6th. was in unattractive condition and no one wanted her. Even the English breeders advised Simpson against buying her. But the Governor had been in the mule trading business, buying 'em thin and selling 'em fat. And it was his business to know what the lean mule would look like if, and when, he had put flesh on him. He bought Dowager 6th. and she turned out one of the great cows of the Gudgell & Simpson herd. Every one of the Dominos, which seem indeed to dominate the Hereford field today, goes back six or eight times to Dowager 6th.

He knew what he wanted too, this shrewd faced Kentuckian from Missouri. He went to England to buy a bull "with an end to him." A hind end was what the Herefords most lacked. He purchased against the advice of the English breeders themselves the bull Anxiety 4th, brought him back with him to Missouri, and put an end on the entire American Hereford breed.

## II

I have said that many range cattlemen were deluded into buying "fancy" bulls, with the result that their herds declined in weight and scale. Yet there were always men who realized the importance of bone and ruggedness for the range. It was to the range man that the great Gudgell & Simpson line of Herefords which today dominates the Hereford field, owed its early growth and success. Something there was in those short-legged, heavy fleshed, yet rugged animals, product of Anxiety 4th. males and North Pole females, that appealed to men of judgment like Murdo McKenzie, W. J. Tod and others.

I have sometimes thought too that the fact of Charles Gudgell, guiding spirit of the Gudgell & Simpson establishment, being connected with the range through an interest in the OX outfit of No Man's Land, may have had some influence in shaping his ideal of a range animal. Charles himself could not spend much time on the ranch, but his brother, J. R., was there a lot, assisting Major Towers, the widely known OX manager. Indeed from an early date Hereford breeders were brought to realize that their principal source of development was selling to Western breeders. During the depression years around 1893, when eastern sales of pedigree stock were low, scores of bulls carried the blood of the most famous sires and dams out West, to be merged, unrecorded, in the great range herds. Texas has more of the good blood of the Hereford breed, past and present, within its borders than any other equal area in the world.

They were men of character, most of those early Hereford importers and boosters: Powell and Miller, and Tom Clark, and George Morgan, who was the first manager of the famous WHR ranch; "Governor" Simpson, importer of Anxiety 4th, Van Natta and the rest. But none cut a wider swath for a while than T. F. B. (Tom) Sotham, whose career as a Hereford breeder affords us a drama of mingled trumph and disaster. Tom came of fighting stock. His father, William Sotham, born in Oxfordshire, England, made the first important importation of Herefords to America, and thereafter did battle for many years for the recognition of the breed. At that date, 1840, the Bates Durham was the supreme ideal of the American cattle breeder, but to the practical eye of a beef buyer for a packing plant, which Sotham was, this elegant breed was ill fitted for the production of profitable beef carcasses. His mind went back to his native Herefords which, though coarse and uneven, were deep-fleshed and readily put on beef on grass. But the American breeders laughed at them, and Sotham was one of the leaders in a bitter fight for recognition. He had at his disposal an acrid tongue and pen, and the courage to match his stuff against all oncomers. But it was forty years before a Hereford herd book even was established.

When the old man passed on at the age of eighty-two he left his son Tom to carry on the fight. Tom too had a ready pen, if less bitter than his daddy's, and he brought to his task two great passions: an inherited love of the Hereford breed and a steadfast devotion to his father. The History of the Hereford which he wrote was largely a vindication of the old man's claim to have introduced the Hereford to America. Tom's chance came when he secured financial backing to establish a breeding farm just out from Chillicothe, Missouri. Always a free spender he built himself a charming home in Chillicothe, placing a young Englishman, Ed. Price, in charge at the farm. He started in with high ideals: to improve the Hereford breed, especially as to refinement of head and horn. He laid in some fine foundation stock along certain lines he liked, being a profound student of pedigrees. His great bull was Corrector. Tom was a past master in the art of publicity and never in the annals of livestock breeding was a bull so highly publicized as "Old Dad," as Tom always called him. I only saw the old bull when he had grown high in the withers and his famous furry coat had lost some of its mellowness, its yellow red faded almost to a dun. People have been known to wonder how much of his great reputation was due to his master's skill in keeping him before the public. Not a letterhead nor a page of any of Tom's elaborate sale catalogs but Old Dad's alert head loomed up on it.

Times went very well for Sotham for some years, especially in the banner years around the turn of the century. He won many championships and got high prices for some of his bulls. He was a somewhat bitter contestant but always took the big view of a situation. After a desperate fight in the great Omaha exposition of 1898 between his Thickset and the grand Scott and Marsh bull, Hesiod 29th, he turned round after the sale and offered Hesiod's owners $2,000 for him. A line breeder but no in-and-out advocate, when old Corrector played out he imported Improver from England to carry on his work.

But Sotham's energy and enterprise proved to some extent his own ruin. Taking a show herd South to Charleston, S. C. they caught tick fever, and Improver with a number of his show mates died. The loss increased for Sotham the financial difficulties of that disastrous year of 1903. His notes were called in. A last-moment-looked-for local effort to keep the concern together having fallen through, the mortagee ordered a sheriff's sale. A friend of mine, an extensive farmer and breeder of Waterloo, Iowa, now living in California, who was present and bought one of the bulls, has often described the scene to me. Under the shock of events—not merely the financial collapse but far more the sudden sweeping away and dispersing of plans of breeding deeply pondered and being carried to success—Tom's mind seems to have become temporarily unsettled. He was an immense man, tall and powerfully built, and he moved about the sale yard stick in hand, as though with some idea of intimidating buyers. He refused to give any identification papers for cattle sold. But a number of deputy sheriffs had charge of the sale and Tom finally became more amenable and helped in the ring. The cattle brought only a fraction of their usual values.

Some of the circumstances of this sale were suppressed in the press accounts at the time. I have related them just as they were, because the story is part of the livestock history of the period, and my friend Tom has been dead a number of years. Many of my readers who are interested in livestock, must know from personal experience how absorbing a life passion the breeding of livestock becomes to some men. Such as these will share with me the sympathy I feel for Tom Sotham, Hereford breeder—alike in his achievement and in his tragic collapse.

### III

In the period I am writing about Hereford breeders still used to consider their problem in terms of certain great foundation bulls: The Grove 3rd, with his mellow flesh, who sold for $7,500 when he was eleven years old; Lord Wilton who gave the breed refinement of head and horn, and imparted stylish carriage to the clumsy forehands; Garfield, the "rich red" bull of the massive substance and constitution of iron, forerunner of Champion Dale and Perfection, who sold for $10,000 and $9,000 respectively; and Sir Richard 2nd, whose blood through

a long line of great dams went into the Prime Lads and Gay
Lads, Prince Rupert and Woodford, the Beau Donalds and
Beau Perfections. These bulls along with Anxiety 4th, are the
five outstanding foundation sires of American Herefords. Although all carried the blood of one common early ancestor,
Sir David 68, the mating of their strains was an absorbing
problem.

Today interest seems to center in one close bred line of
cattle descended from Anxiety 4th. Scrutinizing the tightest
of these Gudgell & Simpson pedigrees even the most casual
student of bovine history is apt to recall the last occasion when
such another fetish for an exclusive line or family swept the
cattle breeders of America. That was a more spectacular happening than the present one, culminating, as it did, in a sale
where ninety-two cows were run up to an average of $3,813,
with a top of $40,600. The story of the Bates Shorthorns would
make a movie. But in the hands of reckless and inexperienced
breeders it didn't take these fancy cattle long to go to wreck.

Now don't anybody run off with the idea that I am trying
to draw a parallel between those elegant overbred Duchesses
and our still virile Dominos. The only signs of decline judges
detect in some of the latter are a lack of scale, a weak hind leg,
and some over-refinement in quality and finish. There are certain facts that seem to me to have helped the Gudgell & Simpson stock to withstand and indeed flourish for a long period,
upon an unprecedented concentration of blood. In the first
place the foundation stock was expertly selected, and from a
large number of different herds and blood lines. Indeed this
latter fact may well have been one reason why Charles Gudgell
found it advisable to keep within narrow lines of breeding and
avoid further outcrosses. You may remark that Gudgell used
intensive Anxiety 4th line breeding but he never bred Anxiety
4th to his own daughters, nor mated full brothers and sisters.
And his greatest bulls, Beau Brummel and Lamplighter, were

out of North Pole, not Anxiety, cows. Yet another point is that the Gudgell and Simpson stock has been scattered in every corner of the United States and Canada, and I have a theory that drastic changes of locality, and climate, and conditions affect the constitution of an animal much as a change of blood does. And finally it is an important feature that great and increasing numbers of registered Hereford herds have for years been raised under natural range conditions in place of the confinement of the corn belt farm of early days.

But the point I want to make here is that, however admittedly superior the Anxiety 4th strain may be to all others, it is a pity that many of the great herds of Western range cattle should lack the benefit of the blood of other great sires and dams that have builded up the whole body of the Hereford breed. For it is in the range country that the passion for an "air tight" Anxiety 4th pedigree is most insistent. It goes without saying that there are good Hereford herds that supply a broader range of breeding. If you have a turn for pedigrees, come with me and we'll pass one or two of them in review.

Suppose we take Hartland Brae 51st, a herd bull on the breeding farm of Paul Thompson at Clinton, Indiana. Each grandparent of this bull carried a strain of Anxiety 4th, but further back he traces to the great Dale, and Dale goes back twice to Garfield, through his sire and on the dam's side through Tom Clark's Peerless Wilton whom Peerless, greatest daughter of Lord Wilton, dropped to the service of Garfield. Then on the dam's side this Thompson bull is full of the blood of Bonny Brae 3rd who made history for Cargill & McMillan of Wisconsin around the turn of the century, and who brings in another strain of Wilton and Garfield, along with one of Sir Richard 2nd, "Old Dick." There you have four of the five great foundation bulls of the breed in one pedigree, incorporated under the dominant strain of Anxiety 4th.

Those who own cattle of the Beau Aster-Domino strain

have useful outcrosses through Beau Aster's dams, tracing back to Maidstone, a grandson of Lord Wilton, who went to the Argentine at $7,500, and Sotham's Thickset, son of Corrector and grandson of the great Fowler. Besides which Beau Aster himself was largely mated with cows of Lord Wilton, the Grove 3rd and Corrector blood.

Or take the pedigree of Brother Regulator, belonging to G. L. Matthews & Son of Kinsley, Kansas, whose herd was founded over forty years ago. Strongly Anxiety 4th on the dam's side, on the sire's it runs back through Repeater and Distributor to Disturber. Disturber was by a Beau Brummel bull but through the female line went directly to Garfield and Lord Wilton, his grandam being the dam of the great Dale. Not far back you find a strain of Hesiod 2nd, famous son of The Grove 3rd, and run onto Fulfiller, who was by Tom Sotham's imported bull, Improver, out of Benison. Improver was the bull, you will remember, Sotham brought over from England to take Corrector's place, and Benison was the loveliest of "Old Dad's" granddaughters and the apple of Tom Sotham's eye.

Up through the northern and northwestern states the straight Anxiety complex seems less exclusive than in some other parts. The great Montana herd of A. B. Cook (dispersed in 1928) and the Chandler herd of Baker, Oregon, still flourishing after forty years of existence, were based on an extraordinarily broad and solid foundation. No breeder ever took greater pains than A. B. Cook to secure only top cows for his foundation herd or sought them over a wider field. Along with his Anxiety sires he used bulls strong in the blood of Perfection, Perfection Fairfax and all that lies behind those names. Chandler's earliest notable bull was Debonair 26th, carrying much of the blood of Fowler, the bull with the dimple which Van Natta pronounced the best bull he ever owned and who left behind him a train of dams almost the equal of Jewel

Fowler herself. The stock of Woodford, in whose veins ran the blood of Garfield and Lord Wilton through concentration in his grandsire, Dale, has played a large part in this herd. "I like," Chandler will tell you, "always to have a strong strain of Garfield in my cattle." There speaks the far-visioned breeder. And these two great herds have developed independent strains like the Panamas, Belmonts, etc., whose influence has spread and persisted in the best breeding tradition throughout the entire Northwest, affording a broad basis for breeding operations.

Over in Idaho the well established herd of Henry Thiessen at Culdesac, contains much of the blood of Perfection; of Prime Lad in whom Anxiety blood mingles with that of Lord Wilton and Sir Richard 2nd; of Bell Metal, imported grandson of that good imported sire, Albion.

I have laid much stress on Garfield because perhaps strains of that rugged, big boned though deep fleshed bull are just what is needed to correct any present over-refinement in our Herefords. Another bull carrying on this bull's blood in the North is Onward Domino, bred by Fulcher & Kepler of Holyoke, Colorado. The Mountcrest herd of Northern California, the WHW herd of Wyoming and the de Berard cattle of Colorado Middle Park are among the many that feature this stock. In conversation recently with one of the de Berard brothers, I commented to him on the fact that his Royal Domino 4th, the nine months bull calf that won the Reserve male championship at San Francisco's Treasure Island and sold thereafter for $2,000 had a healthy double cross of Garfield through Onward Domino.

We people of America are not greatly in the habit of exercising independent judgment. We follow a lead and when we get going are as hard to stop as a flock of sheep going through a gap in a fence. This hurry to join the rush is apt to blur our vision of the situation and impair our judgment.

A year or so ago in my district of California a herd of Herefords was offered at auction showing only slight traces of the popular Domino breeding, but strong in the blood of Perfection Fairfax, great grandson of Dale and carrying a world of famous blood in his veins. In his own right he won nineteen grand championships in his day. Although well advertised the sale attracted few bidders and of these some failed to claim the cattle knocked down to them. True, the stock had been neglected, yet at a 1913 auction at Kentland, Indiana, nine head of Perfection Fairfax bulls had drawn an average of $1,460! I am not offering advice, much less uttering prophecies, but I tell the above story to illustrate the point that while we scramble madly to secure certain lines of breeding, we leave neglected sound and safe lines of Hereford blood. Thereby maybe missing opportunities for later success, should the present vogue in Hereford pedigrees shift somewhat, as lines of breeding do. Not to mention certain risks which highly intensified breeding in inexpert hands incurs.

#### IV

Speaking of the cow Benison a while back brought to my mind others of those good Hereford mother cows I used to know on the farm and in the ring in earlier days. Peerless, who brought both stake and name to good Tom Clark, I think I never saw, but Queenly, get of Beau Brummel out of a Van Natta cow by old Fowler, and Primrose, mother of Prime Lad, and Dollie 2nd, reputed to have sold for $7,000, and a score of others, still seem fresh in the memory. And thinking of them sets me wondering whether the boast that our Hereford of today is so greatly superior to that of forty years ago is so very well grounded after all.

Certainly the breed as a whole in America is more smooth and uniform than it was then; has a good deal more quality throughout, leveler quarters. But I can't help regarding with some misgivings the tight little animals which some judges in conformity with the dictates of our packers and house-keepers place at the head of our show ring classes, and con-trasting them with earlier types. I am reminded how rapidly I have seen whole herds decline in scale and weight. Twice I know, in my own experience, I have had to discard an entire year's crop of heifers for being undersized as a result of an ill-judged attempt on my part to develop an ultra compact "butcher" type.

You cannot in livestock breeding, especially under range operations, maintain a type or quality in an animal permanently at a high point of equilibrium. You have to allow a margin. And in the case of range cattle that margin will be on the side of scale and bone and constitution. The suggestion is sometimes made that under the sparse and precarious range conditions of our western range country, and to meet present market demands, a smaller, smoother breed of cattle would be advise-able. If the point be granted, as it may, certainly such type must not come as a result of a decline of some larger type, but must be conceived and developed purposively. That may be to some extent what is taking place today. Along these lines, among sheep, the Southdown has been developed as a perfect small-sized sheep that can live and put on flesh on the short dry pickings of the English Downs; at the same time fattening rapidly in the feed yard.

But the range cowman, unless he has changed his views since I was one, would like his calves to weigh 400 pounds at weaning time, and his dry cows off the grass in the fall to scale 1000 pounds on the market. If your cattle don't weigh out, they won't pay out, he says. And it takes good big range cattle to make those weights. The Argentine breeders, too, go in for scale, that being one reason why the English keep up the size of their Herefords, since they supply most of the Argentine foreign-bred bulls. Nor are the cattlemen alone in this quest of scale. The range sheepmen in crossing their Merino ewes to get mutton lambs use mainly the biggest mutton rams: Hampshire, Lincoln, Dorset. And with the size must go a certain measure of ruggedness, an absence of over-refinement, in an animal that has to make its way against adverse conditions and, as far as may be, off its own resources.

One thing that strikes me as wrong about the present situation is that our American judges and breeders of pure bred stock tend—more a good deal, I believe, than the British—to use practically the same standards in judging she stock that they use for a bull or steer. They lay an equal stress on smoothness about the tail-head, compactness of build, and other features that have little bearing on the special functions of the female, which I take to be to produce as many good calves as possible, and bring them fat to weaning time off her own bat. Any practical cowman can show you around his herd and spot for you the good "mother cows." They are apt to be fine in the neck, roomy of frame, perhaps a bit uneven in the hind quarters. But they have an imponderable quality about them that stamps them as breeding cows. And though the boss may have more correctly built cattle in his herd, these find favor in his experienced eyes because they are the ones that year in and year out keep him out of the red.

A short while back I saw a calf of almost perfect formation placed low in a heifer class of a great show, and the judge gave as his reason for her place that she was "a little too big." According to what particular standard of weights and measures, I would ask, does this judge limit the size of his Herefords? and from the cattleman's angle what objection would there be to calves at weaning time weighing out forty or fifty pounds extra, and mature cows proportionately? Just that margin would be enough to spell success for him in his business.

Such conditions as the above prevailing, it seems fortunate that we still have some judges and breeders of pure bred stock who adopt the more liberal attitude towards the breeding cow. Such cows as Chandler's Miss Mark 34th, undisputed champion female of 1938, have along with modern finish a fullness and scale reminiscent of some of the great early day matrons. A cow like this can and does produce and support a calf as good as herself. "I wouldn't consider," says her breeder, "keeping a cow in my herd that couldn't produce a good calf and have milk enough to keep it." Miss Mark 34th is no result of inbreeding to get ultra refinement. Strong in Anxiety blood she yet shows a lusty development that recalls such ancestors as Dale and Garfield and the great old cow, Rose Blossom.

It's a heap easier in this breeding business to criticize than to construct. No one knows that better than I do. We used to keep a small herd of pure bred Herefords on the Rafter C Bar ranch, from which to try and breed bulls that we thought were of the right type for our range cows. I had bought these purebreds from the JJ herd on the famous JA ranch in Palo Duro canyon out from Clarendon, Texas. It had been started by Charlie Goodnight in 1881 on a shorthorn foundation and Charlie had spared no money in getting the finest bulls, domestic and imported, for use on it. Those early Texas cowmen got the best that was going. C. C. Slaughter paid $2,500 for imported Ancient Briton and $5,000 for Sotham's Sir Bredwell, which are stiff prices for a range man to pay. As for our bunch John Hinde and I would ride through it often discussing results. I would try to discourage him a little when I thought him too optimistic. I remember at long last we got a heifer that bid fair to grow up into something near our ideal. John pointed her out to me one day. "We'll call her Hope, John!" I said.

It had been just a few years before that I had bought from Ed. Mitchell, the Tequesquite (N.M.) Hereford breeder, a

lovely golden red bull called Laddie. He was a double Garfield. Ed. told me his mother was an extra good milker. So
I brought him to run with our little bunch of pure bred cows.
I wanted to put some more of that "mother" quality into them,
and through them into the range herd. And sure enough, as
long as I ran that herd of cattle I could spot the Laddie touch
in our cows, generation after generation, in the "spread" and
the feminine heads and forequarters. But once in a while we
would have to run in a cow because her young calf could not
take all the milk, which is a drawback in the range business.
As for our modern American type of Hereford cow, you
cannot get her complete story till you've visited the shows
and made the acquaintance of the old black-and-white nursing
sisters that are lined up in the back stalls.

Talking like this leads my thoughts back to the early cows
I was telling you about. I notice that I left out mention then of
the greatest of them all: Mischievous (put the accent on the
middle syllable!). No Hereford cow has given name to so
many and so great strains and families as she has. Gudgell
& Simpson used to name their cattle after the dams; either
using the name itself or the initial letter, as you will see by
a little study of their pedigrees. How well I recall young
Frank Gudgell, who in later days had principal charge of the
show herd, showing me old Mischievous on their beautiful
Independence (Missouri) farm one day. Frank was deploring
that some disease was totally destroying the elms that grow in
that rich soil as big as the elms on Yale College campus, and
under whose shade those great Anxiety cattle used to rest.
What a grand good cow she was, Mischievous. A lightish red,
as I recall her, of the rugged order, roomily built, weighing
a ton in good flesh at six years. But, though a consistent prize
winner, not so overly smooth about the rump. She raised a
great calf every year from her second year throughout a long
life, including twins. I am fairly sure Mischievous would be

placed near the foot of the line in one of our modern show rings, and rightly so, I judge, as today's standards go. But all the same I would like to have a couple of thousand range cows just like her to turn loose on my old ranch. I would be able to quit work and buy Seabiscuit.

# 12

# Who Destroyed the Range?

*"And they've broken up the grama,
And our lives, our hearts."*

THERE has been a vast ideal of publicity given by the press and magazines of the country during the last few years to the wide destruction of our western ranges. Government departments too have dealt exhaustively and sometimes spectacularly with the subject. And the burden of blame seems to have fallen upon the cattlemen. But most of what has been written has been the work of professional journalists without any first hand knowledge of what they were writing about, or else the rather aloof comment of the scientific investigator. It has seemed to me that a brief account of conditions that have accompanied the range business for a number of years by one who has LIVED through it, handling cattle in all denominations from one hundred head to thirty thousand, might give the public a clearer view of the matter, and of the part the stockman has played in it.

When I first struck the West the range business was at its climax. For the past five or six years cattle had just been poured onto the range till the entire west from the line of Mexico to Canada was packed with them. Not to mention sheep and horses. There is no question but the range was disastrously overstocked.

Nevertheless not too much blame should be laid on the cowman for this condition. In the first place the system of open range and community grazing which prevailed afforded him little opportunity for estimating the capacity of range pasture.

He had grown, too, from experience to have unlimited faith in his grama and buffalo grass, his mesquite and sacaton. It might be beaten out or eaten off, but a good rain would bring it back again. Nor was he far wrong. A few years after the breakup of the range boom I was buying the ranches members of the cattle pools had abandoned, and the pasture on the range surrounding them appeared to be as good as ever. Nor must we fail to make allowance for the myth of the marvellous range business which was hypnotizing the imagination of every man in the boom days. Few were the discerning cattlemen who doubted the capacity of the range to support the tremendous problem mapped out for it.

That took place a long time ago, and since then the depletion of the range has proceeded by fits and starts. It is generally ascribed to overloading on the part of the stockmen. Yet there are instances in which the evidence for the charge is shaky, to say the least. Take the sudden invasion of northeastern New Mexico, southeastern Colorado and western Kansas by snake-weed in the early 1900's This wiped out ALL other feed over a wide area. Stock will starve to death rather than eat it. I know I had to move the cattle from a considerable part of our own range to rented pastures elsewhere. It was easy for the Government ecologist to ascribe these conditions to abuse of the range, but in my case he had to meet the fact that the range had been handled for fifteen years with persistent care and conservatism. When the weed had got well established Charlie O'Donel wrote me from the Bell Ranch asking me about it. Charlie had come to the Bells from the panhandle of Texas and knew nothing about snakeweed. I wrote back: "There is nothing we can do about it. The snakeweed will go away in its own good time and the grass come back." Well, that is exactly what happened. The snakeweed disappeared entirely and the grass resumed its old place in equal abundance and, generally speaking, quality. Here were two phenomena, for neither of which the plant ecologists could ever account to me. I put the problem to them in this shape: I said, "If the cowman is to be charged up with the coming of the snakeweed, who gets credit for the return of the grass?"

The years have come and gone since then and I suppose many cowmen have indulged their propensity for eating off a good crop of grass when it comes, which isn't often; and stocking up their range to the limit. If these were faults—which some deny—there are at least many extenuating circumstances we can plead in respect of them. A banking system, for instance, which laid stress on the numerical showing of stock without reference to range.* Land laws-the most futile ever devised by any government in the world having range lands to deal with— that gave the stockman no security of tenure, but encouraged him to get as much as he could out of the range while the getting was good. While the customary low prices, dictated by the packers, put a further premium on numbers, if one was to pay one's way. Who excuses himself, accuses himself, says the Frenchman; and I offer these excuses because I feel that the accusation against the stockman of being responsible for the general range depreciation has some grounds of truth. But the appalling destruction of our national grazing resources which has been the subject of all the recent publicity was brought about, at a comparatively late period, by a movement the stockman did his best to counteract; of which, indeed, he was the victim. He objects to the blame for it being laid upon him.

By the first decade of this century the western stockmen may be said to have built up for themselves a kind of working system for the range, which, failing better, in a general way served their purpose. The grass at this time, though somewhat depleted, was still good in a good season and supported a

*Bank rates of interest for cattlemen likewise were very high, ranging from 3% a month in 1873, 2% in 1882, to 1% well on to the new century.

large amount of stock. Such generally were the conditions when there came about the invasion of the dry farmers. They suddenly swept down upon us like the hordes of the Huns from some remote quarters, and their ways were strange to us. It was useless to tell them you couldn't grow crops in a country where it hardly ever rains. They said it had been that way in Iowa when their folks first went there. Plowing the land had brought the rain.

It took them only a year or two to crowd us off our ranges, cutting up the land into small individual holdings, and breaking up the sod that was the life of the West. The blue grama in our district was so close and tough it took them often two and three years to subdue it. Some of this plow land they would summer fallow, establishing on it a surface layer of several inches of powdery soil which, when the March winds came, blew over and buried the adjoining grass land and, eventually, their houses and barns and machinery. After the first few years the land grew little but Russian thistle, and that wilted and rolled and piled up on the fences, the drifting dust collecting on it and making unsightly hills. It was a sorry looking spectacle these people made of God's good plains.

I don't want to be unfair to the grangers. Most of them were victims of propaganda. In some parts they were successful, but the majority of them lost all. Some had put money into the land and left it buried with their houses and barns in the sand. The real villains of the piece were the promoters and speculators who sold the idea. Some of these brought out school teachers and the like to take up claims, following them up with tractors that broke up whole sections of land at a go. The railroads joined in boosting the scheme. Bankers fell for it; local realtors and Chambers of Commerce. Everybody at the last had a hand in the demolition of our great American breeding grounds.

Everybody except the stockmen. Only a few of them joined in.

And there remains still for us the problem of the future handling of these ranges. Twenty-five years ago I decided that we cattlemen should modernize our ideas and practise. And I tried to put that decision into effect in my own case. I figured that the cow business could not remain the only great industry being run on the pioneer hit-or-miss method. The big industries provide scientific research departments of their own to study their problems. The stockmen have theirs provided for them by state and federal Governments. The progressive stockman of today takes the modern view and cooperates with these agencies. Such cooperation cuts decisively both ways. The stockman gets the benefit of the research and experiment of the scientific investigator and in return keeps the department man in touch with practical problems of the range. Likewise he can test out under range conditions any of the investigator's findings. I have known cases of such cooperation show remarkable results.

# 13
## Cowboy as Comrade

M Y record of the early West is drawing to a close and I look back over it to see if I have in any degree achieved my object in writing it. That object was twofold. First to offer fellow cowmen something that would be a truthful reflection of themselves and their lives. And secondly to correct in the minds of the younger generation the impression of ourselves and our lives which novels and screen plays have firmly established; to make clear to them what we really were like and how we really lived.

In case they should argue that this is not a matter of importance I refer them to where I have shown that the only genuine politico-social organization over the whole of the Western states during a period when the courts and legislatures were corrupt and futile, was that established by the cattlemen. And I will add that taken by and large this work was carried out more effectively and certainly by cleaner, if somewhat high-handed, methods than any other similar movement in American history. This being so, it seems to me a misfortune that the figures of the men who accomplished this should be handed down in the distorted form that has come to be generally accepted. And what I say of the cowmen and cattle owners applies to the cowhands who bore the brunt of the everyday work.

People sometimes ask me why, in view of my upbringing and all, I chose to throw in my lot with men, the majority of whom had had only scant cultural advantages. Certainly their ideas and attitudes on many subjects were different from mine;

THE RAINSTORM

considerable areas of interest and experience we could never touch upon. But if there were drawbacks, there were fully equal compensations. Let me tell you about one day when John Hinde and I were driving a bunch of cattle up on the high lands north of the Escondida. One of those New Mexico semi-tropical storms struck us suddenly. As the rain swept over us in solid sheets, and the wind roared and whistled in our ears, and the lightning following on deafening claps of thunder ran along the horns of the cattle, I remarked to John as we met up behind the herd, "Say, this cowpunching business is not what the story books crack it up to be." John is an inarticulate cuss; he replied with one of his (expressive) grunts. "But," I continued loquaciously, shouting as the rain beat into my face, till my voice overtopped the roar of the storm: "It's — a MAN's — life, John!" Yes, those range fellows one knew and worked with were — they had to be — first and last Men. And that was something. A lot.

Another thing that seemed to me an attractive characteristic of the cowman was a certain quietude, or reserve. He is generally represented as being loud and noisy, and some of the Texans were a bit loud-mouthed, but as a general thing you never heard much noise around a cow camp. Sometimes a song, generally rather subdued, or a tune on the mouth organ, would break the silence and float away over the wide spaces around us. But that silence, those "lost horizons," of the prairies did not breed chatterboxes. Indeed I feel sure if there was one thing a cowboy objected to more than another, it was a feller "shootin' off his mouth." That is one reason why we disliked the young Texas nester kids that came to work with the outfits. They had been differently raised somehow and would get up in camp and lay it off to a campful of old cowhands.

Of course there was no call to be as silent as Stonewall Wilson. Wilson was an Englishman, foreman for Campbell and Austin who ran the Open A, Quarter Circle brand near Liberty,

and the Box Bar brand on the Sapello river in the Rocky
Mountain foothills. Wilson was a top hand but was never
known to speak except to give an order. I recall one of the
boys telling me about him. "Me and Stonewall," he said "was
takin' a long trip one time down to the lower country, and
thinks I, we might as well ride together for company. Well,
I started in talkin', just like I am now, as we jogged along.
Stonewall, he seemed to be takin' in every word I said, but
he never said nuthin' in reply. I tried to kinder strike up a
new subject every once in a while. I thought that might be
the trouble. But it didn't seem to make a particle of difference
to Stonewall; he just kept on sayin' nuthin'. We traveled ten
miles; then ten miles more, without ary a word from Wilson.
When we'd ridden thirty miles, and him still silent, I blew up.
'By God, Wilson' I sez, 'this is all I can stand of you!' I
swung my horse off'n the road we was on and lit out across
the prairie at a high lope, makin' the rest of my ride alone, and
leavin' Stonewall Wilson still sayin' nuthin'."

But when these men did talk—which they did quite freely—
their language was extraordinarily dry and terse, and at
the same time expressive. I know in my own writing the
influence of it has done more than all the "modern" writers
combined to correct false notes in a semi-Victorian style and
habit of thought. And wherever it has been possible in this
chronicle to use the actual words of the range man I have done
so. Their phraseology was original with themselves; the outcome of their own experience. Their speeding horses "burned
the ground" or "hit the high places." If they wished to denote
a man of unusual character they might say that men like him
didn't "run in bunches." There you get a metaphor only a
range man would understand. Frank Hastings, early Manager
of the SMS ranch, quotes a cowboy who called a promissory
note "a slow note." They tried always to take the verbiage out
of an expression, to strip it to the bone. A cowboy's lariat was

his "string" or "line"; his .45 Colt revolver was just his "gun." To "ride line" and "cut trail" were good examples of laconic descriptive terminology. And closely associated, I think, with this condensation of speech was the clearness and steadiness of judgment that has always seemed to me a characteristic of the Western cowman.

This spirit of simplification extended to wearing apparel and horse equipment. The former bore no relation to the fantastic toggery and gaudy colors the Hollywood cowboy affects. The working cowboy's garments were an everyday vest, worn open over an ordinary shirt, often black; with occasionally a handkerchief around his neck. Pants of a heavy closely woven material, worn outside the high-heeled boots. These were higher in the leg than those used now and cut with a square top; the high heels being intended to prevent the foot slipping through the stirrup. Saddle and bridle were stout but severely plain.* Silver conchas and the like were practically unknown, and regarded as tenderfoot stuff. The rawhide lariat was rare among Americans.

These range men drank but little; enough only, on hitting the town after five months on the range, to make some of them feel like doing a little fancy riding or trying out their gun on the saloon lights. The thing that caught the cowboy was the rattle of the poker chips. That was for him the siren song! His profanity was picturesque and practically perpetual. Yet there were fellows I've known who never used a cuss word, or touched drink or tobacco. The usual smoke consisted of a granulated preparation whose name was reputed to have cost a million dollars a word to put on the market, and which was said to be tobacco. This was poured into a brown "cigareet"

*Some riders, myself one of them, used a short chain to connect the line or rein with the bit. This served the purpose of preventing the rein itself from getting wet when the horse was drinking with the bit on. The wetted leather tended to crack. It also lengthened the lines. As we never knotted our lines together it was necessary for us to have them good and long.

paper and lighted with a sulphur match which would choke you if you weren't careful. I could never get anything out of one of them except a lungful of sulphur, a whiff of smoke, and a taste of burnt brown paper. I smoked a pipe and, like most all the fellows, chewed Star or Climax plug. That was food and drink!

The only books we ever read were cattle brands. It was amazing the number of these some fellows knew and their skill in reading them. But those old cowbrands constituted a very history of the West.

I never remember seeing any of the boys show what you might call emotion, but they had a great feeling all of them deep down for horse and cow brute. Over and above the individual mounts of the men, every outfit had some pet like Chuckbox, handsome lead-team sorrel of the Wagon Mound roundup wagon, who used to hang around the camp, looking for scraps of beef the cook would throw out, which he ate. Or some old crippled "sister" that had shown up in every roundup as far back as anyone could remember. Rough and tough as some of our men might be, I was always aware of a certain fineness about a cow camp. We lived nearer to Nature than any other class of people, and Nature has a way of refining, spiritualizing those near her. Add to this that there wouldn't be probably a red cent of money among the lot of us. Our lives were kept free from the sordidness that goes with money deals and barter. Allowing for occasional differences, I never knew such a sense of true comradeship as ours was.

I've told you from time to time about my brother Chris who worked cattle with me in early days. He has lived now many years in England, where he writes successful Western stories and is known as the British Zane Grey! After long years of absence from the range and range men here is what he writes: I think now that no man could have ridden the old ranges and worked with these boys, without being a whole lot the better for it. It brought out all that was best in a man, and made him ashamed of the more common weaknesses.—And I subscribe to that pronouncement of brother Chris.

A DAUGHTER OF THE RANGE

# 14
## Love on the Range

I HAVE described in these pages the various features of the early range as fully as my space allowed and my knowledge extended. And you may wonder that my descriptions reveal so little of the love element. For the love episode, represented by a half-wit supposed to be a cowboy, and a New York ingenue, is the principal feature, I am told, of all western stories. These two meet up and ride about the country on pinto-palomino horses; the girl, having attended Smith College, discoursing in a semi-sophisticated strain, the cowboy responding in a style unbeknown to cowpunchers. Naturally they fall in love, and I suppose the story ends up with their marriage, though on the latter point I speak with no certainty, never having been able to read to that point in any of them.

But in the times that I am in the main writing about there were no such things as the dude ranches which today distort the atmosphere of the West, upset its financial standards, and provide a constant supply of eastern debutantes for the novelists. (As to the origin of the "cowboys" who figure in these dramas I have not even a guess to offer.)

I think the book that started these western tales going was Owen Wister's *The Virginian*. I've known that book to be read by intelligent cowboys at the time of its publication. I don't remember any of them considering it a true picture of range life or character. But Owen Wister merely "picked up" his knowledge of the West. He was followed by Zane Grey, a man who knew the range but found good money in writing travesties of it to a pattern. There have been others who know and write truthfully on the subject, but almost always with an element of exaggeration and an eye to sales. And alongside of these has come an avalanche of balderdash that has perhaps no counterpart in the writing line, and which muchly disgusts the genuine cowman.

I make bold then to say that one of the principal causes of the falsity that pervades our western stories is this love business. For the truth is love played a very small part in our range life. Few cowboys got married young. Many of us spent months and years far from "white" women of any kind. That is what made the average cowboy shy with the feminine sex, and what kept his respect, even reverence, for them constant. Most of you have heard the story of the bunch of cowpunchers who dropped into town one night and went to the theatre. The play was a melodrama, the gist of which lay in the ill-treatment of the heroine by the villain. The boys watched it for some time with growing impatience and finally became so incensed at the villain that they drew their six-shooters and started in a body for the stage, bent on doing away with this maltreater of womankind.

Families containing young women were few and far between. Some of the families lived in the small scattered towns and the boys from surrounding outfits would come around in winter time when jobs were scarce. At such places and times dances were quite frequent. In the gayest ballrooms I've never had such merry times as in those rough, 'dobe dance halls lighted with dim oil lamps. We'd slick the floor up with wax candles. I can still feel the pulse and rhythm of the square dances as we swung to the music of fiddle and guitar, and the "calling" of Mat McCallister or Andy Weist. Yet even here strict decorum prevailed; there was none of that "sitting out" which, in modern ballrooms, leads to many engagements. Indeed these dear ladies between dances sat side by side on a bench along one wall, quite discreet and a trifle demure, while the men occupied a bench along the opposite wall and loitered in groups by themselves. It cannot be said that any great efforts were made among our range folks to render love making easy.

It wouldn't have been so bad if the "white" folk, as we called ourselves, had been permitted by social usage to mingle with the Spanish or Mexican families. But the Texan custom prevailed over most of the southwestern country. We were brought up to regard the natives with some contempt, not to say, repugnance, and to marry one, even of the better families, speaking generally, was considered a bad break. Certainly the peons were of very mixed and doubtful origin, Spanish, Indian of all sorts, negroid. But of the better class of Spanish-speaking people some were of pure and excellent Spanish extraction, and more refined in habit and manner than many of the English speaking community. I myself had excellent and intimate friends among them, and it pleases me to render tribute, here, to their hospitality and charm. Without doubt some of our men could have gotten fine wives from among them. Yet I expect it was better that the mixture of races was limited as it was; their temperaments were greatly different. Certainly the jealous and fiery disposition of the Mexican brought about constant differences at their dances.

There was the case of Ira Duckworth, for instance. Ira was riding for a local cow outfit. He took in a Mexican *baile*, or dance, one night, in Wagon Mound. Ira wasn't a quarrelsome fellow, but the native *vino* is heady, and many of the company besides were probably a bit lit up. He got into an argument with Juan Martinez who was our one and only cobbler. Some of the other Mexicans took Juan's part and Ira got pretty well beaten up. When it was all over he went up to the hotel where he was putting up. He came back with his gun to the dance hall and, walking straight up to Juan, shoved it into his stomach

and shot him dead. Then he made a run for it and got away
from a mob of furious Mexicans. And the town was left minus
a cobbler.

I remember one day riding out into the Turkey Mountains
to hunt cattle. My brother and I had cattle on the Salt Lake,
that lies to the north of this range, and they would stray off
into the mountains. The range itself was controlled by the ZH
outfit which I have told you before had been moved over
bodily from No Man's Land when run out by dry farmers.
The Muscatine Cattle Company, to give it its real title, was a
big concern and brought in a number of riders, most of whom
stayed on in the district. One of the riders was Tom Porter,*
and he and I met up that morning as he was riding his range.
The Turkey Mountains are a small but completely isolated
mountain range, whose higher peaks are clothed in pinabete
timber of medium size, and intersected by lovely grassy valleys
studded with oak brush. The high-lying timber was dense and
cattle were easily lost in it.

Tom was a nice fellow and I was glad of his company as
I rode. I don't remember exactly how, but the conversation
swung around to the subject of Mexicans. Tom wanted to
know how I liked them. "O, I get along with them all right,
Tom," I said; "allowin' always for their bein' kinder dumb,
workin'." Finally he asked me what I thought of a "white"
man marrying a Mexican. Here I had a more decided opinion.
"Tom," I said, "that's plumb ruination. The man's got to become a Mexican himself; and all his children with him." Tom
seemed to hesitate a moment before he answered in a quiet
voice. "I'm sorry to hear you say that, Jack—because I've just
gotten married to a Mexican myself!" That was as bad a break
as I ever made and I think it upset me nearly as much as it did
Tom; but presently he went on; "You know we live up in the
mountain, the wife and I. The company built us a little house.

*This is a fictitious name.

I'd be awful glad, Jack, if you'd come and have a bite of dinner with us and meet Nita." I agreed readily and he broke off into a trail leading up a shoulder of the mountain, which brought us shortly to a clearing in the forest in the center of which was a new log cabin.

I found Nita an attractive young girl, with the refined features and clear high complexion of the Spanish type, speaking excellent English. I couldn't help noticing how wrapped up in each other these two young lovers were, and what a pleasing couple they made. For Tom was a right good-looking boy himself. A nicely prepared meal over, I went on my way alone.

I never saw Tom again, but years after an old ZH man, when I enquired, told me Tom had left his Mexican wife and married an American girl. I suppose Nita returned to the quiet little settlement where her family lived. I don't know whether she is still living or not, but, if she is, you may be sure she looks back always, with longing and heartache, to life in the little Turkey Mountain clearing with her Americano cowboy.

No, the introduction of the love episode as a main motif in our western stories creates a false and artificial atmosphere. Indeed I do not think it possible to construct a story out of range life, with cowboys as the principal characters, at all. Life on the range was so far removed from the ordinary life of the population, tied to it only at rare and scattered points, that it is impossible to use it as a consistent groundwork of a novel. The cowboy with his highly specialized work and his equally highly specialized habit of life and thought, is impossible to bring into focus. He moved and had his being not along the common channels of existence, but on horseback! He and his life were abstractions; one with the wide spaces, the night skies; one with the West Wind that we battled with everlastingly. The most intangible feature of that intangible thing that is the history of our America. It would be a good thing if the story tellers would keep their hands off it.

# Index

# Index

CHINESE IN THE POST–CIVIL WAR SOUTH

# CHINESE IN THE POST-CIVIL WAR SOUTH

A PEOPLE

WITHOUT

A HISTORY

LUCY M. COHEN

LOUISIANA STATE UNIVERSITY PRESS

BATON ROUGE AND LONDON

Manufactured in the United States of America
Designer: Barbara Werden
Typeface: Linotron Bembo
Typesetter: G & S Typesetters, Inc.
Printer and Binder: Vail-Ballou Press

Publication of this book has been assisted by a grant
from the Andrew W. Mellon Foundation.

LIBRARY OF CONGRESS CATALOGING IN PUBLICATION DATA

Cohen, Lucy M.
    Chinese in the Post–Civil War South.

    Bibliography: p.
    Includes index.
    1. Chinese Americans—Southern States—History—19th
century.   2. Chinese Americans—Southern States—Social
conditions.   3. Chinese Americans—Employment—Southern
States—History—19th century.   4. Southern States—
History—1865–        5. Southern States—Foreign
population.   I. Title.
F220.C5C63   1984        975'.004951        83-19626
ISBN 0-8071-1122-8

To Regina Flannery Herzfeld, pioneering anthropologist,

and to 梁 瑞 培 (Leung Milián),

my beloved grandfather

# CONTENTS

# ILLUSTRATIONS

# PREFACE

This book is a study of efforts to introduce Chinese as substitutes for emancipated slaves in the South, and especially in Louisiana, after the Civil War. Relatively small numbers of Chinese were brought to the region, and the contract system under which they were employed was a failure. Because of changing concepts of race relations in the nation and in the region and because of the system of social organization prevalent at the time, the Chinese who remained in the area disappeared from the public awareness as a distinct group.

My interest in the Chinese migration to the southern states is both personal and professional. As the granddaughter of a Chinese immigrant to El Salvador, Central America, I have been particularly aware of the paucity of scholarly work on Chinese settlements in the borderlands of the Caribbean region. While conducting ethnohistoric research on the nineteenth-century settlements of Chinese in the Central American nations, I became interested in the possible connections between the Chinese migrations to Central America and the West Indies and parallel developments in the southern United States. The exchange of peoples and ideas between the South and its Central American and Caribbean neighbors was well established, particularly in the second half of the nineteenth century. Therefore, it seemed important to search for linkages in movements of Chinese and to study the possible implications of these movements for the Chinese and their host societies.

The Chinese were not totally unknown to the post–Civil War South. In the 1840s and 1850s, Christian missionaries to China had brought Chinese men with them on occasional visits back home.

These Chinese visitors had made a favorable impression as they appeared before religious groups throughout the South. In addition, during the 1850s southerners had discussed problems of plantation labor with their counterparts in foreign areas, who had begun to substitute Chinese and East Indians for Negro labor. Some southerners who had lived in the West Indies or had read accounts of the organization of work in the plantation systems there had proposed that Chinese be introduced to work in the South. Yet the idea of drawing on Chinese labor for agriculture was not adopted in the antebellum South. Public opinion in the North as well as in some sectors of the South condemned the international exploitation of Chinese "coolie" laborers. Furthermore, proponents of Chinese labor were also identified with the system of Negro slavery, thus raising northern suspicions of their motives.

The dearth of labor in the Reconstruction period prompted southerners to draw on the West Indian model and, in spite of many obstacles, to introduce Chinese labor. A number of Chinese were imported from Cuba when their contracts there expired. Other Chinese were brought from China, San Francisco, and New York. This influx of aliens was not greeted with equal enthusiasm by all southerners. But note was taken of their contributions as well as the problems encountered in their settlement mainly on the sugar and cotton plantations of Louisiana and the lower South.

Service of Chinese on the plantations and in other labor projects was brief. Misunderstandings over terms of contracts and other difficulties brought these arrangements to a close. Some of the immigrants returned to China or dispersed to other regions of this country. Still others remained near the localities where they had been employed, thereby enriching the mosaic of cultures in the local communities. In the end, however, the Chinese who entered the South during Reconstruction disappeared from history. Their presence went unrecorded in the journals and public documents that had first taken detailed note of their arrival and initial settlement.

My book traces the crucial developments that led to the disappearance of these Chinese from the annals of southern culture and life. It also broadens our understanding of race and labor relations in the early Chinese settlements in the lower South and our perspectives about the social organization of the Chinese in the United States. Previous research on the early history of Chinese in the country has focused on institutions involving the highly visible, urban-based Chinatowns. The present work emphasizes the processes through which the Chinese lost distinctive characteristics in a rural world. My hope is to contribute to an understanding of a little-known chapter in which the Chinese shaped and were in turn influenced by changing local, national, and international forces.

Chapters 1 and 2 describe the contacts of residents of southern communities with individual Chinese brought back by missionaries and the origins of the idea of using Chinese laborers in southern agriculture. The beginnings of international and national policy conflicts over the importation of Chinese laborers are also part of this background.

Attempts to recruit Chinese laborers from Cuba to the lower South after the Civil War met with suspicion from the North and from the federal government that planters were about to introduce a new group of slaves. As described in Chapter 3, the success of proponents of Chinese labor in allaying these fears encouraged some railroad entrepreneurs and their agents, as well as prominent planters, to introduce Chinese to alleviate labor shortages in the postemancipation era.

Chapter 4 presents specific cases of the hiring of groups of Chinese males under contracts, which were intended to be of several years duration, to work on railroad projects, plantations, and other sites. Chapter 5 deals with the conflicts engendered by the contract model, which resulted in the termination of most of the contracts after approximately five months.

Although some Chinese migrated elsewhere, others stayed in the South. Chapter 6 describes the enterprises engaged in by those who remained and uses census data to give a demographic view of their characteristics in selected areas. Within a few decades, the Chinese in the South lost their visibility. Chapter 7 analyzes the process that led to their disappearance from the public view.

# ACKNOWLEDGMENTS

Since this work is based on many primary sources, I wish to acknowledge my appreciation to the staffs of manuscript repositories who were helpful. I am especially grateful to Margaret Fisher Dalrymple and Stone Miller, Department of Archives and Manuscripts, Louisiana State University Library; Evangeline Lynch, Louisiana and Rare Book Room, Louisiana State University Library; Carol Wells, Southern Studies Institute, Northwestern State University, Natchitoches, Louisiana; Dode Platou, Historic New Orleans Collection, New Orleans; and Lilla M. Hawes, Georgia Historical Society, Savannah, Georgia. Albert Blair and William E. Lind, research consultants, United States National Archives, Washington, D.C., offered wise guidance and dedicated service.

Among the librarians and research consultants in church archives and historical societies, I am deeply indebted to Donn Michael Farris, Duke University Divinity School, and Ruth See, Historical Foundation of the Presbyterian and Reformed Churches, Montreat, North Carolina. Other resourceful consultants included V. Nelle Bellamy and Elinor S. Hearn, Episcopal Church Archives and Historical Collections, Austin, Texas; Fred Anderson, Virginia Baptist Historical Society, Richmond; Nancy Nell Stanley and Kirke White, Foreign Mission Board of the Southern Baptist Church, Richmond; and J. Glen Clayton, South Carolina Baptist Historical Society, Baptist Historical Collection, Furman University, Greenville, South Carolina.

Over a number of years of work the staffs of the Georgia Historical Society in Savannah, the Louisiana Room in the Tulane University Library in New Orleans, the Special Collections Division in the University of Georgia Library in Athens, and the Bancroft Library at the University of California, Berkeley, offered patient assistance. Specialized libraries and staff at the Library of Congress, Washington, D.C.; Louisiana State University, Baton Rouge; Northwestern State University, Natchitoches, Louisiana; and San Francisco Public Library were helpful. Jean McElligott of the Catholic University of America Library, Washington, D.C., was particularly patient with my many interlibrary loan requests.

Linnea Back Klee worked wisely in the collection of census data, and she helped develop a code for the analysis of newspaper sources. Muriel Boone of Sante Fe, New Mexico, offered suggestions for special research interests regarding Bishop William J. Boone, and Joan Wu Halpin raised many insightful questions. Dorothy Tierney and her volunteer staff at the Natchitoches Parish Courthouse helped me find valuable documents. Helen White and Monica Yost worked in special bibliographic and editing tasks, and Joan M. Roche generously committed her knowledge and organizational abilities to assist with final tasks. Elizabeth M. Hale typed the first version of the manuscript, and Christine Ochoa patiently prepared the final text. I am also grateful to Louisiana State University Press, especially to Beverly Jarrett, the Executive Editor, and to other members of the staff, particularly Catherine Barton, John Easterly, and Trudie Calvert, for their help in turning the manuscript into a book.

Of the many persons who encouraged me in the pursuit of this research, I wish to give singular recognition to Gunther Barth of the Department of History, University of California, Berkeley. The privilege of sharing scholarly concerns with him enabled me to address complex questions, and his collegial interest in the contributions of anthropology to questions of historic interest was particularly welcome. H. Shelton Smith, James B. Duke Professor Emeritus of American Religious Thought, Duke University, contributed scholarly insights about race relations in the South and offered helpful suggestions regarding the use of documentary sources in the materials and repositories of selected Christian churches. In addition to her perceptive criticisms, Leila Calhoun Deasy of Florida State University contributed helpful observations concerning the character of social life in the lower

South. She and her sister, Elizabeth C. Richey, offered invaluable guidance during my numerous field trips to the region.

For a thoughtful reading of several versions of the entire manuscript and for their many wise suggestions, I am deeply grateful to Regina Flannery Herzfeld, Catholic University of America, and to Sister Frances Jerome Woods, Our Lady of the Lake University, San Antonio, Texas. Jon Wakelyn of Catholic University encouraged me to pursue work on this subject, generously sharing his broad knowledge of southern history.

John M. Price and H. F. Gregory, Northwestern State University, Natchitoches, Louisiana, and Miles Richardson, Louisiana State University, Baton Rouge, shared their scholarly wisdom of the region as well as their hospitality. Roy S. Bryce-Laporte, Research Institute on Immigration and Ethnic Studies, Smithsonian Institution, and Henry F. Dobyns, Newberry Library, Chicago, strongly encouraged the pursuit of this work in light of our shared interests in ethnohistory and race relations in the Americas.

During the course of research, the Catholic University of America provided me with a faculty grant-in-aid award, and its Anthropology Department, through the Connolly Fund, offered a special award toward preparation for publication. A summer senior faculty award from the National Endowment for the Humanities made it possible for me to complete the research and undertake the preparation of a substantial part of the manuscript.

I owe a special debt of gratitude to a group of descendants of Chinese and their families in Natchitoches, Louisiana, and elsewhere. In addition to their generous assistance, they extended the warmth of gracious hospitality. Although it is not possible to cite the names of all those who offered their collaboration, I wish to acknowledge, in particular, Earnest Hongo (deceased), his daughter Ora Hongo Mixon, his niece Oritha Hongo Durel, and their families; David Telsee, his wife Rosa Mae Jackson Telsee, and their family; Octavia Telsede Grayson and her family, together with her sister Lillie Mae Telsede Williams, her daughter Odelle Hayes, and their families; Mary Graham; and Nathanael Wong, Jr. In addition, Eva Rachal (deceased), her son Lloyd Rachal, and Cora Marinovich Balthazar (deceased) were helpful with their wise knowledge of the area.

Descendants of Edward J. Gay in Louisiana have encouraged me to draw on extant written sources and on oral tradition to bring to light family history. I wish to recognize Anne L. Dean, her mother Carolyn G. Labouisse, and her aunt Gladys LeBreton, who nurtured my interest in the study of social relations and the organization of sugar plantations in Louisiana.

CHINESE IN THE POST CIVIL-WAR SOUTH

# 1 / CHINESE AS REMARKABLE CURIOSITIES

 Southerners' attitudes toward the settlement of Chinese in their region before the Civil War have been largely conjectural because of both the paucity of information and the small number of Chinese involved. Protestants from the South, who in the 1840s and 1850s actively contributed to the establishment of missions in China, however, did play a role in influencing the southern image of the Chinese.

Before the Treaty of Nanking between China and Great Britain in 1842, several American Protestant foreign missionary organizations were active in China. These included the American Board of Commissioners for Foreign Missions, whose first representatives went to China in 1829; the General Missionary Convention of the Baptists, also known as the Triennial Convention, who sent its first missionaries in 1836; and the Domestic and Foreign Missionary Society of the Protestant Episcopal Church in the United States, who sent the founder of its China mission in 1840.[1]

These Christian missionaries returned to the United States periodically, and some brought Chinese men and women back with them.

---

1. Kenneth Scott Latourette, *A History of Christian Missions in China* (New York, 1929), 209–27; Alexander Wylie, *Memorials of Protestant Missionaries to the Chinese: Giving a List of Their Publications, and Obituary Notices of the Deceased. With Copious Indexes* (Shanghai, 1867); T. Bronson Ray *et al., Southern Baptist Foreign Missions* (Nashville, 1910); *An Historical Sketch of the China Mission of the Protestant Episcopal Church in the U.S.A. from the First Appointments in 1834 to Include the Year Ending August 31st 1884* (New York, 1885), 6–34.

1

Although these visitors returned to China, their tours through the South gave the public firsthand impressions that facilitated comparisons and contrasts with other "heathen" groups. The opinions of missionaries who had worked in China were valued, and so were those of southerners who had visited the plantations of the West Indies and observed the Chinese who had been introduced there as substitutes for Negro labor.

In the decade of the 1850s small groups of Chinese men were living and working in a range of occupations in several parts of the East and the South. Most were located in such port cities as Boston, New York, Baltimore, Charleston, and New Orleans. They came from China under a variety of circumstances, some as representatives of commercial houses involved in the tea trade, others as seamen and servants. Some came to the East and South after a period of residence in Cuba or other West Indian colonies.

From time to time, an upsurge of missionary interest or a dramatic incident such as the sudden abandonment of a company of entertainers by their sponsor brought the presence of these Chinese residents to the public attention. But unlike the Chinese in California and nearby western territories, their fellow countrymen in the East and the South during this period received limited attention from public officials and legislative authorities. When the eighth census of the United States was taken in 1860, California was the only state that counted Chinese as a separate group. Elsewhere they were included as part of the immigrant population born abroad. In this period there was no special "color" identification to separate the Chinese from the white population.

The work of several pioneering missionaries to China from the Protestant Episcopal and Southern Baptist denominations contributed to southerners' initial efforts to understand the Chinese who entered the Northeast and the Southeast in the 1850s and 1860s. The efforts of these two denominations provide useful illustrations of the interlocking foreign and domestic mission activity among the Chinese.

The Reverend William J. Boone, founder of the American Episcopal Mission in China and its first Episcopal bishop, was one of the pioneering southern missionaries to China. A native of Walterboro, South Carolina, he had studied law with Chancellor Henry William

De Saussure, father of his future wife, and was admitted to the bar in his native state in 1833. He was ordained deacon in Charleston on September 18, 1836, and priest the following year. Boone was appointed as a missionary to China under the sponsorship of the Foreign Committee of the Board of Missions, and in July, 1837, he sailed for the Orient with his wife, Sarah Amelia De Saussure.[2]

From 1837 to 1840, the Boones labored among the Chinese in Djakarta, Java, then known as Batavia. In 1840 they moved to Macao and in 1842 established a mission at Kulang-see, a small island near Amoy. Boone spent these years helping the school of the Morrison Education Society and exploring directions for the new mission. The Morrison Education Society, named after the Reverend Robert Morrison, the first Protestant missionary to reside in China, had been begun on January 6, 1835, by a group of men involved in commerce. Its goal was to establish and support schools in China in which "native youths shall be taught, in connection with their own, to read and write the English language; and through this medium to bring within their reach all the varied learning of the western world. The Bible and books on Christianity shall be read in the schools."[3] Boone made plans for the development of schools for selected groups of Chinese and prepared these proposals for the consideration of the Foreign Committee of the Board of Missions.

Boone's wife, Sarah Amelia, died in China in August, 1842. Upon his first return trip to the United States, he brought back his two small children, Henry William and Mary Eliza, as well as Sin Say, a language teacher, and Wong Kong Chai, a young man who helped to care for the children. Chai, as this family companion was called, was viewed with much interest and curiosity. Although he was considered "strange" because of his long braid of hair, note was taken of his edu-

2. Albert Sidney Thomas, *A Historical Account of the Protestant Episcopal Church in South Carolina, 1820–1957; Being a Continuation of Dalcho's Account, 1670–1820* (Columbia, 1957), 16–48; Muriel Boone, *The Seed of the Church in China* (Philadelphia, 1973), 15–30; Wylie, *Memorials of Protestant Missionaries*, 99–102; "Boone, William Jones," in Charles Dick and James Homans (eds.), *Appleton's Cyclopaedia of American Biography* (New York, 1915), I, 316; *Historical Sketch of the China Mission*, 24–39.

3. William Elliot Griffis, *A Maker of the New Orient: Samuel Robbins Brown, Pioneer Educator in China, America, and Japan. The Story of His Life and Work* (New York, 1902), 59.

cational background. His fair command of English made communication with him relatively easy.[4]

During his visits to churches and religious associations in both South and North, Boone emphasized that his proposals to prepare Chinese youth differed from methods used in other "heathen lands." Boone indicated that "everywhere else, missionaries have found the heathen entirely ignorant, and have therefore been obliged to open schools for thousands in order to raise up a class capable of reading the word of God and other Christian books. In China this preparatory work in the providence of God is already done for us, as six-tenths, perhaps, of the males of this country are able to read."[5]

Boone visited the dioceses of New York, New Jersey, North Carolina, South Carolina, Georgia, Alabama, and Louisiana and succeeded in exciting a deep interest in the China mission and his plans for the education of youth. The Foreign Committee of the Board of Missions, through local societies and individual donors, offered financial support for his plans, as is evident from statements in the annual reports published in the journal *Spirit of Missions*. During Bishop Boone's subsequent return visits to the United States, local mission boards, women's societies, and individual contributors from the South were highly responsive to his pleas. They were pillars of support for the work of missionaries and teachers and for the native Chinese who worked along with them.

On October 29, 1844, in the address from the House of Bishops to Boone, delivered in Philadelphia after his consecration as missionary bishop to China, he and his fellow missionaries were exhorted to "shine as lights in a dark place." He was reminded that the "heathen land" that would be the seat of his episcopate contained a large segment of the population of the globe, and its inhabitants, "though to some good degree enlightened and civilized," were "ignorant of the true God." The House of Bishops supported Bishop Boone's plans to educate Chinese youth because this was considered an important means of extending the influence of the gospel in a heathen land. In

4. "Report of Bishop W. J. Boone to the Board of Missions, February 13, 1847," *Spirit of Missions*, XII (August, 1847), 255–59; Boone, *Seed of the Church*, 106.

5. "Appendix B: Report of the Foreign Committee, China," *Spirit of Missions*, IX (August, 1844), 267.

December of the same year, Bishop Boone returned to China with his children, their two Chinese companions, and several American missionaries and teachers. He was also accompanied by his second wife, Phoebe Caroline Elliot, a childhood friend, who was the sister of the Right Reverend Stephen Elliot, the first Episcopal bishop of Georgia. The Elliots had been in Beaufort, South Carolina, with Boone at the time of a revival in 1831–1832 led by the Reverend Daniel Baker. As a result of the Beaufort revival, Boone and Elliot and a number of other young men entered the ministry.[6]

Upon their return to China, the Boone family settled in Shanghai instead of Amoy because the Board of Missions believed that this city was a strategic place in central China. Boone began to implement his educational plans, although he modified some of the original concepts to conform to prevailing customs in Chinese society. In this connection, the Reverend Edward W. Syle, one of the missionaries who joined Bishop Boone in 1845, wrote that the native Chinese teachers had expressed doubt that parents would give up their children altogether for a period of ten years, notwithstanding the bishop's insistence on this condition for their attendance at his school. Nevertheless, the school was always full. Wong Kong Chai, who was Bishop Boone's first convert, was baptized on Easter Sunday, April 12, 1847. He became the first Chinese deacon, and after thirteen years in this office, on November 8, 1863, he was ordained as the first priest of the Protestant Episcopal church in China.[7]

When the Reverend Samuel Robbins Brown, the first director of the school of the Morrison Education Society in Hong Kong, returned to the United States in 1849, he brought with him three Chinese students, Yung Wing, Wong Shing, and Wong Foon. The young men entered the Monson Academy in Hampden County, Massachusetts. Monson students were noted for their zeal in missionary work. Yung

6. See *Spirit of Missions*, IX (November, 1844), 432–34; Thomas, *Historical Account*, 24-29; H. St. George Tucker and Alexander C. Zabriskie, "Evangelicals and Missions," in Alexander C. Zabriskie (ed.), *Anglican Evangelicalism* (Philadelphia, 1943), 189–200.

7. "Instructions from the Foreign Committee of the Board of Missions to Rt. Rev. the Missionary Bishop to China, and the Other Missionaries Appointed to That Station, December 5, 1844," *Spirit of Missions*, X (January, 1845), 17–25; "Communication," April 20, 1846, *ibid.*, XII (January, 1847), 19–23; "Report of Bishop W. J. Boone," *ibid.*, XII (August, 1847), 255–59.

Wing and his two companions were supported at Monson by contributions from patrons in Hong Kong, including the Scotsman Andrew Shortrede, proprietor and editor of the Hong Kong *China Mail*, A. A. Ritchie, an American merchant, and A. A. Campbell, another Scotsman. The Olyphant brothers, of the American firm Olyphant and Company, had arranged for their passage from Hong Kong to New York.[8]

Wong Shing, the eldest of the three youths, returned to China in 1848 because of poor health. Wong Foon and Yung Wing completed a classical course and graduated from Monson Academy in the summer of 1850. Their Hong Kong patrons offered them continued support for professional studies if they were willing to go to Scotland to attend the University of Edinburgh. Wong Foon accepted the offer, and in 1857 he graduated third in his medical class. He established his practice in Canton and was respected by Chinese and foreigners until his death in 1879.[9]

In the summer of 1850, when Yung Wing completed his secondary-school studies, he solicited the assistance of his former teacher for support of his studies at Yale College. Brown in turn sought help from his southern friends. Although he was a native of Connecticut, he had contacts in the South because he had attended the Columbia Theological Seminary in South Carolina in 1835. While there, he had supported himself for two years by teaching vocal and instrumental music in the Barhamville Young Ladies' Seminary, and one of his students, Phoebe Caroline Elliot, had subsequently become Bishop Boone's second wife. During the summer of 1850, when Brown visited his sister and old friends in the South, he also contacted former students who were members of the Savannah Ladies Chinese Society. He described Yung Wing's needs, and this association agreed to help finance his college education. With additional aid from the Olyphant brothers of New York, Yung Wing became the first person from China to receive a degree from an American university.[10]

8. Latourette, *History of Christian Missions*, 221–22; *Dictionary of American Biography*, II, 153–54; Yung Wing, *My Life in China and America* (New York, 1909), 1–33; Griffis, *Maker of the New Orient*, 25–41.

9. Yung, *Life*, 31–33.

10. Griffis, *Maker of the New Orient*, 50–52; Hennig Cohen (ed.), *A Barhamville Miscellany: Notes and Documents Concerning the South Carolina Female Collegiate Institute,*

In 1853, ten years after his first return trip, Bishop Boone and his family made another visit to the United States. Tong Chu Kiung, a young Chinese originally from Soochow, who had become a candidate for holy orders in Shanghai, also came with the family. Chu Kiung, as he was usually called, was among the first group of students graduated from Boone's Episcopal boys' school in Shanghai.[11]

Reports document the enthusiastic response accorded Bishop Boone and Chu Kiung at such places as Christ Church in Savannah and the Ogeeche River Mission nearby, which was made up almost entirely of blacks who labored on the rice plantations. Chu Kiung and Mrs. Boone visited parishes in South Carolina and Georgia without the bishop. Chu Kiung was invited to address congregations from the chancel, and Boone later reported to the Foreign Committee in New York that his "appeals on behalf of his idolatrous countrymen were believed to have reached many a heart." When Chu Kiung addressed the Board of Missions in New York, he made a deep impression on board members as well as bishops and representatives from the English Society for the Propagation of the Gospel.[12]

Upon his return to China, Tong Chu Kiung continued his work in the missions, and in 1856, at the age of twenty-five, he was ordained a deacon in Shanghai. But in 1861, at the time of his own resignation, Bishop Boone deposed him from the ministry. Chu Kiung was discouraged about the lack of success in his work, which provided insufficient support for his family. Bishop Boone believed that Chu Kiung's

---

1826–1865, Chiefly from the Collection of the Late Henry Campbell Davis (Columbia, 1956); Records of Students and Faculty Members of South Carolina Female Collegiate Institute, Barhamville, South Carolina, 1837–59, Collected and Compiled by Professor Henry C. Davis, Manuscripts Division, South Caroliniana Library, University of South Carolina, Columbia, S.C.; Yung, Life, 34–37.

11. Spirit of Missions, XVII (April, 1852), 137, (May, 1852), 170, (November, 1852), 407–408; Chu Kiung to Bishop Boone, November 22, 1851, in the Domestic and Foreign Missionary Society: China Records, 1835–1951, Archives of the Episcopal Church, Austin, Texas.

12. "Report by Stephen Elliott, Jr., bishop of the Diocese of Georgia, February 13, 1853," in Journal of the Thirty-First Annual Convention of the Protestant Episcopal Church in the Diocese of Georgia, Christ Church, Savannah (Savannah, 1853), 23; see "Appendix G," Spirit of Missions, XVIII (November, 1853), 505; Bishop Boone to P. P. Ewing, August 15, 1853, and Bishop Boone to I. S. Aspinwall, Esq., June 10, 1853, both in Domestic and Foreign Missionary Society: China Records, 1835–1951.

discontent was also associated with perceived disproportions between his salary and that of his former school companions who were employed in such places as the Chinese customhouse and the British consulate.[13]

During the 1850s, other Chinese visited the United States with returned missionaries, and several remained to study. In January, 1855, for example, Nga Yung Kiung and Yang He Ting (He-ding) arrived in New York to complete their education. Nga Yung Kiung graduated with honors from Kenyon College. Upon his return to Shanghai in January, 1862, he joined the mission and became a candidate for holy orders. Yang He Ting studied English in the United States and became a teacher in the missions, after which he worked at the British Consulate.[14]

By the mid-1850s, small groups of Chinese had entered the Northeast and the South as entertainers and as workers in a variety of occupations. The Reverend Edward W. Syle was one of the clergymen called upon to assist several church groups in the East, specifically in New York, in establishing a mission among the Chinese groups there. Records from Syle's journals, published in *Spirit of Missions*, offer rich information on the growth of Chinese settlements in those areas. Syle, a British-born graduate of Virginia Theological Seminary, had first sailed for China with Bishop Boone in 1845. While in Shanghai, he had become familiar with the emigration of Chinese to the United States because he had been instrumental in making available missionary tracts translated into Chinese for newcomers to California. In August, 1851, writing from Shanghai, Syle had reported that he had sent to the Reverend J. L. Ver Mehr, Episcopalian minister in San Fran-

---

13. "Report of the Foreign Committee," *Spirit of Missions*, XXI (November–December, 1856), 612; Bishop Boone to the secretary of the Foreign Committee, May 18, 1861, in *ibid.*, XXVI (September, 1861), 265–67.

14. Extract from a letter of J. T. Points to Foreign Committee, September 30, 1854, *ibid.*, XX (February, 1855), 58–60, 81; "Report of the Foreign Committee," *ibid.*, XX (November–December, 1855), 584; "Journal of Rev. E. W. Syle, September, 1856," *ibid.*, XXII (June, 1857), 276; "Journal of Rev. E. W. Syle, December 4, 1856," *ibid.*, XXII (August, 1857), 385–88; "Report of the Rt. Rev. W. J. Boone, D.D., Missionary Bishop at Shanghai, China, to the Board of Missions of the Protestant Episcopal Church of the United States, New York, October 14, 1857," *ibid.*, XXII (November–December, 1857), 617–19.

cisco, translations into Chinese of the Scriptures, tracts, and catechisms for the "benefit of the hundreds of Chinese" in California.[15]

By 1853, when Syle returned to the United States with his family for reasons of health, groups of Chinese were becoming visible in the East and the South. While on his temporary sojourn in the United States, he acted as agent for the committee formed by the Board of Missions of his church to awaken interest in the mission to China. Upon completion of the year of service at home, he undertook a mission on behalf of destitute Chinese in New York City at the invitation of the Reverend R. H. Dickson, city missionary at Grace Episcopal Church, and of the ladies' mission group at St. George's Episcopal congregation in that city. Dickson wrote to Syle on April 21, 1854, asking if Sunday schools or related activities might be undertaken among some of the Chinese, who were described as "poor creatures who were scattered through the streets, eking out a subsistence by the sale of cigars and fabrics of their own, looking forlorn and neglected."[16]

In May, 1854, Syle carried his survey to the Chinese themselves by visiting their lodgings and making inquiries regarding their occupations. Some Chinese lived at Ward's Island, at the accommodations maintained by the New York commissioners of emigration, who had built several hospitals, a dispensary, and places of refuge there for destitute immigrants. Others were in boardinghouses on Cherry Street, and a few had been long established in this country and had married here. Some worked serving behind counters in tea stores.[17]

Syle met a Chinese salesman in a tea store who spoke English and several Chinese dialects. He had been in the service of Dr. Karl Gutzlaff, the pioneering Prussian missionary, and had accompanied him on

15. Obituary, E. W. Syle, *Journal of the Proceedings of the One-Hundred and Seventh Convention of the Protestant Episcopal Church in the Diocese of Pennsylvania, May 12–14, 1891* (Philadelphia, 1891), 48–49; Obituary, Edward W. Syle, *Spirit of Missions*, LV (December, 1890), 475–76; "Report of the Foreign Committee, August, 1851," *ibid.*, XVI (August, 1851), 357–58; Gunther Barth, *Bitter Strength: A History of the Chinese in the United States, 1850–1870* (Cambridge, Mass., 1964), 161–62.

16. "Proceedings of the Board of Missions," *Spirit of Missions*, XIX (November–December, 1854), 481; Report from E. W. Syle to the editors, July 15, 1854, *ibid.*, XIX (August, 1854), 323–24.

17. Report from E. W. Syle to the editors, June 1, 1854, *ibid.*, XIX (July, 1854), 284–86; Friedrich Kapp, *Immigration and the Commissioners of Emigration* (New York, 1870), 125–41.

his voyages up the coast of China. Eventually, however, he had settled in New York and had married a white woman. Syle also found thirty or so Chinese who occupied two rooms in a boardinghouse. He was able to communicate with eight "Ningpo and Shanghai men," as well as with some "Canton men" who had belonged to a dramatic company brought from California in April, 1853. Members of this company had suffered a series of vicissitudes—"failure of their project, desertion by those who brought them here, forfeiture of their wardrobe, destitution of the means of subsistence, and banishment (as they considered it) to Ward's Island." From this island, the actors had emerged as peddlers of cigars and had become part of the "stock subjects for caricature sketches" in city papers. An "old Canton-man" who spoke some English and who had kept a boardinghouse in New York for some twenty years, told Syle that most of these play actors wanted to return to China rather than remain in the United States.[18]

In three other boardinghouses, Syle found Chinese who worked at sea as cooks and stewards. Although they spoke English, Syle noted that they were "thoroughly Chinese in their thoughts." One of these boardinghouses, home for about fifteen men, was kept by a Chinese man who had been in that business for fifteen years and had been married for some time to a local woman. There were some twelve in another house and three in the third. In total, Syle located about seventy Chinese in the city, which was a larger number than he had expected to find.

A committee of ten members, including one of the Olyphant brothers, was appointed by the churches to take measures for the relief of the destitute. They raised approximately $2,500, which was used to send twenty-two destitute Chinese back to California and four to Canton.[19] Of those who remained in New York, three joined together to open a small store to sell tea and exhibit the "fantastic lanterns" that they constructed. The head of this tea house, Tsung Ze-kway, was a "Shanghai man" who had entered the United States with Syle and accompanied him on some of his visits to parishes. According to Syle,

18. Report from E. W. Syle to the editors, July 15, 1854, *Spirit of Missions*, XIX (August, 1854), 325–26.
19. *Ibid.*, 326–28.

Tsung had considered becoming a Christian minister but had eventually chosen to go into trade instead.

Of the group that remained, those who wished to work "with their hands" were placed in a suburb of Brooklyn. They went to work as day laborers, all in the same employ, in the neighborhood of the tea store, which was located at Gowanus near the Greenwood Cemetery on the road to Fort Hamilton. Six Chinese who wanted to learn English were placed in a special domicile to receive lessons from a theology student.[20]

Syle concluded his written survey of Chinese in New York by reminding readers that contact with the Chinese and their products was becoming "daily more intimate and inevitable." He noted that increasing numbers of Chinese were living in the East and the South, not only in New York but working in the tea rooms in Cincinnati, Dayton, Indianapolis, and Boston and in the iron mills of the Cumberland region of Kentucky. Chinese fans, embroideries, floor mattings, and chests of tea were now often found in American households.[21]

With the onset of the Civil War, the Protestant Episcopal missions to China and to the Chinese suffered heavily because nearly all their American missionaries had connections with the South. Up to this time, eighteen Episcopalian-ordained missionaries had gone to China from the United States. Sixteen were graduates of the Virginia Theological Seminary, most of them natives of the South.[22] Furthermore, Bishop Boone had looked to the South for substantial financial support, and this region was now isolated from mission headquarters in New York. The troubles at home had deeply felt repercussions in this China mission and its activities during the decade of the 1860s.

The Southern Baptists were also active in mission work to China and among Chinese in the United States. The Reverend Jehu Lewis Shuck and his wife, Henrietta Hall, were pioneers in the establishment of missions in China under the auspices of the Baptist Board of For-

20. E. W. Syle to the editors, *ibid.*, XIX (September, 1854), 339–40.

21. *Ibid.*, 341–43.

22. "Report of the Foreign Committee," *ibid.*, XXVI (November–December, 1861), 331–35; Lloyd R. Craighill, "The Work of the Seminary in China," in William A. R. Goodwin (ed.), *History of the Theological Seminary in Virginia and Its Background* (2 vols.; New York, 1923), II, 271–82; Wylie, *Memorials of Protestant Missionaries*.

eign Missions and, after 1845, under the Southern Baptist Convention. In 1845 northern and southern Baptists separated mainly because southerners could not accept the declaration of the Foreign Mission Board of Boston that it would not appoint a missionary if he were a slaveholder. Shuck received the first commission granted by the newly formed Southern Baptist Convention.[23] He had been born in Alexandria, at that time part of the District of Columbia, in 1814. After studying privately at the Lewisburg Academy in Greenbrier County, West Virginia, he decided to read law. A deep religious experience, however, convinced him to enter the ministry. While preparing at the Virginia Baptist Seminary in Richmond, he decided to become a missionary to China. He was a contemporary of Boone, but unlike the latter, who served for a lifetime in China, he worked in the China mission field and among the Chinese in California, where he established the first Southern Baptist mission in that area.[24]

Henrietta Hall Shuck was the first American woman evangelical missionary to go to China and was among the pioneers who opened a school in Macao for Chinese children. The daughter of the Reverend Addison Hall, she was born in 1817 in Kilmarnock, Virginia. She made a profession of faith in a revival when she was not quite fourteen and was baptized by her pastor, Jeremiah Bell Jeter. She developed a yearning to serve the Chinese after reading the memoirs of Ann Hasseltine Judson, the well-known Baptist missionary to Burma.[25]

During the Shucks' ministry, several individual Chinese were bap-

23. Ray et al., Southern Baptist Foreign Missions, 9–50; Rufus B. Spain, At Ease in Zion: Social History of Southern Baptists, 1865–1900 (Nashville, 1961), 3–11.

24. "Rev. J. L. Shuck," in William Cathcart (ed.), The Baptist Encyclopedia (Philadelphia, 1881), 1056; Wylie, Memorials of Protestant Missionaries, 90–93; "Inventory of Church Archives of Virginia: Guide to the Manuscript Collections of the Virginia Baptist Historical Society, Vol. II: Index to Marriage Notices in the Religious Herald, Richmond, Virginia, 1828–1938," in Virginia Baptist Historical Society, Richmond; Margaret M. Coughlin, "Strangers in the House: J. Lewis Shuck and Issachar Roberts, First American Baptist Missionaries to China" (Ph.D. dissertation, University of Virginia, 1972); J. B. Hipps, "John Lewis Shuck," in Encyclopedia of Southern Baptists (Nashville, 1958), II, 1201–1202.

25. Jeremiah Bell Jeter, A Memoir of Mrs. Henrietta Shuck, the First American Female Missionary to China (Boston, 1850); Thomas S. Dunaway, Pioneering for Jesus: The Story of Henrietta Hall Shuck (Nashville, 1930); Henry A. Tupper (ed.), The First Century of the First Baptist Church of Richmond, Virginia (Richmond, 1880), 181; E. C. Routh, "Henrietta Hall Shuck," in Encyclopedia of Southern Baptists, II, 1201.

Yong-Seen-Sang, Chinese teacher and preacher from the First Baptist Church, Shanghai, during his visit to the United States in 1845–1846.

tized and others became prospects. The Shuck household was known to missionaries from other denominations and the Chinese Christians who had returned from abroad. Henrietta Shuck devoted herself to missionary and educational work. She was particularly interested in the instruction of Chinese girls and conducted a school until her death in November, 1844, at age twenty-seven, following the birth of her fifth child. Shuck then returned to the United States in 1845 to arrange for the education of his motherless children. He brought along Yong-Seen-Sang, his teacher of six years and a native preacher, and Mecha, a young Chinese woman who acted as nurse and traveling companion for the children.[26]

Yong-Seen-Sang was a scholar from Hseung Shan, a district not far from Canton, and he was versed in both Cantonese and Mandarin. He was described as having all the attributes of a Confucian gentleman who, without having achieved official rank or owning any property, made his living by various literary endeavors. Yong was in his thirties when Shuck hired him as his teacher. At that time, Shuck described him as a "bigoted adherent to the whole three religions of China—viz, Confucianism, Taoism, and Buddhism." After five years of contact with Shuck, however, Yong became a convert to Christianity.[27]

Secular and religious papers describe Yong's visits in the South. With Shuck he toured Virginia, Mississippi, Kentucky, and Tennessee. In Georgia the two engendered such enthusiasm that some faithful were reported to have traveled fifty miles to meet the missionary and the Chinese preacher. In Alabama they went to Montgomery, Benton, Greensboro, and Tuscaloosa. The students of the Judson Female Institute in Marion, Alabama, who received the missionaries with enthusiasm, donated five hundred dollars for Shuck's projected chapel in Canton.[28]

These evangelists offered to their audiences new perceptions and vivid images of China and the Chinese. Yong-Seen-Sang was usually presented as a "scholar and a cultivated gentleman." He served as an

26. Dunaway, *Pioneering for Jesus*, 67–137, 144–57; Richmond *Religious Herald*, February 4, 1847.

27. Coughlin, "Strangers in the House," 211; Richmond *Religious Herald*, April 2, 1846.

28. Richmond *Religious Herald*, August 20, 1846.

example to support some of Shuck's ideas about missionary work. At a meeting in the Second Baptist Church of Richmond on April 1, 1846, for instance, Shuck emphasized that missionary endeavors among the Chinese did not encompass the task of civilizing the "heathen" because "for ages, the Chinese had been civilized." Yet Shuck pointed out that "civilization had never prepared a sinner for the service of God on earth, nor fitted him for enjoyment in heaven." He raised questions about the belief that a people had to become "literary to have the gospel." Shuck indicated that for ages the Chinese had been literary but had not had the gospel. He described Yong as an educated man with a thoughtful and philosophical mind, who had studied the Christian system very attentively and would be extremely useful in proselytizing among his countrymen. At meetings throughout the South, he was pointed to as an outstanding example of missionary accomplishment.[29]

His responses at meetings in the state of Virginia illustrate these qualities. On March 29, 1846, at the First Baptist Church of Richmond, he was asked, "When the gospel of Christ is first preached to the natives, what do they generally say of it?" Yong answered that the typical response was to say, "This is the religion of foreigners, and may be very good for them but ours is best for us." At a meeting on April 1 held at the Second Baptist Church of that same city, he was asked whether he enjoyed more happiness in believing the gospel than he had in the practice of idolatry. He responded through his interpreter, Shuck, that "since he had received the gospel, his heart had been drawn out in love to God and this cause made him happy." His exhortations appealed to listeners, as noted at a meeting held on April 9, 1846, at Four Mile Creek in this same state. He called on his listeners to keep in mind that "his country and this differ greatly in reference to religion. In his country, there are no churches—no Christian privileges. In this country, there are many Christian privileges." Yong asked his listeners to "appreciate these privileges."[30]

Yong elicited local enthusiasm for the support of promising students and teachers. The Female Missionary Society of the First Baptist

29. *Ibid.*, April 2, 1846.
30. *Ibid.*, April 2, 9, 1846.

Church in Richmond, which had been organized to support a native Chinese teacher or colporteur (a distributor of religious tracts and books) to labor in China, pledged an annual contribution toward Yong's support and continued to finance his work until his death in China in 1886. The Second Baptist Church in that city appointed the Shucks' female companion as its missionary. Since she was proficient in both English and Chinese, the hope was that she would become a religious instructor to Chinese women in China.[31]

Upon their return to China, Shuck helped to organize the First Baptist Church in Shanghai and became its first pastor while Yong-Seen-Sang became a preacher in the Canton mission and its vicinity. In 1851 Shuck lost his second wife, Ann Saxton Shuck, in childbirth. This event contributed in part to his decision to resign from the Board of Foreign Missions to China and to accept appointment by the First Baptist Church in Richmond as missionary to California. For this new work he was sponsored by the Southern Baptist Domestic and Indian Mission Board of Marion, Alabama, and was partly supported by contributions from the Mission Board of the Goshen Association of Virginia, as well as by the Judson Female Institute of Marion.[32]

By 1851–1852, the number of Chinese in the United States had increased rapidly because of the arrival of large groups of laborers attracted by reports of the discovery of gold in California. Missionaries who had direct experience in China, such as Shuck, were asked to interpret the customs and describe the personal characteristics of the newcomers. Works written by these missionaries became valued for the light they shed on the life of the Chinese.

Publicity was accorded increasingly to Chinese in the South. There was, for instance, the attention given entertainers and workers in Ohio, Kentucky, and Tennessee in 1853–1854. On January 9, 1854, an announcement appeared in the Louisville *Courier* for the performance

31. Jane C. Reins, secretary, Female Missionary Society, First Baptist Church, to William Sands, editor, Richmond *Religious Herald*, April 9, 1846; Dunaway, *Pioneering for Jesus*, 142–43; Richmond *Religious Herald*, February 4, 1847.

32. Richmond *Religious Herald*, September 1, 29, 1853; Mission to the Chinese of California, "Eighth Annual Report, Board of Foreign Missions," in *Proceedings of the Southern Baptist Convention, Baltimore, Maryland, May 13–17, 1853* (Richmond, 1853), 37–38.

that evening of a company of Chinese jugglers, acrobats, and magicians that was touring the nation. Comments from the Pittsburgh *Post* were quoted urging people to attend, particularly "those who think the Chinese as a race stupid and incapable of successful competition with European races. . . . It would be hard for Europe or America to produce a boy of twelve years of age, who could as often 'bring down a house,' with his witchcraft and wonderful feats." When the company arrived in Memphis one week later, the public was urged to patronize them because "as natives of a different sphere, they are curiosities, enough, but when connected with their unique performances" they command over a full house.[33]

On February 7, 1854, the Cincinnati *Daily Enquirer* advertised that at Tyson's Tea Store in that city a "real genuine Chinaman" was dealing out tea. Prospective customers were invited to pay a visit to the store to examine the extensive stock of goods as well as the Chinese salesman, billed as a "curiosity in itself." One week after this report, the same newspaper announced that Mr. Tyson was in favor with the Celestials for he now had "three native Chinamen" who drew attention. The owners of the teahouse had indicated that the Chinese costumes and customs were a curiosity and that their polite attention to their customers was "quite remarkable."[34]

In another locality, brief news announcements noted that the proprietors of the Eddyville Iron Works on the Cumberland River in Kentucky had engaged the services of "twenty Chinese coolies as iron workers." William Kelly, one of the inventors of the Bessemer iron-refining process, had hired these Chinese for work at the Suwanee Furnace and Union Forge in Lyon County, Kentucky. As was the case of the Chinese at Tyson's Tea Store, their presence was a novelty and a curiosity.[35]

33. Pittsburgh *Post*, quoted in Louisville *Daily Courier*, January 9, 1854; Memphis *Daily Appeal*, January 16, 1854.

34. Cincinnati *Daily Enquirer*, February 7, 15, 1854.

35. Chattanooga *Gazette*, quoted in Augusta *Daily Chronicle and Sentinel*, November 17, 1853; San Francisco *Daily Alta California*, December 20, 1853; Barth, *Bitter Strength*, 187–88; John Newton Boucher, *A Century and a Half of Pittsburgh and Her People* (4 vols.; New York, 1908), II, 27–41; Joe Creason, "William Kelly of Kentucky—A Maker of Steel," *Courier Journal Magazine*, Louisville *Courier-Journal*, February 27, 1949, pp. 16–21.

In May, 1854, as the Chinese men destined for the Kelly ironworks passed Louisville on a steamer, a local reporter wrote that they were a "tall healthy looking set of Celestials, and we learn that they have sold themselves for a term of years to work at the aforesaid iron works."[36] The term *Celestial* was used, often humorously, to refer to the Chinese people as members of the former Chinese Empire, which in China was referred to as the Heavenly Dynasty.

Gunther Barth has pointed out that little has been reported concerning the outcome of this experiment. One source indicates that Kelly was so pleased with their work that he planned to import fifty additional Chinese to help out at the furnaces. According to Barth, this plan was not pursued further because of "international complications." Other sources suggest that conflicts between some of the Chinese and authorities at the furnace contributed to the demise of the experiment. Less than a year after the Chinese arrived in Eddyville, a writer for the Louisville *Daily Courier* stated that one of the "Chinamen" employed at Kelly's furnace had been "murdered by a Negro," who had done the deed in self-defense. An editor of the Paducah *American* explained that the incident had been precipitated by a "difficulty" between some Chinese and a Negro at Kelly's Suwanee Furnace. He further reported that the Chinese followed "traditional" customs in burying food with the body and with a "heap of muttering and the chanting of what was believed to be a Chinese hymn." After this incident, other Chinese apparently left the furnace. Two months later, on June 26, 1855, the Louisville *Daily Courier* reported that three "long-haired, shallow-faced, small-footed and comically dressed sons of the Middle Kingdom" were seen "perambulating" in the streets of the city. They were reported to appear "as well satisfied as Chinese could be, afar from the land of tea and rats."[37]

Census figures for 1860 show that eight persons born in China resided in Kentucky but only two remained in Eddyville. One was Jim Fo, a twenty-six-year-old forgeman whose birthplace was given as

36. Louisville *Daily Courier*, May 15, 1854.

37. Barth, *Bitter Strength*, 187–88; "William Kelly," in J. Grant Wilson and J. Fiske (eds.), in *Cyclopedia of American Biography* (New York, 1888), III, 509; Creason, "William Kelly," 16–21; Louisville *Daily Courier*, March 28, April 14, June 26, 1855.

"China-Peking"; his wife, Louisa Fo, was twenty years old and had been born in Kentucky. The second, "Eyou," a twenty-eight-year-old Chinese man, listed his occupation as painter and his place of birth as "Peking-China."[38]

Chinese also resided in other parts of the South in 1860, notably in Louisiana, but they are not usually identified as such because of the classifications used in the census for that period. Two census schedules were used in the 1860 census: Schedule 1 for free inhabitants, which included whites, blacks, and mulattoes, and Schedule 2 for slaves, which listed blacks and mulattoes. The 1870 census listed whites, blacks, and mulattoes and added the categories Chinese and Indian. The 1860 census recapitulation of population of the states and territories shows that among the total of 358,110 white persons in California, there were 34,933 "Asiatics." This figure was based on a special count for that state alone.[39]

Other figures on the numbers of Chinese in the United States for this period are based on customhouse reports of arrivals of ships' passengers listed according to country of birth for the cumulative period 1820 to 1860. The total given is 41,443 and of these, 41,397 are reported to have entered between 1851 and 1860.[40] These figures do not distinguish repeated entries by the same persons such as merchants and laborers who went to China and returned and therefore were enumerated more than once.

Nativity data reported by states and territories based on country of birth rather than gross population totals, however, show that 35,565 persons in the United States enumerated in the 1860 census were born

38. "Nativities of Free Population, Recapitulation by States," in U.S. Department of the Interior, *Population of the United States in 1860, Compiled from the Original Returns of the Eighth Census*, 620; U.S. Department of the Interior, Eighth Census of the United States, 1860, Lyon County, Kentucky, Population Schedule, in Record Group 29, National Archives, Washington, D.C. (hereafter NA).

39. Carroll D. Wright and William C. Hunt, *The History and Growth of the United States Census*, Senate Document No. 194, 56th Cong. 1st Sess., 154–57; "Population of the States and Territories by Color and Condition, with the Rate of Increase and Representation in Congress," in *Population of the United States in 1860*, 598–99.

40. "Statement of the Number of Alien Passengers Arriving in the United States by Sea from Foreign Countries from September 30, 1819 to December 31, 1860," in *Population of the United States in 1860*, xix–xxii.

in China. The vast majority were residents of California (34,935).[41] These figures show that small numbers of people born in China re-sided in several states in the East and South, notably in New York (77), Massachusetts (38), Pennsylvania (21), Connecticut (11), and Louisiana (10). A more detailed analysis of some of these figures indi-cates that their counts may be low. Detailed examination of all the legi-ble population schedules for New Orleans in the 1860 census shows, for example, approximately thirty persons born in China, a higher figure than the total of ten found in reports on the nativity of the free population of New Orleans and in the summary for the state of Loui-siana in that census.[42]

The New Orleans population schedule shows that these Chinese lived in households with their spouses and children, and some had a Chinese boarder. Others, such as four kite makers, lived together. These people worked as stewards, cigar makers, kite makers, cotton pickers, and in various other occupations. A group of eight cotton workers retained Chinese surnames such as Wan Chow and Mento Chow. Those in cigar manufacture had Spanish names such as Will Dias and José Martín; typical English names were John Young and John Robinson. The wives of these Chinese had been born in Phila-delphia, China, New Orleans, France, and London. Information about the place of birth of their children suggests that some of these Chinese men had entered New Orleans via New York or Philadelphia; the Spanish names used by others suggest that some of them may have entered via Cuba or the Philippines. All of the Chinese in New Or-leans, together with their families, were classified as white.[43]

41. "Nativities of Free Population," in *Population of the United States in 1860*, 620. There is an error of two persons in the figures published within the volume. The actual total is 34,933, rather than 34,935.

42. "Nativity of the Free Population of the City of New Orleans, Louisiana," in *Population of the United States in 1860*, 615, 620. This analysis of legible schedules for New Orleans does not include three persons born in China who were most probably not Chinese, such as a child of an American tradesman; nor does it include three chil-dren born in the United States of Chinese parents. It includes only Chinese who were born in China, to conform to the nature of the nativity report data.

43. U.S. Department of the Interior, Eighth Census of the United States, 1860, New Orleans, Louisiana, Population Schedule, in Record Group 29, NA.

Southerners were exposed to Chinese in the decades before the Civil War when the Chinese accompanied missionaries on their periodic visits. The missionaries were eager to give local mission supporters the opportunity to meet members of this ancient civilization. As a result, residents of local communities enthusiastically contributed to the southern missionary efforts in China. Chinese individuals and small groups who resided in cities in the East and South were also subject to curiosity and interest. Agents of Christian missions periodically highlighted the plight of Chinese men who had met with ill fortune. For the most part, however, the presence of Chinese was not a subject of major concern to philanthropic organizations devoted to the welfare of immigrants. Their numbers were very small, and in contrast to what happened in California, their presence caused no political outcry in these regions.

Although an experiment using Chinese laborers in the ironworks of Kentucky was not successful, those concerned with agriculture and commerce in the South continued to obtain information about the use of Chinese immigrant labor on plantations, especially those in the West Indies. The problems of plantation labor in the mid-nineteenth century, discussed in the following chapter, led some groups of southerners to evaluate the suitability of Chinese as a new source of labor for the region.

# 2 / REGULATION OF THE COOLIE TRAFFIC

 Before the Civil War, some southerners considered the possibility of using Chinese workers, particularly as an alternative source of agricultural labor. Editors of two well-known journals, Daniel Lee of the *Southern Culti-vator* and J. D. B. De Bow of *De Bow's Review*, wrote articles and exchanged ideas on the introduction of Chinese and East Indian labor into the British and French West Indies, the Spanish colony of Cuba, and Peru.

Daniel Lee, a native of New York State, was a physician but also studied soil chemistry and agriculture. In time he became a leading agricultural journalist well-known in the region and beyond as a representative of the interests of farmers. His scientific study of agriculture and experience in journalism led him to move to the South to become editor of the *Southern Cultivator*, which had been founded in Augusta, Georgia, in 1843. Lee was an early supporter of the establishment of agricultural colleges, and as head of the agricultural division of the Patent Office in Washington, D.C., from 1848 to 1853, he advocated the collection of farm statistics, experimental farming, and the appropriation of public lands for the establishment of agricultural schools.[1]

As editor of the *Southern Cultivator*, Lee wrote in 1854 that the "growing policy of bringing agricultural laborers from Africa, China, and other Asiatic nations into the British West India islands, Cuba, Central America, and the guano islands of Peru, deserves the serious

1. E. Merton Coulter, *Daniel Lee: Agriculturist* (Athens, 1972); see also Clifford Carlton Norse, "*The Southern Cultivator*, 1843–1861" (Ph.D. dissertation, Florida State University, 1969).

consideration of readers."[2] Chinese laborers had been introduced to Cuba and Peru, and the British colonial authorities and British colonists themselves had begun experiments with the use of Chinese as plantation labor. Indeed, in the years 1849–1852, the British Colonial Office and the British West India authorities had put into effect a plan to import Chinese first considered by the West India Committee in 1843. The plan had not been implemented in 1843, however, because approval to reintroduce contract labor from India as well as immigrants from Madeira made it unnecessary.

Reports and letters to the secretary of state for the colonies of Great Britain indicated that the increasing competition between importers of Chinese labor for the Americas had led to serious abuses of the Chinese workers involved. Examples of ill treatment included fraud in recruitment, shortages of food and supplies on the ships, and harsh punishments dealt out by crews during the voyages. These documents reflected the opinion that Chinese labor had economic value and that exploitation could be minimized by official recruitment and regulation of shipment. A contract system was established under the supervision of a government emigration agent. A private firm was given approval to recruit and ship Chinese to the West India plantations. In 1852, the British vessels *Lord Elgin, Glentanner,* and *Samuel Boddington* sailed from China to British Guiana with approximately 790 emigrants, and the *Australia* and the *Clarendon* sailed for Trinidad with approximately 702 Chinese. No Chinese were shipped to the British West Indies in 1853. In 1853–1854, the emigration agent failed to carry out plans to procure 1,550 Chinese, and he was not reappointed. Chinese immigration ceased until 1856, when the next experiment was initiated.[3]

Lee asked readers to consider the wisdom of importing Chinese coolies or Africans to the South under contracts, to serve for a term of years as apprentices or hirelings and then to be returned to their land of nativity. He stressed the value for cotton, sugar, and rice planters of a cheaper supply of agricultural laborers than the slaves from Maryland, Virginia, Kentucky, and Missouri, whom he thought sold for

2. Daniel Lee, "Hireling Labor and Slave Labor," *Southern Cultivator,* XII (June, 1854), 169–80.
3. Persia Crawford Campbell, *Chinese Coolie Emigration to Countries Within the British Empire* (1923; rpr. New York, 1969), 86–117.

extravagant prices. Lee suggested that such a labor pool would be equivalent to that provided the North by the influx of 300,000 or 400,000 immigrants from Europe. With these laborers, 300 million acres of land could be opened, and the wealth of the South would increase "beyond all calculation." Lee knew that the coolie traffic to the West Indies, Cuba, and Peru was viewed as an extreme form of the contract system of labor, which coerced recruits into service. He expected criticism from "anti-slavery men," who would attack any system that found favor with southern planters, although "it is the child of British West India emancipation." He pointed out that in the North, the importation of laborers from Europe was a profitable business, and he saw no reason why the South could not accrue similar advantages through the importation of apprentices.[4]

No doubt aware of experiments to cultivate tea in the South, Lee suggested that Chinese laborers familiar with its culture would increase the chance of its success, thereby adding another staple crop to southern agriculture. He asserted also that the Chinese could work in the South's iron, coal, and copper mines, such as those in Tennessee. The economic advantages of using Chinese laborers were that they would accept wages less than the "interest on the cost of Negro field hands." Noting that the Peruvians, Spanish, and Californians had not treated the Chinese as laboring people "ought to be treated," he stated that under good handling, "hundreds of thousands" of them might be hired for a term of years.[5]

By 1858, however, Lee was involved in the movement to bring Africans to the South and had decided that Chinese would not be suitable. In a series of articles and correspondence on cotton culture and laborers for the South, he stated that experience and observation since 1854 had led him to doubt the wisdom of mixing Chinese with slaves.

4. Lee, "Hireling Labor and Slave Labor," 169–70.
5. *Ibid.*; Abbott Lawrence to Hon. Thomas Ewing, July 11, 1850, in *Report of the Commissioner of Patents for the Year 1850: Part II, Agriculture,* 169; Junius Smith, *Essays on the Cultivation of the Tea Plant in the United States of America: Addressed to the People of the United States Generally, and to the Planters and Farmers of the Southern and Western States Particularly* (New York, 1848); Francis Bonynge, *The Future Wealth of America: Being a Glance at the Resources of the United States and the Commercial and Agricultural Advantages of Cultivating Tea, Coffee, and Indigo, the Date, Mango, Jack, Leechee, Guava, and Orange Trees, etc. with a Review of the China Trade* (New York, 1852).

He now thought African Negroes were best suited for the South, and he supported this position with references to the experience of the French with recruitment of Africans for their Caribbean colonies. Again comparing southern labor needs with northern immigration growth, he indicated that it was no less humanitarian to bring laborers from Africa to the South than to bring immigrants from Liverpool and Bremen to the North.[6]

Arguments against the use of coolie labor in the South also appeared in the records of southern commercial conventions. Such conventions had originated in the late 1830s to discuss questions of direct trade with Europe and later to consider internal improvements and railroads. By the late 1850s they were considering the feasibility of introducing African apprentices or slaves.[7] On August 4, 1857, General William H. Chase of Pensacola reported to the convention assembled in Knoxville, Tennessee, on the necessity for an increased labor force and the means of meeting that need. In his report he acknowledged that the demand for labor exceeded the supply available in Europe and America. One solution to the problem might be to use additional forced labor to supplement the existing free and slave labor. He identified five potential sources of such forced labor: "by contract with the Chinese; by contract with the East Indians; by contract with the African Chiefs and Agents; by smuggling slaves from Africa; and by reopening the African slave trade."[8]

In discussing the disadvantages of coolie labor, Chase explained that although a contract system of labor (in contrast to a slave system) could produce free immigrant laborers from Africa and Asia, the system would not really work effectively. The coercion involved in re-

6. Daniel Lee, "The Future of Cotton Culture in the Southern States, No. 1," *Southern Cultivator,* XVI (January, 1858), 27–28; Lee, "The Future of Cotton Culture in the Southern States, No. 2," *ibid.* (March, 1858), 90–92; L. B. Mercer to Dr. Daniel Lee, March, 1858, and Daniel Lee, "The Future of Cotton Culture in the Southern States," *ibid.* (May, 1858), 137–39; Lee, "Laborers for the South," *ibid.* (August, 1858), 233–36.

7. Herbert Wender, *Southern Commercial Conventions, 1837–1859* (Baltimore, 1930); William Watson Davis, "Ante-Bellum Southern Commercial Conventions," *Transactions of the Alabama Historical Society,* V (1904), 153–202; John George Van Deusen, *The Ante-Bellum Southern Commercial Conventions* (Durham, 1926).

8. William H. Chase, "The Labor Problem," in *Official Report of the Debates and Proceedings of the Southern Commercial Convention, Knoxville, Tennessee, August 10, 1857* (Knoxville, 1857), 41–42.

cruitment of coolies to supply the English, French, and Spanish colonies showed that the contract labor agreements were abused. He concluded that the renewal of the African slave trade was preferable to the introduction of Chinese contract laborers and indeed that this was the only solution for the problem of the labor shortage. Chase further believed that if opposition to slavery continued, the smuggling of slaves from Africa would be extended, finding a market particularly in the cotton-growing states of the South, and the combined navies of England, France, and the United States would be unable to suppress it. He concluded that the demand for labor would continue to increase, and only the restoration of the African slave trade would meet the designs of God, "who in his Providence, created the Africans as the means of equalizing the labor of the world and at the same time of bringing millions of that race into the fold of christianity and civilization." He recommended that the slave trade be reopened "under just, humane, and equitable laws." Chase's communication was referred to the convention's Committee on Business.[9]

Discussion of the suitability of Chinese labor for the South during the late 1850s thus was overshadowed by arguments in favor of reopening the slave trade. Interest in the potential value of Chinese contract labor, however, was not confined to the South. In this period Chinese were settling throughout the world, and the advantages and disadvantages of their labor value became a subject of national and international debate. The themes discussed in this period were to persist well into the 1860s and the 1870s and were influenced by changing conceptions of labor needs. Furthermore, Chinese emigrants of later decades were to face problems regarding their freedom to emigrate and the nature of their work contracts as their legal status changed in response to changing beliefs about them as a race distinct from the whites and the blacks.

Eldon Griffin states that in the 1850s, American consuls in China showed special solicitude with regard to the emigration of Chinese coolies. The consuls had witnessed the abuses in this traffic and were aware of the difficulties in regulating American ships engaged in this commerce. A central problem was that plantation economies through-

9. *Ibid.*, 42.

out the world were experiencing a time of troubles. Changes were taking place in the structures of the labor groups that had worked on these plantations, and Chinese laborers were drawn into the vacuum created by these changes.[10]

The "coolie traffic" consisted of Chinese laborers who were "almost slaves." Vessels from the United States transported many of these Chinese laborers to their new work sites. For example, the United States commissioner to China, Peter Parker, reported that in 1855, a total of 3,050 coolies were carried on five American ships, 1,938 on three British ships, 1,150 on three Peruvian ships, and 250 on a Chilean ship. Swatow, the site of recruitment, was not among the ports that China had opened for trade with the West. Shipmasters, however, often obtained trade goods in a legally open port and then sailed to recruit coolies at the ports that were supposed to be closed to foreigners.[11]

The British had provided for the entry and search by British officials of any ship of any nation transporting Chinese passengers from any port in Hong Kong and of any British ship transporting them from any port in China, if such ships were to be engaged in voyages over seven days long. But American legislation prohibited the entry and search of United States ships outside American ports. The British "Act for the Regulation of the Chinese Passenger Ships" (August 14, 1855), called the Chinese Passengers Act, proclaimed by the governor of Hong Kong, Sir John Bowring, on January 29, 1856, included provisions concerned with conditions under which the entry and search of Chinese passenger ships might take place, regulations for the maintenance of safety in the ships, regulations on provisions and diet, and guidelines for the issuance of permissions and certificates to authorize exit of ships to proceed to sea.[12]

10. Eldon Griffin, *Clippers and Consuls: American Consular and Commercial Relations with Eastern Asia, 1845–1860* (1938; rpr. Wilmington, 1972), 194, 198.

11. Despatch No. 4, Peter Parker to William L. Marcy, secretary of state, February 12, 1856, "Correspondence of the Late Commissioners in China," in *Senate Executive Documents*, 35th Cong., 2nd Sess., No. 22, p. 632.

12. Parker to Marcy, February 12, 1856, pp. 661–69; "An Act to Regulate the Carriage of Passengers in Merchant Vessels," February 22, 1847, *U.S. Statutes at Large*, IX, 127–28; "An Act to Provide for the Ventilation of Passenger Vessels, and for Other Purposes," May 17, 1848, *ibid.*, 220–23; "An Act to Extend the Provisions of All Laws Now

British and American opinion likened the coolie traffic to slavery because of the coercive recruitment practices and inhumane conditions in ships departing from China, the high incidence of illness and bad treatment, and the terms of service provided by the contracts. As Persia Campbell points out, prospective employers or speculators on the profits of selling contracts to employers in the countries that wanted to introduce Chinese, such as Peru and the Spanish colony of Cuba, engaged Chinese firms to hire recruiters (often called "coolie brokers"), who were usually paid per head for the coolies they recruited and brought to the places of detainment, or barracoons—sometimes called "pig-pens." A promise of work, small advances in wages, or debt bondage enticed Chinese to emigrate. During the sea voyage, which lasted up to four months, food and water were often short. Few facilities were provided for exercise, particularly in vessels of small tonnage. Riots and murder were not infrequent.[13]

Griffin points out that the economic drive for profit and power by Chinese procurers, foreign agents, plantation owners, shipowners, and shipmasters superseded considerations of law and humanity. According to Griffin, "it has often been assumed that the coolie traffic was simply a chamber of horrors; it was much more besides." The coolie traffic was part of the worldwide problem of servile labor to which the Congress of the United States paid scant attention. This neglect, together with the fact that profits to owners of vessels who carried these laborers were considerable, heightened the need to regulate the traffic and exercise control over its abuses.[14]

J. D. B. De Bow's articles on Chinese labor provided information about the international context and scope of the coolie trade. Born in Charleston, South Carolina, and a lawyer by training, De Bow worked as an editor most of his life, following a course that marked him as a champion and interpreter of southern social, economic, intellectual, and political institutions and aspirations. Early in his career he became a contributing editor to the *Southern Quarterly Review*. After

---

in Force Relating to the Carriage of Passengers in Merchant Vessels, and the Regulation Thereof," March 3, 1849, *ibid.*, 399–400.

13. Campbell, *Chinese Coolie Emigration*, 95–97.

14. Griffin, *Clippers and Consuls*, 198.

attending the Southern Commercial Convention at Memphis in 1845, he became convinced of the need for a monthly journal devoted to trade, commerce, manufactures, and agriculture. He moved to New Orleans in 1846 and began publication of *De Bow's Review*. In a few years it had attained the widest circulation of any magazine published in the South. De Bow was the first to occupy the chair of commerce, public economy, and statistics at the University of Louisiana in 1848, and in 1850, President Franklin Pierce appointed him superintendent of the nation's seventh census. He was an active contributor of ideas to the commercial conventions held in the South before the Civil War, particularly on the subjects of a transcontinental railroad through the South, direct trade between the South and Europe, and a canal through Central America. Throughout the 1850s, *De Bow's Review* published details of scandals in recruitment and tragedies during the voyages of coolies to the West Indies and Peru, drawing largely on United States congressional reports and British parliamentary papers.[15]

De Bow criticized the British for opposing slavery in the South on humanitarian grounds yet encouraging the use of coolie labor as a means to increase profits: "She has carried away 2,250,000 negroes from Africa, and having destroyed two thirds of them by the rigors of her slavery, frees the pitiful remnant, paying a trifling sum not equal to the interests even of the profits of her slave trade! She is now building up her wealth by destroying the Chinese by thousands with her opium; and lastly, she is filling her coffers, by increasing the greatest iniquity of modern times, the Coolie trade. And this is the nation that raises her hands in holy horror at the cruelty of the Southern States."[16]

He concentrated on economic reasons why the coolie trade would not appeal to southern planters. In September, 1858, De Bow wrote that if a successful abolitionist-inspired insurrection of the Negroes were to result in their freedom, the coolie trade would receive strong impetus. He speculated that under such circumstances, ships from En-

---

15. J. D. B. De Bow, "The Coolie Trade," *De Bow's Review*, XXIII (July, 1857), 30–35; De Bow, "The Coolie Trade; or the Encomienda System of the Nineteenth Century," *ibid.*, XXVII (September, 1859), 296–321; "Asiatic Free Colonists in Cuba," *ibid.*, XXIV (May, 1858), 470–71, Ottis Clark Skipper, *J. D. B. De Bow: Magazinist of the Old South* (Athens, 1958).

16. De Bow, "Coolie Trade; or the Encomienda System," 321.

gland and the northern states would promote the recruitment of thousands of Chinese laborers for the southern plantations. But under the prevailing conditions he dismissed this possibility because of the planters' heavy investment in slaves: "It is cause for satisfaction, that, under present circumstances, the Coolie trade cannot touch the shores of America; no central government has the power to command it, and the interests of the planters are too great to permit a majority of the people in any given Southern States to vote for the introduction of a species of labor so cheap, that it would ruin all the old planters and kill off slavery as well as the slaves by starvation. Hence, the safety of the slaves is their value."[17]

Competition to the agricultural interests of the South resulting from the increased use of Chinese labor in the West Indies merited the attention of American diplomatic representatives to China. On March 8, 1853, Humphrey T. Marshall, United States commissioner to China, wrote from Macao to inform the secretary of state of potential problems arising from the growing interest in Chinese workers for the British West India colonies. Marshall feared potential competition from this labor because estimates of the annual cost of wages for a Chinese laborer under contract were judged to be far lower than that for a slave. He considered the expansion of British planting interests through use of this new "hard working source of labor" a political and economic threat to the United States:

> Should that power [Great Britain] seriously undertake to populate her West India possessions and her colonies on the coast of South America with Chinese laborers, who have no idea whatever of the right of popular participation in the direction of government, the effect to be produced upon the industrial interests of the planting States of the United States, and upon the institutions of the republics of South America, must necessarily be most disastrous to them.
>
> . . . The *terms* for which they engage, and the rates of their wages, with the estimated cost of subsistence and clothing, prove that the experiment is designed to be seriously made, and when made that it must depress the entire planting interest of the United

17. *Ibid.*, 319–20.

States. The total cost of the Chinese laborer is estimated at eighty dollars per annum, which is far below the cost of slave labor, independent of the risk which the planter runs in his original investment. The Chinese lives on rice principally, and that staple will be produced at mere nominal rates in the country to which he is emigrating. He is patient of labor, tractable, obedient as a slave, and frugal. When he shall occupy a leasehold, on which to exert the energy and skill he possesses, he will compel from the earth the maximum production of which it is capable; and under whatever circumstances will create a competition against which it must be difficult to struggle. . . .

I will not elaborate the views which these suggestions develop as occurring to my own mind, but I shall be glad to know whether the President deems any step to prevent the use of American shipping in the furtherance of this emigration proper and politic. . . . If the President should desire to manifest the disinclination of the United States to the progress of this emigration, an order to the American consuls to refuse clearance to any ship under American papers and colors, carrying coolies from China, would at once confine the trade to the shipping of other nations, and might, possibly, induce Great Britain to halt in this scheme so at war with an established principle of American policy.[18]

To meet this competition, Marshall called for an American policy that would give authority to American diplomats and consuls in China to prevent United States ships from transporting Chinese coolie immigrants. His successors, Peter Parker and William Reed, repeatedly sought legal authority to this end. They emphasized that with proper authority, American officials could control the coolie traffic. They could allow embarkation of voluntary emigrants, and they could use the threat of sanctions to prevent the evils of recruitment of Chinese under force.

A few months after his appointment as commissioner to China in August, 1855, Peter Parker sent a dispatch to Secretary of State William Marcy to draw his attention to the Chinese coolie trade: "When I

---

18. Despatch No. 9, Humphrey Marshall to secretary of state, March 8, 1853, *House Executive Documents*, 33rd Cong., 1st Sess., No. 123, p. 78.

came to the investigation of this traffic, I had no adequate conception of its enormities, and the strong terms in which I have described it are fully sustained by official documents and the most reliable testimony."[19] Parker's later reports emphasized the scandals of the trade and the frequent use of United States vessels to transport the coolies.

On January 10, 1856, Parker issued a public notification condemning the traffic in Chinese coolies. In this document, he noted that the traffic was "replete with illegalities, immoralities, and revolting and inhuman atrocities, strongly resembling those of the African slave trade in former years, some of them exceeding the horrors of the 'middle passage.'" He declared that the imperial Chinese government strongly disapproved of the traffic and that it had been carried out "in localities where foreign trade is not permitted by any treaty, and is therefore illegal." Furthermore, the friendly relations between China and the United States were jeopardized, and even the lives of the coolie brokers were "exposed to the vengeance of those whose relations or friends have been bought, kidnapped, or grossly deceived, in the progress of the coolie trade."[20]

The notification sought to stop all American citizens from participating in the coolie trade: "The undersigned therefore calls upon all citizens of the United States to desist from this irregular and immoral traffic; and makes known to all whom it may concern the high disapprobation thereof of the government of the United States, and forewarns all who may hereafter engage therein, that they will not only forfeit the protection of their government while so doing, in whatever consequences they may be involved, but, furthermore, render themselves liable to the heavy penalties to which the traffic, if as hitherto in some instances conducted, may expose them." Parker was careful to distinguish between the forms of Chinese emigration:

> This notification respects the "coolie trade," in contradistinction to the voluntary emigration of Chinese adventurers; between these there exists a wide difference.
>
> Regulations for the business of furnishing Chinese labor to

19. Despatch No. 1, Peter Parker to William L. Marcy, secretary of state, January 14, 1856, *Senate Executive Documents*, 35th Cong., 2nd Sess., No. 22, p. 623.
20. *Public Notification*, Peter Parker, Hong Kong, January 10, 1856, *ibid.*, 625–26.

countries that may desire the same, and for affording facilities to Chinese voluntarily disposed to render such service, in providing outfit and passage, and means, and freedom of return at their option, may be a subject for future treaty stipulation or government arrangement on the part of western nations and China.

The United States consuls will be instructed to convey copies of this notification to the proper Chinese authorities at the five ports.[21]

On February 12, 1856, Parker submitted to the secretary of state information on the coolie trade that had been furnished by British colonial authorities. He noted that on August 14, 1855, the British Parliament had approved the Chinese Passengers Act, which was designed to prevent abuses during the transportation of Chinese emigrants, and he asked for specific instructions to enable the American representatives in China to regulate the coolie traffic through control of United States vessels: "I am apprehensive that something more than leaving United States merchant vessels to their fate, if engaged in this inhuman traffic, will be necessary; and I respectfully suggest the necessity of specific instructions emanating from the navy department to our men of war on this station, authorizing them to prevent resort to illegal ports, and to examine such vessels as do, and ascertain that they do not offend against law, and to make them accountable if they do."[22]

Although Parker's public notification was welcomed by Chinese officials, available records for the year 1856 show that in only one case, that of the house of George R. Sampson and Lewis W. Tappan of Boston, was he able to stop the traffic. Sampson and Tappan had engaged several vessels to carry two thousand coolies from China to Brazil. Under a contract made with the Brazilian government, Sampson and Tappan were promised £2,000 to have their agent in Hong Kong, C. D. Mugford, recruit and deliver two thousand Chinese within eighteen months, beginning in June, 1855. Some of the Chinese were embarked by this agent on board the ship *Sarah*, which sailed for Brazil on December 26, 1855. But correspondence and conversation with Parker and correspondence with Mugford convinced Sampson and Tappan that the coolie trade was wrong. They sent in-

21. *Ibid.*, 626.
22. Parker to Marcy, February 12, 1856, pp. 632–33.

structions to Mugford to "abandon the business at whatever cost, and to divert the ships intended for this business to other branches of trade."[23]

In a dispatch to George R. Sampson on May 24, 1856, Parker recalled earlier conversations and correspondence with Sampson in which they had observed that sometimes men of highest moral and commercial character engaged in ventures with coolie contract labor while not aware of its "true character." He recalled that Sampson and Tappan had with "pains and expense" abandoned this enterprise once they had been "enlightened upon the subject." Parker added that in the future, if the "cause of humanity" could be served by treaties that clearly defined the conditions under which the voluntary emigration of Chinese could take place so as to take away the evils, he would happily endorse it.[24]

Parker's successor, William Reed, focused on the need for a new approach to prevent the employment of American ships for the transportation of coolies to Cuba. In 1858, after a few months in China, Reed wrote to Secretary of State Lewis Cass that the "subject of Chinese emigration is too wide and perplexing." Still, he added, two viewpoints might be considered. On the one hand, because of the "crying want of labor" in several regions of the world and because of the destitution of the Chinese, emigration could be a means of "social relief and benefit to the world at large." But he feared that the system of Chinese contract labor would result in a "new and illegitimate slavery, the practical enslavement of a distant and most peculiar race." On the other hand, if the more than thirty thousand Chinese in Cuba were to increase owing to lower shipping costs and other considerations, then, Reed suggested, the secretary of state and the president should consider the impact of this "new infusion of strength" into Spanish America on the general interests of the United States. He speculated

23. "Coolie Trade," *House Reports*, 36th Cong., 1st Sess., No. 443, pp. 4–8; Alexander H. Rice, A. T. Hall, W. B. Spooner, C. O. Whitmore, and E. Train, *Report of the Committee Appointed by the Government of the "Board of Trade," to Take into Consideration the Communication of Messrs. Sampson and Tappan, Dated April 24th, 1856* (Boston, 1856); C. D. Mugford to Peter Parker, January 7, 1856, *Senate Executive Documents*, 35th Cong., 2nd Sess., No. 22, pp. 657–58.

24. Exhibit A, Despatch No. 13, Peter Parker to George Sampson, Esq., May 24, 1856, *Senate Executive Documents*, 35th Cong., 2nd Sess., No. 22, pp. 837–39.

that one of the results might be the emergence of a new and trouble-some labor force certain to be oppressed by its masters, a situation that might end in a bloody massacre. Like his predecessors, Reed empha-sized the need for the government's condemnation of the traffic "as a matter of humanity and policy" and sought to have the government repress it "so far at least as it is conducted in American vessels." [25]

In an accompanying document, Reed expressed the opinion that "the carrying of Chinese laborers (coolies) in American ships, from any foreign ports to any port foreign or domestic, there to be held to service, is prohibited by acts of Congress, and exposes the master to a heavy penalty, and the forfeiture of his vessel on its arrival in the United States, and this whether the laborers be taken to the United States or not." [26] He instructed United States consular officials in China, therefore, to assume the duty of informing diplomatic au-thorities from other colonial powers, such as Spain and Great Britain, that since he, as chief diplomatic representative of the United States in China, considered the carrying of Chinese coolies in American vessels to be illegal, no official sanction would be given to this trade. Masters of American ships were to be instructed of this policy.

But efforts to implement these instructions were not successful, be-cause consuls did not have the legal authority to implement them. A case in point is that of the American vessel *Flora Temple*. The ship, commanded by American master, Captain J. M. Cole, had been con-tracted to transport a cargo of coolies from Macao to Havana. On Jan-uary 5, 1858, Reed instructed S. B. Rawle, American consul in Macao, to inform the Spanish consular authorities in Macao that the coolie trade was expressly prohibited by law and to "call the attention of the master of the vessel to his responsibility" as an American citizen or resident of the United States not to "take on board, receive, or trans-port from this port [Macao], or any port in China or its dependencies,

25. Despatch No. 1, William B. Reed to Lewis Cass, secretary of state, January 13, 1858, *Senate Executive Documents*, 36th Cong., 1st Sess., No. 30, p. 63; Tyler Dennett, *Americans in Eastern Asia: A Critical Study of the Policy of the United States with Reference to China, Japan and Korea in the 19th Century* (New York, 1922), 311–31; Michael Paul Onorato, "The Mission of William B. Reed, United States Minister to China, 1856–1858" (M.A. thesis, Georgetown University, 1959).

26. Exhibit 5a, Despatch No. 1, William B. Reed to S. B. Rawle, Esq., U.S. consul, January 5, 1858, *Senate Executive Documents*, 36th Cong., 1st Sess., No. 30, p. 75.

any Chinese coolie or laborer, for the purpose of disposing of such person as a slave, or to be held to service or labor in the U.S. or elsewhere." Failure to follow these instructions would expose the shipmaster, on his arrival in the United States, to a "prosecution for a violation of the act of Congress, with the penalty of fine and imprisonment and the forfeiture of his vessel." [27]

On January 8, 1858, William Macy, American deputy consul in Macao, informed Reed that the United States consular authorities in that port had failed to prevent the transportation of Chinese emigrants to Havana on the *Flora Temple*. Their efforts had been rejected both by the Spanish consul general in Macao and by the shipmaster of the *Flora Temple*. On January 7, 1858, the Spanish consul general, Nicasio Cariente y Moral, had responded to Consul Rawle's communication by stating that until he received new instructions from his government, he did not have the authorization to refuse assistance to those involved in the contract and embarkation of Chinese laborers in ships bound for Spanish possessions sailing under any flag. Should he do so, he would act contrary to the provisions of the Spanish royal decree of March 22, 1854, which permitted Spanish subjects and foreigners to engage in "this business which is allowable, just, and legal," as long as a contract is made "spontaneously by one free man with another free man, the one offering his services, and the other accepting them, for a determined space of time, and in consideration of a remuneration, and of certain conditions stipulated between them." The Spanish consul general further asserted that he was not responsible for ascertaining "whether the American ship-owners and captains, in chartering their vessels, infringe the laws of their country or not." They would answer to their government in case of any infraction and accept the consequences. [28]

Captain Cole wrote to Consul Macy that his instructions had come from the owners of the *Flora Temple* in the United States before his departure for China. He felt bound to obey these orders, which directed him to convey passengers from Macao to Havana. Macy con-

27. *Ibid.*
28. Exhibit 5b, Despatch No. 1, William A. Macy to William B. Reed, Esq., January 8, 1858, *Senate Executive Documents*, 36th Cong., 1st Sess., No. 30, p. 76; Exhibit 5c, Inclosure A, Despatch No. 1, Nicasio Cariete y Moral to S. B. Rawle, Esq., January 7, 1858, *ibid.*, 76–77.

veyed Cole's explanation to Reed. Reed in turn prepared a dispatch to Secretary of State Cass, dated January 13, 1858, in which he summarized the dilemmas he and consular officials faced in attempting to control the coolie traffic. He indicated that Commissioner Marshall's statements of March, 1853, on the subject of consular sanctions against Chinese passenger ships under the American flag, as well as Parker's public notification of January, 1856, which condemned the coolie trade, were ineffectual precedents upon which to build policy. In view of this lack of legal authority Reed had searched for legislation upon which to condemn the coolie trade. He thought the act of Congress of April 20, 1818 ("An Act in Addition to 'An Act to Prohibit the Introduction (Importation) of Slaves into any Port or Place Within the Jurisdiction of the United States'"), might serve the purpose. The main features of this act were that Negroes were not to be imported with intent to hold them as slaves and that vessels in which they were imported would be forfeited. No persons were to equip vessels for this trade in the ports of the United States, and any who did so would be subject to a fine. The act further outlined the dispositions to be followed if slaves were imported in violation of it and specified the sanctions to be applied to those who broke the law.[29]

Section 4 of this act prohibited citizens of the United States or other residents in the country from transporting slaves to the United States. The following sanctions were to be applied to violators:

SEC. 4.    That if any citizen or citizens of the United States, or other person or persons resident within the jurisdiction of the same, shall, from and after the passing of this act, take on board, receive, or transport, from any of the coasts or kingdoms of Africa, or from any other foreign kingdom, place, or country, or from sea, any negro, mulatto, or person of colour, not being an inhabitant, nor held to service by the laws of either of the states or territories of the United States, in any ship, vessel, boat, or other water craft, for the purpose of holding, selling, or otherwise disposing of, such person as a slave, or to be held to service or labour, or be aiding or

29. Exhibit 5d, Inclosure B, John M. Cole, master, ship *Flora Temple*, to William A. Macy, Esq., January 7, 1858, *ibid.*, 78; Macy to Reed, January 8, 1858, p. 76; Reed to Cass, January 13, 1858, p. 60.

abetting therein, every such person or persons so offending, shall, on conviction, by due course of law, severely forfeit and pay a sum not exceeding five thousand, nor less than one thousand dollars, one moiety to the use of the United States, and the other to the use of the person or persons who shall sue for such forfeiture, and prosecute the same to effect; and moreover, shall suffer imprisonment, for a term not exceeding seven years nor less than three years; and every ship or vessel, boat, or other water craft, on which such negro, mulatto, or person of colour, shall have been taken on board, received, or transported, as aforesaid, her tackle, apparel, and furniture, and the goods and effects which shall be found on board the same, or shall have been imported therein in the same voyage, shall be forfeited, one moiety to the use of the United States, and the other to the use of the person or persons who shall sue for and prosecute the same to effect; and every such ship or vessel shall be liable to be seized, prosecuted, and condemned, in any court of the United States, having competent jurisdiction.[30]

Although acknowledging that this law was aimed at the "evil" of Negro slavery rather than the coolie trade, Reed sought counsel from Secretary Cass regarding its application to the Chinese by raising two questions: "Is the Chinese cooly a person of color as distinguished from negro or mulatto?" and "Is the contract under which he agrees to go, goes, and is landed in Cuba, a disposal of him to be held to service or labor?"[31]

On the first question, Reed indicated that he had little doubt that "Malays and Javanese" or the "black sepoys" found in Hong Kong were "persons of color" and therefore that the Chinese "cooly" was, "to some sense," also a "person of color." The term *sepoy* usually referred to a native of India serving in the lower ranks of the army. The question of the tenure of labor or service for which the coolies were destined was less of a problem to Reed. He drew on a Spanish ordinance that used the term *laborer* or *imported laborer* rather than *free day laborer*. He further argued that although the Chinese were imported to Cuba under a contract for a term of years, they were subject to trans-

30. *U.S. Statutes at Large*, III, 451–52.
31. Reed to Cass, January 13, 1858, p. 61.

fer of masters, with "no volition of their own, and no provisions were made for their return to their native country." On the basis of this interpretation of the 1818 law, Reed instructed consuls to warn all parties, "especially the owners and masters of vessels who transported Chinese laborers, that they might expose themselves to the penalties of the law." In conclusion, Reed stated that if his interpretation of the 1818 statute was not sustained, he hoped that the subject would attract "the immediate attention of the President and Congress, so that, if they agreed with him in his opinion of this trade, effective legislation would be adopted." As had his predecessors, Commissioners Marshall and Parker, Reed underscored his opinion with arguments about the threat posed to United States interests by the use of coolie labor in the Americas.[32]

A month after this correspondence was sent to the secretary of state, the secretary of the American legation in China, S. Wells Williams, sent instructions to the consuls of the United States in China. He emphasized that the legal problem about recruitment of Chinese was not whether they left willingly or unwillingly but concerned the nature of the work agreement. The legation took the view that "what constitutes the breach of the laws of the United States is the contract for labor or service under which the cooly is shipped." Williams wrote that it was "quite immaterial in point of law, whether the cooly goes with or against his will, if, on his arrival, he is to be disposed of to be held to labor."[33]

Reed's request for counsel about the legislative basis upon which to condemn the coolie traffic continued its course as in April, 1858, the secretary of state sent the dispatch to the attorney general, requesting his opinion "as to whether such employment of our ships is in violation of the laws of the United States for the suppression of the slave trade." Almost one year later on March 11, 1859, the attorney general offered the opinion that the 1818 law could not be used to control the coolie trade and that the only remedy lay with Congress.[34]

32. *Ibid.*, 61–62.

33. Inclosure 2q, Despatch No. 10, S. Wells Williams to U.S. consuls in China and to Sir John Bowring, February 18, 1858, *Senate Executive Documents*, 36th Cong. 1st Sess., No. 30, pp. 204–206.

34. Lewis Cass, secretary of state, to J. S. Black, attorney general, April 28, 1858,

The Committee on Commerce of the House of Representatives was subsequently requested to inquire "into the expediency of prohibiting by law all American vessels from engaging in the coolie trade, or from transporting apprentices, so called, to the West Indies, or other parts of the world." The committee's report, together with a bill, was submitted to the House of Representatives on April 16, 1860. The bill, which became law on February 19, 1862, was the "Act to prohibit the 'Coolie Trade' by American Citizens in American Vessels."[35] (See Appendix I.)

The law prohibited American citizens or foreigners residing in the United States from transporting inhabitants or subjects of China known as coolies to any foreign country "to be disposed of, or sold, or transferred, for any term of years or for any time whatever, as servants or apprentices, or to be held to service or labor." Any ships employed for such purposes would be forfeited to the United States and would be liable to be seized and prosecuted in the circuit or district courts of the United States, where the ship would be "found, seized, or carried." Section 4 of this act clearly stated, moreover, that it was not designed to control the voluntary emigration of any Chinese subject or any vessel that carried voluntary emigrants. In such cases, certificates would be prepared by the consul or consular agent of the United States who resided at the port of embarkation providing the person's name and a statement that his emigration was voluntary. The certificate was to be given to the master of the vessel.

The "Act to Prohibit the 'Coolie Trade' by American Citizens in American Vessels," approved just one year after the secession of the South from the Union, was welcomed by Americans concerned about the regulation of a trade that resembled slavery and posed a threat to American interests. The fact that Section 4 of this legislation continued to allow the "voluntary" emigration of Chinese under proper certification by consular authorities at the port of embarkation is of importance because some students of Chinese overseas emigration have emphasized that most Chinese who departed of their own will under the

---

Record Group 59, Domestic Letters, Department of State, NA; J. S. Black to Lewis Cass, March 11, 1859, Record Group 59, Miscellaneous Letters, Department of State, NA.

35. *U.S. Statutes at Large*, XII, 340–41.

credit-ticket system were bound to their masters or brokers through the ties of debt bondage.

Chinese emigration of the middle and late nineteenth century was conducted by the recruitment of Chinese under two systems of organization, the credit-ticket and the contract systems. The coolie traffic was an extreme form of the contract system.

Under the credit-ticket system Chinese merchants or brokers advanced money for the expenses of the passage of Chinese indentured emigrants to their overseas destination. The broker had a lien on the services of a Chinese emigrant until he paid off his debt or until it was paid by relatives of the emigrants or by their prospective employers. In return, the newcomers worked for those who extended the credit until the debt was paid. The credit-ticket system had long been used by indentured emigrants from South China who left voluntarily to work in what Chinese called Nanyang (South Seas), the region to the south of China that included the Philippines, the former Dutch East Indies, the Malay Peninsula, and Borneo, Thailand, Indochina, and Burma. The Chinese who left for Australia and California also used the credit-ticket system.[36]

Harry Parkes, who was then interpreter in the British Consulate in Canton, described the entry of Chinese to California as an exception to the usual pattern of coolie emigration. They went, he said, in hopes of obtaining gold and high wages. Thus they went not as settlers but as "sojourners" for a brief term of one or two years; "passengers" rather than "coolies" would be a better name for them. He reported that these poor emigrants left for California "with the purposes of returning as soon as they had netted, exclusive of expenses, two or three hundred dollars; which, to the common field-labourer, whose united gains for twelve months do not amount to more than a tenth of that sum, is sufficient inducement for the venture." Parkes stated that most Chinese were sent to California as a speculative venture by "moneyed parties," who paid their passage, which was about fifty dollars, and other expenses amounting to about twenty dollars, on the condition

36. Barth, *Bitter Strength*, 50–51; Victor Purcell, *The Chinese in Southeast Asia* (London, 1965), 1–40; Ta Chen, *Emigrant Communities in South China: A Study of Overseas Migration and Its Influence on Standards of Living and Social Change* (New York, 1940).

of receiving from each of them on their return the sum of two hundred dollars.[37]

Sir W. Pember Reeves and Gunther Barth have emphasized that upon first sight, the credit-ticket system appeared to be "innocent enough." The movement of Chinese to California was characterized as "voluntary" and "free" because they traveled of their own will. But these writers assert that the Chinese who depended on the credit-ticket system to California were often held almost as slaves of their countrymen and that these invisible ties of control were not understood or recognized by their neighbors or by authorities in the places to which they migrated.[38]

Furthermore, under agreements between the Chinese companies that governed the credit-ticket system and the shipping companies, no Chinese emigrant was allowed to return to China until he obtained a permit stating that he was clear of debt. This cooperation was strengthened because the conveyance of Chinese passengers and Chinese merchandise on American ships was highly profitable.[39]

Foreigners and Chinese middlemen played a major role in the contract system, through which laborers were hired for a specific time period ranging from five to eight years, with the promise of a fixed rate of pay, often with advances and usually with provisions for rations and clothes. The first shipment of Chinese under contract to foreigners is believed to have been made in 1845 in a French vessel that departed from the port of Amoy to the Isle of Bourbon. It was undertaken by a Frenchman who speculated that Chinese could be obtained at cheaper wages from their place of birth than in the Straits settlements. In 1847 a Spanish company introduced Chinese laborers to Cuba, and by 1852 close to fifteen thousand had left for Havana and several thousand for the Chincha Islands, off the coast of Peru, to extract guano. A number were introduced into California for agricultural work under contracts.

37. "General Remarks on Chinese Emigration," by Harry Parkes, Inclosure in No. 10, Canton, September, 1852, in Great Britain, *Parliamentary Papers*, Vol. 68 (Accounts and Papers, Vol. XII, 4 November 1852–20 August 1853), "Correspondence with the Superintendent of British Trade in China upon the Subject of Emigration from That Country," No. 263, p. 26.

38. W. P. Reeves, preface to Campbell, *Chinese Coolie Emigration*, ix–xv; Barth, *Bitter Strength*, 55–58.

39. Campbell, *Chinese Coolie Emigration*, 31–32.

But the credit-ticket system soon superseded the contract labor agreements because of the stimulus of the gold discoveries. Chinese introduced to the British West Indies entered under a system of contracts; most were destined for British Guiana.[40]

Persia Campbell states that few contract emigrants returned to China from the Caribbean colonies. This suggestion is puzzling because Chinese who left almost always hoped to return to the home of their ancestors. Abuses occurred under the contract system, and over the years, the status of the indentured Chinese laborer was lowered, as shown by the legislation of the British West Indies. The right of laborers to terminate contracts had been regarded by the British West India planters as subversive to the central purpose of the contract system—to supply a dependable, long-term labor force. When the regulation of contract labor first was considered in 1843, contracts for five years had been allowed on the condition that the laborer could terminate them at the end of six months or at subsequent yearly intervals as a security against injustice or abuses. When the subject was reintroduced in 1850–1852, five-year contracts were again allowed. The Chinese laborers were given the power to terminate these contracts upon repayment of the costs of their introduction less an amount equivalent to their wages for their time of service; or they could terminate them at the end of one year, provided they paid a small periodic tax. Over the next decade, several additional modifications were introduced that made it more difficult for Chinese to terminate their contracts. By 1864, legislation stipulated that contracts were to run for five years without the possibility of termination. Consolidated Ordinance 4 of 1864 thus stated, "No such immigrant shall be entitled to change his employer or to commute any part of his term of service." The planters thus had absolute control over the services of the Chinese for a period of five years. At the end of this term, the newcomers were not bound to enter into a second contract, although efforts were made to induce them to reindenture. A bounty of fifty dollars was offered to persuade those in a "dependent position to refrain from claiming their independence."[41]

40. Charles A. Winchester, Inclosure 3 in No. 8, British Consulate, Amoy, August 26, 1852, in *Parliamentary Papers*, "Correspondence with the Superintendent of British Trade in China upon the Subject of Emigration from That Country," 9–15.
41. Campbell, *Chinese Coolie Emigration*, 133–35.

In summary, emphasis on the difference between voluntary labor under the credit-ticket system and forced labor under the contract system obscured the basic realities of the ties of bondage in effect under both systems. When southern agents and employers began experiments to introduce Chinese laborers to that region after the Civil War, as described in the following chapters, they were to find themselves subject to the law of 1862 and other statutes and to the tests of regulations and interpretations that public officials felt compelled to make.

Southern plans to supplant the emancipated Negro slaves with Chinese roused northern suspicions that a new form of bondage was about to be introduced. It seemed unlikely that southerners, who before the Civil War had defended themselves against the abolitionist charge that slaveholding was a sin, had changed their attitudes.

According to H. Shelton Smith, the major argument of the southerners in defense of human bondage was drawn from the Old and New Testaments, contending that the master-slave relation was sanctioned by God's word. Smith indicates that they had also defended slavery on the grounds that it elevated the Negro from the level of barbarism believed to exist in Africa and that it contributed to the general good of society. In an address to the United States Senate in 1838, John C. Calhoun stated that conflicts between capital and labor could not occur in a bondage society: "Every plantation is a little community, with the master at its head, who concentrates in himself the united interests of capital and labor of which he is the common representative." [42]

The South fought the Civil War with a sense of mission, which the vice-president of the Confederate States of America, Alexander Stephens, clearly enunciated in Savannah, Georgia, on March 21, 1861: "With us, all of the white race, however high or low, rich or poor, are equal in the eye of the law. Not so with the negro. Subordination is his place. . . . It is, indeed, in conformity with the ordinance of the Creator." On January 1, 1863, when through the Emancipation Proclamation, Abraham Lincoln freed all slaves in rebel-ruled territory, religious leaders from eleven denominations in the South declared that abolitionism interfered with the plans of God for the elevation of black

42. H. Shelton Smith, *In His Image But . . . : Racism in Southern Religion, 1780–1910* (Durham, 1972), 129–50; Calhoun quoted in *ibid.*, 149–50.

people and that the South had done more to Christianize the Negro than any other people on the face of the earth.[43]

In view of such attitudes, northern reformers doubted that plantation owners and other entrepreneurs in the South could adopt new views of the relations between plantation owner and worker, and these fears were to be reflected in their efforts to stop plans to introduce Chinese labor to the region.

43. Stephens quoted in *ibid.*, 183; see also 197–98.

# 3 / CHINESE FROM CUBA AND ASIA

Following the Civil War, southern planters seriously considered importing Chinese laborers. In weighing this alternative they were influenced by the West Indian experience with Chinese workers and the encouragement of southerners who had lived in the West Indian islands or in China itself.[1]

In July, 1865, several articles in the Galveston *Daily News* supported using Chinese workers for the cultivation of southern lands. Such laborers would be easy to obtain on a contract basis. They were described as "docile and thrifty, taking good care of themselves, and doing their work without reluctance." The only drawback to a Chinese laborer was that "he will never go in debt to the proprietor and, of course after the contract has expired, the planter has no lien on the laborer, and cannot compel him to remain." In marked contrast was the "idle and thriftless peon, such as the Mexican, the native of Central America, and the negro," whom a proprietor had no trouble in maintaining "in constant servitude."[2]

On July 12, 1865, John S. Thrasher published a letter that later was widely quoted in which he described progress in agriculture and commerce in Cuba as a result of the contract system with Chinese laborers. Born in Maine of an American father and a Cuban mother, Thrasher had lived in Cuba from 1839 to 1851. In the early 1850s,

1. Lucy M. Cohen, "Entry of Chinese to the Lower South from 1865 to 1870: Policy Dilemmas," *Southern Studies*, XVII (Spring, 1978), 5–37.
2. Houston-Galveston *Daily News*, July 5, 1865; see also letter by "Brazos," Houston-Galveston *Daily News*, June 7, 8, 1865.

while a resident of Louisiana, he had taken an active role in Cuban independence and annexation movements. He was also a correspondent for the New York *Herald*, the *Faro de Cuba*, and the New Orleans *Daily Picayune*.[3]

Thrasher believed that planters would find coolie contract labor highly beneficial. He recalled that when Chinese were first introduced into Cuba, some problems had arisen regarding the "ill-defined obligation of the parties to the contract, and in the absence of penalties to enforce those of the laborers." The situation had been remedied, however, by the adoption of an explicit code of "free labor regulations, and the provision of officers for the enforcement of the obligations of each party." Because agricultural conditions were similar in Cuba and in the southern states, Thrasher thought the same labor system would be workable. He suggested that if several planters agreed to take a limited number of Chinese at a maximum cost per head, "parties could probably be found to undertake the importation of a ship-load. The ships engaged in the trade, carry from 300 to 600 Coolies."[4]

John Little Smith, an eminent Mobile jurist, was also widely quoted in the press of neighboring states. Discussions with Thomas M. Boyle, former captain of the American ship *Ticonderoga*, which had taken emigrants from Great Britain to the Australian colonies and had also transported Chinese from China to Cuba, convinced Smith that the Chinese would afford the "best and cheapest labor in the world." They were reputed to make good plantation hands and to be unsurpassed as servants. He proposed to bring Chinese from Cuba, where their contracts were expiring, and afterward from China, in such number as might be required. Smith stated that coolies should not be engaged solely for field labor simply because they had been profitably employed that way in other countries but that they could work in river and swamp lands in which the "caucasian races are not likely to work." He further suggested that the Chinese should work in groups to encourage competition. He thought the Chinese left the

3. Letter by J. S. Thrasher, Houston-Galveston *Daily News*, July 12, 1865; see also New Orleans *Bee*, July 19, 1865; Herminio Portell Vilá, *Narciso Lopez y su epoca, 1850–1851* (Havana, 1958), III, 718; Jorge Quintana, *Indice de extranjeros en el ejército libertador de Cuba, 1895–1898* (3 vols.; Havana, 1953), I, 287–96.

4. Houston-Galveston *Daily News*, July 12, 1865.

fields in Cuba after their contracts expired because they were harshly treated by their masters.[5]

Charles du Gaalon, a Louisiana-born planter who resided in the French West Indian colony of Guadeloupe, was one of the first promoters to attempt to turn these suggestions into reality. He had engaged in sugar cultivation under the system of freed labor inaugurated in French colonies by the French Revolution of 1848. Du Gaalon proposed that southerners introduce Chinese and Hindoo coolies, emphasizing that Hindoo coolies were preferred in the French and British colonies for their docility and quality of work. They were assumed to be moral because they brought their wives and children with them. Chinese from cities in the Celestial Empire had a reputation for insubordination although those drawn from the countryside did not. Furthermore, the Chinese did not bring their wives with them.[6]

Not long after du Gaalon had presented these plans to interested planters, M. F. Reimoning, an agent of Soubry and Company of Paris and Marseilles, arrived in New Orleans with instructions and authority from this company to make contracts for the importation of laborers into Louisiana, preferably from the British and French colonies of the East Indies. Reimoning noted that the act of 1862 prohibiting the coolie trade did not apply to Chinese who emigrated voluntarily or to coolies from India. Soubry and Company had five ships that had brought several thousand immigrants to the French colonies to serve for five-year contracts at about $2.25 a month plus clothing and food.[7]

5. "Smith, John Little," in Thomas McAdory Owen, *History of Alabama and Dictionary of Alabama Biography* (Chicago, 1921), IV, 1584; Great Britain, *Parliamentary Papers*, Vol. 68 (Accounts and Papers, Vol. XII, 4 November 1852–20 August 1853), "Papers Relative to Emigration to the Australian Colonies," No. 1627, pp. 185–90. For record of Cuba voyages, see Griffin, *Clippers and Consuls*, 392; "Asiatic Free Colonists in Cuba," 470–71; Mobile *Daily Advertiser and Register* quoted in New Orleans *Daily Picayune*, September 19, 1865; New Orleans *Daily Picayune*, September 23, 1865; Baton Rouge *Tri-Weekly Gazette and Comet*, September 23, 1865; Mobile *Advertiser and Register*, October 24, 1865.

6. New Orleans *Daily Picayune*, October 17, 1865; Abbeville *Le Meschacébé*, October 21, 1865; Opelousas *Courier*, December 16, 1865; New Orleans *Daily Picayune*, November 23, 1865; New Orleans *Bee*, November 21, 1865.

7. New Orleans *Bee*, November 21, 23, 1865; New Orleans *Daily Picayune*, November 23, 1865; New Orleans *Times*, November 23, 1865; Baton Rouge *Tri-Weekly*

Several large planters and other influential men had met to test public sentiment and to explore the possibility of forming a company. Some advocates desired coolie labor for their fields so that they could recoup their shattered fortunes. Others emphasized that coolie labor would set a good example for the freedmen.[8]

After meeting with interested groups, Reimoning selected Charles du Gaalon as procurator for contracts in New Orleans. A newspaper advertisement announced an "immigration agency": "Mr. R. Reimonenq announces to the planters of Louisiana and neighboring States that he has been appointed agent of the commercial houses of France and the Great Indies, and that he is authorized to sign contracts for the immigration of laborers from India or China. N.B.—Mr. Charles de Gaalon, interested in this agency has charge of the procuration of Mr. Reimonenq."[9]

The efforts of entrepreneurs and planters to introduce Chinese during 1865 and 1866 did not come to fruition. Only one Louisianan, a man named T. Edmonston, is known to have brought in Chinese, and these were from the Philippine Islands. The early failures were associated with the discouraging responses from the office of the commissioner of the Bureau of Immigration, which had been established subject to the Department of State, under the authorization of the Act to Encourage Immigration of July 4, 1864. On August 30, 1865, Samuel Rainey of New Orleans requested permission to import immigrants from China. On September 27 of that same year, H. N. Congar, the commissioner, replied that the act of 1862 did not give him authority to grant special commissions or to give subsidies for the purpose of securing immigrant laborers from any country. Congar gave similar responses to H. F. Stickney and George A. Stewart, both of Alabama.[10]

---

Gazette and Comet, November 25, 1865. The name Reimoning is also spelled Reimonenq, Rimmoning, or Rimoning in some documents.

8. Mobile Advertiser and Register, November 26, 1865.

9. New Orleans Daily Picayune, November 23, 1865; see also New Orleans Bee, November 23, 1865. The name de Gaalon is most frequently spelled du Gaalon.

10. James O. Noyes, Annual Report, Office, Board, [and] Commissioners of Emigration, 1870, to the General Assembly of Louisiana, February 10, 1870 (New Orleans, 1870), 9–11; T. Edmonston to the commissioner of immigration, New Orleans, April 20, 1865, Record Group 59, Letters Received, Bureau of Immigration, Department of State, NA.; "An Act to Encourage Immigration," July 4, 1864, U.S. Statutes at Large. XIII, 385–87;

Reimoning and Hunter and Company, shipping agents, also sought the views of the government on the subject of Chinese laborers for the South. In March, 1866, once again, the commissioner referred to the act of 1862 and stated that "the whole policy of the Government is in accordance with the spirit of this law, and this Office does not feel itself authorized to encourage any scheme for the introduction of coolies into this country."[11]

Commissioner Congar reiterated this policy in his 1866 annual report to Congress, indicating that the "introduction of new races bound to service and labor, under contracts similar to those in the West Indies, is contrary to the true interests, as it is to the laws, of the United States." Congar recommended that if "proper and profitable contracts cannot be made with the freedmen, who are used to the peculiar labor of the Southern States, there is no doubt but that a free, foreign immigration will supply all their necessities." He further noted that his bureau had received complaints that the agents of immigration had grossly misrepresented the nature of the contracts to be entered into, with resulting injustice. The growth and prosperity of these southern states should depend on free immigrant labor bound to no illegal contracts.[12]

Plans to engage Chinese were noted in the press and in immigration reports for several states through 1866 despite this apparent setback. Detailed accounts were published about the cost of recruitment

Samuel Rainey to the commissioner of immigration, New Orleans, August 30, 1865, Series 643, Record Group 59, Letters Received, Bureau of Immigration, Department of State, NA; H. N. Congar, commissioner of immigration, to Samuel Rainey, Esq., September 27, 1865, Record Group 59, Letters Sent, Bureau of Immigration, Department of State, NA; E. P. Jacobson, for the commissioner of immigration, to H. F. Stickney, Esq., December 8, 1865, Series 641, Record Group 59, Letters Sent, Bureau of Immigration, Department of State, NA; William H. Seward, secretary of state, to George A. Stewart, Esq., April 6, 1866, Record Group 59, Domestic Letters, Department of State, NA.

11. F. Rimmoning and Co. to commissioner of immigration, January 3, 1866, Record Group 59, Letters Received, Bureau of Immigration, Department of State, NA; William Hunter and Co. to commissioner of immigration, December 30, 1865, *ibid.*; E. Peshine Smith, commissioner of immigration, to F. Rimoning and Co., and Msrs. Hunter and Co., March 8, 1866, Record Group 59, Letters Sent, Bureau of Immigration, Department of State, NA.

12. H. N. Congar, "Report of the Commissioner of Immigration, February 28, 1866," *House Executive Documents*, 39th Cong., 1st Sess., No. 66, p. 6.

and the positive results that might accrue. Reimoning's advertisement was republished in several newspapers and J. D. B. De Bow suggested that coolies might replace Negro labor. In August, 1866, De Bow published "Coolies as a Substitute for Negroes," an article he had solicited from a "citizen of New York," which presented the history and statistics on the introduction of Hindoo coolies to the British West Indies. The article pointed out that once adopted in an impoverished area, coolie labor raised the region to a highly flourishing state. [13]

In September, 1866, a Chinese emigration agent, Ah Yuc of the House of Ware, Yune and Company, San Francisco, went to Louisiana to explore the feasibility of bringing Chinese to the South. He was accompanied by Robert F. Strickland, a representative of the Chinese Emigrant Companies in California, who had spent some years in China, and by an interpreter, John Marcal, who was well-known in San Francisco. In New Orleans, Ah Yuc and his companions met with Governor James Madison Wells and with Thomas Gottman, the first commissioner of the Louisiana Bureau of Immigration, which had been established in March of that year. They proposed to contract to bring Chinese to the South to work the 1867 crop. Newspapers reported that Ah Yuc hoped to bring from three hundred to twenty thousand Chinese. Throughout 1867, sporadic references to Ah Yuc and his agents appeared in the papers, but no Chinese arrived. Nevertheless, Ah Yuc and the San Francisco Chinese emigration company that he represented retained an active interest in the matter through the 1870s. [14]

In the fall of 1866 the New York *Commercial and Financial Chronicle*

13. "Coolies as a Substitute for Negroes," *De Bow's Review*, After the War Ser., II (August, 1866), 215–17; Houston-Galveston *Daily News*, May 4, 1866; New Orleans *Crescent*, January 3, 1866; New Orleans *Daily Picayune*, January 24, 1866; New Orleans *Bee*, March 6, 1866, September 27, 1866; J. D. B. De Bow to Governor Perry of South Carolina, October 12, 1865, *De Bow's Review*, After the War Ser., I (January, 1866), 6–14.

14. New Orleans *Daily Picayune*, September 8, 12, 14, 1866, October 28, 1866; Mobile *Advertiser and Register*, September 9, 1866, October 25, 26, 1866; New York *Tribune*, September 12, 1866; New Orleans *Bee*, September 14, 1866; New Orleans special to the *Times* quoted in Savannah *Morning News*, September 25, 1866; Charleston *Daily Courier*, September 28, 1866; San Francisco *Daily Alta California*, September 15, 1866; Louisville *Daily Journal*, September 21, 1866; Barth, *Bitter Strength*, 206. In newspaper reports, this Chinese agent's name is also spelled Ayuk, Ah Young, and A. H. Yuc.

announced that several capitalists had formed an association to bring Chinese from Asia for employment on the sugar and cotton plantations of Louisiana and Texas. It was hoped that if these plans proved successful, Chinese would be taken to other states. The capitalists were negotiating with transportation companies in New York on the terms for conveying laborers from Asia to New Orleans. The *Commercial and Financial Chronicle* of New York, however, took the position that if freedmen could not supply the necessary labor, emigration must be relied upon, preferably from Europe. Introduction of "another race of human beings into this country is another matter, demanding the most serious consideration." The paper hoped that "arteries of colonization" of Europe would be tapped before resorting to the half-civilized regions of eastern Asia. If Chinese were imported, however, as seemed likely, their passage should be made as pleasant as possible in an effort to avoid the tendencies to melancholy and suicide to which Chinese often had succumbed upon arrival in new settings such as Panama.[15]

In 1867 the introduction of Chinese laborers to the South finally became a reality. Ironically, the newcomers did not enter as a consequence of the schemes of established entrepreneurs or planters described above. Rather, they were brought in by a small group of planters who were neighbors in the parish of Natchitoches, on the Red River, in northwestern Louisiana.

Natchitoches, the oldest white settlement in Louisiana, had served as a gateway through which travelers from New Orleans and the eastern states passed on their way to Texas. Its population included persons of Indian, French, Spanish, black, Creole, Italian, and German descent and of other ancestries and cultures. In 1860, the total population of the parish was approximately 16,699, of whom 9,434 were slaves, 958 were free blacks, and 6,306 were white. The parish covered an area of 366,000 acres in which rich portions of cultivated land were devoted mainly to cotton and corn. After the Civil War, appeals had been made without success to attract white immigrant settlers, especially Germans from Texas. Thereupon Chinese were brought into

15. "Proposed Importation of Coolies into the United States," *Commercial and Financial Chronicle* (New York), III (October 6, 1866), 418–19.

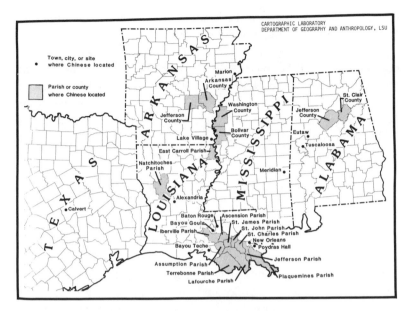

Some places where Chinese located, 1865–1880

the parish of Natchitoches in 1867 to supplement the work of emancipated Negroes.[16]

Terence and Arthur Chaler, cotton plantation owners in Natchitoches Parish, received the first contingent of fifteen Chinese laborers. They were brought by Jules H. Normand, a native of Cloutierville in the same parish and son of Dr. F. M. Normand and Marie Lolette

16. Milton Dunn, "History of Natchitoches," *Louisiana Historical Quarterly*, III (January, 1920), 26–56; Sister Mary Silverius Karnowski, "Natchitoches During the Civil War and Reconstruction Period" (M.A. thesis, Catholic University of America, 1949); "Natchitoches Parish," in *Biographical and Historical Memoirs of Northwest Louisiana* (Nashville, 1890), 293–377; Frederick Law Olmsted, *A Journey in the Seaboard Slave States, with Remarks on Their Economy* (New York, 1856), 624–42; Frederick Law Olmsted, *A Journey Through Texas; or, a Saddle-Trip on the Southwestern Frontier* (New York, 1860), 44–64; J. W. Dorr, "The Parish of Natchitoches," New Orleans *Crescent*, July 11, 1860, reprinted in "A Tourist's Description of Louisiana in 1860," ed. Walter Prichard, *Louisiana Historical Quarterly*, XXI (October, 1938), 1165–70; Roger Wallace Shugg, *Origins of Class Struggle in Louisiana: A Social History of White Farmers and Laborers During Slavery and After, 1840–1875* (Baton Rouge, 1939), 43–45.

Rachal. After his studies in Paris and a brief period in Cloutierville, Normand and his wife, Elizabeth Aurelia Anty, moved to Cuba in 1855. During his stay on the island, Normand worked in planting, photography, and the management of a hospital. In 1867 he brought the Chinese laborers to New Orleans from Havana and Matanzas on the steamer *Liberty* under Captain Thomas A. Bain. The New Orleans *Bee* described the Chinese as "stout, hardy looking young men who will doubtless prove better laborers than the negroes under the present system." Because the newcomers spoke Spanish they were seen as "an intelligent race which learned a foreign language quickly." [17]

Normand announced that within a couple of months he could bring another hundred or so Chinese whose terms of contract had expired in Cuba and who were not satisfied with their situation in that country. According to the 1860 "Regulations for the Introduction of Chinese Workers to Cuba," two months after the termination of a contract a Chinese had to renew it or leave the island unless he was apprenticed to or worked under a recognized teacher or was employed as a domestic or agricultural laborer. The reaction of the Natchitoches press toward the Chinese was guarded. The editor of the *Semi-Weekly Natchitoches Times* stated that although the parish would benefit by this new competition to the labor of the freedmen, the Chinese should be tried before greater numbers of them were recruited. [18]

By the end of March, 1867, Normand and Benjamin W. Bullitt, a successful planter from Natchitoches, brought about fifty-five Chi-

17. "Jules Honorat Normand," in *Biographical and Historical Memoirs of Northwest Louisiana*, 362; Obituary, Jules H. Normand, Natchitoches *Times*, January 18, 1907; Marriage Book 6, Registers of the Parish of St. Jean Baptiste, St. John the Baptist Catholic Church, Cloutierville, La. (hereafter called Cloutierville Registers); Burial Book 11, Cloutierville Registers; Natchitoches *Louisiana Populist*, September 28, 1894; Notarial Record, February 26, 1880, Natchitoches Parish Records, Office of the Clerk of the Court, Natchitoches, Vol. 76, No. 135, p. 91; Sam H. Torrey, U.S. district attorney, to John M. Binckley, assistant attorney general, August 2, 1867, Record Group 60, Letters Received, Louisiana, Attorney General Papers, Department of Justice, NA; Thomas Savage, vice consul general, Havana, to William H. Seward, secretary of state, August 23, 1867, Record Group 59, Consular Despatches, Havana, Department of State, NA; New Orleans *Bee*, January 16, 1867.

18. Natchitoches *Times*, January 30, 1867; Plaquemine *Weekly Iberville South*, April 13, 1867; Artículo 18, *Reglamento para la Introducción de los Trabajodores Chinos en la Isla de Cuba*, August 4, 1860 (Havana, 1860).

nese from Havana to New Orleans. Severin Trichel, another parish cotton planter, hired twenty of these Chinese. The remainder were taken to a plantation on the Mississippi River. Bullitt indicated that when their eight-year terms of service in Cuba expired, Chinese were willing to contract to come to the South "for two or more years for monthly wages of $12.00" plus daily subsistence rations of "2½ lbs. of pork and 4 lbs of rice." The expense of bringing these Chinese from Cuba to Louisiana plantations was estimated to range from forty-five to sixty dollars a person, depending on the distance and route from New Orleans. In interviews with the editor of the *Weekly Iberville South*, the newspaper from the sugar plantation region of Plaquemine, Louisiana, Bullitt said that thousands of Chinese might be contracted under such terms if done before the middle of the next autumn when the Cuban planters made their yearly contracts, after which time laborers would be scarcer and the wages higher. In June, 1867, Bullitt and Normand opened an office to take orders for the new laborers in New Orleans. They advertised that a fast steamer was available to visit Cuban ports to bring Chinese to Louisiana in lots of about two hundred per trip.[19]

Concurrently, another Louisianan, Edward T. Wyches, who was also a resident of Cuba, began to introduce Chinese from that island. The type of contract Wyches entered into with each Chinese laborer can be seen from a blank agreement that is now in the National Archives.

> This agreement entered into between _____ a native of China and J. J. Wyches for and in behalf, of Messrs Lyle and Wyches of New Orleans, Louisiana, Witnesseth:
>
> I _____ aged _____ years having served out my apprenticeship of eight years in the Island of Cuba do hereby agree and bind myself to emigrate to the United States, to labor for the above Messrs Lyle & Wyches or their assigns, under the following conditions:

19. Plaquemine *Weekly Iberville South*, April 13, 1867; New Orleans *Crescent*, March 30, 1867, June 14, 1867; Sam H. Torrey, U.S. district attorney, to John M. Binckley, assistant attorney general, August 2, 1867, Record Group 60, Letters Received, Louisiana, Attorney General Papers, Department of Justice, NA; Thomas Savage to William Seward, August 23, 1867, Record Group 59, Consular Despatches, NA.

1ST   I agree to work on plantation, or do any other kind of labor that may be assigned to me by my employer, for the period of eighteen months beginning at the time I commence to work, for which I am to be paid by him at the rate of fourteen dollars wages per month U.S. currency payable monthly.

2ND   I am to be furnished by my employer with comfortable quarters and rations of ten pounds of rice, and three & a half pounds of pork per week.

3RD   In case of sickness, I am to be furnished with medicine and necessary attention, and for time lost, a pro-rata deduction is to be made from my wages.

4TH   I agree to work from daybreak till dark with an intermission of one hour each, for breakfast and dinner, and during sugar making to stand watch at night, as usual on sugar plantations, but no labor is to be required of me on Sundays, except when necessary to secure the crop, feeding stock, and customary household duties.

5TH   I promise to render strict obedience to my employer, and submit myself to the regulations of the plantation or household, and in all things to conduct myself as a good and faithful servant.

6TH   In case of my failure to comply with the conditions of this contract, I hereby bind myself to reimburse my employer for my travelling and other expenses, paid by him, in bringing me from the Island of Cuba to the United States.

7TH   I hereby authorize the said Messrs Lyle & Wyches to transfer this contract at their discretion.

In witness whereof, we subscribe our names to this contract in duplicate made in Spanish and English. Done at the City of Havana, this 2nd day of July 1867.[20]

Wyches' first group of twelve Chinese arrived in New Orleans from Havana on the steamer *Cuba* on May 18, 1867, and thirty-eight more came shortly thereafter. They were taken by Wyches and his father, J. J. Wyches, to the plantation of Dr. E. E. Kittredge, an estab-

---

20. Agreement between a Native of China Residing in Cuba and J. J. Wyches, enclosed in Torrey to Binckley, August 2, 1867.

lished sugar planter on the Bayou Lafourche, Assumption Parish. They began work the day after arrival, and Dr. Kittredge appeared pleased with their "character of service and general habits."[21]

One month later, the editor of the *Planters' Banner* visited these Chinese as they worked on Bayou Lafourche, under the supervision of a Creole who spoke Spanish and acted as an interpreter and manager. He described them as follows:

> These laborers have served out their time as coolies on the Island of Cuba and now are at liberty to go where they please and hire with whom they please. They receive on this plantation 14 dollars per month the year around. They don't mind the sun while at work, but when walking out on Sundays, each has a red umbrella and a fan. . . . They bathe often, and take good care of clothes and bedding. They are of a light, copper color, have black, straight hair, and look more like Indians than any other people. . . . They wear a white blouse reaching to their hips, a pair of breeches and hat, shoes in dry weather, and in wet, wet weather they go barefoot and roll their breeches above their knees, when working in ditches or mud. Their beds are of matting, and their pillows blocks of wood about as large as a man's hand and three times as thick, with a blouse folded and laid on each. . . .
>
> The rations of these Cuba Chinamen are simply ½ a pound of pork and a pound of rice daily. They abhor corn bread, and will nearly starve before they will touch it. They cook careless weed, and other weeds for greens, and are fond of potatoes and other vegetables. They hang up an opossum till it is juicy and mellow, and then cook it and stuff it with raisins. They speak the Spanish language, and a creole of the Lafourche, who speaks Spanish, manages them and acts as interpreter.
>
> They appear peaceable and satisfied, do anything they are required to do without a murmur, and as freely work in a ditch knee deep in mud as in the field. They are always quiet, and work steadily, all day long but not rapidly. . . .
>
> From what I saw I am favorably impressed with Chinese la-

21. Thibodaux *Sentinel* quoted in New Orleans *Daily Picayune*, June 6, 26, 1867; *La Sentinelle de Thibodaux* quoted in *L'Abeille de la Nouvelle Orleans*, June 5, 1867.

borers, but I would sooner have those direct from China than those from Cuba, who have passed through the hands of labor agents. Labor agents are usually sharp and unscrupulous, and would be likely to pick up the most worthless coolies on the island, loafers, idlers, and those unskilled in agriculture. The agent who furnished Dr. Kittredge's laborers stated that the planters will not let the best of the coolies leave the Island of Cuba. They will pay them 15–25 dollars in gold per month rather than let them go. As to the stealing propensities of these laborers, or their malice, I don't think these will give their employers any more trouble than they would find in white or black laborers. They appear to be less stoical, and much more passionless than either whites or blacks.

They are the laborers for Louisiana.[22]

Reports of similar successes received increased attention. Yet in August, 1867, the importation of Chinese from Cuba was suddenly brought to a halt. The federal government was concerned, once again, with the question of the southerners' possible participation in the prohibited coolie trade.

On July 12, 1867, Thomas Savage, the vice consul of the United States in Havana, brought to the secretary of state's attention the fact that "certain parties in the State of Louisiana had been and were still engaged in the business of importing into that State from Cuba, Chinese or Coolies under contract to serve on stipulated wages for a specified time." The vice consul further indicated that the Chinese were designated as "coolie passengers" and that although they were provided with passports by the Havana government, "there is reason to apprehend that their contracts establish the relation of slavery or servitude which is expressly forbidden by the last clause of Section 2 of the 'Act to encourage immigration' approved 4th of July 1864." Section 2 of this act stipulated that contracts by emigrants pledging their wages to repay expenses of emigration were valid and enforceable in the courts. Furthermore, advances could be a lien upon land after its acquisition by the emigrant. The last clause of this section stated, "But nothing herein contained shall be deemed to authorize any contract

22. Franklin *Planters' Banner* quoted in New Orleans *Crescent*, July 12, 1867.

contravening the Constitution of the United States, or creating in any way the relation of slavery or servitude." Savage told the secretary of state that he had received reports that E. T. Wyches had purchased some of the coolies he brought to Louisiana from their masters. Wyches' father, J. J. Wyches, had been a storekeeper on the Portuguese ship *Josefita Almira*, which had transported Chinese from China to Cuba. The suggestion of guilt by association thus raised suspicions that Wyches was engaged in the illegal coolie trade.[23]

As a result of the correspondence, Samuel H. Torrey, the district attorney of New Orleans, was instructed by the attorney general of the United States to investigate whether the vessel transporting Wyches' Chinese was engaged in the so-called coolie trade. Torrey was directed to ascertain whether the vessel had violated the act of 1862, Section 1, wherein no citizen or resident of the United States could prepare any vessel to procure coolies from China, and Section 4, requiring certificates prepared by the American consul at the port of departure for voluntary Chinese emigrants. In addition, the attorney general mentioned the Thirteenth Amendment to the Constitution of the United States, which abolished slavery, and the second section of the act of July 4, 1864, "An Act to Encourage Immigration."[24]

When on August 7, 1867, E. T. Wyches arrived in New Orleans with twenty-three Chinese on the American brig *William Robertson*, captained by William M. Reed, Samuel H. Torrey ordered the arrest of the captain and instructed the collector of customs to seize the brig. Torrey brought suit against the vessel and Captain Reed was arrested.

23. "An Act to Encourage Immigration," July 4, 1864, p. 386; Thomas Savage to William H. Seward, July 12, 1867, Consular Despatch No. 331, Record Group 59, Department of State, NA; William H. Seward to Thomas Savage, July 23, 1867, Record Group 59, Instructions to Consuls, No. 180, Department of State, NA.

24. William H. Seward to Henry Stanbury, attorney general, July 23, 1867, Record Group 60, Letters Received, Louisiana, Attorney General Papers, Department of Justice, NA; William H. Seward to Hugh McCulloch, secretary of treasury, July 23, 1867, Record Group 59, Domestic Letters, No. 515, Department of State, NA; John M. Binckley, assistant attorney general, to Samuel H. Torrey, July 27, 1867, Record Group 60, Letters Sent, Department of Justice, NA; Samuel H. Torrey to John M. Binckley, August 1, 1867, Record Group 60, Letters Received, Louisiana, Attorney General Papers, Department of Justice, NA; "An Act to Prohibit the 'Coolie Trade' by American Citizens in American Vessels," February 19, 1862, *U.S. Statutes at Large*, XII, 340–41.

Reed gave bonds for sixteen thousand dollars on the steamer and was ordered to appear before the next term of the United States Circuit Court of New Orleans for violating the law against importing coolies.[25]

While the district attorney in New Orleans was investigating the case, Bradish Johnson, an influential sugar planter who had employed Chinese laborers, wrote to Hugh McCulloch, the secretary of treasury, in defense of Wyches. Johnson understood that Captain Reed had been arrested and the vessel bonded for having violated the law of Congress forbidding the introduction of coolies into the United States. He believed that the facts would show that no such law had been violated because the Chinese Wyches had brought from Cuba were voluntary laborers, who had left the island after the expiration of their eight-year contracts. Louisiana planters such as himself were interested in the Chinese because of their skills in sugarcane cultivation, and the Chinese in turn wanted to come. He agreed that the government should oppose the "infamous coolie trade" but called for careful examination of the interpretation of the Wyches' case: "Suppose, on the same considerations, the government should forbid the employment of the thousands of Chinese who are now working on the great Pacific railway, as in the mines and agriculture of California, for the same reasoning must apply, as they are the same people. But there is no reason for such exclusion, as they have been found valuable additions to the country in both these occupations, and the cultivator of cane and cotton, both now in a prostrate condition, should not be made an exception in the deprivation of labor."[26]

McCulloch responded on September 2, 1867, by first referring to the section of the act of 1862 that provided for consular certificates in

25. Sam H. Torrey to John M. Binckley, December 27, 1867, Record Group 60, Letters Received, Louisiana, Attorney General Papers, Department of Justice, NA; New Orleans *Daily Picayune*, August 14, 1867; Charleston *Daily Courier*, August 14, 1867; Savannah *Morning News*, August 20, 1867.

26. Samuel H. Torrey to John M. Binckley, August 2, 1867, Record Group 60, Letters Received, Louisiana, Attorney General Papers, Department of Justice, NA; Hugh McCulloch to William P. Kellogg, collector of customs, New Orleans, August 19, 1867, Record Group 56, Letters Sent, Department of the Treasury, NA; Savage to Seward, August 23, 1867; Special Deputy Collector, Bureau of Customs, to Hugh McCulloch, New Orleans, August 30, 1867, Record Group 36, Letters Sent, Bureau of Customs, New Orleans, Department of the Treasury, NA; Bradish Johnson to Hugh McCulloch, August 28, 1867, in New Orleans *Commercial Bulletin*, October 21, 1867.

cases of voluntary emigration. When his department had received information from a "co-ordinate branch of the Executive concerning an alleged trade in coolies between Havana and New Orleans contravening the laws of the United States," collectors of customs along the Atlantic and Pacific coasts had been sent instructions to inquire into all cases that gave reason to suspect violations of the law regulating the immigration of coolies. McCulloch indicated that his department had "no official knowledge" about the libeled brig *William Robertson* and that it probably had come to the attention of "one of the other executive departments of the government having jurisdiction in such cases."[27]

These letters became the subject of lively debate in the New Orleans papers. The editor of the New Orleans *Commercial Bulletin* criticized "official etiquette" on the allocation of responsibility: "Our public servants are getting to be very much like our private ones. If you call the chamber-maid to answer the bell, she says it is the duty of one of the co-ordinate departments known as the man servant."[28]

Late in September of that year, the district attorney decided not to bring charges against Captain Reed and requested that the case be discontinued. The district attorney pointed out that Thomas Savage, the United States vice consul in Havana, had written to him that same month certifying that Captain Reed had "acted in good faith and under the impression that the Chinese were passengers going to New Orleans as free agents." In the vice consul's presence, Wyches had assured the captain that the Chinese fell into the category of passengers. Savage further remembered telling Captain Reed not to hinder the Chinese from going wherever they pleased after arrival in New Orleans.[29]

Wyches returned to Cuba, and in mid-November, 1867, he brought

27. Hugh McCulloch to Bradish Johnson, September 2, 1867, in New Orleans *Commercial Bulletin*, October 21, 1867. In admiralty practice, the term *libel* means "to proceed against by filing a libel; to seize under admiralty process, at the commencement of a suit" (Henry Campbell Black, *Black's Law Dictionary* [3rd ed.; St. Paul, 1933]).
28. New Orleans *Commercial Bulletin*, October 31, 1867; New Orleans *Crescent*, October 26, 30, 1867; New Orleans *Bee*, October 23, 1867.
29. Sam H. Torrey to Edward Jordan, solicitor of treasury, September 25, 1867, with following enclosure: Thomas Savage to U.S. district attorney for the eastern district of Louisiana, September 10, 1867, and W. M. Reed and William Robertson to Hugh McCulloch, September 21, 1867, Record Group 206, Solicitor of Treasury, Letters, Department of the Treasury, NA.

the vessel *Star of the Union* with twelve Chinese laborers to New Orleans. These Chinese traveled with Spanish passports and had labor
contracts. In addition, they had the certificate of the vice consul general of Havana certifying that each had signed the contract freely and
voluntarily. They spoke Spanish and used Spanish names, as shown by
an extant copy of a certificate of the Chinese Hilario Rivas, who was
said to be known in China by the name of "Alshow." A thirteenth Chinese passenger who entered with this group was an "ordained minister
or Priest" named "Mr. Orr." Orr was actually Tye Kim Orr, the Chinese leader born in the Straits settlements who had resided in British
Guiana until 1867.[30] Tye Kim Orr was to become a leader in the movement to introduce Chinese to the South in 1869.

The Wyches case did not, however, settle the questions raised by
federal government officials about the southern experiments with
Chinese labor. In 1869, when interest in Chinese immigration to the
South had a marked resurgence, planters, entrepreneurs, and their
agents had to test the law once again. By now these southerners had
become aware that not all national officials concurred in their understanding of the distinctions between the categories "coolie" and "voluntary emigrant." Those involved in this labor movement realized
that the purpose of the act of 1862 was not to regulate importation of
Chinese labor to the United States because the Chinese who had entered California were assumed to be voluntary emigrants. It had been
written to prohibit American ships from transporting Chinese coolies
to foreign ports.

Furthermore, several key southerners were well-versed in the law
and in the art of identifying its fine points. They were ready to question the opinions of such national authorities as the secretary of the
treasury and his representatives and the attorney general. By 1869,
leaders and promoters of the introduction of Chinese labor frequently

---

30. Copy of Certificate of United States Consul General Thomas Savage, Havana,
November 9, 1867, Record Group 36, Letters Sent, Bureau of Customs, New Orleans,
Department of Treasury, NA; New Orleans *Daily Picayune*, November 16, 1867; New
Orleans *Bee*, November 16, 1867; Special deputy collector to Sam Torrey, New Or-
leans, November 15, 1867, Record Group 36, Letters Sent, Bureau of Customs, New
Orleans, Department of Treasury, NA; Cecil Clementi, *The Chinese in British Guiana*
(Georgetown, British Guiana, 1915), 284–96.

met with others in the region who were weighing the advantages and disadvantages of immigration as a source of labor. They participated in commercial conventions and organized gatherings to implement large-scale sponsorship of Chinese.

At two commercial conventions held in the Mississippi Valley in May, 1869, delegates from the southern and western states discussed building up trade and new transportation routes. Immigration to the South and West was a related problem, and the question of Chinese labor was of special interest to some of the delegates. At the first of these meetings, which opened in Memphis on May 18, motions in support of the introduction of immigrants other than the "Caucasian race" were opposed. But the delegates recognized that the Chinese laborers who had finished work on the Central Pacific Railroad earlier that month might be engaged for railroad building in the South. The convention therefore approved a resolution stating that "all the railroads in the South be requested to employ upon these roads as many as possible of the Chinamen recently discharged on the Pacific Railroad, and that all companies engaged in building new railroads be especially requested to employ as many of these laborers as they possibly can."[31]

At the second commercial convention held in New Orleans on May 25, James O. Noyes, commissioner of immigration of Louisiana and chairman of the Immigration Committee at the convention, recommended that in the event European immigration should decline or cease, it would be judicious to import coolies and Chinese. A member from Tennessee, supported by the Reverend Dr. Charles K. Marshall of the Methodist Episcopal church of Vicksburg (also a planter himself), led the discussion against this proposition, arguing that the convention ought not to favor the introduction of "pagan and otherwise incongruous races." Noyes's motion was defeated.[32]

31. "Commercial Conventions," in *The American Annual Cyclopaedia and Register of Important Events of the Year 1869* (New York, 1870), 114–18; Louisville *Courier-Journal*, May 19, 20, 21, 22, 1869.

32. "Commercial Conventions," 116; *Proceedings of the Commercial Convention Held in New Orleans, May 24th, 27th, 28th, and 29th, 1869* (New Orleans, 1869); William M. Burwell, "Science and the Mechanic Arts Against Coolies," *De Bow's Review*, After the War Ser., VI (July, 1869), 557–71; New York *Weekly Journal of Commerce*, May 27, 1869; Louisville *Courier-Journal*, May 25, 29, 1869.

Marshall's views may have surprised some of the delegates because in 1860 he had undertaken to educate Dsau Sier Whoa, one of two Chinese students whom the Reverend J. William Lambuth, Methodist Episcopal missionary to China from Mississippi, had brought to the Mississippi Conference. Lambuth hoped that these youth would ultimately "be called of God to preach the gospel to their own countrymen." Dsau (later spelled Sau-tse-zeh) was given the English surname C. K. Marshall, after his sponsor. In 1876 he was ordained as the first Chinese minister of the Methodist Episcopal Church South.[33]

On June 19, 1869, cotton planters in the Arkansas Valley met at Garretson's Landing, Pine Bluff, on the Arkansas River to discuss the need for additional labor. Similar meetings were held in Vicksburg, Montgomery, Mobile, Charleston, St. Louis, and other places in the South. A newspaper report of the Pine Bluff meeting stated that Chinese laborers could be obtained in "great numbers and at cheap rates, and made efficient in the cultivation of cotton, and are proof against the malaria of the climate." The testimony of persons familiar with the Chinese was considered, and it was resolved to organize a joint stock emigration society to be known as the Arkansas River Valley Emigration Company. Subscribers were to invest with a minimum of three hundred bales of cotton, which they promised to deliver by November 1. Officers elected to the Company included Colonel T. C. Flournoy of Arkansas County and Major J. B. Hall of Jefferson County. Directors included Governor R. M. Anderson from Arkansas County and Benjamin F. Richardson from Jefferson County. Committees were appointed to secure subscriptions, concentrating on Arkansas, Jefferson, Desha, and Pulaski counties. The company engaged the services of Captain George W. Gift as agent to procure laborers from China and from California if suitable ones could be found.[34]

33. James Cannon III, *History of Southern Methodist Missions* (Nashville, 1926), 106–107; William Burwell Jones, *Methodism in the Mississippi Conference, 1891* (Jackson, 1951), 398–99; John Buford Cain, *Methodism in the Mississippi Conference, 1846–1870* (Jackson, 1939), 292–93.

34. Memphis *Daily Appeal*, July 14, 20, 1869; see also Vernon Lane Wharton, *The Negro in Mississippi, 1865–1890*, ed. Albert Ray Newsome (Chapel Hill, 1947), 97–99; New Orleans *Daily Picayune*, June 9, 1869; New York *Weekly Journal of Commerce*, June 10, 1869; Louisville *Courier-Journal*, June 3, 1869; Charleston *Daily News*, August 2, 1869; Plaquemine *Weekly Iberville South*, June 12, 1869; St. Louis *Missouri Republican*,

George Washington Gift, a native of Tennessee, had entered the United States Naval Academy in 1847 at the age of fourteen. In 1851, he resigned from the navy to join his father in California, where he served as private secretary to Governor John Bigelow and chief clerk of the State Treasury and in other public positions. He entered the banking business and later turned to civil engineering. He retained his interest in the sea and in the 1850s made several voyages to Mexico and Tahiti. When the Civil War broke out, he returned to the South, served with distinction in the Confederate Army, and achieved the rank of lieutenant commander. After the war Gift lived in Georgia and Tennessee and was an active contributor to several agricultural journals, writing in the *Southern Cultivator* and the *Southern Farmer* about the organization of joint stock associations in seaboard cities, details regarding shipping, and the qualities desirable in the agent who would select emigrants in Hong Kong or Shanghai. His letters in these journals as well as his correspondence with his wife, Ellen Shackelford Gift, show that he had first hoped to appeal to subscribers in Georgia and to introduce Chinese through the port of Savannah.[35]

Gift and some thirty other members of the Chamber of Commerce in Memphis met on June 30, 1869, to plan for a Chinese labor convention, which was proposed for July 13. The Memphis *Daily Appeal* published the proceedings of this meeting. Among those in attendance were a representative of the Pacific Railroad Company and Butler Anderson, who had worked with the Chinese in California for about five years.

---

July 8, 9, 1869; Little Rock *Daily Arkansas Gazette*, June 30, July 7, 1869; Memphis *Daily Appeal*, June 27, 1869; Pine Bluff *Weekly Press*, July 8, 15, 1869.

35. Harriet Gift Castlen, *Hope Bids Me Onward* (Savannah, 1945); J. Thomas Scharf, *History of the Confederate States Navy* (New York, 1887), II, 618–19; George W. Gift, "Cotton Under High Culture," in U.S. Department of Agriculture, *Annual Report, 1867*, pp. 409–12; George W. Gift, *Settlers' Guide Containing All the Circulars and Laws Relating to Pre-Emption Claims in California* (Benicia, Calif., 1854); George W. Gift to the editors, October 7, 1867, *Southern Cultivator*, XXV (December, 1867), 374–75; George W. Gift to the editors, February 15, 1868, *ibid.*, XXVI (March, 1868), 93–94; "Asiatic Labor" (quoting Louisville *Democrat*), *Southern Farmer*, II (October, 1868), 208; "How Our Chinamen Are Employed," *ibid.*, III (May, 1869), 103–105; George W. Gift, "The Labor Question—The Chinese," *ibid.* (June, 1869), 127–28; George W. Gift to Ellen Shackelford Gift, January 12, 1870, in George Washington Gift Letters, Southern Historical Collection, University of North Carolina, Chapel Hill.

Anderson described at length the major obstacle to revival of business and prosperity in the South, which he believed to be the want of efficient and reliable labor in agriculture to increase crop production. He mentioned the steps taken by neighbors in the Arkansas Valley to employ the "reliable, industrious and patient Chinaman" to labor in rice, cotton, sugar, and tobacco fields.

At the request of the participants, Anderson elaborated on his experiences with the Chinese in California. Although he had worked with them in the mines rather than in agriculture, he had no doubt that they would be as skilled and faithful when working for planters as for miners. They tended to carry out contracts scrupulously, and they looked after their money. The Chinese ought not to be rejected on the grounds of their religious beliefs. Although they did not worship "our God" and had contempt for whites and Negroes, they were educated and had their own literature, arts, and professions. Anderson further pointed out that the Chinese left their country with the intention of returning and that they kept to themselves rather than amalgamating with other races. An example of their tightly knit group organization was their tendency to conduct business only with other Chinese. They were imported to this country through their own traders and commercial establishments. Chinese laborers were responsible to their headmen, who maintained ties both with the Chinese recruitment organization and with the employers.

The following resolutions were adopted: (1) to encourage the migration of Chinese laborers, in large numbers, direct from China, to supply the demand in the South for steady and reliable labor; (2) to call a convention on July 13 composed of delegates from the South, especially Georgia, Alabama, Mississippi, Louisiana, Texas, Arkansas, and Tennessee, to accomplish this purpose; (3) to invite Cornelius Koopmanschap, the principal importer of Chinese in California, to attend the convention; and (4) to encourage newspapers in the South favorable to the Chinese migration to publish the proceedings of the meeting.[36]

An Arrangements Committee was appointed to carry out the proposals for the July 13 convention. Planters throughout the South were

36. Memphis *Daily Appeal*, July 1, 1869.

urged to come to learn about the new source of labor supply directly from the merchant from San Francisco, Koopmanschap, who would be present to "ascertain the wants and requirements of planters." Koopmanschap was described as "responsible and able to comply with all his contracts." Railroad companies offered free return tickets for all who would attend.[37]

The purpose of the Chinese labor convention that opened on July 13 was to devise the "best and cheapest means of procuring Chinese laborers." About five hundred delegates, representing planting, railroad, and business interests came from Alabama, Georgia, Kentucky, Mississippi, South Carolina, Louisiana, Arkansas, Tennessee, Missouri, and California, met in the Greenlaw Opera House in Memphis. Isham Green Harris, a lawyer and former congressman from Mississippi, governor of Tennessee, and Confederate officer, was elected permanent chairman of the convention.[38]

Cornelius Koopmanschap arrived on the second day of the convention. Tye Kim Orr, the Chinese preacher who had entered Louisiana from Cuba in November, 1867, was invited to attend by Moses Greenwood, chairman of the Louisiana delegation.[39] Representatives of railroad companies were also present.

A major activity of the convention was making plans for the organization of a joint stock company to be capitalized at $1 million with each share of stock to cost $100. The company was to be called the Mississippi Valley Immigration Labor Company. It was suggested, furthermore, that the books for subscription be kept open till August 14, 1869, and that the company be organized when the sum of $100,000 was subscribed. The proposal was introduced by General Gideon S. Pillow, a native of Tennessee, who was chairman of the Finance Committee and a law partner of Isham Harris. The company was to bring into the United States "as many Chinese immigrant laborers as possible, in the shortest time." The first step was to place reliable agents in San Francisco and New York.[40]

37. *Ibid.*, July 2, 1869.
38. "Harris, Isham Green," in Jon L. Wakelyn (ed.), *Biographical Dictionary of the Confederacy* (Westport, Conn., 1977), 217.
39. Memphis *Daily Appeal*, July 14, 1869.
40. "Gideon Johnson Pillow," in Ezra J. Warner, *Generals in Gray: Lives of the Confederate Commanders* (Baton Rouge, 1959), 241; Memphis *Daily Appeal*, July 15, 1869.

General Nathan Bedford Forrest, president of the New Selma, Marion and Memphis Railroad, pledged five thousand dollars and his support of the employment of one thousand Chinese. A native of Tennessee, General Forrest was a self-made planter and trader, whose military leadership in the Confederate Army had earned him recognition from the South and the North. Impoverished after the Civil War, he returned to planting in Tennessee and became president of the new railroad. He was also the first Grand Wizard of the Ku Klux Klan.[41]

The first guest to address the convention and to answer questions was Tye Kim Orr, described as a "Chinese gentleman whose enunciation was very clear resembling very much that of an educated Spaniard." Tye Kim Orr (also known as O Tye Kim) was a Christian Chinese born in the Straits settlements and educated in a London Missionary Society school at Singapore. He arrived in London about March, 1864, where members of the Strangers' Home for Asiatics and a committee of the Church Missionary Society supported his desire to preach the gospel to the Chinese in British Guiana, paying his passage to Demerara and providing him with enough funds until he arrived there. During his residence in Georgetown, British Guiana, he formed a congregation of Chinese Christians, and in 1865 he established a Chinese agricultural settlement on a tributary of the Demerara River. He left Demerara in July, 1867, and in November, 1867, he entered Louisiana with E. T. Wyches' group of Chinese from Cuba in the vessel *Star of the Union*. He settled in Ascension Parish, in the heart of the sugar-growing area of the state.[42]

In his address Tye Kim Orr explained that he had left his home in 1863 and had traveled through the West Indies and South America. He observed that after emancipation the West Indian Negroes had "degenerated and would not work" and that Chinese had been imported to

41. "Forrest, Nathan Bedford," in Wakelyn (ed.), *Biographical Dictionary of the Confederacy*, 189–90; William R. Majors, "Nathan Bedford Forrest," in Billy M. Jones (ed.), *Heroes of Tennessee* (Memphis, 1979), 83–97.

42. Memphis *Daily Appeal*, July 15, 1869; Barth, *Bitter Strength*, 190–91; Clementi, *Chinese in British Guiana*; [Edward Jenkins], *The Coolie, His Rights and Wrongs: Notes of a Journey to British Guiana* (London, 1871), 116; *London and China Telegraph* (London), September 5, 1866, pp. 469–70; Special deputy collector to master of the *Star of the Union*, November 15, 1867, Record Group 36, Letters Sent, Bureau of Customs, New Orleans, Department of Treasury, NA; *Thibodaux Sentinel*, August 28, 1869.

CHINESE FROM CUBA AND ASIA 69

replace them. Tye Kim Orr indicated that he realized there were objections to the Chinese because they were "heathens" but added that "you want cotton and cane and if he makes them you will not object very much to him." After reactions of applause and laughter from the audience, he challenged convention members to consider "what is the 19th Century for, if not to bring the Word to the people who have it not? Do not spurn these people from you. You may be the means of evangelizing them. . . . The Chinese are a docile, patient, susceptible people and will follow . . . and love those who try to teach and benefit them. Love begets love." Tye Kim Orr then offered concrete suggestions about conducting the emigration process. He warned: "You must not get the wharf rats; you must get them from the rural districts of China where the people are agriculturalists." He cautioned the audience repeatedly not to rely on "speculating agents, but to send agents to China and pick them up there."[43]

Cornelius Koopmanschap arrived with his secretary, Charles Legay, and expressed astonishment that so many people were interested in Chinese labor. He had expected to see only a "few planters and farmers." Questions about his identity and nationality, which had been raised before his arrival, were forgotten when his letters of reference were presented to the eager audience. Such notables as Leland Stanford of the Central Pacific Railroad, for whom he had secured several thousand Chinese laborers, offered high praise for his work.[44]

Information on the career of this merchant is sparse. Cornelius Koopmanschap was born in Weesperkarspel, near Amsterdam, on February 13, 1828. He settled in California in 1850 or 1851, after traveling in the East Indies and China, and became established in San Francisco as an importer of Chinese goods and a commission merchant. In the 1860s he lived in both San Francisco and Hong Kong, where his business partner S. H. M. Bosman resided. His connections with Chinese firms secured for him a role as the major contractor and importer of Chinese laborers to San Francisco.[45]

In his report to the Immigration Committee of the convention, he

43. Memphis *Daily Appeal*, July 15, 1869.
44. *Ibid.*, July 14, 15, 16, 1869.
45. Barth, *Bitter Strength*, 191–97; Marysville *Daily Appeal*, October 26, 1869; St. Louis *Missouri Republican*, July 15, 1869; *The China Directory for 1861* (Hong Kong,

stated that the House of Koopmanschap had imported about thirty thousand Chinese, and he was sure he could supply the South with all it desired. Although he was not able to give final prices on the cost of transportation, he calculated that the cost per man from China to San Francisco would be thirty to forty dollars and from San Francisco to Memphis approximately sixty dollars. He pointed out that although the Chinese who worked on the Pacific railroad had earned thirty-five dollars a month, contracts for labor direct from China with agents, the parties in the "business of furnishing labor," could be made at approximately eight to twelve dollars a month with guarantees that the laborers would follow through on their contracts. Koopmanschap explained that contracts made in China sometimes carried guarantees for faithful performance by the governors of districts. Contracts might extend from two to five years and sometimes even to eight. He reiterated Tye Kim Orr's warnings, adding that the "lower caste of population found in the coasts and seaboard cities were 'worthless' as farm hands."[46]

Koopmanschap's role in furthering large-scale importation of Chinese was given extensive publicity in the local, regional, and national press and has been the major interest of authors who have subsequently described the Chinese labor convention.[47] Not enough attention has been given, however, to alternative proposals presented at this convention, which set the direction for the plans actually followed by representatives of several states in introducing Chinese to the region.

Colonel John Martin of Kentucky proposed that, in keeping with the purpose of the convention to devise the best and cheapest way of procuring a supply of reliable labor, an organization be formed with capital to employ "competent and reliable men to go to China and se-

---

1861); Marysville *Daily Appeal*, December 2, 1869. For references to Koopmanschap's shipping activities see ads in San Francisco *Daily Alta California*, April 3, May 22, June 6, 9, 12, July 26, 27, 1865.

46. Memphis *Daily Appeal*, July 15, 16, 1869.

47. See for example, Charleston *Daily News*, July 21, 1869; St. Louis *Missouri Republican*, July 15, 1869; New York *Times* quoted in Charleston *Daily Courier*, July 24, 1869; Charleston *Daily News*, July 24, 1869; Louisville *Daily Courier*, July 24, 1869; Savannah *Morning News*, July 26, 1869; New York *Journal of Commerce*, July 29, 1869; San Francisco *Daily Alta California*, July 20, 1869; Little Rock *Daily Arkansas Gazette*, July 30, 1869; New York *Evening Post*, July 29, 1869; New York *Herald*, July 22, 1869.

lect laborers, make contracts and arrange transportation." Such a system would save planters the payment of "heavy commissions which an intermediate agent demands." He suggested that a well-known, competent businessman such as John Williams of Louisiana, General Gideon S. Pillow, or Willoughby Williams of Nashville go to China with Tye Kim Orr and that their first effort be the introduction of some one thousand laborers to be distributed over several states. If successful in its first year, the project would be continued.

General Pillow did not believe that Colonel Martin could raise the necessary funds. He promised to go to New York to raise the necessary capital. Moses Greenwood, the delegate of the New Orleans Chamber of Commerce, offered General Pillow "moral support" but emphasized that he could not "bind" himself to any one option because he and his Louisiana representatives had come "simply to seek information." Judge W. H. Sutton of Louisiana took the same view.[48]

Delegates were given information from informed sources not present at the convention and expressed their own opinions on the subject. Walter H. Gibson, a native of South Carolina who had resided in the Far East, especially in the Malay Archipelago, and was now the commissioner of immigration in Hawaii, had written to General Nathan B. Forrest to offer assistance based on his experience with importing Chinese and Japanese to the islands of Hawaii. The delegates from Mississippi were divided. William Spears, editor of the Vicksburg Herald, opposed the movement, whereas General William R. Miles hoped to introduce Chinese to Mississippi under the sponsorship of the Vicksburg Chamber of Commerce. An announcement was made that an agent of the Wills Valley Railroad, the new railroad constructed southwest from Chattanooga, had left earlier in July for San Francisco to employ three thousand Chinese to work on the road.[49]

By the end of the convention, almost all the participants voted to support General Pillow's plan. The convention was adjourned with the expectation that delegates would inform their states and local communities about plans and would secure orders for Chinese through

48. Memphis Daily Appeal, July 16, 1869.
49. Ibid., July 3, 15, 17, 1869; see also Wharton, Negro in Mississippi, 97–102; New Orleans Daily Picayune, July 9, 1869; Knoxville Press and Herald quoted in Baton Rouge Weekly Advocate, July 17, 1869.

subscription to General Pillow's Mississippi Valley Immigration Labor Company.[50]

But states and local community leaders were not unanimous either in support of the idea of introducing Chinese to the South or of the labor recruitment model advocated by General Pillow. In Mississippi, elaborate plans made by General Miles, representative of the Vicksburg Chamber of Commerce, were defeated largely because of opposition to Chinese as "heathen" and the fear that heightened racial conflict might follow their settlement.[51]

General Pillow did not receive the support he had anticipated for his Mississippi Valley Immigration Labor Company, although he raised $100,000 in stocks. The Board of Directors of this company assured those who opposed the movement that only voluntary immigrants brought directly from China or the Eastern countries would be introduced. At the commercial convention in Louisville on October 17–18, 1869, however, opponents to the introduction of "unlimited numbers of Chinese, under contract, to serve for a term of years," won support for a resolution opposing Chinese labor on the grounds that "enlightened public policy" would be best served by blocking further immigration and consequent "antagonism of the races." In December, 1869, the company was forbidden by Tennessee law to bring in Chinese immigrants.[52]

On July 23, 1869, Moses Greenwood, chairman of the Louisiana delegation, submitted his report of the Chinese labor convention to

50. New Orleans *Daily Picayune*, July 27, 1869; Vicksburg *Daily Times* quoted in Memphis *Daily Appeal*, July 26, August 15, September 1, 1869; Pine Bluff *Weekly Press*, July 22, 1869, September 2, 1869; Wharton, *Negro in Mississippi*, 97–99; "Shall We Grow Tea?," *Rural Carolinian* (Charleston, S.C.), I (October, 1869), 34; "The Coolies and Coolie Labor," *ibid.*, (December, 1869), 129–33; Jacksonville *Tri-Weekly Union*, August 28, 1869, quoted in San Francisco *Daily Alta California*, September 16, 1869; Charleston *Daily News*, July 19, 1869; Savannah *Morning News*, August 12, 1869; Savannah *Republican*, August 6, 1869.

51. Vicksburg *Daily Times* quoted in Memphis *Daily Appeal*, September 2, 1869.

52. Memphis *Daily Appeal*, July 21, 26, November 24, 28, 1869; New Orleans *Daily Picayune*, July 28, 1869; Charleston *Daily News*, August 2, 1869; Little Rock *Daily Arkansas Gazette*, August 11, 1869; "Commercial Conventions," 114–18; Louisville *Courier-Journal*, October 17, 18, November 24, 1869; see also "An Act to Encourage Immigration," December 1, 1869, State of Tennessee, *Journal of the House of Representatives*, 36th General Assembly, 1869–70, chap. XIV, 188–89.

the New Orleans Chamber of Commerce. He recommended that the chamber offer full support for importation of Chinese labor but noted that the Louisiana delegates had not committed themselves to any specific procedure. He hoped that a state organization similar to those headed by the "commissioners for immigration" in other states would be formed.[53]

Also on July 23, Secretary of the Treasury George S. Boutwell wrote to the collector of customs in New Orleans, Colonel James F. Casey, reminding him that the act of February 19, 1862, prohibiting American citizens from engaging in the coolie trade was still in force. The secretary mentioned in addition a circular of January 17, 1867, from the Department of State instructing that, at any port where coolies were recruited, United States ministers and consuls were to undertake a "full examination" of each case and to certify that the embarkation was not forced or produced by fraud but was voluntary only after they were satisfied that this was the truth. The collector was directed to exercise "all vigilance in the suppression of this new modification of the slave trade."[54]

As in 1867, the warning of these national officials was subject to much discussion in the southern press and in other areas, such as New York and California.[55] John Williams, a Louisiana planter and capitalist who had attended the Memphis meeting, sought legal counsel to advise him whether he might be aided or thwarted by the existing laws of the United States and of Louisiana. He wanted to know whether contracts entered into in China could be enforced in Louisiana.

After reviewing federal and state legislation, his law firm, Clark, Bayen, and Renshaw, reported that the act of 1862 referred "to an existing trade—one so well known that the acts referred to it in general terms, not defining its character." The coolie trade did not exist in the

53. New Orleans *Daily Picayune*, July 27, 1869.

54. George S. Boutwell, secretary of the treasury, to James F. Casey, collector of customs, New Orleans, July 23, 1869, in New Orleans *Daily Picayune*, July 27, 1869.

55. New Orleans *Daily Picayune*, July 30, August 6, 1869; Baton Rouge *Weekly Advocate*, August 7, 1869; Abbeville *Le Meschacébé*, August 14, 1869; Memphis *Daily Appeal*, August 8, 1869; New York *Journal of Commerce*, July 29, 1869; New York *Evening Post*, July 20, 1869, quoted in San Francisco *Daily Alta California*, July 30, 1869; San Francisco *Daily Alta California*, August 18, 1869; New York *Tribune*, July 29, 1869; San Francisco *Morning Call*, July 27, August 11, 1869.

United States. The attorneys emphasized that the law did not apply to free and voluntary emigration of Chinese certified by the consular office or agent at the port of embarkation. They found that Louisiana statutes contained no objection to the drawing of contracts with Oriental laborers in their own country for a five-year period on specified terms, either as domestic servants or to work on farms, plantations, or in manufacturing. Such contracts could be enforced in the courts of the state. The law firm advised that planters procure full evidence that the contract was "perfectly free and voluntary" and that the regulations prescribed by the secretary of state had been followed.[56] This counsel led John Williams to commission his brother, Nolan Williams, to travel to China in search of laborers, accompanied by Tye Kim Orr. Williams also partially supported George W. Gift's venture to procure laborers from China or California.

Gift left for California in late July, 1869. He first considered obtaining laborers there but found that Chinese were much in demand, and the going wage of thirty dollars in gold per month was more than what he believed could be afforded for plantation labor. Therefore he decided to embark for China. A few months later, Nolan Williams and Orr followed.[57]

Gift sailed from San Francisco on the steamer *Japan* on September 4, 1869, arriving at Hong Kong on October 7. He worked with zest and enthusiasm, eventually recruiting 189 Chinese for his Arkansas company. Excerpts from Gift's descriptions and from consular correspondence on the subject highlight the problems he had to overcome to carry out his pioneering mission.

First, in China the misapprehension arose that recruitment of laborers for the South meant that slavery had been revived and that laborers would be treated as they had been in Peru and Cuba. Gift reported to the Arkansas River Valley Immigration Company:

> In China I found that the laboring classes are much influenced by the superior classes, and that the superior classes are easily warped by European merchants and residents of longstanding who, in

56. New Orleans *Daily Picayune*, August 29, 1869.
57. Pine Bluff *Weekly Press*, August 12, September 9, 1869; Little Rock *Daily Arkansas Gazette*, July 24, 1869; New Orleans *Daily Picayune*, September 1, 1869.

turn, are liable to be prejudiced by untruths and improper reports. Such, at any rate, was my experience. It seemed impossible that we, who had owned slaves, would be more reasonable or humane, than the Spaniard or Peruvian. They had proven themselves infamous, and we only lacked opportunity to do likewise. In fact, our record, according to popular romances was already quite abominable. So under these difficulties I began my work in Hong-Kong.[58]

Second, Gift's mission presented American consular authorities in Hong Kong with a new challenge. Gift reported that the consul initially believed that "it would be illegal and improper to make contracts with Chinese subjects in China, for labor performed in the United States, and it would become his duty to refuse certificates of voluntary emigration to any party or parties who had made any contract of that nature."[59] Charles Goulding, the United States consul, sought State Department advice about extending certification.

On November 19, 1869, Goulding wrote the secretary of state asking for specific instructions because parties were making contracts to take Chinese laborers to the United States for employment for a term of years. He pointed out that his predecessor had customarily given vessels of all nationalities that sailed for ports in the United States with Chinese emigrants a certified list of such emigrants, but that now the consul was required to go on board and through his interpreter personally examine each emigrant. Goulding asked for guidance in conducting this individualized examination. His concerns were based in part on the reality that the Chinese who sailed for California were not subject to individual questioning by the American consular officers because, according to the act of 1862, it was generally accepted that they were emigrating voluntarily. Consul Goulding raised the following questions:

What is a coolie as defined in the law and what is a free emigrant? Has the Consul any discretion further than asking each Chinese

---

58. Report of George W. Gift to the president and directors of the Arkansas River Valley Immigration Company, May 16, 1870, Pine Bluff *Weekly Press*, June 2, 1870.
59. *Ibid.*

who he may find on board a vessel bound to the United States, whether he is a voluntary emigrant or not? Is it or is it not his duty to ascertain whether such emigrant is or is not under contract? . . . To put the question in a still more practical form: Can an individual or Company come here and engage Chinese to be employed for a term of days, months or years in the United States, and legally demand of the Consul the certificate contemplated in the 4th Section of the Act aforesaid?[60]

Assistant Secretary J. C. B. Davis responded: "The State Department is not aware that there is any legal definition of the term Coolie. Its general signification was understood to be a laborer at servile work but the term has received a particular application to the class who have for many years been the subjects of the commerce known as Coolie Trade which was denounced by the unanimous resolution of both Houses of Congress of January 16, 1867, as a mode of enslaving men differing from the African Slave Trade in little else than the substitution of fraud for force in obtaining its victims." With regard to contracts, Davis explained: "The fact that an emigrant embarks under a contract by which he is to reimburse the expenses of his transportation by personal services for a period agreed upon does not deprive him of the character of a free and voluntary emigrant, if the contract is not vitiated by force or fraud." He concluded that "the local knowledge and experience of each consul will enable him to prevent the abuses of the coolie trade without impeding immigration really free and voluntary without more specific instruction."[61]

Gift recruited his laborers in Hong Kong after consultation with British authorities and with selected Chinese. He employed a Chinese merchant to persuade the people to come, and this merchant agreed to accompany them to the South, to reside among them, to look after them, and to act as interpreter for the sum of twenty-five cents per month per man; at the end of three years he was to receive an additional ten dollars per man for every man paid off and discharged. The

60. C. N. Goulding, U.S. consul, to Hamilton Fish, secretary of state, November 19, 1869, Record Group 59, Consular Despatches, Department of State, NA.
61. J. C. B. Davis, assistant secretary of state, to C. M. Goulding, January 20, 1870, Record Group 59, Instructions to Consuls, Department of State, NA.

laborers were to be engaged for three years. The French barque *Ville de St. Lo* was chartered to transport the Chinese to New Orleans. Gift had hoped to send the ship to Savannah, but John Williams and Sons of New Orleans had advanced the necessary funds so Gift was compelled to send the ship to that port. The cost of shipment per man to New Orleans was £13 sterling, including provisions and medicines.[62]

Although the firm of Thomas Hallent and Company had advised Gift to stay in Hong Kong to receive additional orders, he decided that it was prudent to go home to oversee arrival of his first direct shipment of Chinese to the South. He remained in China only long enough to help Nolan Williams with the recruitment of laborers and engagement of a ship. But Williams had problems recruiting Chinese emigrants, and Gift believed it was because Williams placed too much confidence in Tye Kim Orr, who was not finding laborers. Williams and Orr were attempting to obtain Chinese with the promise of lower wages than was customary, and Gift believed that this factor made it more difficult to engage workers.[63] The troubles experienced in the recruitment process were later related by Gift to members of the Arkansas River Valley Immigration Company: "I can describe it as nothing more than a struggle from beginning to end which closed finally on the 9th of February last, when I despatched the bark for New Orleans with 189 men. . . . But it was the best I could do and more than it was predicted I would do." Gift's letters to his wife, Ellen Shackelford Gift, more poignantly capture his own sense of pride: "I have done here what I was told could not be done and I feel correspondingly proud of my achievement. I shall send the first ship to the South. Soon I hope my ships will spread their broad wings and speed away round the Cape of Good Hope with the China boys who are to help our poor country I sincerely trust out of her difficulties. . . . I am the Chinese Immigration."[64]

Consul General Goulding reported that on February 9, 1870, the *Ville de St. Lo* had sailed for New Orleans with two hundred Chinese

---

62. George W. Gift to Ellen Shackelford Gift, January 12, 1870, Gift Letters; Report of George W. Gift, May 16, 1870.
63. George W. Gift to Ellen Shackelford Gift, February 11, 1870, Gift Letters.
64. Report of George W. Gift, May 16, 1870; George W. Gift to Ellen Shackelford Gift, December 18, 1869, January 12, 1870, Gift Letters.

emigrants and that it was probably the first emigrant ship to sail from China to that part of the United States. He declared that the emigrants had been subjected to careful consular inquiry, with the assistance of an interpreter; that they had been carefully examined by the colonial surgeon; and that they had left as free and voluntary agents, willing and anxious to go. The consul stated further that he had not allowed Gift to draw up any contracts before their departure from Hong Kong and that he was satisfied that no such attempt had been made.[65]

Gift's ship arrived in New Orleans on June 1, 1870, after a voyage of approximately one hundred days. Upon their arrival, V. A. King, commissioner and physician to the Louisiana Board of Immigration, noted that twenty passengers had died at sea and that one had died since arrival. He reported that the Chinese were from the interior of China and seemed to be the "better element of the working classes." They were subsequently taken to Arkansas and Mississippi, where they settled to work in the cotton fields.[66] The initial reaction to the Chinese may be gleaned from an excerpt in an Arkansas newspaper:

> River men and others were thrown into some little excitement yesterday on the arrival of thirteen Chinese. . . . Among the number is a sort of head man, or interpreter, through whom orders are given. We have read many descriptions of John but cannot forego a short one of our own.
>
> He is what we would call a cross between an African and an Indian—not so black or stalwart in form as the negro, nor quite as light or straight as the Indian. They are about 5 feet in height, copper-colored, have very small feet, and are slim and dowdy in appearance.
>
> A close-fitting cap covers the head—and their wearing apparel consists of extremely loose-fitting cottonade pants, striking the leg about midway between the knees and ankles—and a blue blouse as a shirt whose folds hang loosely around the body. The "pigtail" striking out from the rear of the cap on the head was a prominent

65. C. N. Goulding to Hamilton Fish, February 9, 1870, Record Group 59, Consular Despatches, Department of State, NA. There are differences in Consul Goulding's and Captain Gift's reports regarding the number of Chinese who embarked on the *Ville de St. Lo.*

66. New Orleans *Times,* June 3, 10, 1870; Pine Bluff *Weekly Press,* June 23, 1870.

feature. John worked quite lustily, though awkwardly, and seemed very unconcerned at the staring multitude.[67]

Just about a month after the arrival of these Chinese at the plantations, President Ulysses S. Grant was asked to respond to a Senate resolution of July 9, 1870, requesting information "in relation to the importation of Chinese coolies into the U.S." The president sent a message to the Senate and transmitted a report from the secretary of state and accompanying papers. The secretary of state, Hamilton Fish, declared that he was not aware that any coolies were being imported into the United States, "in the sense in which the word 'coolies' appeared to be used in the statute." He acknowledged, however, that the department had received two dispatches from the consul notifying it that two shiploads of Chinese emigrants had sailed for New Orleans. The consul described them as voluntary emigrants. The secretary concluded that "there was no further information on this subject in that department," and continued: "The consuls of the United States in China are required to rigidly observe and enforce the provisions of the Act of 1862. The subject continues to occupy the serious attention of the Department, but the instructions which have been issued to the representatives of the U.S. in this respect cannot properly be made public at present."[68]

On October 6, 1870, the ship *Charles Auguste* arrived in New Orleans from Hong Kong with about 220 Chinese recruited by Nolan Williams upon the consignment of his brother, John Williams. About one-half of these men were taken to the plantations of the Williams brothers, and the rest were hired by several other planters.[69] Although there were predictions that the Chinese introduced by the Williams brothers and Gift represented only the beginning of a movement to bring large numbers of laborers directly from China to southern ports, southerners and their agents turned increasingly to California as a site for recruitment and left it to Chinese commercial houses on the West Coast and in China. Thus, although there were other efforts to

67. Little Rock *Daily Arkansas Gazette*, June 19, 1870.

68. Message of the president of the United States, *Senate Executive Documents*, 41st Cong., 2nd Sess. No. 116, pp. 1–4.

69. New Orleans *Daily Picayune*, October 8, 9, 1870.

introduce large groups of laborers directly from China to New Orleans, the only successful efforts were those by Gift and Williams with Tye Kim Orr.

Early in November, 1869, Koopmanschap left San Francisco for China to procure Chinese directly from that country. He hoped to fill orders for Chinese from both the South and East. That same month, his Hong Kong partner, S. H. M. Bosman, arrived in the United States. Bosman had been invited by Prince Sudawana of Japan to accompany the Japanese Embassy, which had visited Washington that month. Newspapers reported that Bosman further developed plans to introduce Chinese laborers to the East.[70]

The unfolding of events in 1869 showed that the Chinese movement to the South was a large-scale enterprise which could not survive solely on the enthusiasm of members of newly formed immigration companies under the direction of impoverished former Confederate leaders. The introduction of Chinese to the South required the interest of employers in local communities together with the investment of capitalists and planters with substantial resources, recognized credit, and an effective network of national and international contacts.

The successful recruitment of Chinese, furthermore, called for an understanding of Chinese views about the southern labor movement, including their ways of handling reciprocity, business obligations, and contractual responsibilities. The procurement of Chinese was ultimately to depend on the active participation of Chinese businessmen and their agents. The Chinese workers and their interpreters and headmen were crucial in assessing the advantages and disadvantages of the workplaces to which they were taken. They would be the final judges of the conditions of work and the systems of social relations in the South.

This perspective was communicated in the late summer of 1869 by two Chinese merchants who visited Chicago and the East on the invitation of prospective employers of Chinese. Choy Chew and Sing Man, two Chinese merchants who were members of commercial

70. Marysville *Daily Appeal*, October 26, November 2, December 2, 1869; New York *Journal of Commerce*, November 4, 1869; San Francisco *Daily Alta California*, November 11, 1869; Charleston *Daily News*, November 15, 1869; Little Rock *Daily Arkansas Gazette*, December 2, 1869; *China Directory for 1861*, pp. 42, 52.

houses with connections in China and the United States, studied labor needs in Chicago and New York. Choy Chew was a member of the firm of Lun Wo and Company, commission merchants, and a passenger agent for the Pacific Mail Steamship Company. Sing Man belonged to the firm of Chy Lung and Company, importers in San Francisco. Their opinions on the Chinese labor movement in the South were widely quoted in the press.[71]

During a visit to New York in August, 1869, Choy Chew was asked for his reactions to the introduction of Chinese labor to the South. He replied that he had some doubts because the Chinese were to be paid low wages and were in competition with Negro labor. Nevertheless, he believed that the experiment should not be evaluated until it was tried. He explained that the Chinese had the "peculiarity" of waiting for the first reports of those who pioneered in new regions before making decisions. If these pioneers sent positive reports, others would follow. Negative letters about a work site, however, would result in the refusal of Chinese to migrate to a new location.[72]

71. Charleston *Daily News*, July 31, August 10, 19, 1869; Marysville *Daily Appeal*, July 21, August 8, 1869; San Francisco *Daily Alta California*, July 23, 1869; New Orleans *Daily Picayune*, August 3, 8, 1869; New York *Journal of Commerce*, August 12, 19, 1869.
72. Charleston *Daily News*, August 19, 1869.

# 4 / CHINESE AT WORK

 Efforts to introduce Chinese laborers to the South increased between 1869 and 1871. Entrepreneurs in public works as well as planters established links with recruiters and labor agents. The idea of drawing on Chinese whose contracts in Cuba and the other West Indian islands had expired continued to be discussed although with less intensity than in past years. The problem of the voluntary or involuntary nature of the contracts with Chinese laborers was less important because recruitment was increasingly undertaken in California.

Chinese intermediaries such as labor contractors, representatives of commercial houses, and language interpreters were crucial connecting links in the recruitment and employment processes. Few of these intermediaries acted as independent agents. They were enmeshed in a tightly knit commercial alliance characterized by strong patterns of mutual protection. Southern employers had to learn how to do business with them. Chinese labor contractors expected to make a healthy profit in the recruitment of their countrymen. Furthermore, the role of the contractors was not limited to the procurement of laborers. Some of them visited the Chinese once they were on the job, and they often expected or put pressure on employers to offer laborers a return passage upon the termination of a contract.

The uniqueness of Chinese as members of an "ancient" and "heathen" civilization made them automatic outsiders in the southern social and economic system. Yet they were expected to produce high-quality work, and their performance as laborers was constantly compared with that of the freedmen. Most Chinese laborers who entered the South in this period came without wives, children, or parents, so their contracts did not include arrangements for dependents such as those made under the contract system tried earlier with freedmen.[1]

Chinese laborers demanded that their employers precisely fulfill the terms of contracts and when these terms were not met, they revolted. When conflicts arose with overseers or other supervisors, the Chinese were willing to resort to rebellions to defend their fellow laborers. As increasing numbers of Chinese settled in the South, sharp disagreements occurred between laborers and employers, which had not been observed during the initial stage of "good feeling."

The Chinese expressed their collective grievances through their interpreters, who not only communicated complaints, but also engaged in negotiations, initiated litigation proceedings, and, if necessary, secured new employment for their men. These headmen served as vital links with employers and local communities, and as such they were the major spokesmen for the Chinese in the South.

Others who played key roles, particularly in the larger settlements, were the Chinese physicians, storekeepers, clerks, and cooks, whose efficient services enabled the laborers to maintain a solid and independent sense of community. Chinese who deserted their work became itinerant peddlers, visited the various communities where their compatriots lived, and, no doubt, played an important role as carriers of news. Some Chinese were employed as servants in the homes of plantation owners. Even though this role separated them from field laborers, they retained communication links with those groups when possible.

Several large-scale projects introduced Chinese laborers from California to Texas, Alabama, and Louisiana. Capitalists in corporations or partnerships, which had been organized as speculative ventures, brought sizable groups of Chinese to work along with freedmen and other hired laborers. More than 200 Chinese were brought to work on

1. Howard A. White, *The Freedmen's Bureau in Louisiana* (Baton Rouge, 1970), 101–53; J. Thomas May, "Continuity and Change in the Labor Program of the Union Army and the Freedmen's Bureau," *Civil War History*, XVII (September, 1971), 245–54.

the Houston and Texas Central Railroad and more than 900 on the Alabama and Chattanooga Railroad. The introduction of 147 Chinese to the Millaudon plantation, a famous sugar estate near New Orleans, was the most publicized of all of the experiments with Chinese labor. A closer look at these three cases gives a picture of the social organization among the Chinese and interactions between them and those with whom they came in contact and clarifies the tensions and conflicts that eventually led to their departure to other work sites in the lower South.

In December, 1869, General John George Walker's plan to bring Chinese to labor on the Houston and Texas Central Railroad was reported in several newspapers. Walker had served in the war with Mexico and lived in California for several years before the Civil War, giving him ample opportunity to observe Chinese laborers. After the Civil War he became a strong advocate of the introduction of Chinese laborers to the South, and officials of the Houston and Texas Central Railroad turned to him when other sources of labor failed them. Previous efforts to use white laborers from New York and New Orleans for this railroad had failed because the men had abandoned their work prior to the expiration of their contracts. Walker negotiated a contract with Captain R. P. Boyce of the railroad for three hundred Chinese laborers through B. J. Dorsey, a labor agent for the Chinese in San Francisco.[2]

Difficulties arose during the negotiation period. Boyce learned, to his surprise, that a Chinese "league" or "union" existed throughout California, the "chiefs of which conduct all negotiations and take care of the interests of the men." He found that the "chiefs" wanted "side contracts and private bargains, just as a Southerner or a Yankee politician does before he can comprehend the true interests of his constituents." Under pressure from these "chiefs," Boyce agreed to establish a Chinese store with three thousand dollars in stock near their place of work. He noted that "great diplomacy" was exhibited in arranging the

2. "John George Walker," in Warner, *Generals in Gray*, 319–20; San Francisco *Daily Alta California*, December 9, 1869, quoted in New York *Weekly Journal of Commerce*, December 23, 1869; *Panama Star*, January 4, 1870; Omaha *Herald*, November 21, 1869, quoted in Marysville *Daily Appeal*, November 30, 1869.

"amount and class of goods the contractors were called upon to supply as stock in the establishment." The provisions for this store included dry goods, clothes, and writing and accounting supplies. The entire list of goods procured was printed in the St. Louis *Democrat*:

Narrow leaves, 500 pounds; bamboo brushes, 5 dozen; foo chuck, or bean curd sticks, 10 boxes, or 400 pounds; 10 boxes vermicelli, 500 pounds; 200 pounds of ginger root; 50 pounds orange peel; 200 pounds cuttle fish; 10 boxes soy; 10 jars ketchup; 20 reams Chinese writing paper; 200 Chinese pencils; 10 daily account books; 5,000 Chinese visiting card papers; 5 pieces paper (for lights); 300 pounds California abalones; 40 pounds red melon seed; 2 dozen frying-pan shovels; 4 dozen copper spoons, (large); 100 pounds pak ko; 10 pairs crape suspenders; 50 pounds sugar candy; 50 pounds red dates; 6 counting boards; 1 pound Chinese ink; 100 Chinese pens; 10 paper boxes pills, 10 bottles medicine powder; 10 boxes (100 gallons) China nut oil; 10 jars or 700 pounds salt turnip; 40 sets bowls; 40 sets chop sticks; 1 dozen knives; 2,000 pounds salt shrimps; 15 bags or 1,950 pounds salt fish; 200 bags fungus; 50 Chinese pass books; 50 Chinese general ledger books; 5 boxes or 50,000 fire-crackers; 2 boxes fire-crackers; jos paper; jos sticks; 1 box or 55 pounds dried oysters; 5 mats or 250 pounds black peas; 2 mats or 100 pounds red peas, 18 large kettles; 16 small kettles; 2 dozen frying-pan shovels; 2 boxes or 120 pairs Chinese common shoes; 20 Chinese purses; 10 buckskin purses.

Additional Goods for Chinese New Year.[3]

Most of the Chinese hired for the railroad were classified as "first-class laborers." They had been in California for several years and had worked in building the Central Pacific Railroad. Under the terms of employment they were to work under contract for three years at twenty dollars a month in coin and to supply their own board. The headmen would receive forty dollars per month. In addition to the stipulated wages, both the laborers and the headmen would be *found*, which means that their employers would pay for their transportation

3. St. Louis *Democrat*, December 30, 1869, quoted in San Francisco *Daily Alta California*, January 11, 1870.

and rations en route. Thus the only cost to the workers was any charge in excess of twenty dollars to return to San Francisco after three years of service. Boyce made the contract, assigning to Walker the task of bringing the Chinese from California. A contract was also made with Chew Ah Heang to serve as interpreter, under salary from the contractors. Boyce hoped that if this first enterprise was successful, additional Chinese could be hired from California and transported via Panama, which route he believed would be easier and cheaper.[4]

Walker set out for San Francisco from Galveston on September 23, 1869, and in December he left San Francisco, accompanied by Major W. H. Rhea, former editor of the Memphis *Avalanche*, and bringing approximately 250 Chinese with them. They stopped in St. Louis, where Walker was much quoted in the newspapers. He pointed out that those who made contracts with the Chinese must exercise a "strict adherence to truth and compliance with promises" because they tended to be suspicious and to lack trust in others. Contrary to rumor, the Chinese were not inexpensive labor. The value of their labor by California standards was known in China, and the Chinese were interested in working overseas only if they were remunerated at a level that would permit their return to China in "comparative affluence." Walker believed that good Chinese laborers could now be hired in California at rates ranging from twenty-six to twenty-eight dollars per month "and find themselves" (pay for their own transportation and rations en route), or seventeen to twenty dollars "and found."[5]

The *Missouri Republican* reported that when the Chinese stopped in St. Louis, they were "somewhat surprised at the curiosity exhibited in connection with their arrival" but reminded readers that this "singular people" were seldom seen. Alla Lee, a Chinese who had lived in the city for twelve years, was visited by the interpreter Chew Ah Heang and another "leading man." He answered many questions about the customs of the Chinese and commented on their religious beliefs and

4. Omaha *Herald*, November 21, 1869, quoted in Marysville *Daily Appeal*, November 30, 1869; St. Louis *Democrat*, December 30, 1869, quoted in San Francisco *Daily Alta California*, January 11, 1870.

5. St. Louis *Missouri Republican*, December 30, 1869, quoted in Little Rock *Daily Arkansas Gazette*, December 31, 1869.

the tradition of wearing the queue. A native of Ningpo, China, Alla Lee had first come to California to serve as interpreter for a missionary of the Episcopal church.[6]

Upon arrival at the Gretna landing in New Orleans, the Chinese were greeted by some 250 bystanders, evidently no less curious than those in St. Louis. The officers of the steamer *Mississippi*, which had brought them to Louisiana, remarked that the passengers had given "no trouble whatsoever." They settled quarrels among themselves, and they had volunteered to help the crew in "doing little jobs seeming to take pleasure in working." They departed for their destination in Texas on Morgan's Louisiana and Texas Railroad.[7]

Calvert, Texas, the town to which they were destined, was a boomtown, having grown in less than a year from "fifty houses and 800 souls, to a population of 6,000 and many new buildings."[8] The Chinese were put to work on the sections under construction beyond Bremond, Texas.

After they had been at work for three months, the president and officers of the railroad expressed the unanimous opinion that the experiment had been a success: Chinese labor was the "only labor" on which they could depend. Newspaper reports described these workers.

> Steady at their work, industrious when contract hours of labor have expired, sober, frugal, willing and mindful of the stipulations of their agreement, but exacting in the fulfillment of those in their favor, is the sum of the evidence in relation to them. They find no inconvenience in the climate, and enjoy good health thus far.
>
> In contrast with this state of affairs among the Chinese stands the fact that a number of Swedes who came to labor on the same work have already given up their contract, and left for Minnesota, declaring that they cannot endure the hot sun, and must seek a colder climate.[9]

6. St. Louis *Missouri Republican*, December 31, 1869; Louisville *Courier-Journal*, December 30, 1869.

7. New Orleans *Daily Picayune*, January 9, 1870; Little Rock *Daily Arkansas Gazette*, January 9, 1870.

8. Marysville *Daily Appeal*, January 7, 1870.

9. Galveston *Daily Civilian* quoted in Opelousas *Journal*, May 7, 1870.

Walker's enthusiasm for the Chinese continued, and he established an agency for recruiting Chinese labor in New Orleans, in association with the firm of O'Fallon and Hatch. He hoped to obtain Chinese workers for the railroads and the Louisiana levees from the same parties in California who had supplied those for the Houston and Texas Central Railroad, and he expected that planters might hire them when their contracts with the railroads expired. He thought Chinese workers from California could be obtained on more favorable terms than the "lot for Texas" because those taken to Calvert had had to be paid "for their boldness" as pioneers.[10] He announced his agency in the New Orleans *Times*, June 1, 1870.

Having made the necessary arrangements with an American house of the highest standing in Hong-Kong, China, the undersigned are now prepared to contract with planters and others for the delivery of any required number of able-bodied, docile and experienced agricultural laborers to be drawn from the interior Chinese provinces, where climate most nearly resembles that of the cotton and sugar regions of the South.

The period of engagement will be from three to five years. Wages for plantation work, $8 coin, per month, $6 payable month, $2 to be retained to the end of engagement to secure fidelity to contract.

Ship charges and other expenses at the lowest figure.[11]

In another newspaper piece, Walker explained that a three-year contract would begin from the date of the worker's arrival on the premises of the employer. The Chinese would be expected to buy their own clothing and to pay for their medical bills and for time lost because of illness. Employers would furnish quarters and food and pay for extra work at prevailing rates. The chief merit of the Chinese laborers was their known "fidelity to their engagements" and that most "responsible parties reimbursed a planter for his advance in cases of violation of contract or desertion."[12]

10. New Orleans *Times*, July 16, 1870; New Orleans *Daily Picayune*, January 9, 1870; John G. Walker to editor, New Orleans *Daily Picayune* quoted in Memphis *Daily Appeal*, February 20, 1870.

11. New Orleans *Times*, June 1, 1870.

12. *Ibid.*, July 16, 1870.

On August 5, 1870, an ad in the New Orleans *Times* announced that Walker was about to leave for California to bring laborers for several well-known Louisiana planters, "Dr. Brickell, Mr. John Davidson, the Messrs. Bringier and others, and is prepared to make satisfactory arrangements for the delivery of one or two hundred more." Before Walker's new shipments of Chinese arrived, reports began to spread that those working near Calvert, Texas, were leaving the railroad to secure work on plantations. Edward Rhoads suggests that these Chinese had come into conflict with other laborers on the railroad and that their employers had tried to change the terms of the contracts during a slow period in railroad construction. In September, 1870, all the Chinese ceased work and entered suit against their employers for "wages and for a failure of compliance with contract." The outcome of this suit is not known. By November, 1870, however, Chew Ah Heang visited New Orleans and placed the following notice in the New Orleans papers: "Chew-Ah-Heang, Chinese, informs the public that he has under his control Two Hundred and Forty (240) CHINESE LABORERS (now in Calvert, Texas) in need of employment, and whose services he offers to the community at large. Mr. Chew-Ah-Heang is to be found at the City Hotel." [13]

At the time Chew Ah Heang was attempting to resettle the laborers from the Houston and Texas Central Railroad, news about the hundreds of Chinese at work on the Alabama and Chattanooga Railroad was spreading. John C. Stanton, superintendent of the Alabama and Chattanooga Railroad, ordered Chinese from Koopmanschap's company in San Francisco to supplement his white and Negro laborers. A resident of Boston, he and his brother Daniel L. Stanton had acquired several bankrupt railroad lines, including the Wills Valley Railroad running out of Chattanooga and the Northeast and Southwest Alabama Railroad, which they had combined to form the Alabama and Chattanooga Railroad. The project was designed to connect Chattanooga, with Meridian, Mississippi, a distance of some 295 miles. The

13. New Orleans *Times*, August 5, November 4, 1870; Savannah *Morning News*, September 24, 1870; Edward J. M. Rhoads, "The Chinese in Texas," *Southwestern Historical Quarterly*, LXXXI (July, 1977), 6; Etta B. Peabody, "Effort of the South to Import Chinese Coolies, 1865–1870" (M.A. thesis, Baylor University, 1967).

brothers manipulated financiers in the East and legislators in Alabama to float bonds to provide capital for their scheme.[14]

On June 17, 1870, Koopmanschap sent a telegram to John C. Stanton stating that he could deliver "in thirty days at Chattanooga one or two thousand good Chinese laborers for sixty dollars per head. Wages sixteen dollars per month and board; free passage back." Stanton wired back that the railroad could take "fifteen hundred able-bodied Chinese" and that he had credit at the First National Bank of Chattanooga. An agreement was reached, and Koopmanschap sent the Chinese from California to Alabama by railroad. When the train stopped at St. Louis, the interpreter for the Chinese, Wong Wing, offered local reporters information about the Chinese and details about the organization of the group. Wong Wing had been hired for seventy-five dollars a month and his board; his sole responsibility was to act as an interpreter. He explained that most of these Chinese had sailed from Canton, Hong Kong, and Macao to San Francisco. The party destined for the Stanton railroad included, in addition to the laborers, a doctor, a storekeeper, and a man who acted as clerk and treasurer. Several Chinese spoke pidgin English, which they had learned in China.[15]

Wong Wing was described by reporters as a "well-informed person." He was twenty-seven years old and had spent about ten years in the United States. As a young boy, he had gone to work in the Australian gold fields of New South Wales and Victoria, where he learned English. He responded to inquiries on such subjects as the religion of the Chinese, their dress, and the meaning of their "pigtails" with the aplomb of an experienced interpreter who was used to explaining Chi-

14. A. B. Moore, "Railroad Building in Alabama During the Reconstruction Period," *Journal of Southern History*, I (November, 1935), 421–41; John F. Stover, *The Railroads of the South, 1865–1900* (Chapel Hill, 1955), 88–94, 135–37; John Witherspoon Du Bose, *Alabama's Tragic Decade: Ten Years of Alabama, 1865–1874*, ed. James K. Greer (Birmingham, 1940), 172–89; Walter R. Fleming, *Civil War and Reconstruction in Alabama* (New York, 1905), 591–600.

15. Chattanooga *Times* and Montgomery *Advertiser* quoted in Savannah *Morning News*, June 23, 1870; Nashville *Banner* quoted in Savannah *Morning News*, July 11, 1870; Chattanooga *Times*, July 15, 1870, quoted in San Francisco *Daily Alta California*, July 21, 28, 1870; Brayfield W. Whilden to M. T. Sumner, November 30, 1870, in *Home and Foreign Journal*, n.s., III (January, 1871), 35.

nese customs to curious Americans. He explained that the Chinese believed in a "Supreme Creator" and also worshiped "inferior gods." He volunteered the information that upon arrival in California he had cut his own queue but had subsequently decided to grow it back to avoid the ridicule of his countrymen.[16]

The Chinese arrived in Alabama in early August, 1870. The approximately 960 laborers were divided into two groups, 463 assigned to the eastern end of the railroad in St. Clair and Jefferson counties (the Chattanooga side), and about 500 to the western end in Greene County, near the Meridian terminus.[17]

As usual, the Chinese newcomers were first described as "steady and industrious," although some were said to be "awkward with the handling of shovel and pick." Two visitors left published descriptions of the encampments and work of the Chinese. Robert Somers, a British economist, visited the South from October, 1870, to March, 1871, and spent most of the months of December, 1870, and January, 1871, in Alabama. His descriptions of southern railroads were detailed because he traveled mostly by rail; he wrote extensively on their role in the rebuilding of the region.[18]

Somers visited the encampments on the Elyton side of the railroad near Eutaw, Alabama, on January 14–15, 1871. He reported that the laborers had been brought to Alabama from California and had formerly been employed on the Central Pacific Railroad. Despite this experience, the group that had first been assigned near Meridian had been found inefficient for "grading" and had been transferred to the Chattanooga end of the road. Like other commentators of the period, he remarked that during the first stages of their work on the railroads, the Chinese did not appear to be "as capable of labor as the Negro," but after their hands had "hardened," they gave satisfaction.[19]

16. Chattanooga *Times*, July 15, 1870, quoted in San Francisco *Daily Alta California*, July 21, 28, 1870; Anonymous writer to editor, March 15, 1871, in Memphis *Daily Appeal*, March 21, 1871.

17. Savannah *Republican*, August 9, 1870.

18. *Ibid.*; Memphis *Daily Appeal*, March 29, 1871; Robert Somers, *The Southern States Since the War, 1870–1871* (1871; rpr. University, Ala., 1965), xvii; Fletcher Green, introduction to Thomas D. Clark (ed.), *The Postwar South, 1865–1900: A Period of Reconstruction and Readjustment* (Norman, 1962), 4. Vol. I of Clark, *Travels in the New South: A Bibliography*, 2 vols.

19. Somers, *Southern States*, 163–64.

During the winter of 1870 and the spring of 1871, the Reverend Brayfield Waller Whilden visited all the Chinese encampments in the vicinity of Tuscaloosa. Whilden had been sent in 1849 by the Southern Baptist Convention as a missionary to Canton, China, where he served for approximately three years. He then preached and taught in South Carolina and Georgia until 1870, when he volunteered to serve as missionary to the Domestic and Indian Mission Board among the Chinese in the South.[20] He found few Christians in the Chinese settlements in Alabama, but he held sabbath services and gave out tracts in Chinese to those who showed interest. Whilden also visited the hospital where the sick Chinese were treated and quoted a local physician as saying that they were "more patient in sickness than the people of our own country." He reported that their principal recreational activities were "playing games of chance" and gymnastics.[21]

On one of his last visits to the Chinese camps in Alabama, in March, 1871, Whilden learned that between four and five hundred Chinese had left the railroad. He heard rumors that they were being taken to the sugar plantations of Louisiana by a white man and a Chinese agent from California. Newspapers described the attempts of an "adventurer" from Louisiana to "entice" the Chinese from their employment with the railroad. This affair roused considerable interest in Tuscaloosa because the railroad was suing to try to prevent the labor agent from wooing the Chinese. According to a reporter's letter in the Memphis *Appeal*, the public hoped that Stanton would get the "benefit of his contract at least until the road was completed."[22]

20. Cathcart (ed.), *Baptist Encyclopedia*, 1237; Henry A. Tupper, *Two Centuries of the First Baptist Church of South Carolina, 1683–1883, with Supplement* (Baltimore, 1889); Ray *et al.*, *Southern Baptist Foreign Missions*; Obituary for the Reverend Brayfield W. Whilden, *Minutes of the Seventy-Eighth Annual Session of the State Convention of the Baptist Denomination in South Carolina, Darlington, S.C., November 30–December 4, 1898* (Greenville, S.C., 1898), 43–44; Obituary for the Reverend B. W. Whilden, *Baptist Courier* (Greenville), January 27, 1898, in South Carolina Baptist Biographies, Baptist Historical Collection, South Carolina Baptist Historical Society, Furman University Library, Greenville, S.C.

21. B. W. Whilden to M. T. Sumner, February 8, 1871, *Home and Foreign Journal*, n.s., III (April, 1871); see also Whilden to Sumner, November 30, 1870, *ibid.*, (January, 1871); Whilden to Sumner, December 19, 1870, *ibid.*, (February, 1871); "Reports on Religious Interests of Chinese in the South," *Proceedings of the Sixteenth Meeting of the Southern Baptist Convention, St. Louis, Missouri, May 11–16, 1871* (Baltimore, 1871), 24–55.

22. B. W. Whilden, "Visit to China in March," *Home and Foreign Journal*, n.s., IV

By the end of March, 1871, however, a major exodus of Chinese took place. The steamer *Jennie Rogers* brought five hundred "heathen Chinese" from Tuscaloosa to Mobile, from whence they were taken to work in Louisiana. The "adventurer" from Louisiana who had lured the Alabama Chinese away from the Stanton railroad was W. A. Kissam, an agent who was recruiting Chinese from the railroads to work on the plantations.[23]

The largest single group of Chinese who were taken to Louisiana from Alabama were employed not on plantations but in the cotton mills of the Louisiana State Penitentiary in Baton Rouge, which was leased to Samuel L. James and Company. In 1870 the state legislature, in awarding James and his partners a twenty-one-year lease, gave them the authority to manage the penitentiary and to work the convicts in return for annual rents that would increase on a graduated scale. James started cotton and woolen factories as well as a large shoe factory and a barrel factory in the penitentiary. He found that the demand for cotton goods far exceeded the supply he was able to manufacture with convict labor, so he decided to double the production. The Joint Report of the Committee on the Penitentiary of 1870 stated that since "it would require five hundred first class skilled operators to work three different establishments up to their normal capacity, and there being only three hundred and forty-two prisoners, the Committee suggested to the Lessees that they employ outside operatives to supply the deficiency." James arranged with W. A. Kissam to introduce Chinese laborers to staff the night shift of the cotton factory. Eventually the offer of higher wages also lured Chinese workers from Louisiana plantations.[24]

On March 1, 1871, the steamer *Robert E. Lee* landed 50 Chinese in Baton Rouge. They were the first installment of approximately 150

(May, 1871); anonymous writer to the editors, March 15, 1871, in Memphis *Daily Appeal*, March 21, 1871.

23. Letter to the editors, March 18, 1871, in Memphis *Daily Appeal*, March 29, 1871; Galveston *Daily Civilian*, April 13, 1871.

24. Act 56, March 3, 1870, *Acts of the Legislature of Louisiana, 1870*, 84–85; Mark T. Carleton, *Politics and Punishment: A History of the Louisiana State Penal System* (Baton Rouge, 1971), 3–31; New Orleans *Daily Picayune*, July 29, 1894; New Orleans *Times-Democrat*, July 28, 1894; Baton Rouge *Weekly Advocate*, April 23, February 5, 1870; Baton Rouge *Tri-Weekly Advocate*, March 1, 27, April 10, 1871.

from the Alabama and Chattanooga Railroad, employed to do night work in the cotton factory at the penitentiary. By April 10, some 156 "first class Chinese laborers" were at work, and the factory was operating round the clock. The group was headed by "Che-fung-che-chung-che," who had arrived with his wife. The presence of a Chinese woman among newly arrived emigrants was unusual and was noted in the Baton Rouge *Tri-Weekly Advocate*, which described her as a "fair specimen of female loveliness." Her feet were small, and she dressed in "bloomer" style—a short dress and pants. With "her natural hair done up in a waterfall," she was "striking, if not either beautiful or picturesque." At the factory, work during the day was done by convicts, and at sunset "the Chinese came in from their quarters outside, and continued the work until six in the morning, when they were in turn replaced by the convicts." Samuel James paid the Chinese twenty-two dollars a month in gold, which he considered as cheap as convict labor.[25]

In the meantime, more than three hundred Chinese who were reported to have remained at work with the Alabama and Chattanooga Railroad were forced to stop in June, 1871, because a bankruptcy judgment against the company was made by the District Court for the Middle District of Alabama. The railroad was seized by the United States marshal at Meridian under a court decree. A "mob" of unpaid, angry employees, which included blacks, whites, and Chinese laborers, seized the trains and refused to allow them to run. It was reported that Stanton owed six months in back wages to his workers.[26]

The bankruptcy decree was reversed in the Circuit Court of the Southern District of Alabama, and Stanton reassumed responsibility for the railroad. He continued to have difficulty raising money to pay the laborers and other debts. Moreover, the Chinese labor agents were aware of the troubles their countrymen were undergoing. Two of

25. Baton Rouge *Tri-Weekly Advocate*, March 1, April 10, 1871.

26. Savannah *Republican*, April 25, 1871; Mobile *Daily Register*, June 9, 15, 16, 1871; Case No. 126, *Alabama and Chattanooga Railroad Company* v. *Jones* (1871), circuit court, S.D. Alabama, in *The Federal Cases: Comprising Cases Argued and Determined in the Circuit and District Courts of the United States*, Book 1 (Case No. 1–564) (St. Paul, 1894), 275–80; Memphis *Daily Appeal*, June 15, 16, 27, September 29, 1871; Barth, *Bitter Strength*, 195–96; Moore, "Railroad Building in Alabama During the Reconstruction Period," 425–34.

them, "Ah Joe" and "Say You," visited the laborers in June, and in early fall 1871 they returned to recruit some seventy of them to work in St. James Parish, Louisiana. Chin Poo, another Chinese agent, was reported to have obtained work for still others on the sugar and cotton plantations. A conflicting narrative suggests, however, that he raised money among local citizens in Tuscaloosa to help the abandoned Chinese but subsequently absconded with these funds for San Francisco.[27]

While waiting in Tuscaloosa, some Chinese sold fruit and others found work as house and yard servants. Some who went to Meridian made and sold cigars. About 330 Chinese settled in a camp outside of Tuscaloosa, where they reportedly were living on blackberries and crawfish. In late July, 1871, Koopmanschap visited the Chinese camp, but he brought them no pay. The Chinese offered to transfer all their claims on the railroad in return for passage to California and to China. But Koopmanschap petitioned for bankruptcy in May, 1872. He was unable to liquidate $160,000 in railroad bonds and $100,000 in notes given by the Chinese for allowances and passage money and was pressed by laborers and storekeepers in Alabama for $260,000.[28]

The failure of the Alabama and Chattanooga Railroad resulted in the dispersion of the largest single group of Chinese brought to the South. There was a demand for their labor, however, and during 1871, several hundred were resettled. W. A. Kissam and various other agents actively worked to place the laborers. Kissam had begun to bring Chinese to Louisiana in the summer of 1870. He offered Chinese labor to John Burnside and Edward J. Gay (see Chapter 5), but one of his most successful efforts was the introduction of Chinese workers to the Millaudon plantation.

On July 4, 1870, the steamer *Great Republic* arrived in New Orleans from St. Louis with 141 Chinese laborers for Millaudon. The plantation, which then occupied about seventeen hundred acres in Jefferson Parish, just above the city of New Orleans, was formerly the property of Laurent Millaudon, a well-known sugar planter who had come to

27. Case No. 126; Mobile *Daily Register*, June 21, September 19, 1871; *Senate Reports*, 44th Cong., 2nd Sess., No. 689 ("Report of the Joint Special Committee to Investigate Chinese Immigration"), 550; Mobile *Daily Register*, July 20, 1871.

28. Barth, *Bitter Strength*, 195–96; Mobile *Daily Register*, July 21, September 26, 1871.

New Orleans from France in 1802. He engaged in commerce and invested heavily in city property during the growth of the second municipality of New Orleans. He became one of the wealthiest citizens of the state, and by the early 1850s his sugar plantation was the largest in the state, with the most extensive manufacturing operation and innovative machinery to experiment in sugar production. His plantation was actually two estates, the Front Place and Estella, stretching for more than a mile along the river and several miles inland.[29] But after the Civil War, many planters in Jefferson Parish were forced to sell their lands because of financial losses and problems with recruitment and retention of plantation labor.

So in 1868 the Millaudon estate was purchased by a group of investors from Massachusetts, including Amos B. Merrill, a retired member of the Boston bar, Henry Joseph Gardner, Know-Nothing governor of Massachusetts from 1855 to 1858, Oakes Ames, a four-term member of Congress from that state, and other capitalists. The new owners continued to cultivate the fields with sugar. Although emancipated slaves were retained on the plantation, Chinese laborers were recruited to provide an additional work force. F. W. Gardner, son of Henry J. Gardner, joined Kissam in San Francisco to procure Chinese labor. They contracted for laborers who had worked in California and had been engaged for Louisiana through Cum Wing (or Kune Wing), "a wealthy Chinese merchant and labor agent connected with a Chinese house in California, and with another in China." Amos B. Merrill paid sixty-four dollars apiece to meet the expenses of the Chinese brought to the plantation.[30]

Under the terms of their contract, Merrill paid the Chinese fourteen dollars in gold for twenty-six working days a month, plus two

29. Wilton P. Ledet, "The History of the City of Carrollton," *Louisiana Historical Quarterly*, XXI (January, 1938), 220–81; Louis Bouchereau, *Statement of the Sugar and Rice Crops Made in Louisiana in 1870–1871* (New Orleans, 1871), III, 28–29; Betsy Swanson, *Historic Jefferson Parish from Shore to Shore* (Gretna, 1975); New Orleans *Daily Picayune*, October 6, 1873.

30. New Orleans *Times*, July 8, 1870; New Orleans *Republican* quoted in Savannah *Morning News*, July 12, 1870; Boston *Every Saturday*, July 29, 1871, quoted in Hammond *Progress*, March 25, 1938; Editorial correspondence of the Franklin *Planter's Banner*, September 15, 1871, quoted in San Francisco *Morning Call*, October 7, 1871; Mobile *Daily Register*, September 19, 1871.

pounds of meat, two pounds of rice, and a quarter of an ounce of tea per day. A certain proportion of their pay was withheld as a guarantee for faithful service, to be returned at the end of the contract.[31]

Lee Fock Wing, their interpreter, also identified as their headman, was a Christian who was licensed to preach. He had lived in China and England, and he was described as a member of the "Chinese aristocracy of learning," who commanded the respect of "plebian" laborers. The *Home and Foreign Journal* of the Southern Baptist Convention reported that he had brought copies of the Scriptures and tracts from California and hoped upon arrival in his new home in Louisiana to build a chapel and to open a Sunday school. He had subscribed one month's salary toward the purchase of a building for a house of worship.[32]

Since the Millaudon contingent came just one month after Captain Gift's arrival from China with the laborers bound for the Arkansas and Louisiana plantations, their physical appearance was compared to that of the earlier arrivals. A reporter who had seen both groups wrote that the Millaudon Chinese first appeared to him to have greater "indication of masculine character in facial expression" than had those brought directly from China by Gift. The Millaudon laborers arrived "dressed in blue blouses and drawers, very much like a Coney island bathing dress, with shaven crowns, beardless faces, and plaited pigtails sweeping the ground, their appearance conveys a first impression of effeminacy, which a close inspection quickly dissipates."[33]

The Millaudon workers established their quarters in a two-story wooden building that had once been used as a distillery on the plantation. Two or three of the Chinese did the cooking, and one served tea to the laborers in the fields. Their food preferences were described by a correspondent for the New York *Herald*, who noted that, unlike "fondly cherished beliefs of his childhood" that saw the Chinese as men who made "daily rounds with a string of rats strung by the tail to

31. Letters from Louisiana to New York *Herald* quoted in Savannah *Republican*, July 16, 1870.

32. New Orleans *Republican* quoted in Savannah *Morning News*, July 12, 1870; New Orleans *Republican* quoted in Savannah *Republican*, August 9, 1870; *Home and Foreign Journal*, n.s., III (August, 1870), 14.

33. Letters from New York *Herald*, n.d., quoted in Savannah *Republican*, July 16, 1870.

one end of a bamboo pole, and three fat puppy dogs dangling at the other," the newcomers' diet included chicken, rice, corncakes, and beefsteak. Thirty of these hands were said to have worked on sugar plantations in their own country, and the rest were praised for their readiness to learn new tasks. They put in an "exceedingly and good average day's work with no signs of fatigue, despite a boiling sun." Merrill indicated that they were good at all work except plowing.[34]

A few Chinese at Millaudon spoke a little English. In an interview with a newspaper correspondent, Lee Fock Wing answered questions about the skills of his brethren:

> I suppose some of your countrymen here can write?
> Certainly; all of them
> What! And read, too?
> Certainly—their own language.
> Well, that's more than can be said of many other laborers in this country. Are they contented?
> Yes.
> Do they like the climate?
> Yes! It is what they are used to.
> Have they written this to their friends in China?
> Yes; all of them. I have to take "much letters" to the city yesterday.
> Whew! We'll have labor enough here directly, when these letters get over.
> Yes; there will be much Chinese here by and by.[35]

Observers soon noted that "John Chinaman" had a "lively sense of his interest in any bargain he makes," as demonstrated by several conflicts that occurred on the plantation. Less than a month after they began to work at Millaudon, the Chinese became "excited" upon discovering that the "colored laborers employed on the plantation stopped work at 12 o'clock on Saturdays while they stopped at the end of the day." Lee Fock Wing requested that the hours be made equitable. At first, the proprietor refused. Later, however, he suggested that

---

34. *Ibid.*; Mobile *Daily Register*, September 19, 1871.
35. Letters from New York *Herald*, n.d., quoted in Savannah *Republican*, July 16, 1870.

they "choose to call five days and a half five days each alternate week and he would consider it six the remainder of the time."[36]

Not long after, a nearby planter sent Merrill a bill for some thirty dollars for vegetables furnished on order from Lee Fock Wing. Although Merrill paid this debt, he notified the headman that meat, rice, and tea were "all he had agreed to furnish them." The Chinese then asked for a plot of ground to raise cabbages and pumpkins, "not for their own consumption but to sell."[37]

While this request was pending, Merrill invited Cum Wing, the Chinese labor contractor from San Francisco, for dinner at the plantation. Cum Wing had arranged for the contract with the Millaudon Chinese. His presence led the Chinese to vent their anger against him for the problems they were experiencing with their working conditions. The Chinese workers rushed to Merrill's house, seized Cum Wing, and took him to their quarters. Merrill called the superintendent of police. A squad of policemen was dispatched to rescue Cum Wing and to arrest sixteen of the "ringleaders," who were confined in a house that had formerly been used as servants' quarters. During the night, the other Chinese attempted to rescue their incarcerated companions. The police repulsed them, and on the following day the conflict was settled. The Chinese agreed to return to work but only under the terms of their original contract.[38]

Several further instances of conflict with their overseer occurred, the most serious one in December, 1870. Elijah White, the overseer, pushed a Chinese worker who was acting "sullen," and when this man retaliated by striking him back, White shot him in the arm and through the body. Some reports indicated that the Chinese laborer died soon afterward. This incident impelled the Chinese workers on the Millaudon plantation to arm themselves with clubs and knives and march to the home of the proprietor to demand that White be given to them. Merrill pretended to inquire into the matter, but he probably

36. New Orleans *Republican*, n.d., quoted in Savannah *Republican*, August 9, 1870; New Orleans *Times*, July 26, 1870.
37. New Orleans *Times*, July 26, 1870.
38. Little Rock *Daily Arkansas Gazette*, July 26, 1870; New Orleans *Times*, July 26, 1870; Editorial correspondence, Franklin *Planter's Banner*, September 15, 1871, quoted in San Francisco *Morning Call*, October 7, 1871.

used this time to permit White to escape. He persuaded the Chinese that White had been arrested by the police and that he would be tried and punished.[39]

Following this incident, the Chinese were constantly on guard against strangers. In July, 1871, one year after their arrival, Alfred R. Waud, an artist for the Boston periodical *Every Saturday*, and Ralph Keeler, a writer, were sent to "inspect the work of cheap Chinese labor in the fields." Waud made sketches of the Chinese, against their protests. Merrill said that they were contemptuous of "barbarian art and its exercise upon themselves" and thus the scenes of their domestic life were made "at no little peril." While Waud and Keeler were at Millaudon, sixteen Chinese left the plantation. Merrill explained that he was still in favor of "cheap Chinese labor" and explained that these Chinese were dissatisfied because they had been demoralized by a railroad company that had worked them without paying them. He also thought that many had come from the "coast cities" of China and therefore were considered not to be faithful.[40]

By the fall of 1871, one year after their arrival, most of the Chinese had left the plantation. A correspondent for the Franklin *Planters' Banner* reported that of the 141 Chinese originally brought to the plantation, only 25 remained. Fifty-one had been enticed by higher pay in the cotton mills run by Samuel James at the Louisiana State Penitentiary in Baton Rouge, 26 had gone to work in St. James Parish for Colonel Alfred Roman, a distinguished Civil War commander and sugar planter, and more than 40 had run away. W. H. Kingsley, manager of the plantation, told the correspondent for the *Banner* that the Chinese laborers had been "unfaithful, and that they cared not a straw whether they did their work or not, provided they got their pay." They showed cunning "in making bargains and in obtaining advantages." For example, "they object to being docked when idle or sick, but tenaciously demand all of their wages, whether they earn them or not." Kingsley further suggested that the "muss" between Cum Wing and the Chi-

39. San Francisco *Morning Call*, October 7, 1871; Savannah *Morning News*, December 9, 1870; Little Rock *Daily Arkansas Gazette*, December 9, 1870; New Orleans *Daily Picayune*, December 11, 1870.

40. Boston *Every Saturday*, July 29, 1871, quoted in Hammond *Progress*, March 25, 1938.

nese was the result of a "preconcerted" plan to obtain "more satisfactory terms" from Merrill. He thought them "crafty enough for such tricks."[41]

Efforts to introduce Chinese laborers as part of a large-scale labor force for railroad building and plantation work were failing because the Chinese protested against employers who withheld wages or who threatened to change the terms of their contracts. Walker, the agent for the Houston and Texas Central Railroad, had pointed out that trouble would arise in dealing with Chinese workers unless agreed-upon obligations were strictly followed.

As the Chinese became involved in large-scale work projects in the South, they refused to conform to the practice exercised by employers of changing the terms of contracts without consulting with their headman, the interpreter, or the laborers themselves. Furthermore, the Chinese were quick to defend their fellow laborers from physical abuse or violence inflicted upon them by overseers or other supervisory personnel. They reacted to conflicts by resorting to rebellions, work stoppages, court suits, or abandonment of a work site.

Employers or their representatives attributed their labor problems to the stereotypical Chinese character rather than to problems within the labor system. When the Chinese protested or rebelled, the qualities of fidelity and exactitude for which they had formerly received praise became cunning and craftiness. Expressions of solidarity among the Chinese work groups in defense of individuals were perceived as exaggerated self-interest and a desire for gain. Dissatisfied employers also linked the Chinese protests with the belief that those who had come from the coastal areas in China were more likely to be disruptive than those from the interior.

A more intensive study of the details involved in the organization of work among the Chinese, described in the following chapter, offers insight on the specifics of the case of the Chinese, within the context of a society that was struggling to devise models of work organization that could continue to meet their demands for a cheap and productive work force to supplant slave labor.

41. Editorial correspondence, Franklin *Planter's Banner*, September 15, 1871, quoted in San Francisco *Morning Call*, October 7, 1871.

# CHINESE LABORERS ON THE MILLAUDON PLANTATION, LOUISIANA

"Our interview with the Chinamen went amicably enough, till the artist began his sketching. Then there suddenly broke forth a tempest of Tartar speech that was fearful to hear. Mr. Kingsley, the business manager of the plantation, called Ah Sing to him and explained that no harm was intended; the 'American man' was just going to take their pictures. This assurance being interpreted to the enraged Mongols, stirred up the verbal earthquake again; an undulatory shock went [through] the whole line of laborers. 'Wah lah, wah la wah la!' they observed, with much fierceness. 'Boys no want, I no likee,' said Ah Sing. We had, however, come miles through a hot sun in the middle of June, and the sketching could not be given up; it was completed in spite of many rounds of remonstrating 'Wah lah, wah la wah la.'" (From "The 'Heathen Chinee' in the South: Millaudon Plantation, Louisiana," *Every Saturday*, July 19, 1871, text by Ralph Keeler, drawings by Alfred R. Waud.)

*Chinamen at work on the Millaudon sugar plantation*: "Mounting horses and spreading our umbrellas, we rode out a mile or more through the fields, past countless negroes and mule-teams ploughing, to the spot off by themselves where the picturesque heathens were hoeing cane. There they were as represented in our engraving. Apart, in the middle of the field stood the imperturbable sinecurist who made a faint show of overseeing his countrymen, and his name, oddly enough, escaped being famous by a single g, it was Ah Sing. . . . The Chinamen went on with their work, hoeing the young cane, and doing it very carefully and precisely. Occasionally they would look up at us, but in a very stolid, careless way. Ah Sing approached and greeted us with a polite, 'Hallo, how do?'"

*A Chinese tea-server:* "At some distance in the road running through the field was a cart from which the mule had been removed and on this cart was a barrel of tea. It was the business of one of the gang to go about among the laborers with two large pots depending from each end of a pole which he carried on his shoulders. From these vessels he dished tea, at the will of the thirsty. The beverage was dark with its own strength, and taking it as they did, without the adulterations of sugar and milk, we found it very good. In the pauses of the tea-server's labors he sticks his pole in the ground, and puts his outside coat or blouse over the stick for shade, covering the pots beside with guinea-corn, a sort of weed that grows in the sugar-fields. You will see him in a separate picture standing guard over his charge."

COURTESY HISTORIC NEW ORLEANS COLLECTION

*Chinamen at home:* "Owing to their contempt for barbarian art, and their intense anger at its exercise upon themselves, the sketch of their domestic life, with which you are furnished, was made at no little peril. They have mosquito-bars, as will be seen in that picture, and they lounge about, and argue, and smoke, and fan themselves in a very loose and scalene way."

HISTORIC NEW ORLEANS COLLECTION

# 5 / CHINESE IN CONFLICT

 As increased numbers of Chinese laborers were settled in Louisiana, control over their employment fell more and more into the hands of planters in different sections of the state who assumed responsibility for direct procurement to their plantations. Conspicuous in the leadership of this group were the wealthy sugar planters John Williams and John Burnside, whose lands extended along the prosperous regions of Bayou Lafourche and the Mississippi River, and Edward J. Gay, who owned properties in Iberville and West Baton Rouge parishes. Many other planters also hired Chinese, beginning in early 1870, about the same time they were first employed to work on the railroads in Texas and Alabama. By the fall of 1870 and in the following year, these planters hired the Chinese who had left the railroads.

The planters were concerned both with the moral qualities and with the economic value of the Chinese. Although the Chinese were not the cheap source of labor they originally had been purported to be, men such as Burnside, Williams, and Gay were willing to try them because of the shortages of labor on their plantations and able to do so because they possessed the wealth to pay the costs of procuring them.

The Chinese who settled on Louisiana plantations, however, did not stay long. Both the plantation owners and the Chinese laborers broke their contracts, and the forms of litigation used to settle conflicts were not effective. In addition, new forces converged to contribute to the demise of the movement to hire Chinese laborers for Louisiana plantations.

First, regulation of Chinese emigration created increasing problems for southern entrepreneurs attempting to import laborers directly from China. Under the Convention of Peking of March 15, 1866, Great Britain, France, and China had agreed to joint supervision of the terms of contracts in the country of destination of the emigrants and to fixed responsibility for contract fulfillment. Contracts were to be limited to five years, at the end of which the emigrant would be guaranteed a free return passage or its equivalent. The convention was not ratified, but from 1866 to 1869 the colonial legislature of Hong Kong issued several ordinances to regulate the departure of Chinese. The culmination of this series was Ordinance No. 4 of 1870 with related instructions from the British secretary of state, which closed the port of Hong Kong to the recruitment of Chinese for labor in areas outside the British colonies.[1]

Second, plantation owners recruited laborers from California and from among those who had left their original places of employment in the South. Recruitment of Chinese from California, however, was not simple, because wages were higher there. Moreover, by the early 1870s, Chinese in California were in demand for work in the East and in cities such as Chicago.

Third, the contract labor model failed to establish satisfactory work agreements between plantation owners and their Chinese employees. Many conflicts arose over the interpretation and enforcement of labor contracts. Plantation owners and the managers and overseers to whom they delegated authority were accustomed to having absolute control over laborers. Sometimes they attempted to introduce changes in the terms of employment, such as the specific tasks to be undertaken, hours of work, and wage scales without consulting the laborers or their headmen. Some dissatisfied Chinese laborers repeatedly rebelled. Others abandoned the sites of settlement in search of better opportunities or to establish their own enterprises. Thus it became in-

---

1. Ordinance No. 4 of 1870, "An Ordinance to Make Further Regulations Respecting Chinese Passenger Ships," March 30, 1870, (Proclaimed August 24, 1870), *The Ordinances of the Legislative Council of the Colony of Hongkong* (Hong Kong, 1890), II, 1048–50; Great Britain, *Parliamentary Papers*, Vol. 70 (Accounts and Papers, Vol. XXXV, 6 February–10 August 1872), "Correspondence Respecting the Emigration of Chinese Coolies from Macao," C. 504, pp. 25–27.

creasingly evident that contracts guaranteeing Chinese laborers for a period of service were unworkable because employers and employees had different expectations about their respective responsibilities. Planters were also discovering that a contract based on sharecropping rather than direct payment of wages was the most efficient model for the survival of the plantation system.

The experiences of Williams, Burnside, and Gay illustrate in detail the difficulties in recruitment, the competition for labor, and the conflict over contracts that led to the demise of the Chinese labor movement. Just before Hong Kong was closed to the recruitment of Chinese for labor outside of the British colonies, John Williams had 220 Chinese sent from there to New Orleans. They arrived on October 9, 1870, after a passage of 181 days on the French bark *Charles Auguste*. At a stop at Martinique, the captain replaced 17 Chinese who had died en route with "emancipated" Chinese whose work contracts in Martinique had expired. They spoke French and were said to be Catholic.[2]

John Williams kept more than one hundred of the total force for his Leighton plantation in Lafourche Parish and sent twenty-four to his son-in-law, Richard L. Pugh, at Dixie plantation in the same parish. Pugh was one of the children of Thomas Pugh, a member of a well-known planter family in Lafourche Parish. The Dixie plantation had been acquired by his youngest sister, Frances Estelle (Fannie) Pugh, at the time of her marriage in 1868 to Taylor Beattie, a well-known lawyer in the area. Richard L. Pugh and his father-in-law John Williams continued to operate the Dixie plantation for some years as lessees of Fannie Pugh Beattie. Of the remaining Chinese, fifty-two went to work for Nolan S. Williams, John's brother, on Ardoyne plantation in Terrebonne Parish, and forty-eight were divided between plantations owned by William L. and Thomas J. Shaffer, a pioneer planting family in Terrebonne and Lafourche parishes. William L. Shaffer's new employees went to work at his Cedar Grove plantation, on Bayou Chacahoula, Terrebonne Parish, and Thomas J. Shaffer's at his plantation in the parish of St. Mary.[3]

2. New Iberia *Louisiana Sugar Bowl*, November 24, 1870, June 8, 1871; T. J. Shaffer to New Iberia *Louisiana Sugar Bowl*, June 14, 1871, in *ibid.*, July 6, 1871.

3. New Iberia *Louisiana Sugar Bowl*, July 6, August 31, 1871; Barnes Fletcher Lathrop, "The Pugh Plantation, 1860–1865: A Study of Life in Lower Louisiana"

The newcomers were to receive $13 currency for 26 days of work per month, "no half Saturday lost," and they were expected to work a total of 312 days a year, even "if it takes eighteen or more months to do it." From each month's wages, $3 were retained, to be held in reserve and paid them upon the expiration of their three-years contract. Their rations consisted of 1¾ pounds of rice and ½ pound of pork per day. They were charged for board when not at work, except when sick, and if ill, they received medical attention and rations.[4]

Upon arrival at the Leighton plantation the Chinese were reported to have some sicknesses that had been treated by two physicians, one Chinese, who soon returned to San Francisco, and the other American. The Chinese workers were reported to have "entire confidence" in the local physician, who was hired to visit Leighton plantation every other day.

The interpreter on Leighton plantation, Tsang Afat, spoke and wrote English well. He was about thirty-seven years of age and had first come to the United States at about age fifteen with the family of a northern merchant, to care for the children. During a four-year sojourn in the United States, he became a Christian. He returned to China, married, and remained there until he came back to the United States with the group imported by John Williams. A second interpreter, William Jones, was hired for the Dixie plantation. He was an Irishman by birth but had resided in China for eleven years and was reported to have mastered Chinese. In each group a Chinese served as cook and performed such duties as the policing of quarters and the preparation of baths.[5]

Their work on the Leighton plantation involved various phases of planting. Williams praised their excellence in handling the hoe and the orderly way they dug ditches. Both he and Shaffer noted that a few had learned to plow as well as the Negroes who had taught them these

(Ph.D. dissertation, University of Texas, 1945), 434–41; "Judge Taylor Beattie," in *Biographical and Historical Memoirs of Louisiana* (Chicago, 1892), I, 271–72; "Shaffer Brothers, Planters," in *ibid.*, II, 376–78; William Henry Perrin (ed.), *Southwest Louisiana Biographical and Historical* (New Orleans, 1891), 382–83.

4. New Iberia *Louisiana Sugar Bowl*, August 31, 1871; Shaffer to *Louisiana Sugar Bowl*, June 14, 1871, in *ibid.*, July 6, 1871.

5. New Iberia *Louisiana Sugar Bowl*, November 25, 1870, June 8, August 31, 1871.

skills. The Chinese also cut cane, loaded carts, and worked with the sugar kettle. Williams and his sugar maker praised their work, especially because it was new to them, and said they did not believe other foreign labor would have succeeded as well.

Thomas J. Shaffer expressed satisfaction with his twenty-five Chinese, noting that they accomplished more within a month than did the same number of Negroes. He offered two reasons for this appraisal: "First, they work much more steady, without the loss of half Saturday; and second, they do not run over their work. What they do is done well." He was so pleased with his Chinese that he expected to hire ten more in the fall. Other planters had also placed orders for Chinese with the hope of becoming independent of black labor and making Louisiana "bloom as it did in ante bellum times." T. J. Shaffer thought their labor could build up "our broken fortunes and regulate this detestable system of black labor." With Chinese labor a planter knew "just how many mouths he had to feed. No women, no children, no hogs, no ponies, no forecastle lawyers, and no howling preachers."[6]

In November, 1870, just over a month after the arrival of the Chinese on the *Charles Auguste*, John Williams stated that he had placed orders through agents in San Francisco for "ten times more Chinamen than can be obtained, although sixteen dollars per month is offered," as opposed to the thirteen dollars a month frequently paid to Chinese recruits from California. He also tried unsuccessfully to bring in Chinese from Martinique. An agent whom William L. Shaffer had met in New Orleans offered to furnish Chinese from Cuba whose contracts there had expired. They were said to be available for work under an eight-year contract at eight dollars a month. Not many Chinese from Cuba entered Louisiana in this period but some went to New York, where they worked as cigarmakers, house servants, and candymakers.[7]

John Williams did hire forty additional Chinese, but they were part

6. *Ibid.*, June 8, 1871; Shaffer to *Louisiana Sugar Bowl*, June 14, 1871, in *ibid.*, July 6, 1871.

7. New Iberia *Louisiana Sugar Bowl*, November 24, 1870, July 13, 1871; Terrebonne *Patriot*, July 22, 1871, quoted in Opelousas *Journal*, August 5, 1871; U.S. Department of the Interior, Ninth Census of the United States, 1870, New York City, Population Schedules, Wards 1–22, Record Group 29, NA; New York *Tribune*, October 8, 1870.

of the group who had been brought for work on the Alabama and Chattanooga Railroad. According to Williams, the advantage in hiring them was that the planter paid less for their procurement than for those recruited directly from San Francisco.[8]

By the early fall of 1871, however, reports of problems with the Chinese began to appear in the newspapers. A few had run away. Others on Nolan Williams' Ardoyne plantation complained because their overseer, James A. Bufford, began to give them work assignments based on the task system that had been used as a means of work organization among slaves. Under the task system, the slave was assigned a specific amount of work within a specific unit for the task. Upon completion of a daily task, the laborers could use the remainder of the day as they wished. The task system contrasted with the gang system, through which slaves had worked in groups under the control of a leader. In its extreme form, the leader or driver of a gang exacted labor by the use of the whip or lash. The gang system was used among Chinese laborers on the southern plantations, but their leader, as specified in contracts, was the Chinese headman. Laborers in a gang worked all day with the exception of time allowed for meals and for rest. The task system, which was used by Bufford, was not specified in the typical work contracts with Chinese laborers in the South. Since the Chinese expected employers to adhere strictly to the terms of contracts, they refused to comply with requirements not spelled out in these documents.

According to a reporter for the New Iberia *Louisiana Sugar Bowl*, when overseer Bufford thought it "best to give them tasks, and although he gave them less than usual—six one acre rows per day, each, they demurred and finally quit work altogether." After several days, however, Nolan Williams "compelled the grumblers, over forty in number, to go to work again." A similar problem arose among the twenty-three Chinese in W. L. Shaffer's plantation, but this dispute was contained before any work days were lost. The *Sugar Bowl* reporter believed that these problems occurred because the Chinese were not familiar with the task system.[9] He also thought that the isola-

8. New Iberia *Louisiana Sugar Bowl*, November 23, 1871; Thibodaux *Sentinel* quoted in Opelousas *Journal*, December 16, 1871.
9. New Iberia *Louisiana Sugar Bowl*, July 13, August 31, 1871; Lewis Cecil Gray,

tion of Chinese groups from other "gangs" of their countrymen was an effective way to prevent both the emergence of conflict and the laborers' subsequent running away. As an example, he noted that the gang of Chinese at T. J. Shaffer's place in St. Mary Parish was the most orderly because of their "isolation from other plantations where their countrymen were employed." He also suggested that the visits of "vagabond Chinese peddlers" to their countrymen "demoralized" the laborers. In fact, some planters or overseers had prohibited these visits.[10]

The most highly publicized Chinese rebellion in this area took place in the early fall of 1871 at W. L. Shaffer's Cedar Grove plantation. The Chinese here stopped work to protest Shaffer's having whipped a Chinese servant. Their head man told Shaffer that his workers did not believe he had the authority to perpetrate such a punishment. Furthermore, the servant had been taken to the town of Thibodaux, and the Chinese requested his return; they feared he had been slain. Shaffer and his friends tried to persuade the Chinese to return to work, promising that the servant would be returned later in the day. The workers would do nothing, however, until they had seen the servant. A scuffle ensued between Lavager Babin, who was the brother of a plantation manager, and the Chinese. Several shots were fired, killing one Chinese and wounding two. At an inquest it was reported that the deceased Chinese man had been shot by an unknown person who had acted in self-defense.[11]

A reporter for the *Sugar Bowl* subsequently wrote an article presenting the "Chinese version" of this conflict, as described by Tsang Afat, the interpreter on the Leighton plantation. The interpreter denied the claim of the plantation authorities that the first blow was struck by the Chinamen whom Lavager Babin was endeavoring to persuade to return to work. According to Tsang Afat, Lavager Babin had dragged a Chinese worker out of his cabin. Being bareheaded the workman wished to return for his hat. He raised his hand to his head

---

*History of Agriculture in the Southern United States to 1860* (2 vols.; 1933; rpr. Clifton, N.J., 1973), I, 545–67.

10. New Iberia *Louisiana Sugar Bowl*, August 31, 1871.

11. New Iberia *Le Sucrier de la Louisiane*, September 21, 1871; Thibodaux *Sentinel*, September 23, 1871, quoted in New Orleans *Daily Picayune*, September 28, 1871.

to indicate what he wanted, because he could not speak English. Babin interpreted this gesture as an intention to inflict a blow, so he struck the worker. The blow was returned, and his fellow laborers rushed in to prevent further violence. The whites misunderstood their motives, however, and opened fire upon the Chinese, wounding three, one of whom died afterward. Some of the excited Chinese then beat Babin with sticks. Tsang Afat also emphasized that none of the Chinese had fired a pistol and that no guns were to be found in their quarters.[12]

A letter to the editor of the *Sugar Bowl* reported that Judge Paul Guidry, the parish judge of Terrebonne, had ordered approximately ten Chinese, Lavager Babin, W. L. Shaffer, and William Stratton, who was also involved in the incident, to appear in court. The interpreter, Tsang Afat, translated the testimony for the prosecution, which was presented in Chinese. The *Sugar Bowl* correspondent stated that the Chinese had sworn to the "most outrageous falsehoods," yet "all was taken as truth by the Judge." Judge Guidry, "contrary to the law and to the expectation of every bystander," ordered Shaffer, Babin, and Stratton to the parish prison in New Orleans, to remain there until the next session of the district court in Terrebonne. The prisoners were released, however, under a writ of habeas corpus, gave bail, and were ordered to appear at the next term of the district court. The judge who permitted their release was Taylor Beattie—the husband of Fannie Pugh of Dixie plantation, where two dozen Chinese laborers were employed.[13]

The outcome of this case led all the Chinese from the Cedar Grove plantation to leave for Houma and ask for protection from Judge Guidry. The correspondent to the *Sugar Bowl* stated that by leaving they had violated their contract and cost the Shaffer family six thousand dollars. The judicial decision was seen as a blow against the efforts to build up the prostrated plantations by introducing Chinese labor. W. L. Shaffer was waiting for sixty additional workers to arrive in New Orleans. He had paid four thousand dollars for their transportation to San Francisco and gone to much expense to prepare the quar-

---

12. New Iberia *Louisiana Sugar Bowl*, October 5, 1871.
13. "A Subscriber" to the editor, September 24, 1871, in *ibid.*, October 12, 1871; "Judge Taylor Beattie" in *Biographical and Historical Memoirs of Louisiana*, I, 271–72.

ters in which they would live on the plantation. He warned that if the Chinese were not compelled to return to Cedar Grove and work out their time according to the terms of their contract, he would not bring any others to the plantation, "as it would be money thrown away."[14]

Efforts to secure Chinese laborers were further hampered by difficulties in procurement and competition for laborers. One example was the case of John Burnside. Burnside had left his native Ireland in early youth and was reported to have arrived in the South "as a peddler with a pack on his back." He had been befriended by Andrew Beirne, of Monroe County, Virginia, who had extensive business interests in Louisiana. Burnside worked his way up through real estate and other business ventures in New Orleans and through sugar planting. In 1858 he purchased land in Ascension Parish known as the Houmas holdings, which had previously belonged to M. S. Bringier, General Wade Hampton, and Colonel J. S. Preston. By 1870–1871, Burnside's holdings on the east bank of Ascension Parish included the plantations formerly known as Riverton, Donaldson, Clark, Conway, and Orange Grove. He also held land on that parish's west bank and on the west bank of St. James Parish.[15]

Burnside placed orders for Chinese with several different labor agents. W. A. Kissam, who had procured Chinese for the Millaudon plantation, contacted him, but Burnside apparently did not hire laborers through him. In August, 1870, he placed orders for 130 Chinese to work his Ascension and St. James parish plantations with the J. M. Hixson Company of San Francisco. Hixson had been an agent for procuring Chinese workers for fifteen years, and he had been a labor agent for a Chinese emigrant society for three years. He had placed Chinese workers in British Columbia, Oregon, and southern California. Hixson had visited the South, and he had assisted in procuring Chinese laborers for Louisiana, Texas, and St. Louis. Other

14. "A Subscriber" to the editor, New Iberia *Louisiana Sugar Bowl*, October 12, 1871.

15. J. Carlyle Sitterson, *Sugar Country: The Cane Industry in the South, 1753–1950* (Lexington, Ky., 1953), 110; Bouchereau, *Statement*, III, 16–20; *Outstanding Facts* (N.p., n.d.), in James Amédée Gaudet Papers, Southern Historical Collection, University of North Carolina, Chapel Hill; Sir William H. Russell, *My Diary North and South*, ed. Fletcher Pratt (1863; rpr. New York, 1954).

agents involved in procuring Chinese from California to the South provided additional laborers for Burnside. From Ben Colton and Too Jam he obtained twenty-nine workers and a foreman for the Armant plantation in St. James Parish and twenty-five for his Riverton plantation in Ascension Parish. In addition, A. Yune, a labor agent, provided him with twenty-six Chinese for the Armant plantation.[16]

Burnside must have been satisifed with Chinese labor because early in 1871 he commissioned George E. Payne, a former manager on the plantation of Mrs. James Porter on Bayou Teche in St. Mary Parish, to go to China to engage up to a thousand more, both to work his own lands and for members of the newly organized Louisiana Immigration Company. Payne was thought to be a suitable agent because he had lived in California for six years and had visited Canton, Macao, and Hong Kong. He was connected with the firms Oakey, Payne, and Hawkins and Payne, Dameron, and Company—two closely related firms of cotton factors and commission merchants. There were several plantation owners who were members of the Louisiana Immigration Company who placed orders with Payne. Mrs. James Porter, whose plantations adjoined T. J. Shaffer's, wanted one hundred Chinese; her neighbor, a Mr. Pringle, wanted sixty for his Mississippi cotton plantation; T. J. Bronson, whose land also adjoined Shaffer's, requested one hundred; and T. J. Shaffer hoped for ten, in addition to the twenty-five he already had.[17]

Payne spent some months in Hong Kong and reportedly recruited one thousand potential emigrants from the rural districts, but he had to depart in late 1871 without them. The British government had closed Hong Kong to recruitment of Chinese labor for work outside

16. S. Cranwill to E. J. Gay, n.d., 1871 (probably January), in E. J. Gay and Family Papers, Department of Archives and Manuscripts, Louisiana State University, Baton Rouge; J. Burnside to J. M. Hixson, August 5, 1870, Gaudet Papers; New Orleans *Times*, June 26, August 12, 1870; Memphis *Daily Appeal*, July 29, 1870; agreement between J. Burnside and Ben Colton, October 10, 1871, agreement between J. Burnside, Too Jam, and Ben Colton, September 7, 1872, agreement between J. Burnside and A. Yune, February 5, 1872, all in Gaudet Papers.

17. Contract between John Burnside and George E. Payne to engage Chinese laborers to emigrate to Louisiana, New Orleans, February 4, 1871, in Gaudet Papers; New Iberia *Louisiana Sugar Bowl*, June 8, 1871; New Orleans *Daily Picayune*, January 10, 1871; Bouchereau, *Statement*, III, 40–58.

of British colonies, and British authorities reported that it was this new regulation that prevented Payne from chartering a vessel to convey the Chinese to New Orleans.[18]

Burnside's success in using some Chinese workers on his plantations and his failure to import a larger number from China were known to Edward J. Gay, another planter who faced the problem of securing workers for each year's planting cycle. Gay was one of the most successful sugar planters in Louisiana, and as was typical of the large sugar planters, he invested in a combination of agricultural, manufacturing, and mercantile interests. As preparations began for the 1870–1871 agricultural season, Gay discussed the use of Chinese labor with other planters and examined copies of the labor contracts John Burnside had used. Agents dealing in Chinese labor visited the offices of E. J. Gay and Company in New Orleans to offer assistance in obtaining workers for the season. But rather than hire outside agents, William T. Gay, Edward's brother, went directly to San Francisco to hire Chinese.

The family and business correspondence documenting the recruitment and employment of fifty Chinese for the plantations of the Gay brothers offers valuable insights regarding the planters' difficulties in securing Chinese labor in California and subsequent troubles competing with other employers who offered the workers more attractive terms. Gay's background may help explain his interest in Chinese labor.

Edward J. Gay established his fortune and financial reputation when in 1838, at the age of twenty-two, he invested in the first direct importation of coffee from Cuba to St. Louis. Marriage in 1840 to Lavinia Hynes, daughter of one of the largest sugar producers in Iberville Parish, Louisiana, further enhanced his prospects. In 1855, six years after Lavinia's father's death, the couple moved to Louisiana from St. Louis. Under Edward J. Gay's management, the Hynes properties were augmented. He purchased land that had been held by other heirs of her maternal grandfather, Joseph Erwin, heirs who had

18. New Iberia *Louisiana Sugar Bowl*, June 8, July 6, 1871; *Parliamentary Papers*, "Correspondence Respecting the Emigration of Chinese Coolies from Macao," 25–27; Ordinance No. 4 of 1870, "An Ordinance to Make Further Regulations Respecting Chinese Passenger Ships."

moved elsewhere or were in financial distress. He made his home on one of these plantations, St. Louis, in Iberville Parish, and settled down to a life of a sugar planter. With purchase of adjoining properties, Gay's holdings eventually embraced some of the best, most fertile sugar properties in the state.[19]

After the Civil War, Gay acquired sugar plantations through foreclosure of mortgages as well as through purchases. From 1866 through 1870, his labor agents, frequently under the supervision of a family member or close associate, engaged in numerous efforts to recruit field hands and specialized workers required for sugar production. They tried to attract Negro labor from Virginia, as well as white European immigrants. His plantation managers also experimented with various labor contract arrangements and with sharecropping agreements among their former slaves.

In August, 1870, E. J. Gay's son, Andrew Hynes Gay, wrote to his father from the Ridgefield plantation on the Bayou Grosse Tête that "city negroes" sent to plantations "do not stay any length of time" and that it would probably be difficult to obtain any extra labor to harvest the crop. Andrew thought that it would be less expensive to send for Chinese from San Francisco "immediately," for he had learned that sugar planters from Ascension Parish, "Messrs. Bringier and Collon," had recruited Chinese. These planters had informed him that some "four hundred Chinese were in the neighborhood" and that John Burnside hoped to obtain a "large portion" of them for his plantations. Indeed, Bringier and Collon were among those who had placed orders for Chinese with the agency that General Walker had organized after his introduction of Chinese for the Houston and Central Texas Rail-

19. Alice Pemble White, "The Plantation Experience of Joseph and Lavinia Erwin, 1807–1836," *Louisiana Historical Quarterly,* XXVII (April, 1944), 343–478; Anna Gay McClung, "St. Louis Plantation, Iberville Parish, Louisiana," MS, February, 1956, in Louisiana Room, Louisiana State University, Baton Rouge; Sophie Mitchell Crow, "Family Genealogies," n.d., in Gay and Price Family Papers, Southern Historical Collection, University of North Carolina, Chapel Hill; "Memorial Addresses on the Life and Character of Edward J. Gay, March 22, 1890," *House Miscellaneous Documents,* 51st Cong., 2nd Sess., No. 108; "Edward J. Gay," in Howard L. Conard (ed.), *Encyclopedia of the History of Missouri: A Compendium of History and Biography for Ready Reference* (New York, 1901), III, 10–13; John Thomas Scharf, *History of St. Louis City and County, from the Earliest Periods to the Present Day: Including Biographical Sketches of Representative Men* (Philadelphia, 1883), II, 1243–47.

road in Calvert, Texas. In promoting Chinese labor to his father, Andrew noted that their usual wages were fourteen dollars a month, that transportation would amount to seventy dollars per head, and that they could be delivered in six weeks. Andrew thought that under these terms Chinese labor would be cheaper than Negroes from Virginia. Furthermore, he indicated that Chinese contracted for three years, whereas Negroes made one-year contracts.[20]

Edward J. Gay's son-in-law, Major Lawrence L. Butler, who was manager of the St. Louis plantation, also wrote to Gay suggesting that the Chinese might be better than "green negroes at $100 a piece with a twelve month contract." He said that the well-known planter John Hampden Randolph had sent for twenty-five Chinese and that other neighbors planned to take similar steps.[21]

Gay was familiar with the idea of using Chinese labor for sugar plantations. His commercial and plantation investments had acquainted him with the trade in the West Indies. One of his cousins, William H. Glasgow of St. Louis, was married to a Cuban woman, Carlota Nestora Fales. After the Civil War, Glasgow had worked at the sugar establishments of his in-laws near San Juan de los Remedios in Cuba, and in his correspondence with Gay, he referred to the Chinese who worked on these estates. Another source of contact was P. O. Daigre, manager of Gay's Olivia plantation at Rosedale in Iberville Parish, who in 1867 had gone to seek his fortune in Matanzas, Cuba, with knowledge of a new system of sugar processing. In the spring of that year, Daigre had written to E. J. Gay regarding plans to introduce Chinese from Cuba to Louisiana and had sent one of the agents for Chinese in Cuba to the E. J. Gay and Company office in New Orleans to discuss the agent's plans.[22]

Other members of E. J. Gay's family viewed China as more than a

20. Bouchereau, *Statement*, III; 16–22; Exchange of property, Mrs. N. Kenner, Mrs. L. Gordon, Mrs. A. Tureaud, and M. D. Bringier, New Orleans, January 13, 1870, before N. B. Trist, notary public, in Gaudet Papers; Andrew H. Gay to Edward J. Gay, August 13, 1870, Gay Papers.

21. L. L. Butler to E. J. Gay, August 14, 20, 1870, in Gay Papers.

22. William H. Glasgow to Edward J. Gay, February 18, March 28, 1868, Gay Papers; William Hyde and Howard L. Conard (eds.), *Encyclopedia of the History of St. Louis: A Compendium of History and Biography for Ready Reference* (New York, 1899), II, 903–904; P. O. Daigre to E. J. Gay, March 24, April 15, 1867, Gay Papers.

source of workers for plantations. They saw it also as a fertile field within which Americans could labor for the conversion of souls to Christianity. Anna Maria Turner Dickinson, a cousin of Lavinia Hynes Gay, had sponsored the education and missionary labors of the Reverend Elias B. Inslee, a Scottish-born carpenter and builder, who became the first missionary sent to China by the Presbyterian Church in the United States (the name of the church's southern branch after the sectional split). Her daughter Mary Augusta had married Andrew Hynes Gay, the oldest son of Edward and Lavinia Gay. She and her husband built Live Oaks plantation on the Bayou Grosse Tête in Iberville Parish, on a tract of land that Dickinson had inherited. When Dickinson died in 1848, Anna Dickinson became the manager of this large estate and was known for her contributions to education, works of charity, and the missions. She gave money to Inslee from 1848 until his death in 1871.[23]

Not all of Gay's associates, however, were interested in the Chinese or their use on plantations. His New Orleans partner, Samuel Cranwill, initially suggested that Gay have "nothing to do with the '*Pigtail*' question more than to investigate it." Cranwill indicated that "planters who have tried Chinese labor have had a surfeit of it, from all we hear." He wanted to engage Negro hands from Virginia, and he noted that Irish, Swedish, and German laborers were also available.[24]

A few days later, Cranwill reported to Gay that W. A. Kissam had called with a letter from W. H. Kingsley, the manager of the Millaudon plantation, to offer his services "to procure Chinese laborers." Kissam appeared to be a "very competent young man" and his partner, F. W. Gardner, was "highly connected," being the son of the former governor of Massachusetts.[25]

23. Penrose St. Amant, *A History of the Presbyterian Church in Louisiana* (Richmond, 1961), 100–101; James E. Bear, Jr., *The China Mission of the Presbyterian Church in the United States* (Richmond, 1965); Summaries, Presbytery of Louisiana 1856–72, in Historical Foundation of the Presbyterian and Reformed Churches, Montreat, N.C.; Death notice for the Reverend Elias B. Inslee, *Missionary* (Columbia, S.C.), IV (May, 1871), 1–12 (see Elias B. Inslee file, Historical Foundation, Montreat, N.C.); "Charles H. Dickinson" in *Biographical and Historical Memoirs of Louisiana*, I, 379–80; Mary Dickinson Gay, "A Complete Life," MS, *ca.* 1871, Gay Papers; Clement, *Plantation Life*, 30–87; White, "Plantation Experience," 343–478.

24. Samuel Cranwill to E. J. Gay, September 3, 1870, Gay Papers.

25. Samuel Cranwill to Edward J. Gay, September 8, 1870, *ibid.*

No business transaction was conducted with Kissam, however, for on September 7, 1870, E. J. Gay informed Cranwill that his brother William had left St. Louis bound for San Francisco to assess at first-hand the Chinese labor question. William hoped to employ hands for his own Oaks plantation on the Bayou Grosse Tête and for E. J. Gay's St. Louis plantation. Cranwill, in turn, obtained more information about contracts with the Chinese. Cranwill's letters about Chinese as substitutes for Negro labor began to sound positive. He hoped that William T. Gay would succeed in California, because the Negroes were becoming "so saucy and unreliable, that they are intolerable." They want "their horse, their cow, their pig, and such extras as people whose time is fully paid for, should not expect. 'Tis well some resort is left to show them the planter is not wholly dependent on their caprice, and obliged to suffer their impertinences."[26]

After his arrival in San Francisco, William Gay wrote that prospects for the procurement of Chinese labor were not very bright. He had learned that B. J. Dorsey, who had helped General Walker to procure the Chinese for the Houston and Central Texas Railroad, and F. W. Gardner, who worked with Kissam the labor agent, were having difficulties in the procurement of Chinese for the South. Gay doubted that Gardner would be able to fill an order for five hundred Chinese, "even at $16 a month." Indeed, he thought that Gardner, Dorsey, and "all the rest of the agents for Chinese labor in the South" in San Francisco were "irresponsible men" who had secured orders for approximately one thousand laborers but were "unable really to get a man." Gay explained that one reason the Chinese were difficult to recruit was that in California they were considered the "best farm hands" that could be procured. They were suitable for "all kinds of farming, mining and manufacturing purposes," and they found no difficulty in "getting employment at from $15 to $20 per month and from 80 cents to $1 per day." He was told that in September, after the fruit crops and small products were gathered, a large influx of Chinese laborers would come to the cities. Many of the farm laborers, however, would go to the mining districts and spend the winter in that business, earn-

---

26. Edward J. Gay and Company to Major L. L. Butler, September 9, 1870, *ibid.* Letters signed E. J. Gay and Company were written by Samuel Cranwill, his New Orleans partner. Samuel Cranwill to E. J. Gay, September 12, 1870, *ibid.*

ing two to three dollars per day. He concluded that success in procurement of Chinese was linked to the contacts one established and particularly the selection of "reliable" Chinese labor dealers. He hoped that the laborers for his plantations would come from the Chinese camps in the countryside and be gathered through the influence of their headman. He believed that trust among planters, headmen, and laborers was crucial because "of all suspicious creatures on the earth, Chinese are amongst the foremost." But "the right kind of men, if properly managed by a proper headman, would be fully as good for our purposes as negro labor."[27]

His transactions with Chinese dealers were troublesome, as illustrated by his first unsuccessful effort to hire one hundred laborers. A local agent, who told Gay he had collected the desired number of men, reported that on the day after he had the Chinese ready for shipment, they had scattered. Gay found another dealer from a Chinese commercial house, who agreed to go into the country and secure Chinese farm workers. These laborers were under the control of Chinese merchants and were guaranteed to carry out their agreements faithfully. Gay turned down this offer, however, because he could not accept a term of the contract that stipulated that two-thirds of the laborers' wages would have to be remitted monthly to the dealer of the Chinese house in San Francisco. Gay wrote that the dealer of this Chinese commercial house compelled the men to accept these terms and that they had no say in making the contracts. Referring to this conflict, he commented that the Chinese dealers "are the sharpest of the sharp, and want everything their own way, trusting no one and wanting security here, that the wages will be paid and contracts carried out." He decided, therefore, to turn to Koopmanschap and Company. At first Gay found that demand was so heavy that Koopmanschap and his "English agents" had difficulty filling all requests for Chinese workers. The only men available were "Coolies from cities in China," who, in contrast to the rural Chinese, were believed to be "worthless for field work." Nevertheless, after his bad experiences with other dealers and agents in the city, he found that Koopmanschap and Company had the best facilities for furnishing the men through connections in China and

27. William T. Gay to Edward J. Gay, September 15, 1870, *ibid.*

in San Francisco. Koopmanschap suggested that they begin by obtaining fifty rather than the desired one hundred laborers. The terms were "a bonus of ten dollars per head for getting the men, and no other costs but the transportation and provisions to Louisiana, the whole amount being collected on delivery at the plantations by this agent."[28]

While Koopmanschap was working at fulfilling this agreement Gay learned that a planter from Arkansas named Lombard had procured one hundred Chinese by payment of "double commissions to representatives of five Chinese houses" and had contracted to pay the Chinese sixteen dollars per month, provide free transportation to and from San Francisco, and give an advance of twenty-six dollars to each man. Gay heard, however, that forty of these men disappeared during the process of boarding the train in San Francisco and that more of them left at Sacramento. He wrote to his brother that this was additional proof of the "tricks these people are up to." Although W. T. Gay believed that Lombard had lost much of the money advanced to the laborers, those who did not escape were taken to the Vista plantation in Carroll Parish, in northeastern Louisiana. This plantation was owned by Judge William H. Sutton, who had been one of the members of the Louisiana delegation at the Chinese convention in Memphis in July, 1869. Several announcements about this new labor force appeared in the Louisiana newspapers in the late fall and winter.[29]

As the fruit-picking season was coming to an end and the Chinese were returning to San Francisco, Koopmanschap began to collect the promised laborers. W. T. Gay agreed to pay Koopmanschap sixty-five dollars in gold for each man he accepted. Koopmanschap would handle delivery to the plantations at his own "expense and risk." Furthermore, they agreed that any supplies on hand at the time of delivery would be paid for by E. J. Gay and Company at invoice cost. Gay thought this was a better contractual arrangement than one in which the planter assumed direct responsibility for freight costs, furnishing provisions, and an extra car for cooking on the train, which cost two hundred dollars to hire and ten dollars for commissions. It also re-

28. William T. Gay to Edward J. Gay, September 21, 26, 1870, *ibid.*
29. William T. Gay to Edward J. Gay, October 3, 1870, *ibid.*; New Orleans *Times*, February 7, 1871.

lieved plantation owners from the risks of losing men, because the men would not be paid until they reached the plantation.[30]

On October 8, 1870, Koopmanschap shipped fifty-two Chinese for the Gay family plantations. Twenty-five were destined for the Oaks plantation and the balance for the St. Louis plantation. The Chinese traveled under the supervision of the Koopmanschap and Company agent, a man named Croom. They arrived in St. Louis on October 18 on the Western Missouri Railroad and left the following day on the steamer *Indiana*.[31] On October 26 they were delivered to the two plantations. On October 31, E. J. Gay's partner, Samuel Cranwill, paid Croom $4,812.04 in gold. A disagreement arose because the amount advanced by W. T. Gay in San Francisco was less than what E. J. Gay had estimated. The expenses for one sick Chinese were also deducted. Cranwill communicated the final settlement, based on payment of sixty-five dollars for every Chinese delivered, to E. J. Gay in a letter.[32]

| | |
|---|---:|
| The statements of his settlement and the request to us to pay him for your account | $2399.94 |
| and for Mr. William T. Gay's account | $2432.16 |
| | $4832.10 |
| Under the circumstances and not having the original papers before us we proposed to pay the amount deducting the apparent error | $ 109.00 |
| He said he was willing provided we added the expense of the one Chinaman which you deducted | $ 65.00 |
| This arrangement leaving the settlement in our favor —gold | $ 44.00 |
| We then gave him check for this amount | $4788.10 |
| for which we paid ½% prem. | $ 23.94 |
| making | $4812.04 |

A copy of Gay's three-year contract with these workers (see Appendix II) shows that the Chinese were to be paid sixteen dollars in gold for a twenty-six-day month. They were guaranteed free passage

30. William T. Gay to Edward J. Gay, October 6, 7, 1870, Gay Papers.

31. Samuel Cranwill to Edward J. Gay, October 11, 1870, R. B. Hanenkamp to Edward J. Gay, October 11, 18, 19, 1870, *ibid.*

32. Statement of receipt of twenty-five Chinese men, Edward J. Gay, October 26, 1870, Samuel Cranwill to Edward J. Gay, October 31, 1870, *ibid.*

to the plantations from San Francisco and, at the end of the contract period, back to San Francisco. The sixteen dollars given to the Chinese upon recruitment was to be taken out of their first wages. Sufficient provisions and weatherproof sleeping quarters were to be provided without charge. The work day was ten hours long, with overtime night work to be paid at eight cents an hour, but they were not to work on Sunday. If they were sick or injured, they would not be paid until they resumed work, but food would be provided during their illness for a reasonable length of time.[33]

As had Williams and many other planters who hired Chinese, the Gay families initially expressed great satisfaction with their new employees. William T. Gay found them "well adapted" and able to perform "task work" about as "quick as the Negro." Major Butler, the manager of the St. Louis plantation, found them satisfactory at plowing. Lavinia Hynes Gay, E. J. Gay's wife, wrote to her children about the Chinese. To her son John H. Gay, Jr., who was away at school in Lexington, Virginia, she said they were "working pretty well. I saw them at a distance. They look a mixture of mulatoes, and Indian and they are dressed in pants and shirts, as the other laborers are. They only wear their Chinese dress on Sundays, and when at work, they twist their que around their head and wear the usual hats."[34]

In a letter to her daughter Nannie (Mary Ann Gay Price), who was in St. Louis, she described the peculiarities of Chinese behavior:

The Chinese are always willing to work and some are very good hands. . . . Yesterday was their Christmas day and they asked for half the day and had prepared themselves a good dinner. The day before, the hands were working near the house when one of the Chinamen came in the yard and asked for Mr. Gay, then Mr. Butler, but the gentlemen were not at home. He then called for Mrs. Gay. I went out on the upper porch to see what he wanted. He took off his hat, got down on his knees, and bowed himself his head touching the ground four times very stately then got up. I

33. "Agreement between Edward J. Gay and William J. Gay and Koopmanschap and Co., October 8, 1870, for Laborers, Native of China," *ibid.*

34. L. L. Butler to Edward J. Gay, January 19, March 27, 1871, Lavinia Gay to John H. Gay, Jr., November 15, 1870, *ibid.*

thought he was drunk but it was a mark of respect he was showing. They had done the same to your Pa at the Sugarhouse.[35]

She later wrote Nannie that she was pleased with the work they had done on her rose garden: "They sent me up three weakly Chinese whom I have set to work and as I have had every other nation the Celestials complete the list. They work quite well and if they could speak our language would like to keep them as they are neat and very quick to learn. Several of the planters are using them now and generally seem pleased with them as laborers."[36]

The Baton Rouge newspapers noted that when the Chinese on the Oaks plantation made occasional appearances in town they attracted much attention—they were "quiet and very cleanly looking." They also were reported to be "winning laurels as field hands," for they were "as good as the negro in all kinds of work": "They are more obedient and industrious than the negro, work as well without as with an overseer, and at the same time are more cleanly in their habits and persons than the freedmen. The same reports come from all the sugar estates where they have been introduced, and all accounts given of them by planters in Arkansas, Alabama and other States where they are employed in the culture of cotton."[37]

A Sunday school was started for them on the Oaks plantation, and four or five men showed interest in "regular attendance." As the Chinese New Year approached, they planned the three-day holiday to which an earlier agreement entitled them.[38]

Although by all reports the Chinese had created a favorable initial impression, E. J. Gay did not bring additional Chinese to his plantations. E. J. Gay and Company in New Orleans was continually approached by agents who could readily supply Chinese workers. Shortly after William T. Gay's return from San Francisco, for example, William Selby, the general agent of the St. Louis Mutual Life Insurance Company in San Francisco, wired that 125 Chinese were

35. Lavinia Gay to Nannie [Mary Ann Gay Price], January 1, 1871, Gay and Price Family Papers.
36. Lavinia Gay to Nannie [Mary Ann Gay Price], April 6, 1871, ibid.
37. Baton Rouge Tri-Weekly Advocate, January 23, February 15, 1871.
38. William T. Gay to Edward J. Gay, February 13, 1871, and L. L. Butler to Edward J. Gay, March 27, 1871, Gay Papers.

available for work in Louisiana. Some of the Chinese who had been brought to Texas and Alabama were offered for hire by W. A. Kissam, who visited the company offices in New Orleans several times to offer Chinese from Galveston as well as others who were of the "Texas lot" that had left the Houston and Central Texas Railroad in Calvert. These workers could be obtained for three-year contracts under the usual conditions, with monthly wages in the range of fourteen to fifteen dollars for a twenty-six-day month. Although E. J. Gay did not hire any of the Chinese Kissam offered, his neighbor, John H. Randolph, agreed to hire "25 Chinese of the Alabama Chattanooga lot of 90." [39]

E. J. Gay did ask T. B. Stevens, a former resident of China and sugar planter in the Philippine Islands, about importation of laborers directly from China. The Baton Rouge *Weekly Advocate* reported that Stevens understood sugar production, particularly the employment of Chinese. Stevens stayed at the Oaks plantation during November 1870, and, after studying labor conditions on several other plantations, he recommended against the importation of Chinese. He wrote Gay that he had consulted with sugar planters John Burnside, Duncan Kenner, and Bradish Johnson, who were skeptical about the feasibility of recruiting Chinese labor and preferred to hire whites. E. J. Gay was among several planters whom a representative of the Oriental Steamship Company of London invited to make a "contract or contracts for not less than 1000 Chinese laborers to be delivered in New Orleans, the contracting party paying $140 passage for each man and $8 gold per month with 5 years contract." The Chinese would come to the South by ship through the isthmus of Suez. In a letter to E. J. Gay, Cranwill indicated that orders were secured for five hundred Chinese, but Gay did not place any order. [40]

By March, 1871, five months after the arrival of the Chinese, both Edward J. and William T. Gay began to fear that their new employees

39. Samuel Cranwill to Edward J. Gay, New Orleans, October 26, September 29, 1870, William T. Gay to E. J. Gay, October 6, 1870, A. Kissam to Samuel Cranwill, September 29, 1870, *ibid.*; Account Book, 1870–71, John H. Randolph with J. W. Burbridge and Co., New Orleans, August 26, 1870, John H. Randolph Papers, Department of Archives and Manuscripts, Louisiana State University, Baton Rouge.

40. Baton Rouge *Weekly Advocate*, November 12, 1870; T. B. Stevens to E. J. Gay, November 27, 1870, Samuel Cranwill to E. J. Gay, March 20 (morning) and March 20, 1871 (afternoon), Gay Papers.

would break the contract and leave. The Chinese at the St. Louis plantation were offered work at the S. L. James factory in the Louisiana State Penitentiary in Baton Rouge at twenty-two dollars a month, six dollars higher than the wages paid by E. J. Gay. At the Oaks plantation, W. T. Gay attempted to reduce the monthly wages of the Chinese, accounting for actual time worked rather than an established monthly wage. He encountered strong opposition, for the Chinese were "bitterly opposed to a change of contract price." In keeping with the terms stipulated in the contract, W. T. Gay wrote to his brother that he thought it best that each man should be paid upon completion of twenty-six days of work.

Yu Kid, the headman, and some of the laborers from the St. Louis plantation left for the Louisiana penitentiary factory, but William T. Gay induced them to come back. He held a long conference with them, assuring them that the basis for payment would remain twenty-six days per month. In mid-April, however, Yu Kid and sixteen Chinese left again for the Baton Rouge factory. E. J. Gay reacted by filing a petition against Yu Kid and the others. Each man was served a summons, ordering him to return to St. Louis plantation, or, if he chose not to do so, to pay a sum that was an estimate of the expenses Gay had incurred for the breach of contract and associated damages, plus 5 percent interest.

The following excerpts from the citation served on Yu Kid show that, as headman, he was blamed for the departure of the Chinese. Yu Kid was sued for $489.20, and the other Chinese laborers were sued for amounts ranging between $200 and $250.[41]

For the Hon. the Judge of the Parish of Iberville State of Louisiana.

---

41. William T. Gay to Edward J. Gay, March 20, 21, 22, 1871, and L. L. Butler to Edward J. Gay, March 27, 1871, Gay Papers; Citation No. 1363, *Edward J. Gay* v. *Yu Kid*, April 27, 1871, Petition no. 189, *Edward J. Gay* v. *Yu Loong*, Petition No. 190, *Edward J. Gay* v. *Yook Chow*, Petition No. 191, *Edward J. Gay* v. *Lee Tai*, Petition No. 192, *Edward J. Gay* v. *Yu Wa Hing*, Petition No. 193, *Edward J. Gay* v. *Yu Sum*, Petition No. 194, *Edward J. Gay* v. *Lee Gee*, Petition No. 195, *Edward J. Gay* v. *Yu He*, Petition No. 196, *Edward J. Gay* v. *Tam You*, Petition No. 197, *Edward J. Gay* v. *Yu Choi*, all filed April 26, 1871, Iberville Parish Court, Plaquemine, Louisiana.

The petition of Edward J. Gay a resident of the parish of Iberville, State of La. Respectfully Represents That Yu Kid a resident of this parish is justly and legally indebted to your petitioner in the full sum of Four hundred and Eighty Nine ²⁰⁄₁₀₀ Dollars, with five per cent interest. . . .

That said Yu Kid, with others, arrived at your petitioners plantation in this parish on or about the 27th October 1870, when petitioner having had the contract fully explained to him and he having acknowledged all advances made to him, petitioner accepted said contract as the whole will more fully appear from the said contract hereto annexed and made part. . . .

That your petitioner has fully and liberally carried out all the obligations assumed by him in said contract and has always been ready to carry out same, but that the said Yu Kid, has proved himself utterly inefficient and incompetent as a foreman and when required to work and fulfill his contract aforesaid, has refused so to do or to work, and has used his influence on other parties of his own role, and prevented their working and complying with said contract, and now said Yu Kid has left petitioner's plantation, and has through his influence caused sixteen other laborers (Chinese) to also leave petitioners plantation and refuse to carry out their agreement with petitioner. That the said action of said Yu Kid in leaving the place of petitioner was without any just cause he being engaged for three years. . . .

By the said illegal acts of said Yu Kid, your petitioner has been greatly damaged and he is indebted to your petitioner in the said amount.

That upon the expectation of having the labor of said Yu Kid and the other parties to said contract for the whole term of three years petitioner engaged and did pay the whole expenses of his and their transportation from the City of San Francisco, which amounted, in fare provisions and compensations to agent, etc. to the sum of Sixty five Dollars each. That since said Yu Kid has been on petitioner's plantation he has paid him the sum of one hundred and Sixty four ²⁰⁄₁₀₀ Dollars for wages, all said sums and payments being in United States Gold coin.

That petitioner has also advanced and furnished said Yu Kid with provisions and as fully set forth, amounting to the Sum of Sixty Dollars.

That the action of said Yu Kid in influencing others to leave, has caused petitioner large damages and he owes at least the sum of Two hundred Dollars, therefor.

That said Yu Kid having as aforesaid quit the employment of petitioner without just cause before the expiration of the time for which he contracted to work, is bound to repay to petitioner the whole of the amount paid him as wages, the transportation and damages aforesaid.

Avers amicable demand without effect.

Wherefore the premises considered your petitioner prays that said Yu Kid may be duly cited to answer this petition that after all legal delay petitioner may hear judgment against said Yu Kid for the said sum of Four hundred and Eighty-nine 20/100 Dollars with legal interest. . . .

The wages and transportation and provisions to be paid in Gold coin.

Notwithstanding this judicial action, Yu Kid and his companions who had gone to Baton Rouge never returned to the St. Louis plantation, and by late June, 1871, most of the other Chinese on this plantation had left. Their departure was noted in a letter from Major Butler to E. J. Gay, who stated that several recently arrived Irishmen had also left.[42]

The Chinese on the Oaks plantation left, too, after disputes about the terms of the contract and difficult relations with the overseer. When W. T. Gay threatened to change the contract by allowing each man "his time in proportion to the way he works," the entire force of Chinese threatened to stop work. Because they were so "bitterly opposed," Gay did not change the contract. Instead, he reiterated that each man would be paid upon completion of the twenty-six-day work period and that each man would pay for his own board.[43]

42. L. L. Butler to Edward J. Gay, June 22, 1871, Gay Papers.
43. W. T. Gay to E. J. Gay, March 22, 1871, ibid.

When Gay was on a trip to St. Louis, Missouri, his overseer, a man named Vance, wrote him that he would have no trouble "getting along without" the Chinese. The extant correspondence does not reveal the reasons for the friction between Vance and the Chinese. Even though he apparently realized that the overseer was at fault, Gay laid off the Chinese. He explained to his brother Edward that since Vance had made himself so "unpleasant to them," he felt it was best to part with the Chinese. He offered their services to his brother and his brother's son, Andrew Hynes Gay, at forty dollars per man, hoping that they could place the Chinese with a party willing to pay for them. But he added that Kissam could "place the contract without difficulty at a fair price," since Chinese from California could not be obtained for less than seventy dollars per head. The family did not accept his offer, however, and on May 13, 1871, the Baton Rouge *Weekly Advocate* announced that the steamer *R. E. Lee* had carried all of the Chinese from the Oaks plantation to New Orleans. The paper reported that despite their three-year contract they had left because "one of the provisions of the contract was violated by their employer."[44]

Despite the failure of this contract, promoters of Chinese labor continued to attempt to interest the Louisiana planters in importing Chinese laborers. The planters, however, were not willing to take the risk. Thus, after John Burnside called at the E. J. Gay offices in New Orleans to introduce Vernon Seaman, one of the best-known importers of Chinese in San Francisco, who was about to depart for Hong Kong to bring Chinese laborers to the South, Samuel Cranwill noted in a letter to E. J. Gay that not even Burnside himself had placed any orders. The interest in Chinese labor clearly had run its course. Cranwill observed that the costs and risks involved in recruiting Chinese laborers had caused Burnside to lose interest in the idea:

Mr. Burnside is not sending for any Chinese by Mr. Seaman—he says because he sent for 200 by W. Payne—formerly Oakey Payne and Hawkins of New Orleans—who left here for Hong Kong about four months ago—with orders for 1,000 Chinese. The fact is

44. William T. Gay to E. J. Gay, April 19, 1871, *ibid.*; Baton Rouge *Weekly Advocate,* May 13, 1871.

I think Mr. Burnside would just as soon he had not sent by Mr. Payne. His views have considerably changed of late in regard to Chinese laborers. It would take about two years in the difference of labor wages to make good the $200 in currency bonus to be paid on the delivery here of the Chinese—and the risk of their dying or leaving unceremoniously before that time, makes the risk greater than the prospective advantages—not to speak of their inefficient labor compared with negroes.

But of these matters no one can better judge than yourself.[45]

For E. J. Gay and Company, the failure of the experiment with Chinese workers was one more disappointment in a series of efforts to maintain an adequate source of labor for the plantations. By the fall of 1871, one year after William T. Gay had traveled to San Francisco to recruit Chinese, his nephew Edward J. Gay, Jr., was sent to Chicago to recruit Scandinavian laborers who were reported to be available for the next planting season.[46] As had his uncle, Edward, Jr., explored various labor sources to meet the growing demands of the plantation.

The system of contract labor used to recruit Chinese for plantations and large-scale works such as building railroads in the lower South did not succeed in spite of the initial enthusiasm of agents and entrepreneurs. The antagonism expressed by the Chinese toward their southern employers, typically manifested after only about five months on the job, could not be resolved by either employer or employees. Several elements inherent to the contract system of labor help to explain the failure of the experiment of using Chinese workers on southern plantations.

Contracts for service, engaging workers for a designated time period during which they were to repay costs of transportation and other advances, were not limited to the Chinese. A labor contract system for freedmen had been established by Louisiana planters under the autho-

45. Samuel Cranwill to E. J. Gay, August 11, 1871, Gay Papers; Testimony, Vernon Seaman, San Francisco, November 13, 1876, "Report of the Joint Special Committee to Investigate Chinese Immigration," *Senate Reports*, 44th Cong., 2nd Sess., No. 689, pp. 548–51.

46. Edward J. Gay, Jr., to Edward J. Gay, September 14, 16, 21, 1871, Edward J. Gay, Jr. to W. T. Gay, November 5, 1871, Gay Papers.

rization of the army of occupation and the Freedmen's Bureau. In the years 1864–1866, for example, Negro laborers were given the opportunity to sign up for a year, and contracts included regulations to ensure maintenance of discipline and control. Freedmen, however, preferred urban employment to work on plantations under a contract that regulated hours and wages, levied fines for disobedience, and stipulated that they could not leave the plantation without the permission of the employer.[47]

The experiences with the Chinese, in which planters changed or manipulated the contract at their pleasure, did not yield positive results either. Moreover, the social organization of the Chinese work groups, in which intermediaries were used to defend the workers' interests, was in basic conflict with southern ideas about labor. Chinese head men or interpreters, who were experts in the fine art of bargaining, expected to use their skills in labor negotiations. Southern planters, however, did not wish to negotiate on terms of employment; they believed themselves to be the sole authority in setting work agreements with employees.

The most serious problem with labor contracts, however, was enforcement. Edward J. Gay unsuccessfully brought suit against the Chinese for failing to fulfill their contracts. The courts did not choose to punish Chinese laborers for deserting from service. The efforts of the Chinese to sue their former employers for violating the contracts or infringing other of their rights were also frustrated. The employers were sufficiently powerful in their communities to influence judges or to manipulate the courts so that judgments were always in their favor, as in the case of the Chinese against Lavager Babin and W. L. Shaffer in Terrebonne Parish.

The southern experiments with Chinese farm laborers failed, therefore, because the employees and employers had nearly opposite views of the meaning of the contract and of social relations between worker and employer. As sharecropping and tenantry replaced the contract labor experiments in the South, some Chinese became part of that labor system. Others established themselves in towns near or in large cities

47. May, "Continuity and Change in the Labor Program," 245–54; White, *Freedmen's Bureau*, 101–33.

such as New Orleans. No further attempts were made to import Chinese directly from China. The Chinese increasingly assumed control over their own lives in the South, as is shown by descriptions of early settlements in New Orleans and outlying towns and rural areas, presented in the following chapter.

# 6 / TOWNSMEN AND COUNTRYMEN

In the early 1870s there were many reports that the Chinese who had broken their contracts had left the plantations for towns and cities. Some, however, remained in the countryside, working the cotton plantations as sharecroppers. Others lived and worked in the sugar-growing areas. New Orleans was the commercial center, where representatives of Chinese firms from California established businesses and were seen by the public as representative of their countrymen. By the beginning of the 1880s, New Orleans had become a stopping place for Chinese travelers such as the merchants who traded between Hong Kong, California, and the West Indies.

In 1871, New Orleans had become a magnet for Chinese who left the plantations. The best-known Chinese-owned commercial establishments, however, were not in the hands of these former agricultural laborers but were managed by representatives of Chinese commercial houses from San Francisco. Their goal was to bring Chinese laborers as well as Chinese goods to the area.

The first shipment of goods directly from China and Japan to New Orleans arrived in 1870, on the American bark, *Lawrence*, from Hong Kong. Ads in the New Orleans papers announced the auction of goods from the bark, and thereafter Chinese articles were offered for sale in stores.[1]

Not far from the offices of the New Orleans *Bee*, on 98 Chartres

1. New Orleans *Daily Picayune*, November 19, December 4, 1870.

Street near Conti, Messrs. Fou Loy and Company had a store that was a center of attraction for "hundreds who delight to gaze upon the curious manufactures of China, and the pig-tail of John himself." The company's newspaper ads reveal that these wholesale and retail merchants dealt in groceries, teas, and a great variety of Chinese goods such as firecrackers, Chinese smoking tobacco, Chinese shoes, toilet articles, Japanese workboxes, and "thousands of Chinese curiosities."[2]

A New Orleans *Times* reporter described Fou Loy and Company as a "stock company, each member of which takes a part in the management of affairs" and continued:

> One wise-looking old chap is constantly engaged in pretending to write in a large ledger-like book, with a view no doubt to delude himself and the public into the belief that business is heavy. Another old fellow appears to occupy the position of financial agent of the concern; he receives the cash for certain curious-looking articles which form a part of the general stock in trade. An interview with John's family fails to reveal the presence of any of the female portion of Chinese humanity, and we doubt much if any lovely women have yet made their appearance in our Southern country. However, the "heathen" is so thoroughly a domestic animal that housekeeping suffers none per consequence of the absence of the fair one.[3]

The firm took a twenty-thousand-dollar policy from the Salamander Insurance Company on its stock, which newspapers saw as tangible proof that "the Celestials had a real tact for business, and that Fou Loy looked indeed 'like a business.'"[4]

Another facet of Fou Loy's business was to supply provisions for Chinese laborers at work on plantations. By special arrangement Fou Loy provided food and supplies to these laborers, charging and collecting from them on a monthly basis. The fee was one dollar per head per month. In addition, the firm attempted to attract Chinese laborers from California. In the fall of 1871, a newspaper noted that a Mr. Ton of the firm was going to California for laborers who would be hired

2. New Orleans *Times*, June 28, 1871; New Iberia *Louisiana Sugar Bowl*, June 8, 1871.
3. New Orleans *Times*, June 28, 1871.
4. New Orleans *Bee*, December 5, 1871.

by sugar planters at twenty-two dollars per month in gold, with the laborers furnishing their own food and clothes. James Wood, the largest rice dealer in New Orleans and supplier of rice to the company, had persuaded Fou Loy that since California was intent on restricting Chinese immigration, Louisiana would soon have an abundance of these good laborers and with them a return to prosperity.[5]

A small Chinese shop was operated by Yut Sing as agent for two San Francisco firms, Fook Hing and Company and Tong Wo and Company. Located at 40 Royal Street, Yut Sing and Company advertised that it imported and dealt in "Japan and China teas, lacquer ware and fancy goods." Its main product was teas "of the best qualities, and on favorable terms." The teas could be delivered to St. Louis and in New Orleans. The company was also prepared to furnish Chinese laborers through S. L. Jones and Company of San Francisco and Thomas M. Converse and Son of New Orleans.[6]

In addition to the stores, Chinese businesses in New Orleans included a large laundry on Carondelet Street owned by Lung Too. A reporter for the New Orleans *Times* described the launderer's unusual technique: "Instead of a flat iron in ironing, there is used an implement the exact counterpart of what housekeepers term a 'spider,' and this, filled with coals, is moved to and fro over the garment, while John ever and anon sprinkles the same by sending a fine spray of water through his teeth, which operation, though strange to the uninitiated, is yet most entertaining to behold."[7]

Public awareness of the presence of Chinese was reflected in an article in the New Orleans *Bee* in December, 1871, which stated that only a year earlier, few Chinese were settled in the city, but "now we see them everywhere in the streets of New Orleans." A few months later, the New Orleans *Times* reported: "From a *rara avis*, John has come to be looked upon as a well-behaved member of society in our city." Chinese were said to hold an "even tenor" of their ways and to have learned "the most difficult of all accomplishments—the minding of his own business."[8]

5. New Iberia *Louisiana Sugar Bowl*, October 19, 1871.
6. New Orleans *Times*, November 8, October 10, December 18, 1871.
7. *Ibid.*, June 28, 1871.
8. New Orleans *Bee*, December 4, 1871; New Orleans *Times*, June 28, 1871.

The New Orleans *Times* observed that the Chinese preferred to work in "small trades and industries in the city" rather than the "plodding work of the plantations." They could also meet the demand for small industries and for menial service, and a reporter thought they might displace the "immense surplus of lazy, loafing negroes" who had left the countryside where they could have been "usefully and profitably employed."[9]

As Chinese settled in the city in the 1870s, Fou Loy and his partners became intermediaries and interpreters of Chinese customs, consulted by reporters wishing to learn more about the Chinese. Newspaper writers, in turn, came to the defense of the company when official authorities did not seem to treat it fairly. When Fou Loy brought charges of larceny against two Chinese, for example, and an officer dismissed the charges, a writer for the New Orleans *Bee* expressed "outrage." The officer had fined Fou Loy twenty dollars for bringing the charge and threatened imprisonment for ten days if the fine was not paid. The *Bee* reporter likened the fine to theft, stating that Fou Loy had been robbed just as if a "professional rogue had picked his pocket."[10]

In 1880, the tenth census of the United States for Louisiana listed 489 Chinese, 95 of whom resided in Orleans Parish. Eight of the Chinese men in New Orleans had established households with wives and children; among the others were a widower, a divorced man, and one whose wife was absent. The rest were listed as single men, residing in congregate or boarding houses or as boarders in private homes. Of those listed as married, two had wives who had been born in France and two had Chinese wives. Of the remaining four, one had married an Irish-born woman, another had chosen a wife whose parents had been born in Ireland, and a third had married a woman born in Louisiana of French parents. The only wife of a Chinese man who was from Louisiana and both of whose parents had also been born in that state was a Negro woman, and they lived on or close to a plantation on the outskirts of the city.[11]

The occupations of the Chinese in New Orleans listed in the 1880

---

9. New Orleans *Times*, November 8, 1871.

10. New Orleans *Bee*, November 5, 1871.

11. U.S. Department of the Interior, Tenth Census of the United States, 1880, New Orleans, Louisiana Population Schedule, Record Group 29, NA.

census included laundry work or related activities (eighteen), cigar-making or cigar store salesman (twelve), cooking (ten), and a range of other activities, including bookkeeping, shoemaking, wood carving, and an interpreter.

There was no tightly knit "Chinatown" in New Orleans such as existed in the urban centers of San Francisco and New York. The stores and other business establishments owned by the Chinese were not close to their residences. The Chinese of New Orleans in 1880 were part of the white immigrant communities of the city. They lived as boarders in private homes and in boardinghouses owned by white European immigrant families, or they ran boardinghouses that offered housing to white European immigrants as well as to Chinese.

Four cigarmakers, Young Ching, Ah Tong, Ah Sang, and Ah Sing, boarded in the home of a Swiss cook whose wife was from southern Germany. Their home was located between those of a shoemaker born in France and his Bavarian wife, and a German "collector" whose wife was born in Louisiana of parents from Baden. William Yod, a forty-year-old Chinese whose occupation was an "eating house keeper," had three Chinese men and one Irishman as boarders. Married men tended to reside in the ethnic enclaves of their wives, as shown by the case of William Francis, a Chinese cook, and his wife, Eugenie, who was born in Louisiana of French parents. All of their neighbors had been born in France.[12]

In the 1880s, the Chinese Mission of the New Orleans Presbytery was established, largely through the efforts of Lena Saunders and the Canal Street Presbyterian Church. Lena Saunders was a Boston-trained missionary, sponsored by the Congregational Home Mission Board, who had originally come to New Orleans about 1879 to work among the Negroes. She sought the assistance of the Canal Street Presbyterian Church and founded the Chinese Mission, the only such establishment in Louisiana, on February 19, 1882. By April, 1882, she had a Chinese audience for preaching.[13]

12. Ibid.
13. J. H. Nall, Obituary for Lena Saunders, Southwestern Presbyterian, April 30, 1896, in Biographical Files, Lena Saunders, Historical Foundation of the Presbyterian and Reformed Churches, Montreat, N.C.; Letter to editor, New Orleans Times, n.d., from S. L. Carey, n.d., in Sylvester L. Cary Scrapbook, 178, Department of Archives and Manuscripts, Louisiana State University, Baton Rouge.

Saunders began her mission work with five Chinese, one of whom served as interpreter for the others. In the next five years, more than two hundred students attended classes at the mission, though few stayed long. The transient character of the New Orleans Chinese community was highlighted by Saunders in her 1887 report to the presbytery. She noted that of the original five, only one still lived in the city; three had returned to China, and one had gone to Florida. The mission had "40 resident scholars on their Sunday School list." Between 1886 and 1887, twelve of the men connected with the school had returned to China and seven others had sought employment in other states. Nineteen new names were added to the school roll, and fifty-six were listed as occasional visitors or transient scholars. The men had organized the Chinese Society of the King's Sons to visit their fellow countrymen who were sick and to aid travelers in need.[14]

Saunders also reported that New Orleans had become a stopping point for Chinese traveling between Hong Kong, California, and Cuba. In June, 1887, for example, two companies of Chinese merchants bound for Havana from Hong Kong had visited the Chinese mission several times on their stopover in New Orleans. Through an interpreter, the merchants expressed their appreciation for the work of the church among the Chinese. Saunders wrote that these "proud men of middle-age, and the merchant class in China" had returned after an initial visit, to hear a converted Chinese laundry worker tell them "how they wandered away from God, their Father, who now asked them to come home." A regular attendant at the services asked the merchants to take a letter with them to Havana to spread the message of this Christian mission. "May be, one be there who love Jesus," he said. The merchants were given religious books in Chinese to take to Havana with them.[15]

Lena Saunders' work with the Chinese Christian mission in New

14. Lena Saunders to Friends, Chinese Mission, February 20, 1887, in *Southwestern Presbyterian*, February 24, 1887, p. 4; Annual Reports of the Chinese Mission, Records of the Presbytery of New Orleans, Vol. III (October 9, 1878–April 21, 1892), Historical Foundation of the Presbyterian and Reformed Churches; Wai Kin Che, "The Young American-Chinese in New Orleans in the 1960s" (M.A. thesis, Mississippi College, 1966).

15. Lena Saunders, "Annual Report of the Chinese Mission to the Presbytery of New Orleans, 1887," *Southwestern Presbyterian*, October 20, 1887.

Orleans extended her influence beyond the local community. In the 1880s, when Congress passed legislation restricting Chinese immigration, she labored actively on behalf of the Chinese. She was particularly concerned that families would be permanently separated as a result of the Chinese restriction law, approved on May 6, 1882. Section 1 of this act suspended immigration of Chinese laborers to the United States for ten years beginning ninety days after its passage. The remaining fourteen sections enumerated penalties for violation and exemptions for listing Chinese passengers residing in the United States who left the country and returned, gave a form for listing Chinese passengers in transit through the United States, stated that Chinese were prohibited citizenship, and defined the term *Chinese laborer* to include both skilled and unskilled workers.[16]

Married Chinese emigrants typically left their wives behind. But those who wanted to bring their wives to New Orleans found an ally in Lena Saunders. Her attempts, however, were unsuccessful. She wrote, for example, to the secretary of the treasury on April 11, 1888: "A Chinese member of this mission, a laborer, is a convert to the Christian faith. He speaks and writes both his native language and ours, fairly well. I need his help in reaching others of his countrymen in our city. He will remain providing that his wife now in China, can come and learn of me the Christian faith. There are no children. Will you kindly inform me if I have the privilege of sending to China for her, and what obligations to my country I can assume in order to bring the Chinese wife to this Mission?"[17]

The office of the secretary of the treasury responded later in the same month: "You are informed that under the decisions of the Department and the United States Circuit Court of California, the wife of a Chinese laborer is a person whose *original* entry into this country is prohibited by the Chinese Restriction Act of May 6, 1882, and consequently that the person in question, who is understood not to have

16. "An Act to Execute Certain Treaty Stipulations Relating to Chinese," May 6, 1882, *U.S. Statutes at Large*, XXII, 58–61.

17. Lena Saunders to secretary of the treasury, April 11, 1888, Preliminary Checklist of the Segregated Records Relating to Chinese Immigration, in Records of the Immigration and Naturalization Service, 1882–1908, Department of Justice, Record Group 85, NA.

resided in the United States prior to the expiration of 90 days after the passage of said Act, cannot be allowed to come into this country on any terms." [18]

Saunders was not easily defeated, however. She joined others throughout the country in the battle against additional anti-Chinese legislation. She wrote letters, visited influential people, and did everything she could to oppose legislation excluding Chinese and their families. All these efforts failed. The passage of the Act to Prohibit the Coming of Chinese Persons into the United States, of May 5, 1892, which became known as the Geary Act, continued for ten years all laws in force prohibiting and regulating the entry of Chinese persons and persons of Chinese descent. This act also denied bail to the Chinese in habeas corpus proceedings and spelled out requirements concerning certificates of residence. The Chinese resisted the enforcement of this new law. Saunders was profoundly distressed at the law's passage. She suffered a physical and psychological breakdown and spent the last two years of her life in retirement. Following her death in Jackson, Louisiana, on April 17, 1896, more than one hundred Chinese men attended her funeral in New Orleans. Six of them acted as pallbearers, including the one remaining scholar she had met five weeks after she had opened her mission school in 1882. [19]

The New Orleans Chinese community of the late 1870s and 1880s centered around several Chinese families connected with commercial houses from California. The city also served as a refuge where the Chinese who left the rural areas and small towns where they had originally been settled could disappear into relative anonymity, working as launderers, merchants, and cooks. The passage of anti-Chinese legislation that denied Chinese men the right to bring their wives to the United States or to travel to China to seek a wife undoubtedly influenced their personal lives as well as the course of their resettlement in the midst of the immigrant communities of New Orleans.

A central feature of Chinese life in the port city of New Orleans

18. Secretary of the treasury to Lena Saunders, April, 1888, *ibid.*
19. "An Act to Prohibit the Coming of Chinese Persons into the United States," May 5, 1892, *U.S. Statutes at Large*, XXVII, 25–26; *Southwestern Presbyterian*, April 23, 1896; Nall, Obituary for Lena Saunders.

was its role as a stopping point for Chinese who were traveling internationally, especially from Cuba and other Caribbean islands to California and Chinese ports, and vice versa.

In another city in Louisiana a unique experiment in the employment of Chinese workers was undertaken. In Baton Rouge, the capital, for the first time in the lower South a sizable group of Chinese was employed in manufacturing. In March, 1871, W. A. Kissam and a Chinese companion had recruited Chinese formerly working on the Alabama and Chattanooga Railroad as night workers in the cotton and woolen mills of the state penitentiary. Chinese laborers from the Millaudon plantation and those formerly under contract to E. J. Gay also joined this force. Dissatisfied with working conditions on the railroad and plantations, they no doubt were attracted to the mills by the promise of higher wages and the possibility of more congenial tasks.

The convicts worked from morning until sunset, when the Chinese took over and continued until daybreak. Thus the factory was run continuously, producing a steady supply of cloth for the St. Louis market. The Chinese learned quickly, and some reporters suggested that they might surpass the output of the more experienced convict weavers. As production increased, a plan to establish an outside factory that would employ regular residents of the city was discussed but apparently never implemented.

All the Chinese lived together in a brick building located diagonally across from the office of the Baton Rouge *Tri-Weekly Advocate* on Front Street. They were directly responsible to their headman, Koo Lock, who was assisted by three foremen. Ten or fifteen of these Chinese workers spoke a "pidgin English" described as a mixture of Chinese and English. Local citizens were not used to this language form, and it was said that only men of "clear perceptions and keen imaginations" could understand it. Indeed, the unfamiliar sounds of Chinese, a tonal language, were described as a "strange chop mixture of low gutterals and subdued howls, with a few catawauls thrown by way of giving variety to the otherwise monotonous flow of sound."[20]

Documentation of the reasons for the termination of this experiment with Chinese labor at the state penitentiary is slim. Several con-

20. Baton Rouge *Tri-Weekly Advocate*, March 1, 27, April 10, 1871.

flicts occurred in the summer of 1871, which may have contributed to the laborers' moving on to other work such as construction and repair of the levees outside of Baton Rouge. When Koo Lock was accused of "want of honesty," he was replaced by Lee Fock Wing, the former interpreter for the Chinese at the Millaudon plantation. A riot ensued, and adherents of Koo Lock attempted to assassinate Lee Fock Wing. The guilty parties were arrested and sent to jail, but Koo Lock was reported to have absconded with a large sum of money that belonged to the laborers.[21]

The Chinese who had been brought to work in the sugar country of Louisiana tended to congregate in nearby towns while they sought new sites for work. The town of Donaldsonville, the seat of Ascension Parish in the heart of the sugar country, was frequently visited by Chinese from outlying plantations. They gathered in Lafourche Street, along the river.

The Donaldsonville *Chief* carried several articles in the fall and winter of 1871 regarding the difficulty in pronouncing the names of the Chinese, their "fearful and wonderful cognomen." Labor conflicts on the plantations were also described. The newspaper gave details of the funeral customs followed by the Chinese who had buried one of their number named Ah Pou with "all the ceremonies customary with the race, his money, clothing, bed and bed–clothing and a quantity of victuals being interred with the body." The suicide of a Chinese who had been accused of larceny was also reported.[22]

As the Chinese became familiar in Donaldsonville, the *Chief* exhorted its children to refrain from ridiculing them:

> The pig-tail Celestials are again flocking to town and their old haunts on Lafourche street, which have for many months been deserted, are filled with the busy hum of Chinese life. The heathens are a quiet and cleanly set, and make good neighbors if accorded fair treatment. Small boys should refrain from jolting them in the back with brick bats as they peacefully wander along the streets. Such pernicious conduct is apt to conjure up horrible bald-headed

21. *Ibid.*, June 23, 1871; New Orleans *Daily Picayune*, June 30, 1871.
22. Donaldsonville *Chief*, October 7, November 18, December 16, 1871, January 13, February 17, May 18, 25, 1872.

specters before the slumbering juvenile's imagination and render his night's repose a continuous torture instead of sweet rest from the tiresome sports and duties of the day.[23]

Finally, in the spring of 1874, the *Chief* announced that the Chinese had "folded their tents like the Arabs, and suddenly stole away, and the precincts of 'China Town' are silent as the tomb." The "musical beat of the tom-tom was heard no more in the land." The "pig-tail celestials" had left for work on a new plantation.[24]

The best-known Chinese who resided in Donaldsonville was Tye Kim Orr, who had come to Louisiana from Cuba with E. T. Wyches in November, 1867, and had subsequently gone to China to recruit Chinese for John Williams. Tye Kim Orr directed the first school for Negro children in Donaldsonville. His work was praised in the annual report of the state superintendent of public education for 1875, which described the school as in "satisfactory operation" and the teacher, "Mr. Tye Kim Orr, as one of the best qualified in any parish." He was a "universally esteemed gentleman of Chinese descent, who received a thorough education in England, and would fill the position of professor in a college with honor and ability."[25]

When the Reverend Brayfield W. Whilden, the Southern Baptist missionary who had preached among the Chinese working on the Alabama and Chattanooga Railroad, visited Donaldsonville in July, 1871, he held religious services and distributed tracts among the Chinese. In subsequent correspondence with the secretary of the Southern Baptist Home Mission Board, Whilden suggested that this town would be the "best centre for possible missionary labor among the Chinese in the state since they could be reached in three directions for about sixty miles each way."[26] But he was not able to continue his labors among the Chinese in the South, and the only other person to direct missionary attention to them was Lena Saunders.

23. *Ibid.*, January 17, 1874.

24. *Ibid.*, March 14, 1874.

25. Thibodaux *Sentinel*, August 28, 1869; Sydney Marchand, *The Flight of a Century in Ascension Parish, Louisiana* (Baton Rouge, 1936), 176; William G. Brown, *Annual Report of the State Superintendent of Public Education to the General Assembly of Louisiana for 1875*, 99; Donaldsonville *Chief*, April 18, 1874, March 20, 1875.

26. B. W. Whilden to M. T. Sumner, n.d., *Home and Foreign Journal*, n.s., IV (July, 1871), 11.

The Chinese in the cotton country of northeastern Louisiana, as well as those in Arkansas and Mississippi, were isolated from the attractions of New Orleans. Most of them had been brought by Captain Gift and other entrepreneurs to work under contract on cotton plantations in the Mississippi River delta area and in the adjoining territories of Bolivar County in Mississippi, southeastern Arkansas, and the northeastern parish of East Carroll in Louisiana.[27] Several years after their arrival, these laborers became sharecroppers, one labor form that survived in the cotton plantation system. Other Chinese settled in small towns nearby, working in various commercial enterprises.

According to the United States census, all sixteen Chinese in Mississippi in 1870 lived in Bolivar County and worked as farm laborers. The 1880 census listed fifty Chinese for Mississippi, of whom twenty-eight were in Washington County and none in Bolivar County. The rest were scattered in several counties, mostly in the delta area. The occupations of those in Washington County, as listed in the tenth census, included farm laborers, grocers, launderers, farm hands, and hucksters.[28]

The Chinese in Chicot County, Arkansas, in the southeastern corner of the state, were described in 1875 by the Natchez *Democrat-Courier* as worthy of admiration for their work habits and their adeptness in the cultivation of vegetables in their own gardens. In this cotton-growing area, the Chinese appeared "far more serviceable as tenants than as employees." They paid the planter by the hundredweight of cotton picked, "usually one hundred pounds of lint cotton to the acre." In return the planter furnished a mule with which to cultivate the crop, and the tenant could keep whatever part of the crop was not due the

27. James W. Loewen, *The Mississippi Chinese: Between Black and White* (Cambridge, Mass., 1971); Robert Seto Quan, *Lotus Among the Magnolias: The Mississippi Chinese* (Jackson, Miss., 1982); George Albert Rummel III, "The Delta Chinese: An Exploratory Study in Assimilation" (M.A. thesis, University of Mississippi, 1966); Kit-Mui Leung Chan, "Assimilation of the Chinese-Americans in the Mississippi Delta" (M.A. thesis, Mississippi State University, 1969); Pao-Yun Liao, "A Case Study of a Chinese Immigrant Community" (M.A. thesis, University of Chicago, 1951); Shi-Shan Henry Tsai, "The Chinese in Arkansas," *Amerasia Journal*, VIII (Spring–Summer, 1981), 1–18.

28. Ninth Census, 1870, Mississippi Population Schedules; Tenth Census, 1880, Mississippi Population Schedules.

planter. The neatness and personal appearance of the Chinese were praised, and landowners found that they were so industrious that it was difficult to restrain them from working on Sundays.[29]

The changes in occupational activity of the Chinese during the early period of their settlement in Arkansas are reflected in census reports. In 1870, 98 Chinese lived in Arkansas; 96 worked as farm laborers, the remaining 2 as house servants. Most of these people (74) lived in Arkansas County. Ten years later, of the 133 Chinese enumerated, 59 were in Chicot County and 43 in Jefferson County. The rest had settled in small groups in the delta area. Over half of those in Chicot County were listed as "partners" (sharecroppers), 16 as farm or day laborers, and the remainder in miscellaneous occupations.[30]

In testimony before the special congressional committee to investigate Chinese immigration in San Francisco in 1876, Vernon Seaman, a labor agent from California, mentioned the Chinese employed by Colonel Richard A. Sessions to raise cotton near Luna Station in Chicot County. He recalled that in 1872, during his travels through the South, Colonel Sessions had reported that he employed one hundred Chinese and one hundred Negroes. "Each class cultivated one half of his cotton plantation." Each Negro was said to produce an average of five and a half bales but each Chinese produced eight bales.[31]

The Chinese who picked cotton in the neighborhood of Marion, Crittenden County, Arkansas, near Memphis, were admired for their skills, industry, and success in the production of cotton. Their headman was Ah Maun, a Chinese described as a "man of education," who had "gathered up some knowledge of English." He was popular in the countryside, where he had become known as John Ormond. Ah Maun organized five of his countrymen and rented a piece of ground to plant

29. Natchez *Democrat-Courier* quoted in Memphis *Daily Appeal*, October 10, 1875; "Chinamen as Farmers," Natchez *Democrat Courier* of a "recent date," quoted in *Rural Carolinian*, VII (March, 1876), 114–15.

30. Ninth Census, 1870, Arkansas, Population Schedules; Tenth Census, 1880, Arkansas, Population Schedules.

31. Testimony, Vernon Seaman, San Francisco, November 13, 1876, "Report of the Joint Special Committee to Investigate Chinese Immigration," *Senate Reports*, 44th Cong., 2nd Sess., No. 689, pp. 548–51.

corn and cotton. He hired additional Chinese hands during picking time. The quality of the corn and cotton he produced received praise.[32]

In Carroll Parish, in the northeastern corner of Louisiana contiguous to Chicot County, Arkansas, the Chinese were well known. Lombard had brought them from California in 1870, as described in correspondence between William T. Gay and his brother, Edward J. Gay, and in newspaper notices in New Orleans. Sixty-five Chinese from California were the first among this group, taken to work on the Vista plantation several miles outside of the parish seat. In late January, 1871, William Sutton, owner of this plantation, reported that the Chinese had picked seven bales of cotton per hand. Sutton expressed "entire satisfaction" with their work in all the duties "imposed upon them, such as plowing, hauling, ginning, bailing, etc., and in fact everything about the plantation." His statements were quoted in advertisements for Chinese labor by the Chinese Emigration Company located at 39 Perdido Street, New Orleans.[33]

Lake Providence was the center of activity for the Chinese in this parish. A young visitor to this town wrote to a friend in 1875 that her reaction to these strangers was "to laugh at them so much." A reporter for the Lake Providence Carroll Watchman stated that the "Chinamen" were "quite thrifty." He believed that their frugality had motivated the "heathen Chinee" to decide against returning to the "celestial land." Special events, such as the funeral of a Chinese man, were subject matters of newspaper interest. When "John Chinaman" died in a fisherman's shanty on the river bank, he was buried in the public cemetery. The Watchman reported that many Chinese attended the funeral, having rented all the public conveyances in town for the occasion.[34]

A reporter boasted that the best restaurants in Lake Providence were kept by two Chinese men, Sam Sing and Marcee. Sam Sing's advertisements appeared regularly in the local papers. His restaurant was located in the Leonard Building on Levee Street. The meals in-

32. Memphis *Appeal* quoted in Donaldsonville *Chief*, October 26, 1872.

33. William T. Gay to Edward J. Gay, October 3, 1870, Gay Papers; New Orleans *Times*, February 7, 1871.

34. Katie (last name unknown) to Ellie C. Knighton, March 21, 1875, Josiah Knighton and Family Papers, Department of Archives, Louisiana State University, Baton Rouge; Lake Providence *Carroll Watchman*, January 29, 1876.

cluded a range of "meats, fruits, games, fish, and vegetables." Service was provided "at all hours in first-class style." Marcee, described as a "gallant little Chinaman," was known for his enthusiasm for horse races in addition to his restaurant business. His skirmishes were frequently cited in the papers, such as the beating he administered to a customer who had tried to avoid paying for his dinner.[35]

Joe Collins, another Chinese man in Lake Providence, had an "excellent family grocery on Levee Street," according to the *Carroll Watchman*. He was one of the few who had a Chinese-born wife. The tenth census for Louisiana showed, for example, that among the 489 Chinese in the state, 35 were married, had a spouse absent, or were widowed or divorced. Only three of those listed as married had a native-born Chinese wife. Joe and Mary Collins had apparently entered the United States through New York, where their first child was born. They had probably anglicized their names shortly after their arrival. The two other native-born Chinese couples resided in New Orleans. One of these, John and Mary Ashon, had apparently also entered the country at New York, birthplace of their first son. The other couple, Pablo and Isabel Trynaz, had probably come to New Orleans from Cuba, as suggested by their Spanish name and by his work in a cigar store. Of the remaining Chinese men who were listed as married, one had a Chinese spouse born in the United States, four had mulatto wives, and twelve had married Negro women. Eight Chinese men had chosen white spouses, and of these, six were of Irish or French immigrant background. The remaining seven men were listed under the categories of spouse absent, widowed, or divorced.[36]

These patterns of marriage between Chinese men and women of diverse cultural backgrounds emphasize the necessity of understanding the social organization of Chinese settlements in local communities. Most of the Chinese newcomers settled within established and distinctive non-Chinese cultural enclaves and intermarried with members of these groups, thus dropping from the public attention. Like some of their counterparts in Cuba, who have been described by Juan

35. Lake Providence *Carroll Watchman*, April 8, 1875, March 4, 1876; Lake Providence *Carroll Conservative*, November 23, 1878.
36. Tenth Census, 1880, New Orleans, Louisiana, Population Schedules.

Pérez de la Riva, they became "a people without a history."[37] These patterns are identified in the final chapter of this work, in analysis of processes through which the descendants of the Chinese from Cuba became part of the population of Natchitoches Parish, Louisiana.

37. Juan Pérez de la Riva, "Contribución a la historia de las gentes sin historia: Los Culíes chinos y los comienzos de la inmigración contratada en Cuba (1844–1847)," *Revista de la Biblioteca Nacional "José Martí,"* V, (January–December, 1963), 35–76, and "Documentos para la historia de las gentes sin historia: El viaje a Cuba de los culíes chinos," *ibid.*, VI (July–December, 1964), 47–86.

# 7 / A MIXED NATION

Students of the Chinese in the United States have given considerable attention to the institutions that helped them to maintain solidarity and retain their cultural identity, notably in San Francisco and New York. The studies have focused on settlement patterns (creation of Chinatowns), mutual aid associations, trade guilds, and commercial houses and have described the conflicts and struggles of groups within these organizations. These studies have contributed to an understanding of Chinese men, who, whether as sojourners or settlers, were set apart from the host society by their distinctive social behavior, speech, values, and other cultural attributes.

This emphasis on the social organization of Chinese men has been shaped, no doubt, by the fact that these laborers typically were not accompanied by their wives. Those who were married left their wives in China in accordance with the tradition that a wife remained in the ancestral village. Most of these wives were left in the home of the emigrant's parents. The Chinese restriction law of 1882 prevented Chinese men in the United States from bringing their wives to join them. Stanford M. Lyman states that the Chinese men who remained in the United States after 1882 or who were permitted to return to this country after a brief home visit had to "content themselves with a celibate life, seek outlet with prostitutes, or attempt interracial marriage."[1]

Interracial marriage has received limited attention in the literature of the early settlements of Chinese in the United States. And there has

1. Stanford M. Lyman, *Chinese Americans* (New York, 1974), 87.

149

been little attention paid to the processes through which descendants of a Chinese father and a non-Chinese mother adopted local values and lost distinctive national characteristics. The case of a single community can cast light on the complex realities of social classification of the Chinese. A fuller understanding of how the Chinese in Louisiana virtually disappeared from the consciousness of the public that had been so eager to use their services can be gained through a detailed examination of that small group through time in the cotton-growing country of Natchitoches Parish. Census data, church registries, and newspaper accounts can never fully explain what happened to a group of Chinese of whom no traces seem to remain in an area they had settled. I filled in some of the gaps by interviewing descendants, mostly of the third and fourth generations, of the original Chinese settlers. Oral tradition, which includes, according to Jan Vansina, "all verbal testimonies which are reported statements of the past," provides crucial facts to supplement and enrich the documentary data.[2] The testimony of descendants is particularly important for this rural area because local histories on their cultural heritage and social organization have not been written.

The first group of Chinese brought to Natchitoches Parish had arrived in New Orleans in January, 1867. They were hired by Terence and Arthur Chaler, residents of Isle Brevelle in the southern section of the parish. These Chinese bore Spanish first names, as indicated in the list of passengers of the steamer *Liberty* on which they had traveled from Havana and Matanzas to Louisiana. They were identified as "Messrs. Hilario, Clemente, Phillipi, Francisco, Antonio Simon, Castro Bedall, Byforso, Eulatorio, Migel, Julio Baltosar, Seraphine, and Leno."[3] This enumeration was unusual; Chinese laborers who arrived at other ports in the Americas, including California, were usually referred to simply as a group of a particular number.

The reaction of the press in Natchitoches to these newcomers was guarded. The editor of the *Semi-Weekly Natchitoches Times* stated that although the competition they would provide to the freedmen would

2. Jan Vansina, *Oral Tradition: A Study in Historical Methodology*, trans. H. M. Wright (Chicago, 1961), 19–20.

3. New Orleans *Bee*, January 16, 1867; New Orleans *Times*, January 16, 1867.

be beneficial, no more of them should be imported until the usefulness of their labor was tested. The planters were initially pleased with their new workers. Arthur Chaler reported that the Chinese were industrious and frugal and performed any amount of work "provided their contracts were carried out to the letter, particularly with regard to monthly wages and rations."[4]

The twenty Chinese hired by Jules Normand and Benjamin Bullitt for the cotton plantation of Severin Trichel in March, 1867, were praised for their "deportment and their assiduity at work." The *Semi-Weekly Natchitoches Times*, having received favorable reports from all employers of the Chinese, decided to encourage further immigration. The Chinese were particularly desirable because "of all the other foreign laborers received in this Parish, very few have remained faithful to their contracts."[5]

The New Orleans *Crescent* noted that the Chinese were inexpensive to hire and that, since they brought no women with them, they would not encumber the contracting planter with their offspring or helpless relatives. The Chinese were praised for their frugality. The paper remarked that they independently set traps for fish and game and that during their leisure hours they made "fishing nets, bird snares, or domestic implements."[6]

In September, 1867, however, the *Semi-Weekly Natchitoches Times* reported that the planters were disappointed with Chinese labor. Although they had first found the Chinese "hardworking, robust, and honest," the newspaper said the planters now saw them as a "sorry substitute for former slaves." At first their "inefficiency" was attributed to their reaction to a new climate and their lack of familiarity with agricultural implements and local modes of cultivation. Later, the planters described the Chinese as "lazy, mutinous, obstinate, and thievish." The *Times* eventually decided that the use of "cooley labor" had been a "dead failure in Natchitoches."[7] The Chinese who re-

4. *Semi-Weekly Natchitoches Times*, January 30, 1867; *Semi-Weekly Natchitoches Times*, quoted in New Orleans *Daily Picayune*, February 6, 15, 1867.
5. *Semi-Weekly Natchitoches Times*, April 10, 1867; New Orleans *Crescent*, March 30, 1867.
6. New Orleans *Crescent*, March 30, 1867.
7. *Semi-Weekly Natchitoches Times* quoted in *L'Avant Coureur*, September 21, 1867;

mained in the parish—for example, those recruited by Severin Tri-chel—became sharecroppers. Trichel reported in 1869 that the Chinese who worked on his cotton lands did so for a "share of the crop" and that they were "superior to the African" in almost every respect, "being careful, industrious, respectful, and regular in their labor."[8]

During their first year in the parish, three Chinese died. Peo and Crispino were found drowned in the Cane River, near where they lived on Isle Brevelle. They were buried in the local Catholic cemetery. The third Chinese, who was not identified by name in the newspaper, attempted to commit suicide after he was kicked by a mule. Terence Chaler and Ignacio, the Chinese "chief," prevented him from cutting his throat with a razor, but he still maintained that "death was preferred to his sufferings." Later, Chaler and Ignacio saved him again upon finding him "hung by the neck to one of his bedposts." Soon afterward, he apparently drowned in a river. Some parties believed that he had been murdered, and the *Semi-Weekly Natchitoches Times* called for an inquiry into the death.[9] The deaths of all three of these Chinese were reported as homicides, but they may have been suicides. The suicide rate was high among Chinese in the Americas, particularly during the initial period of adaptation.

Several years after their entry, official census figures gave the numbers of Chinese, their reported ages, occupations, and form of household organization. Census figures for Louisiana in 1870 gave a total of seventy-one Chinese, of whom nineteen resided in Natchitoches Parish. Thirty-five had been brought to the area in 1867. The difference can be accounted for by the three deaths and by the migration of others to adjoining parishes such as Rapides and Sabine. In addition, some Chinese may not have been enumerated.

The average reported age of the Natchitoches Chinese at the time of enumeration was thirty-nine years. They were older than Chinese subsequently brought to Louisiana directly from China or from Cali-

*Semi-Weekly Natchitoches Times* quoted in Savannah *Morning News*, October 8, 1867; *Semi-Weekly Natchitoches Times* quoted in New Orleans *Times*, October 22, 1867.

8. New Orleans *Daily Picayune*, June 23, 1869.

9. *Semi-Weekly Natchitoches Times*, quoted in New Orleans *Daily Picayune*, June 8, 15, 1867; *Semi-Weekly Natchitoches Times*, August 3, 1867, quoted in New Orleans *Bee*, August 11, 1867.

fornia, probably because they had spent at least eight years in Cuba, where they had contracted to work. All of these newcomers except a cook and a servant were listed as farm laborers.

The household arrangements these Chinese made varied. In 1870 one group of agricultural laborers lived near the "Wash-Hole," beside Clear Lake and a spring, west of the present-day town of Clarence and ten miles from the town of Natchitoches. These men bore such names as Clemente, Domingo, Carlos, Arturo, Pedro, and Seraphino, which they had adopted during their residence in Cuba. They were hired by Severin Trichel for work in the cotton-growing areas in the northern section of the parish.[10]

The census of 1870 lists two Chinese living in the households of employers in Isle Brevelle in the southern section of the parish. One of them, Gregorio Pedroso, worked as a cook in the home of Francina Normand de Vargas and her family. She was the daughter of Jules Normand, the labor agent who had imported the Chinese from Cuba. The other Chinese, Ignacio Portico, was employed as a house servant in the home of Arthur Chaler, who, along with his brother Terence, had hired the Chinese in January, 1867. In the contract negotiations, Ignacio had been listed as the headman of these Chinese.[11]

Only one Chinese man lived in an independent household at the time of the 1870 census. He was Dr. Hilario Hongo, also known as Dr. Eli or Hilaire Hongo or Hilaire Hong, of Isle Brevelle, who was to become the best known of the early Natchitoches Chinese. Hongo eventually established himself as a healer and was certified as a physician in 1883. In the census of 1870, however, he was listed as a farm laborer.[12]

In 1880, the United States census for Natchitoches reported that thirty-three Chinese resided in the parish. This total included both the first-generation Chinese men and their children; though the latter

10. Ninth Census, 1870, Natchitoches Parish, Louisiana, Population Schedule.

11. *Semi-Weekly Natchitoches Times*, August 3, 1867, quoted in New Orleans *Bee*, August 11, 1867; Ninth Census, 1870, Natchitoches Parish, Louisiana, Population Schedule.

12. Ninth Census, 1870, Natchitoches Parish, Louisiana, Population Schedule; Affidavit of Dr. Eli Hongo, February 12, 1883, in Book I of Medical Certificates, Natchitoches Parish Records, Natchitoches Parish Courthouse, Natchitoches, Louisiana; *Biographical and Historical Memoirs of Northwest Louisiana*, 308.

were of mixed ancestry, they were classified as Chinese. The Chinese adults consisted of thirteen farm laborers and one farmer. Seven of them had established independent households, and an equal number boarded in other homes.

Examination of the ways surnames were formed gives insight into how official documents shaped the identity of the Chinese and their descendants. Scholars in the United States have given limited attention to this process; therefore my analysis is influenced by research conducted by Edgar Wickberg on the Chinese in the Philippines and by Maurice Freedman on Chinese kinship and marriage in Singapore.[13] Sometimes a Chinese surname such as Hong or Wong was retained. Officials in local communities, who were not accustomed to these sounds, altered the spelling. In the 1870 census, for example, Hilario Hong was listed as Ely Conker, no doubt the closest phonetic approximation to an unfamiliar Spanish first name and a Chinese last name.[14] Over the ensuing years, his direct line of descendants introduced minor variations to the surname. Most of them to the present day use the slightly modified surname Hongo.

While living in Cuba, these Chinese adopted Spanish names through baptism in the Catholic church or through popular usage. Upon settlement in Louisiana, some of them used Spanish first names as surnames. A forty-seven-year old Chinese farm laborer hired by Trichel, recorded as Arthur Moret in the census of 1880, for example, was originally listed as Arturo. His descendants adopted the anglicized version as a last name, Arthur or Archie (a local variant). Two of his sons were known as Emanuel Arthur and Louis Archie.[15]

Surnames of other Chinese in the census are evidence of local officials' ignorance of the Chinese custom of following the surname by the given name, as well as the problem of proper phonetic transcription. The census of 1880 listed a forty-eight-year-old Chinese farm laborer as John Philip. His family and circle of friends, however, knew him as Philip Wong, Sr.[16] His descendants use the surname Wong. Fol-

13. Edgar Wickberg, *The Chinese in Philippine Life, 1850–1898* (New Haven, 1965), 31–34; Maurice Freedman, *The Study of Chinese Society: Essays by Maurice Freedman* (Stanford, 1979), 84–92.
14. Ninth Census, 1870, Natchitoches Parish, Louisiana, Population Schedule.
15. Tenth Census, 1880, Natchitoches Parish, Louisiana, Population Schedule.
16. Interview with Nathaneal Wong, Sr., April, 1976.

lowing Chinese custom, Wong probably gave his name as Wong Philip, and the enumerator listed him as John, a name commonly given to Chinese newcomers to the United States.

Another practice was to adopt parts of the name of a local family, such as that of relatives of a spouse, or to combine the name of the family hiring the immigrant with a name used upon entry. This pattern can be seen in the family of Carlos Potillas, who became known as Carlos or Charles Telsis. He was listed as Carlos in the 1870 census, and he worked for Severin and Marcellite Trichel. Carlos married Mary Adeline Padilla, a local resident who was a member of a Spanish family. Descendants report that members of some branches of the Padilla family also intermarried with Indians.[17]

Catholic church registers chronicle some of the modifications that took place in the wife's and children's surnames. Mary Adeline Padilla's last name was modified to Padie, Padee, or Pardee. Her grandchildren and other descendants remembered her as a "Spanish lady whose name was 'Miss Odelle' or 'Miss Adele.' "

Carlos and Mary Adeline had four children—Joseph, Charles, Marcellite, and Julia. The registers of Catholic church rites for these children show that the last name Telsis came into use over time. In the early 1870s, the father, Carlos, was also listed as Charles or Karl Potillas. His son Joseph was baptized as Joseph Telsite Potillas. There were planters in the area who used Telsite as a first or middle name; it was also used by some of Mary Adeline's relatives. Carlos and Mary Adeline's daughter, Mary Marcellite, was baptized in 1878, and her last name was recorded as Potillas.[18] Throughout their adult lives, Mary Marcellite and her brother Joseph used different versions of their last names. Joseph became known as Joseph Virgis Telsede and his sister became known as Marcellite Telsee.

In the decade of the 1880s, the children increasingly used the name Telsede or Telsite as a surname, although the church continued to list their father as Carlos Potillas. By 1900, the name Potillas no longer

17. Ninth Census, 1870, Natchitoches Parish, Louisiana, Population Schedule; Interview, confidential source, May, 1977.

18. Record of baptism of Joseph Telsite, December 18, 1872, Record of baptism of Mary Marcellite Potillas, July 1, 1878, both in Church of the Nativity, Campti, Louisiana, Record of Baptisms, Burials, and Marriages, 1860–1914.

appeared on records. The surname Telsis, with such variations as Telsea, Telside, Telsede, Telsiad, Telcide, Telsa, Telsite, and Telsee, had been fully adopted by the various branches of the descendants of the original couple. These variations are still used.

The Chinese introduced from Cuba to Natchitoches brought no spouses. There were no Chinese women in Natchitoches, and the first generation of men married or established households with white, black, Creole, and Indian women.[19] The granddaughter of one of these Chinese said: "They settled down and some of them had children and some of them didn't. They married all kinds of people . . . Creoles, blacks, whites. Some of them married; others at first just 'took up' with their wives. They were a very 'mixed nation.'"[20]

Hilario Hongo, for example, married Azelie Phillip, who was classified as black in the 1870 census although she was really Indian. Carlos Telsis married Mary Adeline Padilla, who was a white woman of Spanish ancestry. Philip Wong's wife, Lillie James, was black. Cecile Grappe, Philip Chaplin's wife, was Creole.

Family accounts reveal that Azelie Phillip Hongo, Dr. Hongo's wife, was taken to Oklahoma when Indians were removed from Louisiana. A descendant remembered hearing that "when they drove the Indians away to Oklahoma, Azelie was taken." This woman's classification as black in the 1870 census was not unusual in Louisiana. Gary B. Mills, who has discussed the practice of classifying persons of Indian background as black, writes, "Because of the ambiguity of the Indian's position in colonial Louisiana, and because of the forced emancipation of Indian slaves in the 1780s, some confusion has existed as to whether certain individuals were of Indian or Negro descent." He found persons classified in civil records in one racial category such as

19. The term *creole* was used in Natchitoches to refer to persons native to the area, who were of French and Spanish background with admixture of Negro. Sister Frances Jerome Woods indicates that the term is generally used in the Western Hemisphere to apply to native-born descendants of French or Spanish colonists, regardless of racial admixture. In the United States, the term is most commonly used in reference to the descendants of persons with French or Spanish extraction who were born in Louisiana. (Sister Frances Jerome Woods, *Marginality and Identity: A Colored Creole Family Through Ten Generations* [Baton Rouge, 1972], 7).

20. Interview, confidential source, May, 1977.

"mulattress" and in church registers in another such as an Indian of a specific tribal group.[21]

The children born into the families of the Chinese men who had married white, black, Creole, and Indian women were all classified as Chinese in the census of 1880. This second generation also chose partners of varied backgrounds, as is illustrated by the Hongo and Telsis families.

Dr. Hongo and Azelie had five children, Eli, Joseph, Victoria, Mary, and John, all of whom remained in the area until their deaths. Eli, nicknamed Buddy, is not known to have married. Joseph married Marcellite Telsee, who was also half Chinese. Victoria married Joe Lee, a full Chinese, who had been born in California. Mary married Overton Perot, a member of a Creole family. John married Hattie Chapman, a black woman, and moved to the neighboring parish of Rapides.

The oldest son of Carlos Telsis and Mary Adeline Padilla, Joseph Telsede, married Mary Lee Aires, a black, who was a member of a family long resident in the Bayou Bourbeux area. Charles, Jr., married Virginia Prudhomme, a local Creole. Marcellite married Joseph Hongo, who was half-Chinese. Julia never married but lived in the home of her sister Marcellite for most of her life.

The censuses listed the occupations of most of the descendants of the second generation as farm laborer or farmer. Some, however, had a range of skills. Dr. Hilario Hongo, listed in the census as a farm laborer, was a healer who obtained certification as a physician in 1882. Marcellite Telsee, daughter of Carlos Telsis, was a household manager and a midwife and was noted for skilled sewing and quilting. Her descendants suggested that her interest in midwifery came from Dr. Hongo's medical practice and her own father's interest in herbal medicine.

Joseph Virgis Telsede, oldest son of Carlos Telsis, worked as a farmer but had a reputation as a skillful coffin and casket maker. He was also well known for his religious convictions. Although he had been baptized in the Catholic church, he became a founding member and a

21. Gary B. Mills, *The Forgotten People: Cane River's Creoles of Color* (Baton Rouge, 1977), 86–87.

First generation: Dr. Hilario Hongo, Chinese physician who immigrated to Natchitoches from Cuba in 1867.
COURTESY ORA HONGO MIXON

Second and third generations: Joseph Virgis
Telsede, son of Carlos Telsis, a Chinese
immigrant from Cuba, and Odelle Padilla
Telsis, a native of Louisiana, with Joseph, Jr.,
his son, in about 1911.
COURTESY ODELL HAYES

hird generation: Mary Lee Aires Telsede, a
ative of Louisiana and wife of Joseph Virgis
Telsede, with her daughter Octavia, third-
eneration Chinese, in about 1911.
OURTESY ODELL HAYES

Third generation: Lillie Mae Telsede
Williams, daughter of Joseph Virgis Telsede
and Mary Lee Aires Telsede, in 1979.
PHOTOGRAPH BY THE AUTHOR

Third generation: Octavia Telsede Grayson
daughter of Joseph Virgis Telsede and Mary
Lee Aires Telsede, in 1978.
PHOTOGRAPH BY THE AUTHOR

Third generation: Ora Conant, daughter of
Mary Hongo Perot and Overton Perot,
granddaughter of Dr. Hilario Hongo and
Azelie Phillip Hongo, in the early 1940s.
COURTESY MARY CHEVALIER

Second and third generations: Marcellite Telsee Hongo, daughter of Carlos Telsis and Odelle Padilla Telsis, with her three sons, Moise (*below left*), Zenon (*above left*), and Earnest (*above right*), in 1956.

Third and fourth generations: Earnest Hongo with his daughter Ora Hongo Mixon in 1979.
COURTESY ORA HONGO MIXON

Third and fourth generations: Moise Hongo with his wife, Ida Pickett Hongo (*below center*), and their daughters, Dorothy (*left*) and Oritha (*above center*), in 1944.
COURTESY ORITHA HONGO DUREL

Fifth generation: Valerie Durel, daughter of Oritha Hongo Durel and Joseph N. Durel, Jr., in 1970.

COURTESY ORITHA HONGO DUREL

Third, fourth, and fifth generations: David Telsee (*center*), grandson of Carlos Telsis and Odelle Padilla Telsis, with his wife, Rosa Mae Jackson Telsee (*second from right*), in 1976. Others pictured are, *left to right*, Frank Rachal, their son-in-law, Tyrone Rachal, their grandson, and their children Barbara Ann Telsee and Patricia Telsee.

COURTESY ROSA MAE JACKSON TELSEE

Fourth generation: Hury Lee Telsee, daughter of David Telsee and Rosa Mae Jackson Telsee, in 1976.
COURTESY ROSA MAE JACKSON TELSEE

Fifth generation: Tyrone Rachal (*left*), son of Bessie Ann Telsee Rachal and Frank Rachal, with Monica Farley (*above right*) and Kitha Farley (*below right*), daughters of Edith Telsee Farley and Roy Farley, in 1976.
COURTESY ROSA MAE JACKSON TELSEE

deacon in Mount Pilgrim Baptist Church in Bayou Bourbeux, which served the local black community. According to accounts of his descendants, the Mount Pilgrim church was established by the black families of Choctaw Island, south of Bayou Bourbeux, as that community had grown and needed a nearby church. Other second-generation Chinese were active leaders in their churches. Philip Wong, Jr., was a prominent preacher in his community. Marcellite and Julia Telsee were lifelong participants in the activities of Catholic church associations.[22]

In urban areas of the United States the Chinese developed business and commercial establishments. Few in Natchitoches did so. Joe Lee, a California-born second-generation Chinese, who married Victoria Hongo, established a laundry. In the early period of Chinese settlement, there were no Chinese restaurants in Natchitoches, but Dier Sudick, a Chinese who had probably moved from Natchitoches to neighboring Rapides Parish, opened one in the city of Alexandria in that parish. Dier Sudick was remembered by a resident of Isle Brevelle in Natchitoches Parish, Cora Marinovich Balthazar, who as a child in 1900 had boarded for several years with the Sudick family when she had been sent away to school in Alexandria. Dier Sudick had married Stella Jones, a friend of the Marinovich family. Mrs. Balthazar recalled that she and other children in Alexandria looked on the Chinese with curiosity and that adults remarked that Sudick and his Chinese companions were hardworking. On weekends Sudick and his family often visited his in-laws at Isle Brevelle.[23]

In the third generation, as in the second, intermarriage occurred, although some married people of Chinese ancestry. Irma Perot, one of the daughters of Mary Hongo and Overton Perot, married Felix Chaplin, son of the Chinese Philip Chaplin (nicknamed Matassa) and Cecile Grappe (nicknamed Sis). Ora Perot, another daughter of Overton Perot and Mary Hongo, married Willie Conant, a Creole. The marriage witnesses were Felix Chaplin and Alphonse Balthazar.[24] The latter was the son of Baltosar, a Chinese from Cuba. Baltosar was his

22. Interviews with Octavia Telsede Grayson, May, 1977, August, 1978; Interview with Nathaneal Wong, Sr., April, 1976; Interviews with Ora Hongo Mixon, April 1976, July, 1982.

23. Interviews with Cora Marinovich Balthazar, April, 1976, May, 1977.

24. Interview with confidential source, April, 1978; Earnest Hongo to the author,

Spanish first name, and he was recorded as being among Chinese imported by Jules Normand in 1867.[25] Following common practice, this first name became a surname.

Intermarriage was a path through which the descendants of the Chinese merged into the existing groups in society. Official census classification by color shows how the second generation of Chinese was viewed. The impact of these changes on the descendants and on the interpretation of population statistics of Chinese in the United States has not been a subject of scholarly discussion.

Persons of mixed Chinese ancestry in the United States were not classified in specific color categories as were blacks and Indians at certain times. Gary B. Mills points out, for example, that Louisiana had a distinctive and complex classification for Creoles of African descent, with special terminology to denote nonwhites' ratio of Negro blood to Caucasian blood. The most common classifications in the colonial and antebellum periods were Negro (full Negro blood), sacatra (seven-eighths Negro, one-eighth white), griffe (three-fourths Negro, one-fourth white), mulatto (half Negro, half white), quadroon (one-fourth Negro, three-fourths white), and octoroon (one-eighth Negro, seven-eighths white). In the seventh census of the United States (1850), enumerators were instructed to use the color categories white, black, and mulatto. The mulatto category included quadroons, octoroons, and all persons with any perceptible trace of African blood. In 1890 the word *black* was used in the census to describe persons who were three-fourths or more black; *mulatto*, those persons who were three-eighths to five-eighths black; *quadroon*, those persons who were one-fourth black; and *octoroon*, those persons who were one-eighth or had any trace of black blood. Indians were classified as full-bloods of their own tribe, mixed bloods with another tribe, mixture with white, mixture with black, mixture with mulatto, white person adopted into a tribe, and Negro or mulatto adopted into a tribe.[26]

No term existed, however, to designate the native-born descendant

March 7, 1976; Record of marriage of Willie Conant and Ora Perot, May 12, 1908, in Immaculate Conception Church, Natchitoches, Louisiana, Book 14, Marriage Records, 1902–38.

25. New Orleans *Bee*, January 16, 1867.

26. Mills, *The Forgotten People*, xiii–xiv; Wright, *History of the Census*, 154–57.

of a Chinese who was of a mixed Chinese-native ancestry. Other areas of the world had such terms. In the Philippine Islands, for example, Chinese mestizos were formally and legally recognized as a separate group. According to Wickberg, the son of a Chinese father and an indio or mestiza mother was classified as a Chinese mestizo. Subsequent male descendants were Chinese mestizos. The status of female descendants was determined by their marriages. A mestiza marrying a Chinese or mestizo remained in the mestizo classification, as did her children. But by marrying an indio, she and her children joined that classification.[27]

In the absence of a separate color category for the Chinese before the census of 1870, the group was classified as white. Statistics on the Chinese in California for 1860 were obtained through a special count, and this total is usually quoted erroneously as the total number of Chinese in the United States at that time. In the 1870 census, enumerators were instructed to use the separate category Chinese for all persons of that ancestry. There were no special instructions for classifying children born to a Chinese man and a non-Chinese woman. Nevertheless, in 1880, the census enumerators in Natchitoches Parish classified as Chinese the Hongo and Telsis children and all the other children of Chinese men married to non-Chinese women.

This categorization of the children of a Chinese man and a non-Chinese wife as Chinese, however, was not uniform throughout the state of Louisiana. In New Orleans, as discussed in Chapter 6, all but one of the married Chinese men listed in the 1880 census had white wives. Some of their children were classified as white; others were listed as Chinese. For one family, the census enumerator reclassified the children from white to Chinese. The child of the Chinese man married to a black woman was classified as mulatto.[28]

In 1900, the color category used for second generation was changed. A review of all population schedules for Natchitoches Parish in 1880

27. Edgar Wickberg, "The Chinese Mestizo in Philippine History," *Journal of Southeast Asian History*, V (March, 1964), 65–66.

28. Tenth Census, 1880, New Orleans, Louisiana, Population Schedule; U.S. Department of the Interior, *Ninth Census of the United States, 1870: Population and Social Statistics*, Vol. I (1872), xii–xvii; Ninth Census, 1870, Natchitoches Parish, Louisiana, Population Schedule.

and 1900 shows that the same people who were listed as Chinese in the 1880 census were given different color classifications two decades later. In 1900, for example, the children of Carlos Potillas, also known as Charles Telsis, and Mary Adeline Padilla, who had been classified as Chinese in the 1880 census, were listed as black. The children of Dr. Hongo and Azelie Phillip were also categorized as black. Indeed, the entire second generation who had been listed as Chinese in 1880 was classified as either black or white. The only persons listed as Chinese in Natchitoches Parish were those who had been born in China or those born of Chinese parents in the United States, such as Joe Lee, the California-born Chinese who married Victoria Hongo.[29]

The census enumerators who worked in New Orleans followed practices somewhat similar to those in Natchitoches. The category Chinese was designated for people born in China or people born in the United States with two Chinese parents. Census enumerators in New Orleans, moreover, reclassified some Chinese as white, as illustrated by a few instances on the census schedules in which the designation "Chinese" after a name was crossed out and the classification "white" entered. A few other Chinese men were simply listed as white.[30]

Because these changes in color classification reflected shifts in the public concept of the Chinese who had intermarried, it is important to examine how changing classifications affected public perception and influenced the cultural identity of descendants. Some "passed" into white society, others merged into the black communities, and a few took advantage of "Mexican/Indian" categories to be considered white in some situations or black in others. Nevertheless, all retained a vague sense of Chinese ancestry even though branches of the same family had adopted separate values and identities and had grown apart.

Some of the descendants of the Chinese from Cuba who settled in Natchitoches Parish believe that war in China led their ancestors to move to Louisiana and eventually to their parish. The great-granddaughter of Dr. Eli Hongo said, "I used to hear grandmother [Marcellite Telsee] talk all the time about young Chinese who had come over from the war; they were fighters; she said they were tired

---

29. Twelfth Census, 1900, Natchitoches, Louisiana, Population Schedule.
30. *Ibid.*

of fighting." The granddaughter of Philip Wong, another Chinese from Cuba, stated: "My grandfather [Philip Wong] and his people used to talk to their children about the fact that they [Chinese] came over in the wartime; that's why they had been scattered about and come to this country. It was hard times."[31]

These comments may have referred to the participation by Chinese laborers in rebellions and insurrections in Cuba or to the aftermath of the Civil War in Louisiana. It is possible that these accounts stemmed from the conditions of hardship in China at the time the emigrants departed for Cuba. The Taiping Rebellion (1851–1864) had stimulated emigration from the villages of the Pearl River delta in South China to the overseas communities of Southeast Asia and the Americas.[32]

Oral tradition does not mention that the Chinese ancestors came from Cuba. Some descendants had heard that their forebears came from Mexico, but most believed that they had entered directly from the "old country," China. The idea of a Mexican origin may have been linked with the traces of Hispanic culture the Cuban Chinese brought with them, as well as with perceived similarities in physical appearance.

Three major concepts of cultural identity were important to the descendants of Chinese in Natchitoches. They knew they belonged in a clearly distinct category. Some grandchildren of the Chinese settlers remembered them as the "old ones," who were called "Chinese" and looked "Chinese." As one granddaughter of a Chinese stated: "They didn't call them nothing but Chinese; I remember that —— and others also called them Chinese. They called the old folks Chinese, not the young ones." This same descendant laughingly recalled that all those Chinese "from the old country looked alike." When she was growing up, they all had "short hair." One friend who visited from "far away" wore a "long braid." She had felt pangs of sadness when this Chinese visitor had given her a silk handkerchief upon his departure for the "old country."[33]

The children of the Chinese who settled in the parish and some of their grandchildren who were of mixed ancestry were occasionally

31. Interview with Ora Hongo Mixon, April, 1976; Interviews with Mary Graham, April, 1976, May, 1977.
32. Barth, *Bitter Strength*, 25–31.
33. Interviews with confidential source, May, 1977, August, 1978.

classified as Mexican. These descendants consciously used this assignation of Mexican identity to pass as white and to become submerged in white society. Those who have passed do not acknowledge their Creole, black, or Chinese background.

The grandson of one of the Chinese, whose ancestry was mixed, vividly recalled his own views of the dynamics of his cultural identity and its use in social interaction. In one of my visits to the sites of settlement and work of his Chinese ancestor, he recalled scenes of his childhood and youth and his own contacts in and out of the white world in settings that were closed to blacks: "Up in this area, they didn't allow any colored people, but my father traveled all through here with us when we were little and we could go through any time we were ready. They never bothered us." As a young adult, this man traveled through these towns again. He was allowed to enter stores that had "white only" signs on the doors. Some of his kin were worried that his boldness might cause him harm because community residents had a reputation for putting nonwhite trespassers in prison. "People called me crazy because I used to go to some of those places myself when I would be traveling. It would say 'white only,' and a cousin would say, 'You're cool, don't you see that it says, "White only?"'" He told his cousin that after paying for his purchase, he had thanked the owners and they invited him to come back again. This man believes that most people categorized him as a Mexican, although some took him for an Indian. He never discussed his mixed heritage in public. To him, a Mexican was one who could "pass for what he wants." Some "passed for white," and some "passed for colored."[34]

Some of this man's relatives have passed as white, and they deny kinship ties with his branch of the family. He has made a conscious decision, however, to remain with the "colored community, rather than to pass for white." In his words: "I could have passed [for white]. But I know I had colored in me and I wouldn't try to pass for white. Plenty of people told me, 'You're just a damn fool. You go where they feed you, and then, you won't pass. I'd go ahead.' I said, 'Yeah.' I said, 'You can go ahead but I know what's best.' I said, 'I can make a living

34. Interviews with confidential source, May, 1977, August, 1978.

just as good as the other white man. All I have to use is my head. And I know how to use my head.'"[35]

As the Chinese heritage has become submerged through time and in view of the values and norms that shape race relations in Natchitoches, it is understandable, perhaps, that the public appears to have forgotten the Chinese who entered the area over a century ago. In private discussions and during periods of conflict, however, the descendants of Chinese have kept alive the fact of their Chinese ancestry. Past heritage comes to the fore when conflicts, normally hidden from the public, take place, as in an incident described by the granddaughter of a Chinese settler who had intermarried. One branch of this settler's descendants passed for white, and denial of kinship with her family has precipitated conflicts between them. This woman described an incident that took place between children of the families when one of her sons was in his youth: "Years ago, my boy became involved in a fight with a 'white' boy. The white playmate suddenly yelled 'nigger' at my boy. That made me angry, and I told him: 'My daddy and your daddy are first cousins, you half-white b——— . Our grandparents were Chinese and Creole.'" The woman remarked that the boy never returned to her home. She observed with amusement and anger that her own child was lighter skinned than the boy who had insulted him.[36]

Specific forces had a profound impact on the social organization and the course of settlement of Chinese in the region. Several factors militated against the retention of a distinct cultural identity among the descendants of the Chinese who first entered Natchitoches. Descendants of the second and third generations remained in the parish but lived in a dispersed settlement pattern rather than in "Chinatowns" such as were found in towns and cities. The Chinese language was abandoned by the first generation. Surnames were changed, and even among brothers and sisters names varied. There were no formal associations based on occupation such as merchant guilds and commercial houses. Children of intermarriage had physical features that were not clearly Chinese, and they typically became identified with the groups

35. *Ibid.*
36. Interviews with confidential source, May, 1977, April, 1978.

already established in the parish such as Indians, Mexicans, Creoles, blacks, and whites.

Finally, official documents such as the United States census recorded for posterity an ambivalence about the cultural identity of the children of Chinese who married out. When the twentieth century dawned, these children, who had previously been classified as Chinese, were de facto given a new official color classification in the census that erased their Chinese identity from history. But in the pluralistic society of Natchitoches, which had long harbored a rich mosaic of cultural traditions filled with positive and negative evaluations, memories of the presence of individual Chinese and of their descendants were kept alive. The wisdom of these family historians was drawn upon to reconstruct this neglected chapter in Chinese ethnohistory and thus enrich our understanding of the dynamics of race relations in an embattled period in the South.

# CONCLUSION

After the Civil War, as new patterns in the organization of southern labor were developed to address the demands of a postemancipation society, enterprising men in plantations and large-scale public works introduced Chinese hired under contract to replace the Negroes. Their knowledge of the use of Chinese labor in the British, French, and Spanish colonies of the West Indies led southerners to this alternative to fill the labor vacuum created by the end of slavery.

Residents of the South had come in contact with Chinese in the 1840s and 1850s, when southern missionaries brought some Chinese companions when they made visits back to their local communities. These long-braided men from a distant land roused intense curiosity even though, as subjects for possible conversion to Christianity, they did not fit the image of the uneducated "heathen" who were becoming the target of Christian foreign mission concern. Elements of Chinese civilization as expressed by these visitors commanded respect from both the missionaries and the southerners who saw the Chinese.

By contrast, little attention was paid to the individuals and small groups of Chinese who during this early period had settled permanently in the South and in eastern seaboard cities. Unlike the transient visitors who accompanied the missionaries, these established residents had settled, for the most part, among populations of foreign-born white immigrants. Census officials did not enumerate them as a separate racial type. In the countryside and towns of California, however, thousands of Chinese immigrants were a conspicuous presence and became subject to differentiation and segregation on the basis of their appearance and color.

Furthermore, diplomats and consular officers, who were expected to distinguish between a Chinese coolie laborer and an emigrant who traveled independently, helped shape American opinion about the Chinese. In their search for legal means to avoid American involvement in the notorious coolie traffic, these officials reviewed statutes controlling the slave trade. The attorney general's office gave the opinion that a statute addressed to blacks could not be applied to Chinese and thus laid the basis for the subsequent classification of Chinese as a separate race. After the Civil War, the views formed by earlier government officials were partially responsible for the belief that freedmen and white European immigrants rather than Chinese should be recruited as laborers for the South.

Nevertheless, experiments with Chinese labor did take place in the post–Civil War South. The cultural and social organization of the Chinese in the South differed from that found in the work camps and Chinatowns that had encapsulated the Chinese in California into self-enclosed communities. In the South, they were not typically bound by the strict norms and sanctions of commercial houses and their networks of intermediaries and agents, which were characteristic of California. Unlike their countrymen in the western United States, who came almost exclusively from a few districts of the province of Kwangtung, China, the Chinese in the South came as single men, in small groups, not only from China, but also from the Philippines, Cuba, other West Indian islands, New York, Philadelphia, and California. Their widely scattered origins explain the organization of flexible work groups within which individuals adapted and changed according to the circumstances of their conditions of work and social life.

These Chinese did, however, retain cultural patterns and practices such as the celebration of the Chinese New Year and the observance of rituals associated with funerals. Within the work groups, the traditional roles of cooks, practitioners of Chinese medicine, and tea servers were filled. The peddler who carried his wares across communities served as a major source of information and thereby strengthened bonds among the scattered Chinese groups.

The central unifying link of the work group with the outside society was the Chinese interpreter. Although hired by non-Chinese employers to serve as translator and alternatively as headman, he also acted as representative for the Chinese and as advocate for their interests. The interpreter, who in most cases had been trained in schools organized by Christian missionaries, understood both the world of Chinese tradition and that of the non-Chinese employers. He helped to maintain control within the Chinese work group and was also a skilled negotiator when conflict threatened employer-laborer relations. Under adverse circumstances, the interpreter was a leader of protest. Indeed, as he became increasingly involved in advocacy roles for his countrymen, he emerged as a central figure who led the Chinese out of the plantations and other sites of first arrival to new areas of settlement and work.

Problems in interpreting and carrying out labor contracts between the Chinese and their employers contributed to the demise of these experiments. The negative reactions of federal authorities to the idea of Chinese workers supplying labor for the South also militated against their widespread use. In the postemancipation colonial societies of the West Indies, upon which southerners had first modeled their experiments with Chinese, planters and public officials had agreed that they were needed to supplement the work force of emancipated Negroes. In the South, by contrast, federal officials always opposed such a move. Even after southern leaders obtained favorable legal interpretations in support of their efforts to introduce the Chinese, national officials remained suspicious that they were attempting to introduce a new form of slavery.

Furthermore, the Chinese were not a source of cheap labor. The impoverished planters and merchants who had hoped to find in the Chinese a solution to the adverse economic conditions that they faced during Reconstruction did not have the capital required to recruit Chinese. The few planters and speculators who did have capital found problems in retaining the Chinese for the duration of a three-year contract.

Finally, the basic difference in their orientations to work and the management of work groups set Chinese and their employers apart. Although radical changes in the relations between employers and workers could be expected during the Reconstruction period, planters continued to attempt to exercise strong control over their laborers. They expected to be able to change terms of contracts without consultation or negotiation with workers. The intentions of the employers were diametrically opposed to the Chinese expectation of negotiation through their own intermediaries. The experiment with Chinese contract labor gave evidence, on the one hand, of the struggle of planters to maintain values and a system of social organization that they were convinced would assure the survival of the plantation system and, on the other hand, the determination of Chinese to retain their own norms about work and the inviolability of contracts.

After the Chinese moved from the places of first employment to scattered sharecropping sites or locations in towns and cities, few symbols of their culture remained except Chinese stores. The stores provided outsiders with a range of goods and services. Chinese merchants in local communities were highly visible, and, like the interpreters who had preceded them, they became spokesmen for their fellow Chinese.

The Chinese store was owned and operated by the Chinese and served as a center of social exchange as well as a supplier of goods and special services. Typically, the store as a cultural institution was a mirror that reflected two sets of images. One set of images was turned toward the outsiders—the curious customers—who admired its imported goods and exotic products. The second set was turned to the Chinese, who sought the staples for everyday consumption and the social bonds.

In time, the Chinese who remained in the region and their descendants were forgotten, in part because no single standard of classification for them evolved. In the post–Civil War years, the South reaffirmed its view of the superiority of Caucasians over blacks. A complex system of classification delineated whites, blacks, Indians, Creoles, and Mexicans. Chinese newcomers appeared to the white southerners to look like a mixture of these long-established groups. Subsequently, the affiliation of the Chinese men with these groups through marriage and residence in the wife's community hastened the processes through which they disappeared from the attention of the public. With few or no Chinese women available, the first and succeeding generations blended through intermarriage with previously recognized ethnic groups. They became truly a "mixed nation."

# APPENDIX I

## AN ACT TO PROHIBIT THE "COOLIE TRADE" BY AMERICAN CITIZENS IN AMERICAN VESSELS

FEBRUARY 19, 1862

*Be it enacted by the Senate and House of Representatives of the United States of America in Congress assembled,* That no citizen or citizens of the United States, or foreigner coming into or residing within the same, shall, for himself or for any other person whatsoever, either as master, factor, owner, or otherwise, build, equip, load, or otherwise prepare, any ship or vessel, or any steamship or steam-vessel, registered, enrolled, or licensed, in the United States, or any port within the same, for the purpose of procuring from China, or from any port or place therein, or from any other port or place the inhabitants or subjects of China, known as "coolies," to be transported to any foreign country, port, or place whatever, to be disposed of, or sold, or transferred, for any term of years or for any time whatever, as servants or apprentices, or to be held to service or labor. And if any ship or vessel, steamship, or steam-vessel, belonging in whole or in part to citizens of the United States, and registered, enrolled, or otherwise licensed as aforesaid, shall be employed for the said purposes, or in the "coolie trade," so called, or shall be caused to procure or carry from China or elsewhere, as aforesaid, any subjects of the Government of China for the purpose of transporting or disposing of them as aforesaid, every such ship or vessel, steamship, or steam-vessel, her tackle, apparel, furniture, and other appurtenances, shall be forfeited to the United States, and shall be liable to be seized, prosecuted, and condemned in any of the circuit courts or district courts of the United States for the district where the said ship or vessel, steamship, or steam-vessel, may be found seized, or carried.

SEC. 2. *And be it further enacted,* That every person who shall so build, fit out, equip, load, or otherwise prepare, or who shall send to sea, or navigate, as owner, master, factor, agent, or otherwise, any ship or vessel, steamship, or steam-vessel, belonging in whole or in part to citizens of the United States or registered, enrolled, or licensed within the same, or at any port thereof, knowing or intending that the same shall be employed in that trade or business aforesaid, contrary to the true intent and meaning of this act, or in anywise aiding or abetting therein, shall be severally liable to be indicted therefor, and, on conviction thereof, shall be liable to a fine not exceeding two thousand dollars and be imprisoned not exceeding one year.

SEC. 3. *And be it further enacted*, That if any citizen or citizens of the United States shall, contrary to the true intent and meaning of this act, take on board of any vessel, or receive or transport any such persons as are above described in this act, for the purpose of disposing of them as aforesaid, he or they shall be liable to be indicted therefor, and, on conviction thereof, shall be liable to a fine not exceeding two thousand dollars and be imprisoned not exceeding one year.

SEC. 4. *And be it further enacted*, That nothing in this act hereinbefore contained shall be deemed or construed to apply to or affect any free and voluntary emigration of any Chinese subject, or to any vessel carrying such person as passenger on board the same: *Provided, however*, That a permit or certificate shall be prepared and signed by the consul or consular agent of the United States residing at the port from which such vessel may take her departure, containing the name of such person, and setting forth the fact of his voluntary emigration from such port or place, which certificate shall be given to the master of such vessel; but the same shall not be given until such consul or consular agent shall be first personally satisfied by evidence produced of the truth of the facts therein contained.

SEC. 5. *And be it further enacted*, That all the provisions of the act of Congress approved February twenty-second, eighteen hundred and forty-seven, entitled "An act to regulate the carriage of passengers in merchant vessels," and all the provisions of the act of Congress approved March third, eighteen hundred and forty-nine, entitled "An act to extend the provisions of all laws now in force relating to the carriage of passengers in merchant vessels and the regulation thereof," shall be extended and shall apply to all vessels owned in whole or in part by citizens of the United States, and registered, enrolled, or licensed within the United States, propelled by wind or by steam, and to all masters thereof, carrying passengers or intending to carry passengers from any foreign port or place without the United States to any other foreign port or place without the United States; and that all penalties and forfeitures provided for in said act shall apply to vessels and masters last aforesaid.

SEC. 6. *And be it further enacted*, That the President of the United States shall be, and he is hereby, authorized and empowered, in such way and at such time as he shall judge proper to the end that the provisions of this act may be enforced according to the true intent and meaning thereof, to direct and order the vessels of the United States, and the masters and commanders thereof, to examine all vessels navigated or owned in whole or in part by citizens of the United States, and registered, enrolled, or licensed under the laws of the United States, wherever they may be, whenever, in the judgment of such master or commanding officer thereof, reasonable cause shall exist to believe that such vessel has on board, in violation of the provisions of this act, any subjects of China known as "coolies," for the purpose of transportation; and upon sufficient proof that such vessel is employed in violation of the provisions of this act, to cause such vessel to be carried, with her officers and crew, into any port or district within the United States, and delivered to the marshal of such district, to be held and disposed of according to the provisions of this act.

SEC. 7. *And be it further enacted,* That this act shall take effect from and after six months from the day of its passage.

# APPENDIX II
## AGREEMENT BETWEEN CHINESE LABORERS
## AND KOOPMANSCHAP AND COMPANY

This Agreement, entered into between _____ Labor _____ , native of China, and KOOPMANSCHAP & CO as agents for *Edward J. Gay of Louisiana and William T. Gay of Missouri* .

We, whose names are hereunto affixed, agree to labor *faithfully & satisfactorily* upon the following terms:

1st. We agree to work for *William T. Gay & E. J. Gay* or *their* assigns, for the period of *three (3)* years, beginning the day after our arrival at *their plantation in Louisiana*, for which we are to be paid by said *William T. Gay or Edward J. Gay* or their assigns, at the rate of *Sixteen (16)* dollars U. S. Gold Coin for each man, per month of twenty-six days, payable monthly.

2d. A free passage is to be given to us to *their plantations in Louisiana* and at the end of this contract, a free passage back to San Francisco, and all advance amounting to *$16* , in gold, we hereby obligate to pay out of our first wages or earnings.

3d. We are to be furnished by our employers under this contract, with sufficient provision, consisting of rice, pork, fish or beef, vegetables and tea, water, fuel, good quarters and weather-proof sleeping places, free of charge.

4th. All tools and implements to be furnished by our employers under this contract.

5th. We agree to work ten hours per day. *Night work to be paid 8¢ per hour.*

6th. No labor to be required of us on Sunday.

7th. If any of us *usually* fall sick or are injured so that he is unable to work, wages are to cease till he resumes work, but provisions are to be furnished at the expense of our employers. *for a reasonable length of time.*

In Witness Whereof, we subscribe our names to this contract, in duplicate, in this City of San Francisco, this *8th* day of *Oct* , 1870.

*Signed on other side by men. Accepted on arrival in Louisiana Oct 29 1870 for such as come to my place.* *Edward J. Gay*

180

許杰　Yu kid ＄50
許釵　Yu choy ＄24
許喜隆　Yu hee ＄24
許淼　Yu loong ＄24
許森　Yu sum ＄24
許連　Yu lin ＄24
許和開　Yu wo hoey ＄24
許華慶　Yu wa hing ＄24
譚年　Tam nin ＄24
譚其　Tam kee ＄24
譚達克　Tam yuk ＄24
卓安　Chick on ＄24
梁舉　Ran away first Chuml by Kee Oo ＄24
李貴　Lee Dai ＄24
林　Lum hing
周中　Chu ming ＄16
蔡簪

賴周　Lai chow
福桔保滿棠栗志容　Fook
陳隆　Chun long
羅羅　Lo lo
張張　Cheung cheung
馮騤　Fung koey
庚　Kang
何　Ho
顏越李羅　Gan
情懷福容灘

×Lee fook ＄16
√Chow hun ＄16
√Chun po ＄16
√Ting moon ＄16
√So chow ＄16
√So sook ＄16
√Chung chee ＄16
√Chung yong ＄16
√Tong ngow ＄16
√Sok kong ＄16
√Sue wa ＄16
√Ho jim ＄16
Gan ching
√Suet wng ＄16
Lee fook ＄16
√So yong ＄16
Lee Gue ＄16
√So wo sum

魏玉　Gai Yuk ＄16
亞二　Ah gee ＄16
林轎　Lum Lu ＄21
貴李義　Lee Guai ＄16
　Lee ＄16
　Gai sun ＄16
望　Guan ching ＄16
業　Chu sun
陳成　Chun sing ＄16
麥倫義　Mek lun ＄16
傅祿　Fun look
黎田　Lai
羅祥
陳南
程毓醇　Jook chow ＄25
倫　26
　Wong hin ×

× Thin 2 did not reach Omaha.

# NOTE ON SOURCES

Since the ethnohistory of the early Chinese in the South has received limited attention, the major sources for this study have been manuscripts, missionary accounts, letters, and church records. Newspapers and journals, public documents, contemporary accounts and studies, and accounts from oral tradition have also been of central importance. Although there are no written records by the early Chinese in the South, the interpreters who accompanied Chinese laborers, visitors, and agents of commercial houses offered impressions of the region and descriptions of the Chinese that were published in some newspapers and journals.

The following discussion of sources does not include all the items cited in the notes. It offers a critical assessment of the most important sources in various categories.

## I. MISSIONARY AND CHURCH SOURCES

Missionary reports, letters, and newspapers of the Protestant churches of the South were valuable sources of information. Many of these materials are found in denominational libraries and archives. The library of the Divinity School, Duke University, is rich with minutes, reports, and proceedings of state and regional conferences and conventions of the Christian churches. The records and summaries of the presbyteries of Louisiana, Mississippi, and New Orleans, found in the Historical Foundation of the Presbyterian and Reformed Churches, Montreat, North Carolina, contain helpful information, particularly on the ministry of Lena Saunders. The *Southwestern Presbyterian* offered newsworthy accounts as well as a wide range of reports and records.

Alexander Wylie's *Memorials of Protestant Missionaries to the Chinese: Giving a List of Their Publications, and Obituary Notices of the Deceased. With Copious Indexes* (Shanghai, 1867) is a reference work of value. The journal *Spirit of Missions* has useful accounts of the relations between missionaries and Chinese both in China and in the United States. Materials on the Southern Baptist foreign and domestic missions to the Chinese were consulted at the Virginia Historical Society, University of Richmond, and Southern Baptist Foreign Mission Board, Richmond. The *Religious Herald* published a number of contemporary accounts on Chinese life, as well as reprints of articles from local Southern Baptist associations. The portrait of Yong-Seen-Sang done in oil by an unknown artist (1845–1846?) in Richmond is found in the Virginia Baptist Historical Society. This is the earliest known oil portrait of a visitor from China to the United States.

Biographies and accounts of the lives of missionaries who dealt with issues of interest to the present work are few. They include the following: Jeremiah Bell Jeter, *A Memoir of Mrs. Henrietta Shuck, the First American Female Missionary to China* (Boston, 1850); Margaret M. Coughlin, "Strangers in the House: J. Lewis Shuck and Issachar Roberts, First American Baptist Missionaries in China" (Ph.D. dissertation, University of Virginia, 1972); Muriel Boone, *The Seed of the Church in China* (Philadelphia, 1973); and William Elliot Griffis, *A Maker of the Orient: Samuel Robbins Brown, Pioneer Educator in China, America, and Japan, the Story of His Life and Work* (New York, 1902).

H. Shelton Smith's scholarly publication, *In His Image, But . . . : Racism in Southern Religion, 1780–1910* (Durham, 1972), was the most valuable work I found on the evolution of Christian thought in the South with regard to white supremacy and various aspects of the race question. Among the denominational histories, those of use included the following: Henry A. Tupper (ed.), *The First Century of the First Baptist Church of Richmond, Virginia* (Richmond, 1880); James E. Bear, Jr., *The China Mission of the Presbyterian Church in the United States* (Richmond, 1965); Rufus B. Spain, *At Ease in Zion: Social History of Southern Baptists, 1865–1900* (Nashville, 1961); Albert Sidney Thomas, *A Historical Account of the Protestant Episcopal Church in South Carolina, 1820–1957, Being a Continuation of Dalcho's Account, 1670–1820* (Columbia, 1957); and Alexander C. Zabriskie (ed.), *Anglican Evangelicalism* (Philadelphia, 1943).

Nineteenth-century Roman Catholic parish records in Natchitoches Parish, Louisiana, which is part of the Diocese of Alexandria, provided helpful information on basic population and census data for Chinese and their descendants in that particular region.

## II. NEWSPAPERS AND JOURNALS

Newspapers provide a view of the context in which the recruitment of Chinese occurred as well as details about their coming and subsequent settlement. The political perspectives of newspaper editors and reporters during Reconstruction must be taken into account because they shaped the views put forth about Chinese laborers. For overall reporting, the most valuable newspapers include the Memphis *Daily Appeal*, New Orleans *Daily Picayune*, New York

*Journal of Commerce,* San Francisco *Daily Alta California,* St. Louis *Missouri Republican,* and Savannah *Morning News.* The foreign newspapers of importance to this research were the *London and China Telegraph* and the *Panama Star.* In addition to regular reporting, these newspapers frequently reproduced news items from local papers, which give important insights, although the dates and other identifying factors are not always correct.

Extant local newspapers are a rich reference source even if the files are incomplete. The following were particularly valuable: Abbeville *Le Meschacébé,* Baton Rouge *Weekly Advocate, Tri-Weekly Advocate, Tri-Weekly Gazette,* and *Comet,* Charleston *Daily News,* Donaldsonville *Chief,* Little Rock *Daily Arkansas Gazette,* Louisville *Daily Courier, Semi-Weekly Natchitoches Times* in French and English (title sometimes *Semi-Weekly Times*), New Iberia *Louisiana Sugar Bowl* in French and English (French title, *Le Sucrier de la Louisiane*), and New Orleans *Bee* in French and English (French title, *L'Abeille de la Nouvelle Orleans*).

Ads in newspapers were important sources of supplementary information for details concerning the recruitment, availability, and terms under which Chinese were hired and for information concerning the Chinese who went into business. Ads were an established medium for communication regarding the search for and availability of a work force, and they reflect a mode of popular expression.

A few journals were of special importance in the fields of commerce and agriculture. These include *De Bow's Review,* the *Rural Carolinian,* the *Southern Cultivator,* and the *Southern Farmer.*

### III. MANUSCRIPTS

Valuable information on southern experiments with Chinese labor may be found in a small group of papers, letters, and related records of plantations. These include the following: the Domestic and Foreign Missionary Society: China Records (1835–1875) in the Archives of the Episcopal Church, Austin, Texas; James Amédée Gaudet Papers, Gay-Price Papers, and George Washington Gift Letters at the University of North Carolina; Edward J. Gay Papers, Andrew Hynes Gay Papers, and Benjamin Tureaud Papers at Louisiana State University.

### IV. PUBLIC DOCUMENTS

A wide range of public documents in different branches and departments of government offered crucial data to understand how law and policy shaped the outcome of the Chinese movement. Records of the original returns of the federal census from 1850 to 1900 formed the basis for much of the discussion in Chapters 1 and 7 on the population of Chinese in the United States. The returns based on nativity and occupation, by state and county (or parish), are particularly useful. The problems with reliability of these data for enumeration of Chinese have been discussed in light of the lack of precise standards of classification for Chinese and their descendants. Carroll D. Wright and William C. Hunt's *The History and Growth of the United States Census* (Senate Document No. 194, 56th Cong. 1st Sess.) is a useful guide.

Consular and diplomatic correspondence of the United States, most of which is located in the National Archives, Washington, D.C., sheds light on the problems involved in recruitment of Chinese from foreign areas to the South. The quality of the correspondence and details vary by author, topic, and time period. The letters reflect much of the commercial as well as the political character of consular work. These State Department records, particularly Record Group 59, must be consulted along with the complementary correspondence—U.S. State Department, Letters Sent and Instructions to Consuls, as well as correspondence in the Departments of Justice and Treasury, found in Record Groups 56, 60, and 206.

The reports and correspondence of British officials in China, London, and the West Indian colonies found in the *British Parliamentary Papers* offer important perspectives on the international scope of the experiments with Chinese labor.

Further analysis of the rationale and arguments in favor of or in opposition to the introduction of Chinese labor and to the use of contracts is found in House and Senate documents and reports and in statutes. House Report No. 443, 36th Congress, 1st Session, "Coolie Trade," and Senate Report No. 689, 44th Congress, 2nd Session, "Report of the Joint Special Committee to Investigate Chinese Immigration," were of interest, although Report No. 689 did not include direct testimony from the major figures involved in the Chinese experiments to the South. Statutes of special interest are "An Act to Prohibit the 'Coolie Trade' by American Citizens in American Vessels," February 19, 1862 (see Appendix I), "An Act to Encourage Immigration," July 4, 1864, and "An Act to Execute Certain Treaty Stipulations Relating to Chinese," May 6, 1882.

Federal reports of direct concern to the Chinese in the South for the 1860s and 1870s are the annual reports of the Office of the Commissioner of Immigration (Department of State) and the reports of the secretaries of state and agriculture found in congressional documents. The reports of the New York commissioners of emigration and the commissioners of immigration in the southern states show changing state-level policy on the subject of immigration to the East and the South. Friedrich Kapp's *Immigration and the Commissioners of Emigration of the State of New York* (New York, 1870), based on the minutes and annual reports of the New York commissioners of emigration and other state documents contains a wealth of data. Robert Ernst's *Immigrant Life in New York City, 1825–1863* (New York, 1949) contributes to an understanding of the central role of New York as a major entry point for immigrants in these years.

## V. CHINESE IMMIGRATION TO THE SOUTH AND ITS BACKGROUND

Although there are a number of studies on the history of Chinese in the United States, the story of their early entry and settlement in the South has received very limited attention. Gunther Barth's *Bitter Strength: A History of the Chinese in the United States, 1850–1870* (Cambridge, Mass., 1964) is invaluable because it offers rich historical detail. His accounts of the movement of Chinese from the West to the East and the South, although brief, are points of departure for aspects of the present work.

Publications on the Chinese in the lower South have focused almost exclusively on the sociological aspects of racial boundaries between blacks, Chinese, and whites in the Mississippi delta area in the twentieth century, with limited work done on early history. These include the following works: James W. Loewen, *The Mississippi Chinese: Between Black and White* (Cambridge, Mass., 1971); Robert Seto Quan, *Lotus Among the Magnolias: The Mississippi Chinese* (Jackson, Miss., 1982); George Albert Rummel III, "The Delta Chinese: An Exploratory Study in Assimilation" (M.A. thesis, University of Mississippi, 1966); and Kit-Mui Leung Chan, "Assimilation of the Chinese-Americans in the Mississippi Delta" (M.A. thesis, Mississippi State University, 1969).

Pao-Yun Liao, "A Case Study of a Chinese Immigrant Community" (M.A. thesis, University of Chicago, 1951), offers useful data on the community organizations of the twentieth-century Chinese in Arkansas. For Texas, an important source on the early Chinese is Etta B. Peabody's "Efforts of the South to Import Chinese Coolies, 1865–1870" (M.A. thesis, Baylor University, 1967), and Edward J. M. Rhoads, "The Chinese in Texas," *Southern Historical Quarterly*, LXXXI (1977), 1–36. Also of interest is Wai Kin Che, "The Young American-Chinese in New Orleans in the 1960's" (M.A. thesis, Mississippi College, 1966).

The studies of overseas Chinese in the West Indies are important in efforts to understand the Caribbean connections and their influence on the experiments with Chinese labor in the South. The most useful were Persia Crawford Campbell, *Chinese Coolie Emigration to Countries Within the British Empire* (1923; rpr. New York, 1970); and Cecil Clementi, *The Chinese in British Guiana* (Georgetown, British Guiana, 1915), which offers insightful historical material based largely on colonial and other government documents, with some emigration accounts by notable Chinese families in Demerara. Also of use is *The Coolie, His Rights and Wrongs: Notes of a Journey to British Guiana* (London, 1871), by Edward Jenkins. Works on the early Chinese in Cuba that were of value were Juan Pérez de la Riva, "Contribución a la historia de la gente sin historia: Los Culíes chinos y los comienzos de la inmigración con-tratada en Cuba (1844–1847)," *Revista de la Biblioteca Nacional "Jose Martí"*, V (January–December, 1963), 35–76, and "Documentos para la historia de las gentes sin historia: El viaje a Cuba de los culíes chinos," *Revista de la Biblioteca Nacional "Jose Martí,"* VI (July–December, 1964), 47–86.

As background for studies of overseas Chinese, Eldon Griffin's *Clippers and Consuls: American Consular and Commercial Relations with Eastern Asia, 1845–1860* (1938; rpr. Wilmington, 1972) offers unmatched detail on the com-mercial and diplomatic aspects of international trade with China within which the Chinese labor movement developed. Victor Purcell, *The Chinese in South-east Asia* (London, 1965), and Jerome Ch'en and Nicholas Tarling (eds.), *Stud-ies in the Social History of China and South-East Asia: Essays in Memory of Victor Purcell* (Cambridge, 1970), are also useful.

VI. CONTEMPORARY MATERIALS

Most contemporary works do not mention Chinese labor or do so only briefly. Discussion about experimenting with Chinese labor appears in the minutes and proceedings of conventions and meetings. Notable among these are the official reports of the southern commercial conventions (1840–1869). Most of the proceedings of the Chinese Convention, July 13–15, 1869, and related meetings were published in the Memphis *Daily Appeal* and the St. Louis *Missouri Republican*. The names, owners, and locations of Louisiana sugar plantations are available in Louis Bouchereau, *Statement of the Sugar and Rice Crops Made in Louisiana* (New Orleans, 1869–77).

Few of the travelers who visited the South in the post–Civil War period visited the sites where Chinese were found. The brief account of the Chinese on the Alabama and Chattanooga Railroad by the British observer Robert Somers in *The Southern States Since the War, 1870–1871* (1871; rpr. University, Ala., 1965) is of value, together with the reports of visits to the Chinese in this same site by the Southern Baptist missionary Brayfield W. Whilden. His let-ters to the corresponding secretary of the domestic missions are reprinted as "Letters to M. T. Sumner," *Home and Foreign Journal*, III–IV (1871), and "Visit to China in March," *Home and Foreign Journal*, IV (1871).

The sketches of Chinese on the Millaudon plantation by the English-born artist Alfred R. Waud, found in the Historic New Orleans Collection, are of recognized value as the only known representations of the Chinese at work in that region. These sketches, which were done as part of an assignment for the Boston periodical *Every Saturday*, are in a collection that includes perhaps the most perceptive reproductions of people and places along the Mississippi in that period.

## VII. MONOGRAPHS AND SPECIAL STUDIES

There are a number of studies on the social life and organization of work on sugar and cotton plantations after the Civil War. Two works of importance for this research were J. Carlyle Sitterson, *Sugar Country: The Cane Sugar Industry in the South, 1753–1950* (Lexington, Ky., 1953) and Roger Wallace Shugg, *Origins of Class Struggle in Louisiana: A Social History of White Farmers and Laborers During Slavery and After, 1840–1875* (Baton Rouge, 1939). For an understanding of the history and aspects of race relations in northwestern Louisiana, two works stand out: Gary B. Mills, *The Forgotten People: Cane River's Creoles of Color* (Baton Rouge, 1977), and Sister Frances Jerome Woods, *Marginality and Identity: A Colored Creole Family Through Ten Generations* (Baton Rouge, 1972).

## VIII. ORAL TRADITION

The reconstruction of the Chinese past in Natchitoches Parish, Louisiana, involved the use of a range of written sources and, more important, information and anecdotes derived from oral tradition. I first selected a few key older respondents, most of whom were grandchildren of the original Chinese who entered the area in the 1860s. Other respondents were married to the descendants of Chinese with whom they had grown up in the parish. In all cases I told respondents of my own Chinese family background, which added a personal dimension to the research.

During a number of visits to Natchitoches, at intervals over seven years, I conducted informal interviews in homes, or during drives, or while visiting places that had important associations with past events. The narrative material thus elicited threw light not only on what they knew or did not know about the past of the particular family but also on the complicated network of social relations and the varying conditions of the work environment in which historical events of concern to them had taken place.

By the time the present manuscript was completed, most of the older respondents had died. The full text of Chapter 7 has been read, however, by at least one younger descendant of each of the families involved.

# BIBLIOGRAPHY

PRIMARY SOURCES

*Manuscripts*

Archives of the Episcopal Church, Austin, Texas
    Domestic and Foreign Missionary Society: China Records, 1835–1951.
Baptist Historical Collection, South Carolina Baptist Historical Society, Furman University, Greenville, South Carolina
    South Carolina Baptist Biographies.
Church of the Nativity, Campti, Louisiana
    Record of Baptisms, Burials, and Marriages, 1860–1914.
Duke University Manuscript Department, Durham, North Carolina
    Butler, E. G. W. Papers.
Historical Foundation of the Presbyterian and Reformed Churches, Montreat, North Carolina
    Biographical Files: Elias B. Inslee; Lena Saunders.
    Records of the Presbytery of New Orleans, 1878–1892.
    Summaries, Presbytery of Louisiana, 1856–1872.
Immaculate Conception Catholic Church, Natchitoches, Louisiana
    Marriage Records, 1902–38.
Louisiana State University Department of Archives and Manuscripts, Baton Rouge
    Cary, Sylvester L. Scrapbook.
    Gay, Andrew Hynes and Family. Papers.
    Gay, E. J. and Family. Papers.
    Knighton, Josiah, and Family. Papers.
    Randolph, John H. Papers.
    Tureaud, Benjamin. Papers.
Louisiana State University Louisiana Room, Baton Rouge
    McClung, Anna Gay. "St. Louis Plantation, Iberville Parish, Louisiana." February, 1956.
St. John the Baptist Catholic Church, Cloutierville, Louisiana
    Registers of the Parish of St. Jean Baptiste.

South Caroliniana Library, Manuscripts Division, University of South Carolina, Columbia
South Carolina Female Collegiate Institute, Barhamville, South Carolina: Records of Students and Faculty Members, 1837–59, Collected and Compiled by Professor Henry C. Davis.
Southern Historical Collection, University of North Carolina at Chapel Hill
Gaudet, James Amédée. Papers.
Gay and Price Family. Papers.
Gift, George Washington. Letters.
Virginia Baptist Historical Society, Richmond
"Inventory of Church Archives of Virginia: Guide to the Manuscript Collections of the Virginia Baptist Historical Society"

*Unpublished Government Documents*

LOCAL RECORDS

Iberville Parish District Court Records. Office of the Clerk of Court, Plaquemine, Louisiana.
Natchitoches Parish Records. Office of the Clerk of Court, Natchitoches, Louisiana.

UNITED STATES GOVERNMENT DOCUMENTS, NATIONAL ARCHIVES, WASHINGTON, D.C.

U.S. Department of Justice. Letters Received. Record Group 60.
———. Letters Sent. Record Group 60.
———. Records of Immigration and Naturalization Service, 1882–1908. Record Group 85.
U.S. Department of State. Domestic Letters. Record Group 59.
———. Consular Despatches. Record Group 59.
———. Instructions to Consuls. Record Group 59.
———. Letters Received, Bureau of Immigration. Record Group 59.
———. Letters Sent, Bureau of Immigration. Record Group 59.
———. Miscellaneous Letters. Record Group 59.
U.S. Department of the Interior. Eighth Census of the United States, 1860. Lyon County, Kentucky, Population Schedule; New Orleans, Louisiana, Population Schedule. Record Group 29.
———. Ninth Census of the United States, 1870. Arkansas Population Schedule; Louisiana Population Schedule; Mississippi Population Schedule; Population of New York City in 1870, Wards 1–22. Record Group 29.
———. Tenth Census of the United States, 1880. Arkansas Population Schedule; Louisiana Population Schedule; Mississippi Population Schedule. Record Group 29.
———. Twelfth Census of the United States, 1900. Louisiana Population Schedule. Record Group 29.

U.S. Department of the Treasury. Letters. Solicitor of the Treasury. Record Group 206.

————. Letters Sent, Bureau of Customs. Record Group 36.

————. Letters Sent. Record Group 56.

*Published Government Documents*

LAWS: FEDERAL, STATE, AND FOREIGN (LISTED CHRONOLOGICALLY)

"An Act in Addition to 'An Act to Prohibit the Introduction (Importation) of Slaves into any Port or Place Within the Jurisdiction of the United States, from and after the First Day of January, in the Year of Our Lord One Thousand Eight Hundred and Eight,' and to Repeal Certain Parts of the Same." April 20, 1818. *U.S. Statutes at Large*, III, 450–53.

"An Act to Regulate the Carriage of Passengers in Merchant Vessels." February 22, 1847, *U.S. Statutes at Large*, IX, 127–28.

"An Act to Provide for the Ventilation of Passenger Vessels and for Other Purposes." May 17, 1848. *U.S. Statutes at Large*, IX, 220–23.

"An Act to Extend the Provisions of All Laws Now in Force Relating to the Carriage of Passengers in Merchant Vessels and the Regulation Thereof." March 3, 1849. *U.S. Statutes at Large*, IX, 399–400.

*Reglamento para la Introducción de los Trabajadores Chinos en la Isla de Cuba*. August 4, 1860. Havana, 1860.

"An Act to Prohibit the 'Coolie Trade' by American Citizens in American Vessels." February 19, 1862. *U.S. Statutes at Large*. XII, 340–41.

"An Act to Encourage Immigration." July 4, 1864. *U.S. Statutes at Large*, XIII, 385–87.

"An Act to Encourage Immigration." December 1, 1869. State of Tennessee, *Journal of the House of Representatives*. 36th General Assembly, 1869–70.

Act No. 56. March 3, 1870. *Acts of the Legislature of Louisiana, 1870*.

"An Ordinance to Make Further Regulations Respecting Chinese Passenger Ships." March 30, 1870 (proclaimed August 24,1870). *Ordinances of the Legislative Council of Hongkong*, II. Hong Kong, 1890.

"An Act to Execute Certain Treaty Stipulations Relating to Chinese." May 6, 1882. *U.S. Statutes at Large*, XXII, 58–61.

"An Act to Prohibit the Coming of Chinese Persons into the U.S." May 5, 1892. *U.S. Statutes at Large*, XXVII, 25–26.

CONGRESSIONAL DOCUMENTS

*House Documents*, 54th Cong., 2nd Sess., No. 353.

*House Executive Documents*. 33rd Cong., 1st Sess., No. 123; 39th Cong., 1st Sess., No. 66.

*House Miscellaneous Documents*. 51st Cong., 2nd Sess., No. 108.

*House Reports*. 36th Cong., 1st Sess., No. 443.

*Senate Executive Documents*. 35th Cong., 2nd Sess., No. 22; 36th Cong., 1st

Sess., No. 30; 41st Cong., 2nd Sess., No. 116; 44th Cong., 2nd Sess., No. 689.

*Senate Reports.* 44th Cong., 2nd Sess., No. 689.

Wright, Carroll D., and William C. Hunt. *The History and Growth of the United States Census.* Senate Document No. 194, 56th Cong., 1st Sess.

OTHER UNITED STATES GOVERNMENT REPORTS

Gift, George W. "Cotton Under High Culture." In *U.S. Department of Agriculture, Annual Report 1867,* pp. 409–12.

U.S. Commissioner of Patents. *Report of the Commissioner of Patents for the Year 1850: Part II, Agriculture.*

U.S. Department of the Interior. *Population of the United States in 1860, Compiled from the Original Returns of the Eighth Census.*

———. *Ninth Census of the United States, 1870: Population and Social Statistics.* Vol. I.

———. *Statistics of the Population of the United States, 1880.*

STATE GOVERNMENT REPORTS

Brown, William G. *Annual Report of the State Superintendent of Public Education to the General Assembly of Louisiana for 1875.*

New York State Legislature. *Annual Reports of the Commissioners of Emigration of the State of New York, 1851–60.*

Noyes, James O. *Annual Report of the Commissioners of Emigration to the General Assembly of Louisiana, February 10, 1870.* New Orleans, 1870.

BRITISH PARLIAMENTARY PAPERS

Great Britain, *Parliamentary Papers.* Vol. 68 (Accounts and Papers, Vol. XII, 4 November 1852–20 August 1853). "Papers Relative to Emigration to the Australian Colonies," No. 1627, and "Correspondence with the Superintendent of British Trade in China upon the Subject of Emigration from That Country," No. 263.

———. Vol. 70 (Accounts and Papers, Vol. XXXV, 6 February–10 August 1872). "Correspondence Respecting the Emigration of Chinese Coolies from Macao," C. 504.

*Newspapers and Periodicals*

Abbeville (La.) *Le Meschacébé,* 1865–69.

Augusta (Ga.) *Daily Chronicle and Sentinel,* 1853.

Baton Rouge *Weekly Advocate,* 1869–71.

Baton Rouge *Tri-Weekly Advocate,* 1871.

Baton Rouge *Tri-Weekly Gazette and Comet,* 1865.

Charleston *Daily Courier,* 1866–69.

Charleston *Daily News,* 1869.

Cincinnati *Daily Enquirer*, 1854.
Donaldsonville (La.) *Chief*, 1871–75.
Galveston *Daily Civilian*, 1871.
Hammond (La.) *Progress*, 1938.
Houston-Galveston *Daily News*, 1865–66.
Lake Providence (La.) *Carroll Conservative*, 1878.
Lake Providence (La.) *Carroll Watchman*, 1875–76.
Little Rock *Daily Arkansas Gazette*, 1869–70.
*London and China Telegraph* (London), 1866.
Louisville *Courier-Journal*, 1869, 1949.
Louisville *Daily Courier*, 1854–69.
Louisville *Daily Journal*, 1866.
Marysville (Calif.) *Daily Appeal*, 1869–70.
Memphis *Daily Appeal*, 1854–75.
Mobile *Advertiser and Register* (*Mobile Daily Register*), 1865–71.
Natchitoches *Louisiana Populist*, 1894.
Natchitoches *Semi-Weekly Natchitoches Times* (Natchitoches *Semi-Weekly Times*), 1866–67.
Natchitoches *Times*, 1907.
New Iberia *Louisiana Sugar Bowl* (French title: *Le Sucrier de la Louisiane*), 1870–71.
New Orleans *Bee* (French title: *L'Abeille de la Nouvelle Orleans*), 1865–71.
New Orleans *Commercial Bulletin*, 1867.
New Orleans *Crescent*, 1866–67.
New Orleans *Daily Picayune*, 1865–94.
New Orleans *Southwestern Presbyterian*, 1887–96.
New Orleans *Times*, 1865–71.
New Orleans *Times-Democrat*, 1894.
New York *Evening Post*, 1869.
New York *Herald*, 1869.
New York *Journal of Commerce*, 1869.
New York *Tribune*, 1866–70.
New York *Weekly Journal of Commerce*, 1869.
Opelousas (La.) *Courier* (French title: *Le Courrier des Opelousas*), 1865.
Opelousas *Journal* (French title: *Le Journal*), 1870–71.
*Panama Star*, 1870.
Pine Bluff (Ark.) *Weekly Press*, 1869–70.
Plaquemine (La.) *Weekly Iberville South* (French title: *Le Sud d'Iberville*), 1867–69.
Richmond *Religious Herald*, 1846–53.
St. Charles (La.) *L'Avant Coureur*, 1867.
St. Louis *Missouri Republican*, 1869.
San Francisco *Daily Alta California*, 1853–70.

San Francisco *Morning Call*, 1869–71.
Savannah *Morning News*, 1866–70.
Savannah *Republican*, 1869–71.
*Spirit of Missions* (New York), 1835–90.
Thibodaux *Sentinel* (La.). (French title: *La Sentinelle de Thibodaux*), 1869.

*Books and Pamphlets*

Bonynge, Francis. *The Future Wealth of America: Being a Glance at the Resources of the United States and the Commercial and Agricultural Advantages of Cultivating Tea, Coffee, and Indigo, the Date, Mango, Jack, Leechee, Guava, and Orange Trees, etc. With a Review of the China Trade.* New York, 1852.

Boucher, John Newton. *A Century and a Half of Pittsburgh and Her People.* 4 vols. New York, 1908.

Bouchereau, Louis. *Statement of the Sugar and Rice Crops Made in Louisiana.* New Orleans, 1869–77.

*The China Directory for 1861.* Hong Kong, 1861.

Cohen, Hennig (ed.). *A Barhamville Miscellany: Notes and Documents Concerning the South Carolina Female Collegiate Institute, 1826–1865, Chiefly from the Collection of the Late Henry Campbell Davis.* Columbia, S.C., 1956.

Condit, Ira M. *The Chinaman as We See Him, and Fifty Years of Work for Him.* Chicago, 1900.

Crallé, Richard K. (ed.). *Reports and Public Letters of John Caldwell Calhoun.* 6 vols. New York, 1968. Reproduced from the edition of 1851–56.

*The Federal Cases: Comprising Cases Argued and Determined in the Circuit and District Courts of the United States.* Book I. St. Paul, 1894.

Gibson, Otis. *The Chinese in America.* Cincinnati, 1877.

Gift, George W. *California: Being a Short Account of the Climate, Health, Wealth, Productions, Fruits and Values of Property.* Memphis, 1874.

———. *Settlers' Guide Containing All the Circulars and Laws Relating to Pre-Emption Claims in California.* Benicia, Calif., 1854.

———. *Something About California . . . and Paragraphs Describing the Sanatorium of San Rafael.* San Rafael, Calif., 1875.

Gutzlaff, Charles Karl Friedrich August. *Journal of Three Voyages Along the Coast of China in 1831, 1832, and 1833, with Notices of Siam, Corea, and the Loo-Choo Islands.* London, 1840.

*An Historical Sketch of the China Mission of the Protestant Episcopal Church in the U.S.A. from the First Appointments in 1834 to Include the Year Ending August 31st, 1884.* New York, 1885.

[Jenkins, Edward.] *The Coolie, His Rights and Wrongs: Notes of a Journey to British Guiana.* London, 1871.

Jeter, Jeremiah Bell. *A Memoir of Mrs. Henrietta Shuck, the First American Female Missionary to China.* Boston, 1850.

*Journal of the Proceedings of the One-Hundred and Seventh Convention of the Protes-*

tant *Episcopal Church in the Diocese of Pennsylvania, May 12–14, 1891.* Philadelphia, 1891.

Kapp, Friedrich. *Immigration and the Commissioners of Emigration of the State of New York.* New York, 1870.

*Minutes of the General Assembly of the Presbyterian Church in the United States.* Memphis, 1866.

*Minutes of the Seventy-Eighth Annual Session of the State Convention of the Baptist Denomination in South Carolina, Darlington, S.C., November 30–December 4, 1898.* Greenville, S.C., 1898.

*Official Report of the Debates and Proceedings of the Southern Commercial Convention, Knoxville, Tennessee, August 10, 1857.* Knoxville, 1857.

Olmsted, Frederick Law. *A Journey in the Seaboard Slave States, with Remarks on Their Economy.* New York, 1856.

———. *A Journey through Texas; or, a Saddle-Trip on the Southwestern Frontier.* New York, 1860.

*Proceedings of the Commercial Convention Held in New Orleans, May 24th, 27th, 28th, and 29th, 1869.* New Orleans, 1869.

*Proceedings of the Sixteenth Meeting of the Southern Baptist Convention St. Louis, Missouri, May 11–16, 1871.* Baltimore, 1871.

*Proceedings of the Southern Baptist Convention, Baltimore, Maryland, May 13–17, 1853.* Richmond, 1853.

Rice, Alexander H., A. T. Hall, W. B. Spooner, C. O. Whitmore, and E. Train. *Report of the Committee Appointed by the Government of the "Board of Trade," to Take into Consideration the Communication of Messrs. Sampson and Tappan, Dated April 24th, 1856.* Boston, 1856.

Russell, Sir William H. *My Diary North and South.* 1863; rpr. New York, 1954.

Scharf, J. Thomas. *History of the Confederate States Navy.* 2 vols. New York, 1887.

———. *History of St. Louis City and County, from the Earliest Periods to the Present Day, Including Biographical Sketches of Representative Men.* 2 vols. Philadelphia, 1883.

Smith, Junius, *Essays on the Cultivation of the Tea Plant in the United States of America: Addressed to the People of the United States Generally, and to the Planters and Farmers of the Southern and Western States Particularly.* New York, 1848.

Somers, Robert. *The Southern States Since the War, 1870–1871.* 1871; rpr. University, Ala., 1965.

Spear, William. *The Oldest and the Newest Empire: China and the United States.* Hartford, 1870.

Tupper, Henry A. *Two Centuries of the First Baptist Church of South Carolina, 1683–1883, with Supplement.* Baltimore, 1889.

——— (ed.). *The First Century of the First Baptist Church of Richmond, Virginia.* Richmond, 1880.

198 BIBLIOGRAPHY

Williams, Albert. *A Pioneer Pastorate and Times Embodying Contemporary Local Transactions and Events*. San Francisco, 1879.

Wylie, Alexander. *Memorials of Protestant Missionaries to the Chinese: Giving a List of Their Publications, and Obituary Notices of the Deceased. With Copious Indexes*. Shanghai, 1867.

Yung, Wing. *My Life in China and America*. New York, 1909.

*Articles*

"Asiatic Free Colonists in Cuba." *De Bow's Review*, XXIV (May, 1858), 470–71.

"Asiatic Labor." *Southern Farmer*, II (October, 1868), 208.

Burwell, William M. "Science and the Mechanic Arts Against Coolies." *De Bow's Review*, VI (July, 1869), 557–71.

"Chinamen as Farmers." *Rural Carolinian*, VII (March, 1876), 114–15.

"The Coolies and Coolie Labor." *Rural Carolinian*, I (December, 1869), 129–33.

"Coolies as a Substitute for Negroes." *De Bow's Review*, After the War Ser., II (August, 1866), 215–17.

Death Notice, Reverend Elias B. Inslee. *Missionary*, IV (May, 1871), 1–2.

De Bow, J. D. B. "The Coolie Trade." *De Bow's Review*, XXIII (July, 1857), 30–35.

———. "The Coolie Trade; or the Encomienda System of the Nineteenth Century." *De Bow's Review*, XXVII (September, 1859), 296–321.

———. Letter to Governor Perry of South Carolina, October 12, 1865. *De Bow's Review*, After the War Ser., I (January, 1866), 6–14.

Dorr, J. W. "The Parish of Natchitoches." New Orleans *Crescent*, July 11, 1860. Reprinted in "A Tourist's Description of Louisiana in 1860," ed. Walter Prichard, *Louisiana Historical Quarterly*, XXI (October, 1938), 1165–70.

Elliot, Stephen, Jr. "Report by the Bishop of the Diocese of Georgia, February 13, 1853." In *Journal of the Thirty-First Annual Convention of the Protestant Episcopal Church in the Diocese of Georgia, Christ Church, Savannah*. Savannah, 1853.

"The Future of Cotton Culture in the Southern States." *Southern Cultivator*, XVI (May, 1858), 137–39.

Gift, George W. "The Labor Question—The Chinese." *Southern Farmer*, III (June, 1869), 127–28.

———. Letter to the Editors. *Southern Cultivator*, XXV (December, 1867), 374–75.

———. Letter to the Editors. *Southern Cultivator*, XXVI (March, 1868), 93–94.

"How Our Chinamen Are Employed." *Southern Farmer*, III (May, 1869), 103–105.

Lee, Daniel. "The Future of Cotton Culture in the Southern States, No. 1." *Southern Cultivator*, XVI (January, 1858), 27–28.

———. "The Future of Cotton Culture in the Southern States, No. 2." *Southern Cultivator*, XVI (March, 1858), 90–92.

———. "The Future of Cotton Culture in the Southern States (Remarks)." *Southern Cultivator*, XVI (May, 1858), 137–39.

———. "Hireling Labor and Slave Labor." *Southern Cultivator*, XII (June, 1854), 169–80.

———. "Laborers for the South." *Southern Cultivator*, XVI (August, 1858), 233–36.

"Proposed Importation of Coolies into the United States." *Commercial and Financial Chronicle*, III (October, 1866), 418–19.

Saunders, Lena. "Annual Report of the Chinese Mission to the Presbytery of New Orleans." *Southern Presbyterian*, October 20, 1887.

"Shall We Grow Tea?" *Rural Carolinian*, I (December, 1869), 34.

Whilden, B. W. Letters to M. T. Sumner. *Home and Foreign Journal*, n.s., III–IV (1871).

———. "Visit to China in March." *Home and Foreign Journal*, n.s., IV (May, 1871).

*Interviews and Correspondence*

Balthazar, Cora Marinovich. April, 1976; May, 1977.

Graham, Mary. April, 1976; May, 1977.

Grayson, Octavia Telsede. May, 1977; August, 1978.

Hongo, Earnest. April, 1976; May, 1977; August, 1978.

Hongo, Earnest, to the author. March 7, 1976.

Mixon, Ora Hongo. April, 1976; July, 1982.

Wong, Nathaneal, Sr. April, 1976.


SECONDARY SOURCES

*Books*

*The American Annual Cyclopaedia and Register of Important Events of the Year 1869*. New York, 1870.

Barth, Gunther. *Bitter Strength: A History of the Chinese in the United States, 1850–1870*. Cambridge, Mass., 1964.

Bear, James E., Jr. *The China Mission of the Presbyterian Church in the United States*. Richmond, 1965.

*Biographical and Historical Memoirs of Louisiana*. 2 vols. Chicago, 1892.

*Biographical and Historical Memoirs of Northwest Louisiana*. Nashville, 1890.

Black, Henry Campbell. *Black's Law Dictionary*. 3rd ed. St. Paul, 1933.

Boone, Muriel. *The Seed of the Church in China*. Philadelphia, 1973.

Cain, John Buford. *Methodism in the Mississippi Conference, 1846–1870.* Jackson, 1939.

Campbell, Persia Crawford. *Chinese Coolie Emigration to Countries Within the British Empire.* 1923; rpr. New York, 1969.

Cannon, James, III. *History of Southern Methodist Missions.* Nashville, 1926.

Carleton, Mark T. *Politics and Punishment: A History of the Louisiana State Penal System.* Baton Rouge, 1971.

Castlen, Harriet Gift. *Hope Bids Me Onward.* Savannah, 1945.

Cathcart, William (ed). *The Baptist Encyclopedia.* Philadelphia, 1881.

Chen, Ta. *Emigrant Communites in South China: A Study of Overseas Migration and Its Influence on Standards of Living and Social Change.* New York, 1940.

Clark, Thomas Dionysius (ed.). *The Postwar South, 1865–1900: A Period of Reconstruction and Readjustment.* Norman, 1962. Vol. 1 of *Travels in the New South: A Bibliography.* 2 vols.

Clark, Willie Thorburn. *Handmaidens of the King to Foreign Lands.* Richmond, 1932.

Clementi, Cecil. *The Chinese in British Guiana.* Georgetown, British Guiana, 1915.

Conard, Howard L. (ed.). *Encyclopedia of the History of Missouri: A Compendium of History and Biography for Ready Reference.* 6 vols. New York, 1901.

Corbitt, Duvon Clough. *A Study of the Chinese in Cuba, 1847–1947.* Wilmore, Ky., 1971.

Coulter, E. Merton. *Daniel Lee: Agriculturist.* Athens, 1972.

Dennett, Tyler. *Americans in Eastern Asia: A Critical Study of the Policy of the United States with Reference to China, Japan and Korea in the 19th Century.* New York, 1922.

Dick, Charles, and James Homans (eds.). *Appleton's Cyclopedia of American Biography.* 6 vols. New York, 1915.

DuBose, John Witherspoon. *Alabama's Tragic Decade: Ten Years of Alabama, 1865–1874.* Edited by James K. Greer. Birmingham, 1940.

Dunaway, Thomas S. *Pioneering for Jesus: The Story of Henrietta Hall Shuck.* Nashville, 1930.

*Encyclopedia of Southern Baptists.* 2 vols. Nashville, 1958.

Erickson, Charlotte. *American Industry and the European Immigrant, 1860–1885.* Cambridge, Mass., 1957.

Ernst, Robert. *Immigrant Life in New York City, 1825–1863.* New York, 1949.

Fleming, Walter R. *Civil War and Reconstruction in Alabama.* New York, 1905.

Fortier, Alcée. *Louisiana: Comprising Sketches of Counties, Towns, Events, Institutions and Persons Arranged in Cyclopedia Form.* Atlanta, 1909.

Freedman, Maurice. *The Study of Chinese Society: Essays by Maurice Freedman.* Stanford, 1979.

Goodwin, William A. R. (ed.). *History of the Theological Seminary in Virginia and Its Historical Background.* 2 vols. New York, 1923.

Gray, Lewis Cecil. *History of Agriculture in the Southern United States to 1860.* 2 vols. 1933; rpr. Clifton, N.J., 1973.

Griffin, Eldon. *Clippers and Consuls: American Consular and Commercial Relations with Eastern Asia, 1845–1860.* 1938; rpr. Wilmington, 1972.

Griffis, William Elliot. *A Maker of the New Orient: Samuel Robbins Brown, Pioneer Educator in China, America, and Japan, the Story of His Life and Work.* New York, 1902.

Helly, Denise. *Idéologie et ethnicité les chinois Macao à Cuba, 1847–1886.* Montreal, 1979.

Hyde, William, and Howard L. Conard (eds.). *Encyclopedia of the History of St. Louis: A Compendium of History and Biography for Ready Reference.* 4 vols. New York, 1899.

Jones, Billy M. (ed.). *Heroes of Tennessee.* Memphis, 1979.

Jones, William Burwell. *Methodism in the Mississippi Conference, 1891.* Jackson, 1951.

Knight, Franklin W. *Slave Society in Cuba During the Nineteenth Century.* Madison, 1970.

Latourette, Kenneth Scott. *A History of Christian Missions in China.* New York, 1929.

Loewen, James W. *The Mississippi Chinese: Between Black and White.* Cambridge, Mass., 1971.

Lyman, Stanford M. *Chinese Americans.* New York, 1974.

Marchand, Sydney. *The Flight of a Century in Ascension Parish, Louisiana.* Baton Rouge, 1936.

Mills, Gary B. *The Forgotten People: Cane River's Creoles of Color.* Baton Rouge, 1977.

Owen, Thomas McAdory. *History of Alabama and Dictionary of Alabama Biography.* 4 vols. Chicago, 1921.

Perrin, William Henry (ed.). *Southwest Louisiana Biographical and Historical.* New Orleans, 1891.

Portell Vilá, Herminio. *Narciso Lopez y su epoca, 1850–1851.* 3 vols. Havana, 1958.

Purcell, Victor. *The Chinese in Southeast Asia.* London, 1965.

Quan, Robert Seto. *Lotus Among the Magnolias: The Mississippi Chinese.* Jackson, 1982.

Quintana, Jorge. *Indice de extranjeros en el ejército libertador de Cuba, 1895–1898.* Vol. I of 3 vols. Havana, 1953.

Ray, T. Bronson, *et al. Southern Baptist Foreign Missions.* Nashville, 1910.

St. Amant, Penrose. *A History of the Presbyterian Church in Louisiana.* Richmond, 1961.

Shugg, Roger Wallace. *Origins of Class Struggle in Louisiana: A Social History of White Farmers and Laborers During Slavery and After, 1840–1875.* Baton Rouge, 1939.

Sitterson, J. Carlyle. *Sugar Country: The Cane Sugar Industry in the South, 1753–1950.* Lexington, Ky., 1953.

Skipper, Ottis Clark. *J. D. B. De Bow: Magazinist of the Old South.* Athens, 1958.

Smith, H. Shelton, *In His Image But . . . : Racism in Southern Religion, 1780–1910.* Durham, 1972.

Spain, Rufus B. *At Ease in Zion: Social History of Southern Baptists, 1865–1900.* Nashville, 1961.

Starr, Edward Comfort. *A History of Cornwall, Connecticut, a Typical New England Town.* New Haven, 1926.

Stewart, Watt. *Chinese Bondage in Peru.* Durham, 1951.

Stover, John F. *The Railroads of the South, 1865–1900.* Chapel Hill, 1955.

Swanson, Betsy. *Historic Jefferson Parish from Shore to Shore.* Gretna, La., 1975.

Thomas, Albert Sidney. *A Historical Account of the Protestant Episcopal Church in South Carolina, 1820–1957; Being a Continuation of Dalcho's Account, 1670–1820.* Columbia, 1957.

Van Deusen, John George. *The Ante-Bellum Southern Commercial Conventions.* Ser. XVI of Historical Papers of the Trinity College Historical Society. Durham, 1926.

Vansina, Jan. *Oral Tradition: A Study in Historical Methodology.* Translated by H. M. Wright. Chicago, 1961.

Wakelyn, Jon L. (ed.). *Biographical Dictionary of the Confederacy.* Westport, Conn., 1977.

Warner, Ezra. *Generals in Gray: Lives of the Confederate Commanders.* Baton Rouge, 1959.

Wender, Herbert. *Southern Commercial Conventions, 1837–1859.* Baltimore, 1930.

Wharton, Vernon Lane. *The Negro in Mississippi, 1865–1890.* Edited by Albert Ray Newsome. Chapel Hill, 1947.

White, Howard A. *The Freedmen's Bureau in Louisiana.* Baton Rouge, 1970.

Wickberg, Edgar. *The Chinese in Philippine Life, 1850–1898.* New Haven, 1965.

Wilson, J. Grant, and J. Fiske (eds.). *Cyclopedia of American Biography.* 6 vols. New York, 1888.

Woods, Sister Frances Jerome. *Marginality and Identity: A Colored Creole Family Through Ten Generations.* Baton Rouge, 1972.

Zabriskie, Alexander C. (ed.). *Anglican Evangelicalism.* Philadelphia, 1943.

*Articles*

Cohen, Lucy M. "Entry of Chinese to the Lower South from 1865 to 1870: Policy Dilemmas." *Southern Studies,* XVII (Spring, 1978), 5–37.

Davis, William Watson. "Ante-Bellum Southern Commercial Conventions." *Transactions of the Alabama Historical Society,* V (1904), 153–202.

Dunn, Milton. "History of Natchitoches." *Louisiana Historical Quarterly*, III (January, 1920), 26–56.

Krebbs, Sylvia. "The Memphis Chinese Labor Convention of 1869." *Annals of the Southeast Conference Association for Asian Studies*, II (1980), 112–17.

Ledet, Wilton P. "The History of the City of Carrollton." *Louisiana Historical Quarterly*, XXI (January, 1938), 220–81.

May, J. Thomas. "Continuity and Change in the Labor Program of the Union Army and the Freedmen's Bureau." *Civil War History*, XVII (September, 1971), 245–54.

————. "The Freedmen's Bureau at the Local Level: A Study of a Louisiana Agent." *Louisiana History*, IX (Winter, 1968), 5–19.

Moore, A. B. "Railroad Building in Alabama During the Reconstruction Period." *Journal of Southern History*, I (November, 1935), 421–41.

Pérez de la Riva, Juan. "Contribución a la historia de las gentes sin historia: Los Culíes chinos y los comienzos de la inmigración contratada en Cuba (1844–1847)," *Revista de la Biblioteca Nacional "José Martí,"* V, (January–December, 1963), 35–76.

————. "Documentos para la historia de las gentes sin historia: El viaje a Cuba de los culíes chinos." *Revista de la Biblioteca Nacional "José Martí,"* VI (July–December, 1964), 47–86.

Rhoads, Edward J. M. "The Chinese in Texas." *Southwestern Historical Quarterly*, LXXXI (July, 1977), 1–36.

Tsai, Shih-Shan Henry. "The Chinese in Arkansas," *Amerasia Journal*, VIII (Spring–Summer, 1981), 1–18.

White, Alice Pemble. "The Plantation Experience of Joseph and Lavinia Erwin, 1807–1836." *Louisiana Historical Quarterly*, XXVII (April, 1944), 343–478.

Wickberg, Edgar. "The Chinese Mestizo in Philippine History." *Journal of Southeast Asian History*, V (March, 1964), 62–99.

*Theses and Dissertations*

Chan, Kit-Mui Leung. "Assimilation of the Chinese-Americans in the Mississippi Delta." M.A. thesis, Mississippi State University, 1969.

Che, Wai Kin. "The Young American-Chinese in New Orleans in the 1960s." M.A. thesis, Mississippi College, 1966.

Coughlin, Margaret M. "Strangers in the House: J. Lewis Shuck and Issachar Roberts, First American Baptist Missionaries to China." Ph.D. dissertation, University of Virginia, 1972.

Karnowski, Sister Mary Silverius. "Natchitoches During the Civil War and Reconstruction Period." M.A. thesis, Catholic University of America, 1949.

Lathrop, Barnes Fletcher. "The Pugh Plantations, 1860–1865: A Study of Life in Lower Louisiana." Ph.D. dissertation, University of Texas, 1945.

Liao, Pao-Yun. "A Case Study of a Chinese Immigrant Community." M.A. thesis, University of Chicago, 1951.

Lumio, Lucien Casta. "Etude historique sur les origines de l'immigration réglementée dans nos anciennes colonies de la Réunion, la Guadeloupe, la Martinique et la Guyane." J.D. thesis, Faculté de Droit de Paris, 1906.

Norse, Clifford Carlton. "*The Southern Cultivator*, 1843–1861." Ph.D. dissertation, Florida State University, 1969.

Onorato, Michael Paul. "The Mission of William B. Reed, United States Minister to China, 1856–1858." M.A. thesis, Georgetown University, 1959.

Peabody, Etta B. "Effort of the South to Import Chinese Coolies, 1865–1870." M.A. thesis, Baylor University, 1967.

Postell, Paul E. "John Hampden Randolph: A Southern Planter." M.A. thesis, Louisiana State University, 1936.

Rummel, George Albert III. "The Delta Chinese: An Exploratory Study in Assimilation." M.A. thesis, University of Mississippi, 1966.

# INDEX